Gender Perspectives on Industry 4.0 and the Impact of Technology on Mainstreaming Female Employment

Shashi Bala
V. V. Giri National Labour Institute, India

Puja Singhal
National Centre for School Leadership-NIEPA, India

A volume in the Advances in Human Resources Management and Organizational Development (AHRMOD) Book Series

IGI Global
PUBLISHER of TIMELY KNOWLEDGE

Published in the United States of America by
IGI Global
Business Science Reference (an imprint of IGI Global)
701 E. Chocolate Avenue
Hershey PA, USA 17033
Tel: 717-533-8845
Fax: 717-533-8661
E-mail: cust@igi-global.com
Web site: http://www.igi-global.com

Library of Congress Cataloging-in-Publication Data

Names: Shashi Bala, editor. | Singhal, Puja, 1978- editor.
Title: Gender perspectives on industry 4.0 and the impact of technology on mainstreaming female employment / Shashi Bala, Puja Singhal.
Description: Hershey, PA : Business Science Reference, [2022] | Includes bibliographical references and index. | Summary: "This book is timely and highly relevant for making a significant contribution to a better understanding of the labor market impact of technological progress from a gender perspective"-- Provided by publisher.
Identifiers: LCCN 2021038893 (print) | LCCN 2021038894 (ebook) | ISBN 9781799885948 (hardcover) | ISBN 9781799885955 (paperback) | ISBN 9781799885962 (ebook)
Subjects: LCSH: Women--Employment. | Women--Economic conditions. | Finance--Technological innovations. | Industry 4.0.
Classification: LCC HD6053 .G4632 2022 (print) | LCC HD6053 (ebook) | DDC 331.4--dc23/eng/20211006
LC record available at https://lccn.loc.gov/2021038893
LC ebook record available at https://lccn.loc.gov/2021038894

This book is published in the IGI Global book series Advances in Human Resources Management and Organizational Development (AHRMOD) (ISSN: 2327-3372; eISSN: 2327-3380)

British Cataloguing in Publication Data
A Cataloguing in Publication record for this book is available from the British Library.

Advances in Human Resources Management and Organizational Development (AHRMOD) Book Series

ISSN:2327-3372
EISSN:2327-3380

Editor-in-Chief: Patricia Ordóñez de Pablos Universidad de Oviedo, Spain

MISSION

A solid foundation is essential to the development and success of any organization and can be accomplished through the effective and careful management of an organization's human capital. Research in human resources management and organizational development is necessary in providing business leaders with the tools and methodologies which will assist in the development and maintenance of their organizational structure.

The **Advances in Human Resources Management and Organizational Development (AHRMOD) Book Series** aims to publish the latest research on all aspects of human resources as well as the latest methodologies, tools, and theories regarding organizational development and sustainability. The **AHRMOD Book Series** intends to provide business professionals, managers, researchers, and students with the necessary resources to effectively develop and implement organizational strategies.

COVERAGE

- Corporate Governance
- Human Resources Development
- Worker Behavior and Engagement
- Coaching and Mentoring
- Collaborative Method
- Process Improvement
- Organizational Behavior
- Personnel Retention
- Executive Compensation
- Training and Development

IGI Global is currently accepting manuscripts for publication within this series. To submit a proposal for a volume in this series, please contact our Acquisition Editors at Acquisitions@igi-global.com or visit: http://www.igi-global.com/publish/.

The Advances in Human Resources Management and Organizational Development (AHRMOD) Book Series (ISSN 2327-3372) is published by IGI Global, 701 E. Chocolate Avenue, Hershey, PA 17033-1240, USA, www.igi-global.com. This series is composed of titles available for purchase individually; each title is edited to be contextually exclusive from any other title within the series. For pricing and ordering information please visit http://www.igi-global.com/book-series/advances-human-resources-management-organizational/73670. Postmaster: Send all address changes to above address.

Titles in this Series

For a list of additional titles in this series, please visit:
www.igi-global.com/book-series/advances-human-resources-management-organizational/73670

Ergonomics and Business Policies for the Promotion of Well-Being in the Workplace
Mildrend Montoya-Reyes (Autonomous University of Baja California, Mexico) Ismael Mendoza-Muñoz (Autonomous University of Baja California, Mexico) Gabriela Jacobo-Galicia (Autonomous University of Baja California, Mexico) and Samantha E. Cruz-Sotelo (Autonomous University of Baja California, Mexico)
Business Science Reference • © 2022 • 303pp • H/C (ISBN: 9781799873969) • US $195.00

Handbook of Research on Key Dimensions of Occupational Safety and Health Protection Management
Snežana Živković (Faculty of Occupational Safety, University of Niš, Serbia) Bojan Krstić (Faculty of Economics, University of Niš, Serbia) and Tamara Rađenović (Faculty of Occupational Safety, University of Niš, Serbia)
Business Science Reference • © 2022 • 512pp • H/C (ISBN: 9781799881896) • US $295.00

Analyzing Telework, Trustworthiness, and Performance Using Leader-Member Exchange COVID-19 Perspective
Michael A. Brown Sr. (Right Fit Communications LLC, USA)
Business Science Reference • © 2022 • 263pp • H/C (ISBN: 9781799889502) • US $215.00

Future Advancements for CSR and the Sustainable Development Goals in a Post-COVID-19 World
Andrea Pérez (University of Cantabria, Spain)
Business Science Reference • © 2022 • 355pp • H/C (ISBN: 9781799880653) • US $225.00

Building Competencies for Organizational Success Emerging Research and Opportunities
Donta S. Harper (University of Washington, USA)
Business Science Reference • © 2021 • 217pp • H/C (ISBN: 9781799865162) • US $195.00

Role of Leadership in Facilitating Healing and Renewal in Times of Organizational Trauma and Change
Lynda Byrd-Poller (Thomas Nelson Community College, USA) Jennifer L. Farmer (Renewed Mindset LLC, USA) and Valerie Ford (ISP Global Communications LLC, USA)

IGI Global
PUBLISHER of TIMELY KNOWLEDGE

701 East Chocolate Avenue, Hershey, PA 17033, USA
Tel: 717-533-8845 x100 • Fax: 717-533-8661
E-Mail: cust@igi-global.com • www.igi-global.com

Editorial Advisory Board

Table of Contents

Section 3
Mainstreaming Women Through Good Governance in the Digital Era

Detailed Table of Contents

indicators have been used to explore the prevailing gender dimensions and issues pertaining to digital financial accessibility. This chapter also focuses on how the initiatives taken by the Indian government and banks, and FinTech start-ups are bridging the financial gender gap and attaining the goal of sustainable growth in India.

Increase in enrollment of women in higher education also had an impact on the choice of subjects. Science, technology, engineering, and maths (STEM) subjects also attracted a large number of women as their professional choices. However, employment for women in STEM domain has largely remained inadequate and contributed to the overall declining employment trend for women. There are several socio-cultural barriers seriously impeding women's development as professionals in the field of STEM. The government facilitated re-entry of women in science through dedicated women scientist schemes, but domination of life sciences indicates professional gendered segregation. Women in India are largely employed in the unorganized sectors, and improving women participation in the STEM domain can enable women's participation in the organized industry sector institutions. The emergence of Industry 4.0 provides an opportunity to not contribute further to the widened gender disparities and gender stereotypes. This will be a big leap for the emergence of a gender-inclusive work culture in the industry sectors.

Section 2
Future of Work and Employability

This section provides information on challenges in access to the digitized labour market from a gender lens. It also discusses issues on leadership through ICT interventions, corporate social responsibility, and mobile wallets in order to mainstream women in the world of work.

With a view to understanding the changes taking place, studying their impact, and identifying potential opportunities for achieving gender equality, the chapter aims to look at women in the labour market and at the gender digital divide. It discusses the structural change for equality in the information and knowledge society and analyses women's autonomy in the new technology paradigm. It provides four different gendered perspectives to understand women in the labour market in the era

The purpose of this chapter is to examine how gender diversity affects corporate social responsibility disclosure. Considering the socio-economic impact of the deployment of the fourth industry revolution (Industry 4.0), firms have a moral obligation to disclose information on how different stakeholders may be affected by the extensive use of smart technologies in their value-adding activities. The study used multiple regression analysis with 176 publicly traded Indian service sector organizations for the financial year 2020-21. The findings revealed that GD has a negligible impact on CSR filings. By focusing on Indian public firms in the service sector, this study fills a vacuum in the literature. It is the first study to evaluate the impact of women on boards on the scope of CSR reporting in an Indian context. The findings of this study have crucial implications for future board composition as they show that women's representation on boards did not affect CSR disclosures.

In the recent past, the idea of mobile wallets was very new to the world, but it is now becoming popular due to the expansion and development of smartphones with robust and sophisticated facilities. However, the literature on mobile wallets does not deeply identify and discuss how gender is significant in the business world with the power of mobile wallets and how it is helping to adopt the best strategies to incorporate it into the business through e-commerce activities. Therefore, this research contributes to knowledge by exploring mobile wallet users in Sri Lanka from a gender perspective and their significance in business development. The research adopts a qualitative research method to gather the primary data with a case study strategy. So, the case study found that mobile wallet has many inhibitions constraining its adoption and diffusion about gender. Also, it found that mobile wallets provided many social benefits that contributed to overcoming most of the gender-exclusive activities in e-commerce.

Foreword

Gender relations are characterised by unequal power dynamics which assign specific entitlements and responsibilities to men and women as per the expectation of the society. For example, women might be expected to take on caring or domestic duties and remain close to home, while men may be expected to be the main breadwinner, working outside the home, with greater freedom to move around in public places. It reflects a public-private dichotomy where, women are confined in the unrecognized sphere generally unpaid in nature, whereas men go out in the recognized sphere generally paid in nature. This results in widening existing Gender inequality gaps.

Formal equality of treatment between men and women merely emphasized eliminating disability and protecting women. Later the idea of 'Substantive Equality' was developed by expressing it in terms of women's own experience rather than in comparison with a male standard. Substantive equality thus provides a basis for recognizing protectionist measures to eliminate disadvantages and gender-based discrimination, without perceiving them as related to stereotypical attitudes on women's weakness and vulnerability The substantive equality approach recognizes that women and men cannot be treated the same, and for equality of results to occur, women and men may need to be treated differently. The challenge is to know when to take note of difference, and to decide on appropriate measures for different treatment that will facilitate equal access, control and equal result. Such measures will have to be assessed to ensure they promote autonomy rather than protection or dependency. This has to be done without compromising the claim for equal rights and equality as a legal standard. Apart from this we need to raise a generation where equality exists via shift in our attitudes while bringing up our children in our homes and schools.

It is in this context, the present book is an attempt to mainstream gender issues in the employment with the aim to strengthen the roles and responsibilities each one of us have to perform with dedication in treating each other as human beings with empathy. As we are all aware that technology is gender neutral and future of work is majorly technology related.

The book is divided into three broad sections. The first section is termed as "Gender and Digitalisation" followed by "Future of Work and Employability" and finally "Mainstream Women Through Good Governance in the Digital Era."

The first section is about the role of digitization which talks about women in digital society, and how the digital divide can hamper women employability and also how the closing of digital distance between men and women will help empower women. The second section is regarding the relationship between future work and employability. Looking at digital labour market through gender point of view, its influence on women's employment, and how gaining access to digital employment has lead to leadership. This has been talked about using examples from Indian service sector and Sri Lanka. The last section is about bringing women into mainstream through digital era and talks about different strategic imperatives in judicial diversity in India, construction industry and finally about how to expand financial literacy amongst working and non-working women in India.

Overall, the book covers the recent developments in the world of work and talks not only about how women are affected by the digitized area of work, but also about how more women can be brought into digital arena through better management and governance.

The book is aimed at the wider circle of scholars, researchers and those interested in the understanding the realities of recent changes in the sphere of work. It also encourages us to come up with refreshing possibilities and alternatives in unpacking the rather limited area of women's work that remain s invisible in the South Asian region.

The authors and editors are congratulated for their endeavour to bring out the rather less researched area of digital era and women's work.

Saraswati Raju
Jawaharlal Nehru University, India

Saraswati Raju is a Superannuated Professor in Social Geographer at the Centre for the Study of Regional Development (CSRD), Jawaharlal Nehru University, New Delhi. Her teaching and research interests are in issues related to social development with focus on gendered marginalities in labour market, access to literacy/education/skills, empowerment, and gender and space. She has published extensively on these issues in national and international journals of repute. She is one of the founding members for the International Geographic Union (IGU) Commission on Gender and Geography. Member of editorial boards of Annals of Association of American Geographers, Antipode and Progress in Human Geography, amongst others, she has been at the forefront in introducing gender studies in Indian geography—her co-edited publication of the Atlas on Women and Men in India has been praised as a landmark in this direction. Her recent co-edited books include Women Workers in Urban India (2016, Cambridge University), Colonial and Post-colonial Geographies of

India (2006, Sage Publications), Doing Gender, Doing Geography: Emerging Research in India (2011, Routledge), Gendered Geographies: Space and Place in South Asia (2011, Oxford University Press) and her co-authored book titled NGOs and the State in 21st Century: India and Ghana (2006, INTRAC, UK). Prof.Saraswati has received many visiting awards and fellowships in her long and illustrious career. She is a recipient of Janet Monk Service Award (2010) given by the Women Specialty Group of Association of American Geographers for exemplary contribution to the study of gender/ feminist concerns in geography. This is the first ever award outside the Anglo-Saxon world. She has also been awarded the 2012's Distinguished Service Award for Asian Geography, instituted by the Asian Geography Specialty Group, Association of American Geographers. USA. The award honours 'outstanding scholars in the field of Asian geography who have demonstrated exceptional scholarship as well as service to the specialty group'.

Preface

Society is the result of a gradual evolution and development from less humane to more humane which is presently on the way towards being gender sensitive. Gender, as we know is a social expectation from individuals born in different sexes. It is a societal expectation from individuals for the sex they are born with. Perhaps this was true when society was evolving during primitive era and division of labour was decided by different communities, subsequently societies and the countries wherein men were considered as masculine and was expected to perform outdoor activities and women to perform reproductive roles and subsequently attend to the family needs but with the evolution of education system, skill, technology, it has been observed that women are also able to make their own choices. Sociocultural evolution and various other factors have helped in these developments over the period of time. Technological revolution and Globalization have been instrumental in this journey.

Access to technology has led to access of information in almost all the households. This revolution of access to the information is gender neutral. Now both men and women including transgenders can access the same information through a device called mobile which was not the case earlier. In absence of information women were dependent on men for taking decision regarding education carrier and livelihood. This is perhaps not the case in the era of 4th IR. Emergence of Fourth Industrial Revolution has resulted in changing the employment situation. These have resulted in both positive environment for economic transactions as-well as in the exchange of all the information's. Atmosphere of self-learning using artificial intelligence (AI) has been evolving. Technological innovations have given us a glimpse of a society that was a distant dream which we can now witness with the possibility of industrial and employment structural changes across the globe. Technologies such as AI and robotics are labour saving and are expected to generate new forms of employment not only in the field of routine jobs but also in the field of non-routine jobs thereby helping resolve the issues pertaining to the quality of work among pink- and blue-collar jobs via continuous skill development. It is predicated that white-collar and green-collar jobs requiring high-level skills may become costly considerably unless technical education is integrated in all the school's curriculum and is inclusive in nature.

The employment structure triggered by the Fourth Industrial Revolution is expected to generate the need for new or revised affirmative policies to help individuals from different ethnic backgrounds to receive quality education and employment at a dignified level. Affirmative action yields many positive advantages for a workplace such as increasing opportunity, diversity, creativity and productivity but only for skilled manpower. The matter was taken up as a major theme at the World Economic Forum Annual Meeting in Davos, with attention paid not only to the benefits of productivity improvement due to the Fourth Industrial evolution but also to the impact on employment. Behind the recent rise of populism of technological innovations are the strong concerns of people left behind by technological innovations. Several participants pointed out the importance of continuously providing, retraining, and ensuring transparency. In the future scenario creation of a continuous atmosphere for updated training and accordingly reframing of affirmative policies is also essential as per the changes desired in the surrounding for working environment.

Till date, the laws, rules, regulation and policies are to large extent framed for the population appointed at the visible workplaces where they have written employer and employee's documents. With the changing nature of work in the absence of written documents, these regulations will only act like a fish out of water. Who will be taking care of the social security provisions during the dependency phase of Individuals? What kind of social and demographic structure will be emerging out of these changes in the future of work? Advanced structural planning is required for harnessing the benefit of technology and human race. Otherwise, it would be like aiming for a fair globalization but resulting in monopolizing of markets only benefitting the developed nations with decent Jobs conditions at the cost of many nations witnessing jobless growth or indecent working conditions especially for the women, universally.

Parity in access to opportunities for optimum utilization of human resource is essential for achieving inclusive and sustainable growth. Patriarchal mind set, roles and responsibilities assumed by the society often place women in inequitable positions, which are frequently replicated at the workplaces. Therefore, facilitating working environment for all is essential for achieving gender parity. Globally, gender mainstreaming is an important part of policy discussions. Many nations including India are recognizing the importance of gender parity and taking necessary steps to bridge these gaps. Access to quality education, digital literacy, skill development, decent jobs, sharing of family responsibilities and effective implementation of existing affirmative policies are some of the initiatives taken for narrowing this gap. Implementation of affirmative policies will positively change the individual mind sets and inculcate positive behavior in the World of Work and this will be positively reflected in the behavior of Individuals in the Family, Community, Society, Nation and in the Ether subsequently.

Digital technologies are tangible tools for women to overcome lasting inequalities. ICT can help women to gain employment, obtain cost effective health services and education and to increase their income Due to entrenched patriarchal attitude of society in less developed countries, women are at a natural disadvantage to benefit from the digital revolution and add a new dimension to the already existing vicious circle between discrimination and women's backwardness. Therefore, UNESCO also considers the gender divide as "one of the most significant inequalities to be amplified by the digital revolution"

It is in this context that the present book is an attempt to promote gender equity and parity at workplaces.

This book looks into these aspects in detail through various chapter:

Chapter 1: How Closing the Digital Divide Can Improve Women's Employability

This chapter illustrates the significance of addressing gender inequity for women who seek education, training, and governmental resources for employment just as their male counterparts by comparing the culture of different counties such as Bangladesh, Israel, Kenya, and the United States of America. The authors also explained that how Women with technological skills bring new skills to the workplace, reduce economic needs, boost welfare and growth, and better provide for their homes and families. Readers will gain a better understanding of how governmental agencies and policies, educational institutions, and employers all can work toward the same goal and that is closing the Gender Digital Divide.

Chapter 2: Bridging the Digital Gender Divide – Prerequisite for Women Empowerment

Chapter is an attempt to throw sufficient light on prerequisite for women empowerment. Author concludes with the way forward which will lead us to a more digitally gender inclusive and sustainably developed society.

Chapter 3: Woman in Digital Society and Entrepreneurship of the Republic of Belarus

Chapter highlights the role of involvement of women in digitalisation and information technologies for development of business and the development of new competitive advantages in the perspective of Republic of Belarus. Author also signifies that the main goal of digitalization development is to increase interaction between consumers and manufacturers, between business representatives and state regulatory and control bodies, and between business entities.

Chapter 4: Digital Financial Inclusion Through FinTech

This chapter is an attempt to explore new digital financial technologies including FinTech which can transform the lives of women. G20 Financial Inclusion indicators have been used to explore the prevailing gender dimensions and issues pertaining to digital financial accessibility. This chapter also focuses on how the initiatives taken by Indian Government, Banks, and FinTech start-ups are bridging the financial gender gap and attaining the ultimate goal of sustainable growth in India.

Chapter 5: Addressing Low Female Participation in STEM for an Inclusive Industry 4.0 – Mainstreaming Gender

Chapter addresses the issues related to female participation in STEM areas. Author highlights several socio-cultural barriers which seriously impeding women's development as professionals in the field of STEM. Women in India are largely employed in the unorganized sectors and improving women participation in STEM domain can enable women participation in the organized industry sector institutions. The emergence of Industry 4.0 provides an opportunity to not contribute further to the widened gender disparities and gender stereotypes. This will be a big leap for the emergence of a gender inclusive work culture in the industry sectors.

Chapter 6: Understanding Digitised Labour Market Through a Gendered Lens

This chapter discusses the structural change for equality in the information and knowledge society, and analyses women's autonomy in the new technology paradigm. A gendered perspective on new forms of employment highlights how job markets can be opened up in new and inclusive ways to women. The chapter explains that if the digital gap is bridged, then it can provide new sources of global economic growth.

Chapter 7: Issues, Challenges, and Impact on Women Employment of Industry 4.0

This chapter explores how Industry 4.0 will change the process and management of work and how it will impact all the dimensions of labour market. Author tries to explain some of the queries related to Industry 4.0 such as -What kind of employment opportunities will it generate for the labour force? Will it solve the problem of unemployment of the people present in developing and develop world? As purchasing power parity of people is equally important along with the production of goods. Till what extents will the industry 4.0 will be sustainable? Chapter also talks about other factors which we need to consider with these issues like cyber security, data protection climate change, impact on women empowerment and achieving gender balance in this sector of economy.

Chapter 8: Gender, Leadership, and ICT

In this chapter, authors look forward to analyze in-depth the significance of positive leaderships in motivating inclusive growth and sustainable development. Chapter also includes various case studies on leadership styles which is being adopted in various organizations that motivated women to be a part of the active labour market without facing any discrimination on the grounds of her sex.

Chapter 9: Gender Diversity on Board and Corporate Social Responsibility Disclosure in the Digitalisation Era – A Study of the Indian Service Sector Industry

The purpose of this chapter is to examine how gender diversity affects Corporate Social Responsibility disclosure. Considering the socio-economic impact of the deployment of the fourth industry revolution (Industry 4.0), firms have a moral obligation to disclose information on how different stakeholders may be affected by the extensive use of smart technologies in their value-adding activities. The study used multiple regression analysis with 176 publicly traded Indian service sector organizations for the financial year 2020-21. The findings revealed that GD has a negligible impact on CSR filings. By focusing on Indian public firms in the service sector, this study fills a vacuum in the literature.

Chapter 10: Cashless Society and Development of Gender Friendly Services Through Mobile Wallet – A Case of Sri Lanka

This chapter discusses how gender is important in the business world with the power of mobile wallet and how it is helping to adopt the best strategies to incorporate it into business through e-commerce activities. Therefore, this research contributes to knowledge by exploring mobile wallet users in Sri Lanka from gender perspective and their significance in business development. Author also found that mobile wallet provided many social benefits that contributed in overcoming most of the gender exclusive activities in eCommerce.

Chapter 11: Gender Bias in Science and Technology – A Medico's Perspective

This chapter is a medico's perspectives on the impact of gender bias on Science & Technology. It is entirely about what a female doctor feels about the society and the struggles a female faces in her journey, the lacunae in our system, how we should deal with the people and the system for the betterment of humanity in general. Her experiences in the Medical College as a student, as a doctor, as a researcher and as a teacher has been shared. How to maintain a perfect work life balance and still be happy and content in life without being stressed.

Chapter 12: Judicial Diversity in India – A Strategic Imperative

Chapter deals with digi-revolution in India that needs to be more inclusive. From the educational institutions to sports, politics, governance, corporates, military and Parliament, the institutions of all kinds are facing the challenges of ensuring greater gender inclusiveness. Along the similar lines, Judiciary cannot be an exception either. In a country like India wherein the women constitute 50% of the population and where there are already good number of women members in bar available to be elevated, presence of only a handful women in judiciary raises multiple questions. This chapter reflects towards the underrepresentation of women in the Indian judiciary. It uncovers the existence of Glass Ceiling in Indian judiciary. It advocates for the case for the judicial diversity using the judicial lens from the prism of some of the landmark Supreme Court judgements.

Chapter 13: Continuous Struggle for Existence of Female in Construction Industry in the 21st Century

Construction industry in India holds the second important place in the development of the country after the agriculture industry. Construction industry consists of the employment of the most diverse culture of people employed and the issue of gender inequality is one of the main problems associated with this industry. This chapter focuses on various issues related to the diversity of the people employed and the gender inequality prevailing among them.

Chapter 14: Boosting Financial Literacy in 4th IR Amongst Working and Non-Working Women in India

The concept of financial literacy is of vital importance both for the individual and the economy as a whole. The present chapter analyses the different components of financial literacy from the Indian perspective. it is an attempt to throw light and carry out a comparative analysis between the financial acumen of working and non-working Indian women. The results of the study may serve as important inputs to the policy makers to develop strategies to enhance financial literacy among Indian women in particular and thereby help in nation building.

The above discussion is all the more timely because the ILO Centenary Initiative on women at work has been launched as part of the preparations for the ILO's 100thAnniversary during 2019. This book is therefore timely and highly relevant and will make significant contribution to a better understanding of the Impact of Technological Progress on the Labour Market from the Gender Perspective.It is hoped that the present book would be useful to the researchers, the policy makers, and other academicians who can contribute towards successful handling the challenges pertaining to digital gender gap in the world of work.

In summing up, we would be failing in our duty if we do not express our heart-felt gratitude to the authors and imperceptible angels for sharing their experiences in this journey meant towards achieving a level playing field.

DISCLAIMER

The views expressed by the authors in this book are their personal, not necessarily of the organisations they represent.

Shashi Bala
V. V. Giri National Labour Institute, India

Puja Singhal
National Centre for School Leadership-NIEPA, India

Acknowledgment

We would like to acknowledge the support provided by all the people involved in this project and more specifically, the authors and reviewers who took part in the review process. Without their support, this book would not have become a reality.

First, we would like to thank each author for their contributions. Our sincere gratitude goes to the chapter's authors who contributed their time and expertise to this book.

We as editors wish to acknowledge the valuable contributions of all the reviewers and Prof. Saraswati Raju, Professor at Centre for the Study of Regional Development (CSRD), Jawaharlal Nehru University, India, Ms. Francisco Cordova Arauz, Coordinator of National Scholarships Programs, Ecuador , Prof. Farida Siddiqui, Hod, Department of Economics, Maulana Azad National Urdu University Hyderabad, Prof.C. Devendiran, Department of Social Work, Mizoram University, Aizawl, Dr Nidhi Saxena, Assistant Professor, Dept. of Law, Sikkim University (A Central University) Gangtok Sikkim, Dr. Rashmi Maini Assistant Professor, Jaipuria Institute of Management, Ghaziabad, Dr. Veer Mayank, Assistant Professor, Department of Law, Sikkim University, Dr. Nisha Saxena, Assistant Professor, LMN University, Darbhanga, Bihar, Dr. Litty Denis, Assistant Professor, Central University of Gujarat, Central University of Gujarat, Gandhinagar, Gujarat, regarding the improvement of quality, coherence, and content presentation of chapters. Most of the authors also served as referees; we highly appreciate their immeasurable task.

We also wish to acknowledge the valuable help we received from our Seniors, Colleagues and friends who came forward to extend their support. We wish to place our deep appreciation and thanks to (Ms) Jan Travers, Director of Intellectual Property and Contracts, IGI Global, Katelyn McLoughlin, Assistant Development Editor-Book Development, IGI Global for their support, cooperation and attention to details to bring out the publication of this book in time. For enhancing the quality of manuscripts by proofreading, we are grateful to Dr. Bhoomika Batra, CEO of EdBhoomi: Ground for Education, India.

Lastly, we wish to thank our families for their understanding and support in providing us all the necessary facilities and affectionate environment to enable us to complete our work and above all we are immensely thankful to the Almighty for providing us supportive environment during this COVID-19 pandemic phase.

Shashi Bala
V. V. Giri National Labour Institute, India

Puja Singhal
National Centre for School Leadership-NIEPA, India

Section 1
Gender and Digitalisation

This section focuses on gender issues in the digitalisation era, financial literacy, digital divisions in terms of access to digital devices, and quality training for women who have access to the devices in order to utilize the services effectively with confidence while continuing with them in the future.

Chapter 1
How Closing the Digital Divide Can Improve Women's Employability

Paula E. Faulkner
North Carolina Agricultural and Technical State University, USA

Robert Cobb, Jr.
https://orcid.org/0000-0002-4249-0701
North Carolina Agricultural and Technical State University, USA

Thomas Korir Kipkurgat
Moi University, Kenya

Salwa Omar Alinat-Abed
Open University, Israel

ABSTRACT

The authors of this chapter provide a lens of the challenge women face with being successful in the labor force. Readers will learn about the importance of addressing gender inequity for women who seek education, training, and governmental resources for employment just as their male counterparts. The authors also detail how women of different countries and cultures such as Bangladesh, Israel, Kenya, and the United States of America face the challenges for closing the digital divide. When women's employability increases, societies improve. Women with technological skills bring new skills to the workplace, reduce economic needs, boost welfare and growth, and better provide for their homes and families. Readers will gain a better understanding of how governmental agencies and policies, educational institutions, and employers can work toward the same goal, and that is closing the gender digital divide.

DOI: 10.4018/978-1-7998-8594-8.ch001

INTRODUCTION

Women in the skilled labor market face numerous challenges. Despite some progress, the gaps in labor force participation between men and women remain large. For example, no advanced or middle-income economy has significantly reduced the gender gap (Lagarde & Ostry, 2018).

In this chapter, the authors present an overview of women and their participation in the labor force and the challenges they face keeping pace with their male counterparts while struggling with urbanization and globalization headwinds. The chapter provides a cultural lens from four different countries and cultures and how each identifies challenges and develops strategies for increasing females' participation in technology fields amidst gender inequity. Readers will learn the importance of addressing gender inequity, as it affects the degree to which women participate in the labor force. The main objective of this chapter is to discuss how important it is to close the Digital Divide so that women across the globe can obtain the necessary education and training for increased employability in technology.

BACKGROUND

Women's role in the labour market is globally decreasing, widening financial disparities between the genders (World Economic Forum, 2019). This trend is because women are employed in increasingly automatized sectors (i.e., drones, cognitive technologies, and artificial intelligence (AI). Women comprise a significant source of untapped talent in the global workforce and increasing their digital fluency can help move them into the jobs that employers have trouble filling (Sweet, 2016).The low participation of women in the labor force is at times impacted by girls being encouraged to marry at early ages and urban and rural families preferring to invest more in men than women for career skill development. In addition, flexibility is needed, especially since women remain the primary caregivers in the home globally. Therefore, flexible work and part-time employment options are required to help to reduce attrition and increase the number of women who enter and remain in the workforce over the long term (Schomer, & Hammond, 2020).

Women lacking a formal education also affect employability. The barriers faced by women may also include attitudinal, social, and financial constraints, inappropriate training environments, hazardous job environments, lack of security in access and accommodation including sexual harassment and information and knowledge gaps, low prospects for decent work, and low self-confidence, and fear of challenging the status quo (International Labour Organization, 2012).

Women often face gender-specific challenges to their full participation in the labor force, which may require policy interventions beyond those aimed at promoting economic growth and the efficiency of rural labor markets (Food and Agriculture Organization of the United Nations, 2011). For example, the International Labour Organization (2009) offered, "They [women] are rarely provided with any formalized training for these occupations and learn through exploitative practices that do not value (i.e., monetarily) their participation in labour across sectors" (p. 10). But a rising tide lifts all boats. When women gain knowledge and skills for urbanization and industrialization, it makes for a more skilled labor force (Faulkner, et al., 2019).

Women have often been considered undereducated and untrainable compared to their male counterparts. However, in a report by Accenture (2016), it is predicted that if the pace is doubled at which women become frequent users of technology (i.e., digital technologies), the workplace could reach gender equality by 2040 in developed nations and by 2060 in developing nations.

At the current pace, such equality will not be achieved until 2065 in developed nations and 2100 in developing countries. For each of these goals, leveling the pathway for women in infrastructure sectors requires changes at all levels of engagement—in national policies, educational systems, sectors and industry levels, and workplaces.

Getting more women in the door can also change societal gender norms about the kinds of careers that are "appropriate" for women and those in which women can excel (Das & Kotikula 2019). When considering different countries, it was found that nations with higher rates of digital fluency among women have higher rates of gender equality in the workplace. For example, the United States, the Netherlands, the United Kingdom, and the Nordic countries (Sweden, Denmark, Norway, and Finland) have the highest digital fluency scores and rank among the top performers in workplace equality. On the other hand, the largest gaps between the digital fluency of men and women appear in Japan, Singapore, France, and Switzerland. Therefore, increasing women's fluency to the level of men's will help drive equality in the workplace, though as indicated above, Japan has additional challenges to overcome (Das & Kotikula, 2019).

The International Labour Organization (2018) discovered that women who want to work outside of the home experience a harder time finding a job than their male counterparts. This issue is particularly marked in Northern Africa and Arab States, where unemployment rates for women exceeds 16%. Thus, the lack of employability continues to be a central issue faced by women across the world. To address these issues, most countries provide education and training skills and resources for women, which is imperative for their well-being, especially as we enter Industry 4.0, where closing the Digital Divide is crucial to the up mobility of women in the workplace.

What Is The Digital Divide?

Digital Divide is defined as the gap between people who have sufficient knowledge of and access to technology and those who do not-can perpetuate and even worsen socioeconomic and other disparities for already underserved groups (Moore, et al., 2018).

The term digital divide, initiated during the early 1990s (Cruz-Jesus et al., 2012), typically relates to sociodemographic differences in one's use of information and communication technology (Vehovar, et al., 2006). However, the digital divide also addresses the gap between individuals, households, businesses, and geographical areas experiencing different socioeconomic levels, concerning access to information and communication technologies (ICTs) and use of the Internet for a wide variety of activities (Organisation for Economic Cooperation and Development, 2001). As a result, fewer women reach top levels in careers, resulting in a majority employed at lower levels working with computers performing data entry.

Women need digital resources so that they can thrive in a digital information economy. If women are not present at all levels in this growing industry, society will experience marginalization that could undermine the advances made by women and men in other fields (Pande, 2008). In today's society, it is imperative to improve gender equality for all as it is a main indicator of a society's democratization and the level of its civilization (Sibirskaya, 2019).

CULTURAL LENSES: ROLES COUNTRIES PLAY WITH ADDRESSING GENDER EQUITY AND THE DIGITAL DIVIDE

This section provides a cultural lens for Bangladesh, Kenya, Israel, and the United States, with different cultures and how they address gender equity and how best to address the digital divide to improve women's employment. While each country is different, each detail the best strategies and practices for allowing women to gain knowledge, resources, support, and access to technologies.

Bangladesh is one of the world's most densely populated countries, with its people primarily located within a delta of rivers that empty into the Bay of Bengal (BBC News, 2018). The total population is 166,334,118 as of July 2021 (Worldometer, 2021). Currently, 38.6% (62,865,820) of the population is urban (Worldometer, 2021); with many being landless and forced to live on cultivated, flood-prone land (Central Intelligence Agency, 2021). Regarding literacy, a majority of the population 15 and older can read and write. However, the participation of women in the skilled labor force continues to face challenges with keeping pace with the changing demands of the competitive market of urbanization and globalization (Faulkner, et al., 2019).

Figure 1. Bangladeshi Lens
Source: Infoplease, n.d.

In Bangladesh, women earn less than their male counterparts in almost all cases. However, due to the countries' urban population growth, and increased urbanization, it is expected that by 2025, its labor force will reach 76 million. Youth 18 to 24 are considered the most productive labor force segment (Rashid, 2017).

Females' low participation in the labor force can be attributed to societal factors, such as girls being encouraged to marry early. In addition, families in both urban (formal sectors) and rural (informal sectors) areas encourage more males than females to receive education and training skills development. As a result, most females are often forced into typical trades, such as sewing, typing, and entering into informal work agreements, and hazardous and exploitative forms of employment, such as manufacturing (i.e., Ready-Made Garments) domestic work, or as farmworkers. The most preferred job for female college graduates is education, which accounts for 32% of the female college graduate workforce. That is followed by Ready-Made Garments (RMG) at 24%, and lagging behind is the Information Communication and Technology (ICT) industry at 14% (World Bank, 2017). Since employability in technology continues to be an issue faced by women in Bangladesh, providing education and training skills in ICT is recognized as one of Bangladesh's national priorities. Therefore, Technical Vocational Education and Training (TVET) Programs are being offered to meet women's employability needs. Governmental institutions operated by various ministries and directorates and private institutions, industries, companies, and international non-government organizations (NGOs) provide TVET courses. While the government courses offered are formal, the private courses are both formal and informal.

TVET Programs are considered the most important driving force for empowering the marginalized section in the society, with special skills, especially for those from lower socioeconomic backgrounds who cannot afford long-term formal education for various social and financial reasons. Moreover, while people mostly migrate from rural areas, good numbers migrate from urban areas. Therefore, TVET Programs are considered essential for those who face challenges to meet the new demands of the changing economies, new technologies, and the market competency in globalization through improved Education and skills.

Table 1 provides several key governmental policies and procedures supporting increasing Technical Vocational Education Training (TVET) programs. These policies and procedures emphasize TVET programs for promoting productivity growth, self-employment, and, most importantly, employability for women.

Table 2 details major employment industries for females ages 15 and older during 2005, 2010, and 2013. The agriculture industry is the major employment industry for females, followed by manufacturing, wholesale, retail, repair of motor vehicles, and construction. While ICT is shown during the years 2010 and 2013, it is insignificant, which shows ICT as an area in need of change for including women for employment options.

Table 1. Government policies and procedures to increase TVET programs

Policy or Procedure
Vision 2021
The Poverty Reduction Strategy II (PSR II), 2009-2011
The National Education Policy (NEP), 2010
The Seventh 5-Year Plan, FY2016-FY2020
The National Strategy for Promotion of Gender Equality (NSPGE)

Source: (International Labour Organization, 2012)

The COVID-19 pandemic has caused new challenges and has moved rapidly beyond an international health pandemic to heralding a global socioeconomic crisis not seen since the Great Depression of the 1930s. In addition to the threat to public health, the economic and social disruption on a global basis threatens the long-term livelihoods and well-being of millions of people. Therefore, to improve how gender equity for women, The Bangladeshi Government has also implemented three major external assisted projects to promote TVET reforms, which include:

1. The European Union Assisted TVET Reform Project (2008–2012)
2. The Asian Development Bank Skills Development Project (2008–2013)
3. The World Bank Assisted Skills and Training Enhancement Project (STEP) (2010–2015)

Table 2. Major Industries of employment for females ages 15 and over

Industries	Share of Employed Persons (%)		
	2005	2010	2013
Agriculture: Forestry and fishing	48.1	47.6	45.1
Manufacturing	11.0	12.5	16.4
Construction	3.2	4.8	3.7
Wholesale, retail, repair of motor vehicle	15.0	14.0	13.0
Transportation	8.4	7.4	6.4
Information and Communications Technology (ICT)	---	0.1-0.2	0.1-0.2

Source: (World Bank, 2017)

Bangladesh's mission should be to encourage a significantly higher ratio of female participation in the labor force to realize its vision of reaching middle-income status

Figure 2. Kenyan lens
Source: Infoplease, n.d.

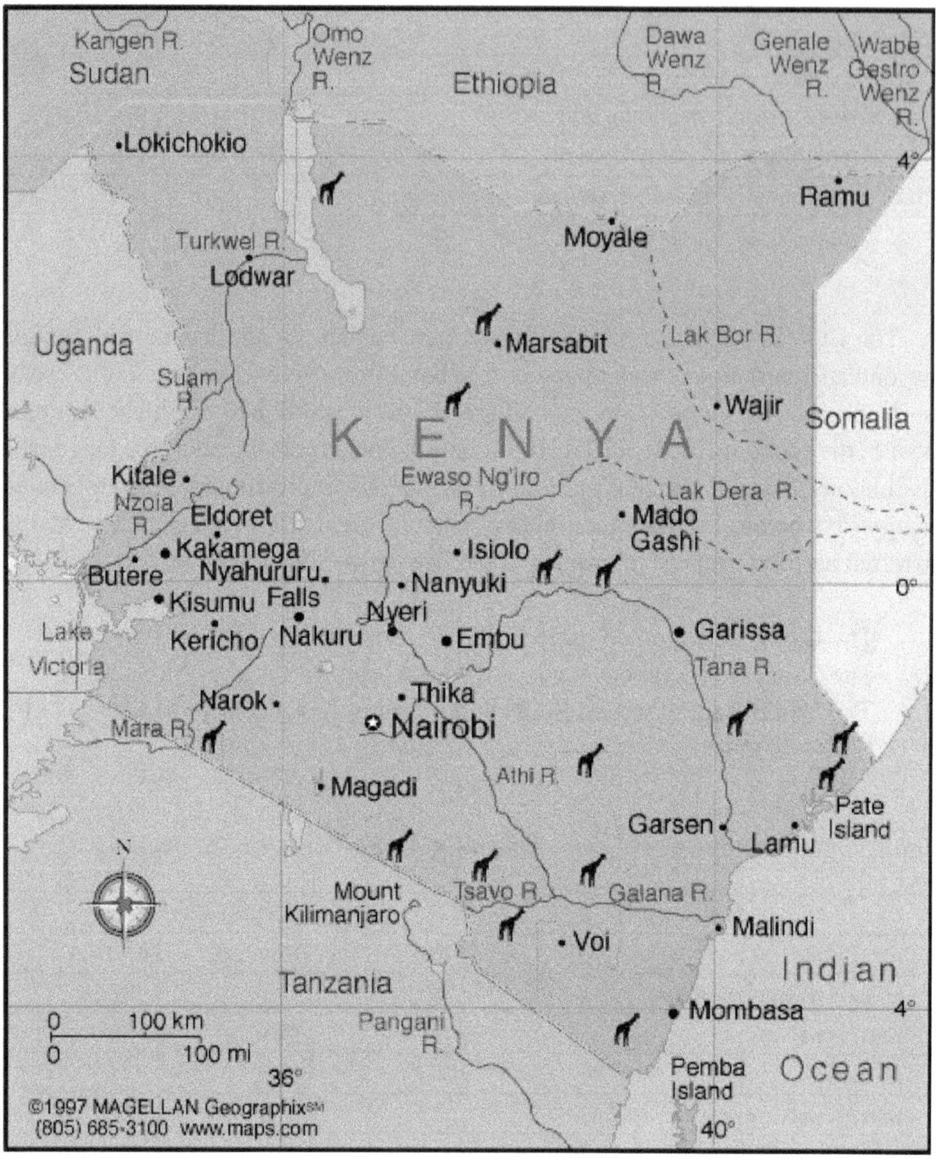

by 2021. In addition, ICT can play an important role in job creation for women (World Bank, 2015).

Kenya is a large multi-ethnic country, with over 42 different ethnic groups and many overlapping conflicts. Its total population is 53,771,296 as of July 2021 (Worldometer, 2021). The country has high sexual and gender-based violence incidents, intercommunal violence, and low levels of persistent violence. In conflict settings, rural youth are mostly affected. Both young men and women often seek migration. Conditions for young women are particularly harmful in remote fragile and conflict-affected areas, especially concerning their access to farmland that in many cases serves as the only source of income.

For several reasons, women are more constrained in accessing employment opportunities than their male counterparts in the Kenyan job market. One primary reason is Constraints on their mobility and less access than men to financial resources and financial institutions such as banks (Filmer & Fox, 2014). Social norms concerning childcare duties and the desire to gain employment shaped women's willingness to labor force participation (employability).

One significant challenge women face for obtaining employment is gender inequity, which results in a lack of access to social protection acquired through work, such as pensions, unemployment benefits, and maternity protection. However, despite employment opportunities for women receiving greater attention in the country over the past decade, few programs have emphasized the importance of targeting young women in employment (Chakravarty, et al., 2017).

It is important to note that women represent the primary economic force in most developing countries. They comprise an estimated 43% of the agricultural labor force producing 60-80% of the foodstuffs. As economies become more Information and Communications technology (ICT)-driven, women's access to and use of ICTs increases, particularly in Kenya. However, despite Kenyan women's critical role in their countries' economies, many still do not have limited access to technology. Access to mobile technology offers women a wealth of social and economic support, empowering more female entrepreneurs in Kenya and other developing markets that benefit from the ever-expanding mobile value chain.

In Kenya, ICTs have infused almost all aspects of people's lives in urban and rural communities. Moreover, advancements in technology have increased the countries' innovations, such as mobile phones; for instance, in today's society, women have access just as their male counterparts in every community in the country. Many Kenyan women, especially those employed in the informal sector, experience challenges accessing office computers and the Internet, limiting gainful employment. Because of limited ownership of assets, women have none or less collateral to offer to banks. They are also constrained in their capacity to access credit and other financial services needed to succeed. Another challenge Kenyan women encounter is access to education (technology education), which is more significant than their male counterparts. Most of the training or educational institutions in Kenya have male trainers who are biased toward female students and have negative perceptions about women's knowledge, skills, and capabilities for using technology.

Another challenge is access to finances. Women consider the lack of finance to be very discouraging when attempting to gain employment in Africa. Women fail to have full access to forms of capital, such as loans or grants to open a bank account. For example, a study found that young Egyptian women face substantial inequalities in the labor market regarding employment opportunities and wages. Young women's labor force participation is low, and unemployment is high (Constant, et al., 2020). In another study related to Egyptian women, over 70% reported that access to finance presented a challenge in beginning their business, while 73% reported expecting that this inequality would be a challenge in growing their business further (International Labour Organization, 2016).

However, fast technological advancement is reshaping the future of work by increasing the demand for different types of human capabilities, such as working with ICT and artificial intelligence (AI). Therefore, training for women must focus on technical skills and advanced cognitive skills (critical thinking and problem solving), and non-cognitive skills to adapt to complex demands. Gaining the training will increase their chance of successful employment (Baliki, et al., 2019), particularly the agri-food and value chain system, which employs young women.

Information and communication technologies (ICTs) expansion across Kenya is a key driver of the economic growth noted in the country in the last decade (International Trade Administration, 2021). In addition, ICTs have the potential to enable many enterprising individuals, firms, communities to address economic and social challenges with greater efficiency and imagination (UNESCO, 2003).

To summarize, the Gender Digital Divide remains an issue in Kenya. However, it is gaining more agreement that women in urban and rural regions can benefit significantly from training and ICT access to improve employment opportunities. As a result, the Kenyan government provides more training programs to close the Digital Divide for women's access to ICT. In today's society, it is now more accepted that today's women should possess technical skills, affecting ICT work (Chastain, et al., 2014). In addition, various forms of digital expression, such as blogging, can amplify women´s voices, increasing their self-esteem.

Kenya has planned strategies for addressing the Digital Divide, such as The Kenyan government proposal of a Five-point Action Plan to improve the Internet infrastructure. The Government is prioritizing the construction and modernization of Internet infrastructure to ensure 100% network coverage in the entire country to access the network, increasing access and affordability. In addition, the government is working with mobile operators and Internet Service Providers to lower tariffs.

In addition, free public Wi-Fi initiatives are being offered in all public places, including schools, prioritizing Digital Education. As a result, all citizens will have access to governmental services and data and engage with governmental leaders in online settings. Endings to online gender-based violence is occurring, especially since online violence against women is a key concern considering Kenya is envisioned to be fully digital by 2030.

The COVID-19 pandemic has shed light on the inequalities in access to the Internet and digital technologies across the globe. Unfortunately, the measures taken to control the pandemic make these inequalities more visible, but they amplify the threat of the digital divide on people, namely women's basic livelihoods (Colum, 2020).

Technology has great potential to create new job opportunities for Kenyan women, which can also help address the persistent gender divide in the labor market. Technology has brought numerous job opportunities involving remote, online, flexible work that can help women overcome mobility constraints, challenge restrictive gender norms, and reduce long-standing occupational segregation in traditionally male-dominated industries (Goos & Manning, 2007).

It is important to note that ICTs, especially the Internet, are essential to women's empowerment in Kenya. This is because ICTs offer immense possibilities, including overcoming isolation, giving women a voice, improving governance, advancing gender equality, and reducing poverty. However, this potential will only be realized when the barriers contributing to the current Gender Digital Divide are recognized and efficiently addressed. Therefore, there is an increasing call for more actions and organizations to bridge the gender digital divide to allow women to benefit fully from technology for their livelihood.

Israel's population is 8,790,286 as of July 2021 (Worldometer, 2022), with 93.2% being urban residents and a median age of 30.5 years. Job security is more challenging for women to obtain in comparison to their male counterparts. Israel's labor force equaled million people during 1990 – 2020. During that period, the average value for Israel was 3.11 million people, with a minimum of 1.89 million people in 1990 and a maximum of 4.16 million people in 2019. The latest number from 2020 is 4.13 million people.

During 1990 – 2019, females made up 44.9% of the labor force ranging from 39.77% in 1990 to 47.6% in 2019 (The Global Economy.com, 2021). It is important to understand that when women are employed, the job is generally low-paying, low quality, and or located in hazardous conditions. While vulnerable employment can be widespread for both women and men, women tend to be overrepresented in certain types of jobs. For example, men are more likely to gain employment by choice while women are more likely to gain employment in the household or relatives' businesses (International Labour Organization, 2018).

The gender gap continues to create barriers for women gaining employment in cultures such as the Middle East. Studies conducted by Banerjee (2019), International Labour Organization (2018), Organisation of Economic Co-operation and Development (2016), and World Economic Forum (2017) detail the negative

Figure 3. Israeli lens
Source: Infoplease, n.d.

effects of the Digital Divide, especially those in the Middle East, India, and Africa. The problem is particularly marked in Northern Africa and the Arab States, where unemployment rates for women can exceed 16% (International Labour Organization, 2018).

A 2018 Organisation of Economic Co-operation and Development Report provided an overview of technological literacy, inherent gender biases, and socio-cultural norms being the root of women's Gender-based Digital exclusion regarding technology, education, and access. While the global digital divide related to gender's Internet usage remained unchanged from 2013-2017, the gap between developed and developing countries has increased. The cause can often be attributed to an increase in the gender Internet usage gap, which is 3% points in the least developed countries.

The digital transformation has the potential to offer women opportunities to benefit their economy. However, digital transformation fails to be equal in societal groups, among gender, and access, use, and ownership of digital tools are not gender-neutral. The term "digital gender divide" is frequently used to refer to types of gender differences in resources and capabilities to access and effectively utilize ICTs within and between countries, regions, sectors, and socioeconomic groups (United Nations, 2015).

Heruti-Sover (2019) offered that in current-day Israel, only 12% of the top positions at companies traded on Israel's leading Tel Aviv-125 Index are held by women, as of 2017, according to a study conducted by Idit Cohen, reported that women hold 62 of these positions, while men have the remaining 461. Heruti-Sover continued by noting banking institutions had a relatively higher percentage of women as top managers, at 30%. Other sectors, however, were male-led. For example, 94% of executives in industrial companies were men and 93% in technology companies. Moreover, these sectors did not have a single female CEO, and the only female chairwoman was one of the controlling shareholders.

The sectors with the broadest pay gaps between men and women were industry and technology, respectively, at 144% and 105%. Male top executives earned 3.3 million shekels ($940,000) a year, versus women, who earned 1.6 million, on average. Thus, women make up a small percentage of top executives in these sectors, and those who do hold posts, earn significantly less than their male counterparts.

In a study conducted by Rafaeli, et al. (2018), the researchers compared technology use based on gender and found male users exhibited higher usage volume than female users. Significant differences in usage volume were also observed between Hebrew, Arabic, and Russian speakers. The usage volume among Hebrew speakers was two times larger than Arabic speakers and 2.4 times larger than native Russian speakers. Stark spatial differences in usage volume were found between users from the Core ("Center") region (Tel Aviv District) and the country's periphery (North

Figure 4. United States of America's Lens
Source: Infoplease, n.d.

and South Districts), with the usage volume characterizing Core residents being five times larger than the one characterizing users from the Periphery.

In terms of Internet content diversity, male users were more diverse than female users concerning internet content consumption. Spatial differences concerning the diversity level were also significant. Users from the Tel Aviv metropolitan and Jerusalem metropolitan regions exhibited the highest diversity levels and were statistically different from users in other regions. In terms of content usage, the findings of the research reveal a high degree of compatibility between the results of this digital trace exercise and various findings reported in the literature from self-report sources:

The United States of America (U.S.) population was 332,974,024 as of July 2021 (Worldometer, 2021), equivalent to 4.25% of the total world population. Approximately 82% of the population is located in urban sectors (273,975,139 in 2020) (Worldometer, 2021).

Women have made notable changes in their labor force activities regarding the labor force, over the past four decades. For example, labor force participation is significantly higher among women today than in the 1970s, particularly among women with children. In addition, a more significant number of women were working full-time and year-round (U.S. Bureau of Labor Statistics, 2014). Women in the labor force peaked at 60% in 1999 (Fry & Stepler, 2017). In 2019, 76,852,000 women aged 16 and over in the labor force, representing close to half (47%) of the total labor force (U.S. Bureau of Labor Statistics, 2021). Recently released projections from the Bureau of Labor Statistics indicate that women's share of the labor force will peak at 47.1% in 2025 and then taper off to 46.3% by 2060, meaning that women will remain a minority of the labor force.

In 2015, U.S. women made up 57% of professionals but only 25% of computer professionals. As a result, there is a need to provide education, training, and support for women in the technological field, as they are more likely than their male counterparts to leave. One of the most common reasons concerns workplace conditions, a lack of access to key creative roles, and a sense of 'feeling stalled in their career' (UNESCO and Equal Skills Coalition, 2019).

In the artificial intelligence (AI) sector, which is expanding rapidly, from 2015 to 2017, the number of workers worldwide with AI skills increased by 190%

(World Economic Forum, 2017). Furthermore, it is important to note that 'industries with more AI skills present in employees' in their workforce are considered the fastest-changing industries.

In the U.S, AI has the highest-paid employees of any field of technology. According to the U.S. Bureau of Labor Statistics and the Census Bureau, the pay gap in computer science is one of the smallest between men and women, with women earning 94% of what their male counterparts take home. However, although the top multinational technology companies are making progress, they are still not close to closing the Gender Gap in technical and leadership roles. For example, Facebook fares better than its fellow technology competitors for the number of women holding senior leadership positions. Still, the percentage of women employed in technical roles remains low (UNESCO and Equal Skills Coalition, 2019). Therefore, the question is posed, "Why are women still a minority among employees of digital tech giants, even in the U.S.? According to data collected by LinkedIn visitors and published in the World Economic Forum's Global Gender Gap Report, only 22% of professionals working in AI worldwide are female. This gap is visible in all of the top 20 countries with the highest concentration of AI employees. It is particularly evident in Argentina, Brazil, Germany, Mexico, and Poland, where fewer than 18% of women professionals have Artificial Intelligence (AI) skills.

Table 3. Statistics of Women in Technology

Statement	%
Computing-related jobs held by women	26
Computing-related jobs held by African-American women	3
Computing-related jobs held by Asian-American women	6
Computing-related jobs held by Hispanic women	2
Women reported they had experienced gender discrimination at work	50
Americans believe women create a safer, more respectful work environment than men.	43
Americans believe men create a safer workspace	5
Women's earnings are outpacing those of men's when it comes to high-skill jobs	---
Women were 22% more likely to experience "Imposter Syndrome" in the workplace (the overwhelming feeling of being out of place compared to colleagues)	---

Source: (Daley, 2021)

What Does The Future Hold For Women Being Employed In Technology?

Daley (2021) offered, "let's face it; tech still has an issue with gender diversity. The tech sector sadly lags behind the rest of the job market when it comes to hiring women" (p.1). As the percentage of employed women across all job sectors in the U.S. has increased to 47%, the five largest technology companies on the planet (Amazon, Apple, Facebook, Google, and Microsoft) women only make up about 34.4% of the workforce (Daley, 2021). Table 3 provides statistical examples of women working in technology-related jobs.

Additional practices for increasing women's employability include: requiring diverse candidate pools for hiring, promotions, and board seats, hiring should be based on potential, offering gender bias training for hiring officers and others in hiring positions, and increasing flexible working options (Daley, 2021).

SOLUTIONS AND RECOMMENDATIONS

To identify solutions for combating Gender Inequity by providing women with the education, training, and resources needed to be competitive in the labor force, society must establish legislation, policies, economic relief, and social programs (Sibirskaya, 2019).

Networking is one recommendation. Singh (2019) recommends, "Networks which promote and reward skills and productivity are helpful. There should also be equal representation of gender in terms of participation in works and skill development" (p. 1). Another recommendation is crucial Skill development. For example, in India, an emphasis for greater skill development efforts in the country was addressed by Prime Minister Narendra Modi, who launched a campaign "Skill India" in July 2015, which focused on skill development in various government and non-government initiatives (Deka, 2019), to address gender equity.

The future of technology is ever-changing. While the types and uses of technologies vary based on gender, knowledge, access, geographical location, and need, it can also depend on one's culture and residence. Each of these factors can significantly affect a woman's employability achievement. Therefore, future research studies on how to assess these factors would significantly improve the future body of knowledge.

Today's society is evolving, and the focus on Industry 4.0 is increasing. Industry 4.0 is defined as "a name for the current automation and data exchange trend in manufacturing technologies, including cyber-physical systems, the Internet of things, cloud computing and cognitive computing and creating the smart factory" (I-SCOOP, 2017, p.1).

Further, Industry 4.0 is often used interchangeably with the concept of the fourth industrial revolution and is characterized by, among others, as:

1) Even more automation than in the third industrial revolution,
2) The bridging of the physical and digital world through cyber-physical systems, enabled by Industrial IoT,
3) A shift from a central industrial control system to one where smart products define the production steps, 4) closed-loop data models and control systems, and
4) A personalization/customization of products (I-SCOOP, 2017).

While progress is occurring in some career fields for women to be involved, they continue to be at risk of exclusion from employment in other fields. The world is undergoing a fundamental transformation that is changing the way we live, work and think. These changes have far-reaching implications for the role of women, especially in science, technology, engineering, and mathematics (STEM) (I-SCOOP, 2017).

The future benefits of Industry 4.0 are significant. Whether it is Industry 4.0, Smart Industry, or the Industrial Internet, there are ample benefits for manufacturers to transform the way they work. However, most benefits of Industry 4.0 are similar to the Digital Transformation of manufacturing, the usage of the IoT in manufacturing, operational and business process optimization, information-powered ecosystems of value, and the Industrial Internet.

DISCUSSION AND CONCLUSION

In this chapter, it has been shared that in many societies, gender bias reduces economic opportunities for women (girls, young and older) (Chandra, 2019).

All over the globe, most women are in health, education, and the caring sector but remain underrepresented in engineering, manufacturing, construction, science, and technology. Therefore, the quality of a nation's workforce is vital for economic growth and social development. The critical determinants of the quality of the labor force include its flexibility, namely the ability of the workers to move across sectors of the economy and between industries. This is because of the changing structure of the economy in the highly competitive and rapidly globalizing world economy in recent years. In addition, providing skills and flexibility are becoming increasingly crucial for faster growth, impacting welfare improvement. Furthermore, they improve a country's ability to acquire and adapt technology to lower the cost of production of goods and services to meet the requirements of new markets.

Flexibility depends partly on the technical and vocational skills acquired by an individual.

It is important to remember that Women must not miss out on the jobs of the future. This is the central message of a new study on women in science released by UNESCO this month, entitled to be smart; the digital revolution will need to be inclusive. A fundamental transformation is underway in the workforce. The Fourth Industrial Revolution, or Industry 4.0, is disrupting industries and the Labour market as cyber-physical systems proliferate and become more sophisticated (UNESCO, 2021).

As reported by the International Labour Organization (2021)

The COVID-19 pandemic has moved rapidly beyond an international health Pandemic to heralding a global socioeconomic crisis not seen since The Great Depression of the 1930s. In addition to the threat to public health, the economic and social disruption on a global basis threatens the long-term livelihoods and well-being of millions of people. (p.1)

Modern democracies take pride in their capacity to secure equality for all citizens regardless of their age, gender, religion, or ethnic origin. However, all societies have to deal with the issue of gender inequality, and, in almost all cases, it is an ongoing process (Mitrevska, 2017). Therefore, it can be concluded that countries, government agencies, educational institutions, and especially job placements should involve both men and women in decision-making processes, as it will improve the likelihood of achieving gender-sensitive and equity.

The idea connects with the concept of empowering women, defined as a "bottom-up process of transforming gender power relations, through individuals or groups developing awareness of women's subordination and building their capacity to challenge it (Mitrevska, 2017). Gender is the socially constructed difference between men and women. This is different from sex, which are the biological differences between men and women. Therefore, when we say that men and women are not the same, we refer not only to differences in biology (biological/sex differences) but also to the different roles (gender differences) created by society (Mitrevska, 2017).

Technology can create new job opportunities for Kenyan women and help address the persistent gender disparity in the labor market. Technology has brought numerous job opportunities involving remote, online, flexible work that can help women overcome mobility constraints, challenge restrictive gender norms, and reduce longstanding occupational segregation in traditionally male-dominated industries (Goos & Manning, 2007).

In 2020, the world embraced digital transformation at an expedited pace, reimagining technology's critical role in how we work, learn and live. Yet, at the same time, the COVID-19 pandemic illuminated a long-standing issue: billions of people remain without the universal human right of internet access (Roese, 2021).

This chapter shows that while women from various cultures and countries may experience Digital Divide challenges for employment differently and gain education, governmental support, and resources, the result provides solutions for aiding them to succeed as society evolves to Industry 4.0.

ACKNOWLEDGMENT

This research received no specific grant from any funding agency in the public, commercial, or not-for-profit sectors.

Figure 5. The Nine Digital Technologies of Industry 4.0 framework (I-Scoop, 2017)

REFERENCES

Accenture. (2016). *Getting to equal: How digital is helping close the gender gap at work*. https://instituteforpr.org/wp-content/uploads/Accenture-IWD-2016-Research-Getting-To-Equal.pdf

Apple. (2018). *Employer Information Report EEO-1*. Apple.

Baliki, G., Bruck, T., Ferguson, N. T. N., & Stojetz, W. (2019). *Rural youth in the context of fragility and conflict.* 2019 Rural Development Report. International Fund for Agricultural Development (IFAD). https://www.ifad.org/documents/38714170/41187395/14_Baliki+et+al._2019+RDR+BCKGROUND+PAPER.pdf/a0003ba0-3e4f-3fbd-8d2b-654bf75176e8

Banerjee, M. (2019). Gender equality and labour force participation: Mind the Gap. *Indian Journal of Women and Social Change*, *4*(1), 113–123. doi:10.1177/2455632719831827

BBC News. (2018, February). *Bangladesh country profile.* https://www.bbc.com/news/world-south-asia-12650940

Bureau of Labor Statistics. (2016). *Labor force participation: What has happened since the peak?* https://www.bls.gov/opub/mlr/2016/article/labor-force-participation-

Central Intelligence Agency. (2021). *South Asia, Bangladesh.* https://www.cia.gov/library/publications/the-world-factbook/geos/bg.html

Chakravarty, S., Das, S., & Vaillant, J. (2017). *Gender and youth employment in Sub-Saharan Africa: A review of constraints and effective interventions.* Policy Research Working Paper No. 8245. World Bank. https://openknowledge.worldbank.org/handle/10986/28905

Chandra, A. (2019). Gender Gap in skill development: An analytical review. In S. Bala & P. Singhal (Eds.), *Gender issues in technical and vocational education programs* (pp. 158–182). IGI Publishers. doi:10.4018/978-1-5225-8443-8.ch008

Chastain, E., Thickett, B., Unnikrishnan, S., & Woods, W. (2014). *Bridging the entrepreneurship Gender Gap: The power of networks.* Boston Consulting Group.

Colum, A. (2020). *COVID-19 and what digital divide means for people's livelihoods in Kenya.* https://www.heart-resources.org/blog/covid-19-and-what-the-digital-divide-means-for-peoples-livelihoods-in-kenya/

Constant, L., Edochie, I., Glick, P., Martini, J., & Garber, C. (2020). *Barriers to employment that women face in Egypt: Policy challenges and considerations.* https://www.rand.org/pubs/research_reports/RR2868.html

Cruz-Jesus, F., Oliveira, T., & Bacao, F. (2012). Digital divide across the European Union. *Information & Management*, *49*(6), 278–291.

Daley, S. (2021). *Women in tech statistics show the industry has a long way to go.* https://builtin.com/women-tech/women-in-tech-workplace-statistics

Das, S., & Kotikula, A. (2019). *Gender-based employment segregation: Understanding causes and policy interventions*. Jobs (Working Paper No. 26). https://documents.worldbank.org/curated/en/483621554129720460/Gender-Based-Employment-Segregation-Understanding-Causes-and-Policy-Interventions

Dastin, J. (2018). *Amazon scraps secret AL recruiting tool that showed bias against women.* Thomson Reuters. https://www.reuters.com/article/us-amazon-com-jobs-automation-insight/amazon-scraps-secret-ai-recruiting-tool-that-showed-bias-against-women-idUSKCN1MK08G?feedType=RSS&feedName=topNews&utm_source=twitter&utm_medium=Social

Deka, S. J. (2019). Vocational education and training for Women: A gender Divide perspective. In S. Bala & P. Singhal (Eds.), *Gender issues in technical and vocational education programs* (pp. 158–182). IGP Publishers. doi:10.4018/978-1-5225-8443-8.ch008

Facebook. (2019). *Diversity Report 2019: Advancing diversity and inclusion.* Facebook. https://about.fb.com/news/2019/07/2019-diversity-report/

Faulkner, P., Begam, S., & English, C. (2019). How Bangladesh is increasing the employability of females with technical training programs. In S. Bala & P. Singhal (Eds.), *Gender issues in technical and vocational education programs* (pp. 158–182). IGI Publishers. doi:10.4018/978-1-5225-8443-8.ch008

Filmer, D., & Fox, L. (2014). *Youth employment in Sub-Saharan Africa. Africa Development Forum.* Washington, DC: World Bank and Agence Française de Développement. https://openknowledge.worldbank.org/handle/10986/16608

Food and Agriculture Organization of the United Nations. (2011). *The state of food and agriculture: Women in agriculture, closing the gender gap in development.* https://www.fao.org/3/i2050e/i2050e.pdf

Fry, R., & Stepler, R. (2017). *Women may never make up half of the U.S. workforce.* https://www.pewresearch.org/fact-tank/2017/01/31/women-may-never-make-up-half-of-the-u-s-w0orkforce/

Google. (2018). *Google Diversity Annual Report 2018.* Google.

Goos, M., & Manning, A. (2007). Lousy and lovely jobs: The rising polarization of work in Britain. *The Review of Economics and Statistics, 89*(1), 118–133.

Heruti-Sover, T. (2019). *Study: Women run only 12% of top Israeli companies.* https://www.haaretz.com/israel-news/business/study-women-run-only-12-of-top-israeli-companies-1.6999800

Huawei. (2019). *2018 Sustainability Report: Bring digital to every person, home and organization for a fully connected, intelligent world.* Huawei Investment & Holding Co, Ltd.

I-SCOOP. (2017). *Industry 4.0: The fourth industrial revolution–guide to Industrie 4.0.* https://www.i-scoop.eu/industry-4-0/

Infoplease. (n.d.a). *Bangladesh.* https://www.infoplease.com/world/countries/bangladesh

Infoplease. (n.d.b) *Israel map.* https://www.infoplease.com/atlas/middle-east/israel-map

Infoplease. (n.d.c). *Kenya map.* https://www.infoplease.com/atlas/africa/kenya-map

Infoplease. (n.d.d). *Map of the United States.* https://www.infoplease.com/atlas/north-america/united-states

International Labour Organization. (2009). *Final report: Survey and assessment of formal and informal apprenticeships in Bangladesh.* http://www.ilo.org/ wcmsp5/groups/public/@asia/@ro-bangkok/@ilodhaka/documents/publication/wcms_106575.pdf

International Labour Organization. (2012). *Bangladesh Skills Vision - 2016.* http://www.ilo.org/wcmsp5/groups/public/@asia/@ro-bangkok/@ilo-dhaka/documents/publication/wcms_176772.pdf

International Labour Organization. (2018). *The Gender Gap in employment: What's holding Women back?* https://www.ilo.org/infostories/en-GB/Stories/Employment/barriers-women#intro

International Labour Organization. (2021). *COVID-19 and the world of work.* https://www.ilo.org/global/topics/coronavirus/lang--en/index.htm

International Trade Administration. (2021). *Kenya-Country Commercial guide: Information, Communications and Technology (ICT).* https://www.trade.gov/knowledge-product/kenya-information-communications-and-technology-ict

Lagarde, C., & Ostry, J. D. (2018). *Economic gains from gender inclusion: Even greater than You thought.* https://blogs.imf.org/2018/11/28/economic-gains-from-gender-inclusion-even-greater-than-you-thought/

Microsoft. (2019). *Corporate Social Responsibility Report 2018.* Microsoft.

Mitrevska, T. C. (2017, March). *Land and gender: Macedonian experience.* Paper presented at the 2017 World Bank Conference on Land and Poverty, Washington, DC.

Moore, R., Vitale, D., & Stawinoga, N. (2018). *The Digital Divide and educational equity: A look at students with very limited access to electronic devices at home.* https://files.eric.ed.gov/fulltext/ED593163.pdf

Organisation for Economic Cooperation and Development. (2001). *Understanding the Digital Divide.* https://www.oecd.org/sti/ieconomy/1888451.pdf

Organisation for Economic Cooperation and Development. (2016). *Closing gender gaps in the labour markets of emerging economies: The unfinished job.* https://www.oecd.org/employment/oecd-employment-outlook-19991266.htm

Organisation for Economic Cooperation and Development. (2018). *Bridging the Digital Gender Divide: Include, upskill, innovate.* https://www.oecd.org/digital/bridging-the-digital-gender-divide.pdf

Pande, R. (2008). Digital Divide, gender, and the Indian experience in IT. In E. Trauth (Ed.), *Encyclopaedia of Gender and Information Technology* (pp. 191–199). IGI Global Publishers. doi:10.4018/978-1-59904-939-7.ch105

Rafaeli, S., Leck, E., Albo, Y., Oppenheim, Y., & Getz, D. (2018). *An innovative approach for measuring the Digital Divide in Israel: Digital trace data as means for formulating policy guidelines.* https://www.neaman.org.il/Files/Measuring_the_Digital_Divide_%20in_Israel_Final_July_29.pdf

Rashid, L. (2017). *Enhancing decent employment opportunities for women and marginalized groups in growth sectors.* https://www.un.org/development/desa/dspd/wp-content/uploads/sites/22/2017/04/BRAC-Skills-present

Roese, J. (2021). *COVID-19 exposed the Digital Divide. Here's how we can close it.* https://www.delltechnologies.com/en-us/perspectives/covid-19-exposed-the-digital-divide-here-s-how-we-can-close-it/?gacd=9643275-1040-5761040-266682520-0&dgc=st&gclid=CjwKCAjwoZWHBhBgEiwAiMN66eQ0xNIcBEqodudgWf8aH6NjUq4v1RyZQmnUKrLN0K1Q_PEj0rfuRoC7YQQAvD_BwE&gclsrc=aw.ds&nclid=vmlAo9V_McM-fNsg2vhYo6-FXU6B5npe066lyRCEAhTzIrCssL85yE2ty_gM9xjL

Samsung Electronics. (2019). *A Fifty Year journey towards a sustainable future. Sustainability Report 2019.* Samsung Electronics. https://images.samsung.com/is/content/samsung/assets/ve/our-values/resource/SustainabilityReport2019v2-en.pdf

Schomer, I., & Hammond, A. (2020). Stepping up women's STEM careers in infrastructure: An overview of promising approaches. ESMAP Paper. Washington, DC: World Bank.

Sibirskaya, A. (2019). Gender issues and priorities in Republic of Belarus. In S. Bala & P. Singhal (Eds.), *Gender issues in technical and vocational education programs* (pp. 158–182). IGP Publishers. doi:10.4018/978-1-5225-8443-8.ch008

Singh, D. (2019). Gender issues in Vocational Education and Training in India: Imperatives and challenges. In S. Bala & P. Singhal (Eds.), *Gender issues in technical and vocational education programs* (pp. 158–182). IGP Publishers. doi:10.4018/978-1-5225-8443-8.ch008

Sweet, J. (2016). *Access to digital technology accelerates global gender equality.* https://hbr.org/2016/05/access-to-digital-technology-accelerates-global-gender-equality

The Global Economy.com. (2021). *Israel: Labor force: Percent female.* https://www.theglobaleconomy.com/Israel/Labor_force_percent_female/

UNESCO. (2003). *Towards a more equitable information society: How and why of gender mainstreaming.* http://portal.unesco. Org/ci/en/file_ download. Php/ 250561f24133814c18284feedc30bb5egender_issues. Pdf

UNESCO. (2021). *Women a minority in Industry 4.0 fields.* https://en.unesco.org/news/women-minority-industry-40-fields

UNESCO and Equal Skills Coalition. (2019). *I'd blush if I could: Closing gender divides in digital skills through education.* Policy paper. UNESCO. https://en.unesco.org/Id-blush-if-I-could

United Nations. (2015). *The World's Women 2015: Trends and statistics.* https://unstats.un.org/unsd/gender/downloads/worldswomen2015_report.pdf

U.S. Bureau of Labor Statistics. (2013). *Women in the labor force: A Databook.* https://www.bls.gov/cps/wlf-databook-2012.pdf

U.S. Bureau of Labor Statistics. (2014). *Women in the Labor force: A Databook.* https://www.bls.gov/cps/wlf-databook-2013.pdf

U.S. Bureau of Labor Statistics. (2021). *Labor force statistics from the current population survey.* https://www.bls.gov/cps/cpsaat03.htm

Vehovar, V., Sicherl, P., Hüsing, T., & Dolnicar, V. (2006). Methodological challenges of digital divide measurements. *The Information Society, 22*(5), 279–290.

WEF. (2018). *The Global Gender Gap Report 2018.* World Economic Forum. https://www.weforum.org/reports/the-global-gender-gap-report-2018

World Bank. (2015, May). *Bangladesh's ICT industry: A boon for Women's employment.* https://www.worldbank.org/en/news/feature/2015/05/08/bangladeshs-ict-industry-a-boon-for-womens-employment

World Bank. (2017). *Breaking the glass ceiling challenges to female participation in technical diploma education in Bangladesh.* South Asia Region, Education Global Practice Report. http://documents.worldbank.org/curated/en/717771486560820977/

World Economic Forum. (2017). *The Global Gender Gap Report.* https://www3.weforum.org/docs/WEF_GGGR_2017.pdf

World Economic Forum. (2019). *Global Gender Gap Report 2020.* https://www3.weforum.org/docs/WEF_GGGR_2020.pdf

Worldometer. (2021a). *Bangladesh population (Live).* https://www.worldometers.info/world-population/bangladesh-population/#:~:text=Bangladesh%202020%20population%20is%20estimated,(and%20dependencies)%20by%20population

Worldometer. (2021b). *Israel population (Live).* https://www.worldometers.info/world-population/israel-population/

Worldometer. (2021c). *Kenya population (Live).* https://www.worldometers.info/demographics/kenya-demographics/

Worldometer. (2021d). *United States population (Live).* https://www.worldometers.info/world-population/us-population/

ADDITIONAL READING

Cihak, M., & Sahay, R. (2018). Women in finance: An Economic case for gender equality. https://blogs.imf.org/2018/09/19/women-in-finance-an-economic-case-for-gender-equality/

International Labour Organization. (2010). Women in labour markets: Measuring progress and identifying challenges. http://www.ilo.org/wcmsp5/groups/public/---ed_emp/--- emp_elm/---trends/documents/publication/wcms_123835.pdf

Maclean, R., Jagannathan, S., & Sarvi, J. (2012). *Skills development for inclusive and sustainable growth in developing Asia-Pacific.* Springer.

Mammen, K., & Paxson, C. (2000). Women's work and economic development. *The Journal of Economic Perspectives, 14*(4), 141–164. doi:10.1257/jep.14.4.141

Norris, E. D., & Kochhar, K. (2018). Women, technology and the future of work. https://blogs.imf.org/2018/11/16/women-technology-and-the-future-of-work/

UNESCO. (2021). The race against time for smarter development. https://www.unesco.org/reports/science/2021/en

Women, U. N. (2005). Gender equality and empowerment of women through ICT. https://www.unwomen.org/-/media/headquarters/media/publications/un/en/w200009dot05icte.pdf?la=en&vs=956

Women, U. N. (2020). Gender and the Digital Divide in situations of displacement: The experiences of Syrian refugee women in Al-Azaraq and Al-Za'atari Camps. https://www2.unwomen.org/-/media/field%20office%20jordan/attachments/publications/2020/gender%20and%20the%20digital%20divide%20in%20situations%20of%20displacement.pdf?la=en&vs=2054

KEY TERMS AND DEFINITIONS

Digital Divide: This applies to those individuals who have access to digital devices such as the Internet, computers, and other technologies and those who have no access.

Employability: An individual's ability to be employed and maintained based on their skills, knowledge, and experience.

Gender: Term used to determine an individual's role and responsibilities as female and male. These roles are learned and vary among cultures across the world. Gender is not sexual or biological; instead, it is a social being.

Gender Inequality: Term used for stating females and males are not equal.

Gender Mainstreaming: A strategy based on public policy that values input from females and males regarding concerns and experiences on implementing programs and legislation.

Gender Responsive: The act of being aware of, providing for, and valuing the particular needs of women, such as with gender-responsive prisons.

Industry 4.0: Refers to the new age networking system including machines in the ICT industry.

Labor Force (Labour Force): Refers to individuals working along with those who can work but are not; basically, it accounts for individuals employed and unemployed.

APPENDIX I

Figure 6. Depicts women in technical and leadership roles in selected top multinational technology companies, 2018-2019.
Source: Apple, 2018, Dastin, 2018, Google, 2018, Huawei, 2019, Facebook, 2019 Microsoft, 2019, Samsung Electronics, 2019

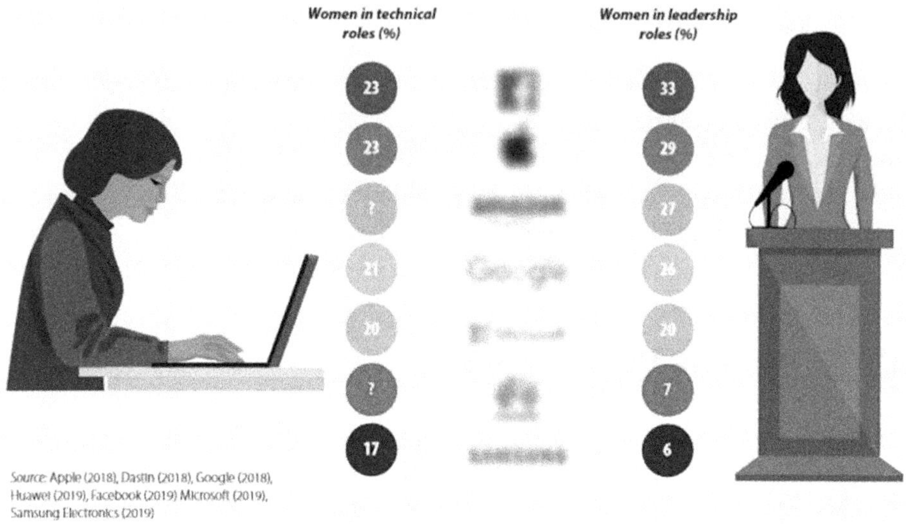

Figure 7. Depicts percentage share of women in top 20 countries for the share of professionals with Artificial Intelligence (AI) skills in 2017.
Source: WEF, 2018

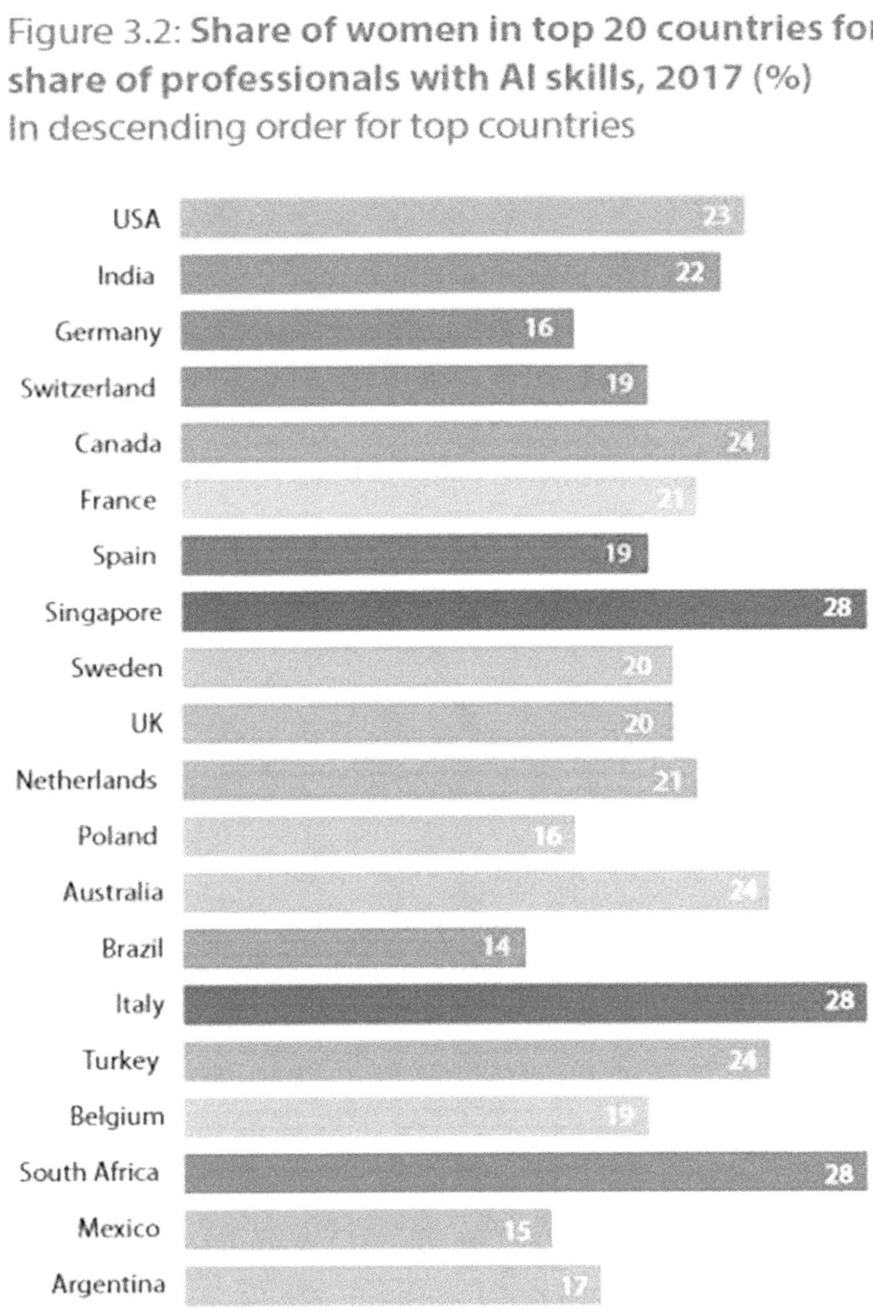

Figure 8. Depicts labor force growth projection for U.S. men and women, 1950-2050. Source: Bureau of Labor Statistics, 2016

Going forward, men's and women's labor force growth projected to be similar to each other

Average annual labor force growth rates (%)

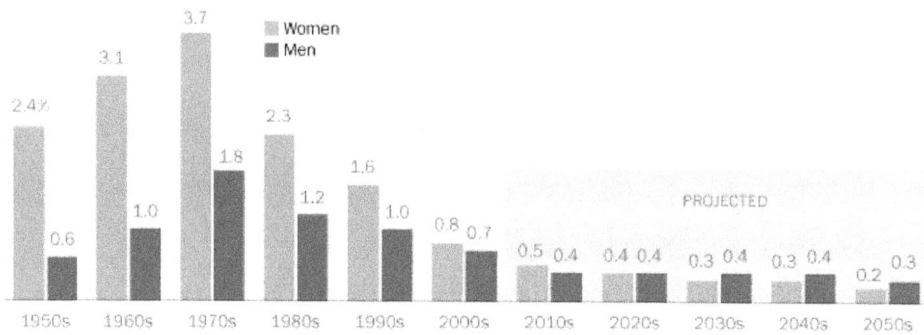

Note: 1950 to 2015 based on historical data. 2016 to 2060 projected.
Source: Bureau of Labor Statistics historical data and labor force projections.

PEW RESEARCH CENTER

Chapter 2
Bridging the Digital Gender Divide:
Prerequisite for Women Empowerment

Anjuli Chandra
The Gandhigram Rural Institute (Deemed), India

ABSTRACT

Women empowerment as a concept was introduced at the International Women Conference in 1985 at Nairobi, but it is yet to be achieved. Living in 21st century where both the genders are being taught and trained on women empowerment all over the world, there is a massive divide and an evident gap, both in terms of power and resources given to the women. Women are lagging behind men in almost every area. This gap become bigger if one looks into the digital realms and digital professions where women do not have the equal accessibility, affordability, and ICT-based education as compared to their male counterparts. In this backdrop, the chapter, by utilizing various national and international reports and inquiring various factors of digital gender divide, is an attempt to shed sufficient light on this prerequisite for women empowerment. The chapter concludes with the way forward which will lead us to a more digitally gender inclusive and sustainably developed society.

INTRODUCTION

Ever since, women empowerment as a concept was introduced at the International Women Conference in 1985 at Nairobi, which defined it as redistribution of social power and control of resources (material, human and intellectual) in favour of women, more than three decades have been passed and still it is far yet to be achieved.

DOI: 10.4018/978-1-7998-8594-8.ch002

Living in 21st Century where both the genders are being much taught and trained on women empowerment all over the world, still there is a massive divide and an evident gap, both in terms of power and resources given to the women. Women are lagging behind men in almost every area. This gap become more bigger if one looks into the digital realms and digital professions where women are not having the equal accessibility, affordability and ICT based education as compared to their male counterparts. The persistence of growing digital skills gender gaps, even in countries that rank at the top of the World Economic Forum's global gender gap index (reflecting strong gender equality) demonstrates a need for interventions that cultivate the digital skills of women and girls (UNESCO, EQUALS Skills Coalition, 2019). Though there are some silver linings but still it is a long journey of bridging the gap. In this backdrop, the present paper by utilizing various national and international reports and inquiring various factors of digital gender divide is an attempt to throw sufficient light on this prerequisite for women empowerment. The paper concludes with the way forward which will lead us to a more digitally gender inclusive and sustainably developed society.

In this review-based research paper, the author by utilizing various national and international reports on digital gender divide attempts to fulfil the following objectives:

1. To understand the development of the concept of women empowerment
2. To understand the concept of gender digital divide
3. To inquire into the factors responsible for digital gender divide
4. To suggest ways leading to more digitally gender inclusive society

DEVELOPMENT OF THE CONCEPT OF WOMEN EMPOWERMENT AND DIGITAL DIVIDE

The issue of 'women empowerment' is now a global phenomenon. Since the origin of the United Nations Organization, the issue of women's development has attracted the attention from the scholars worldwide, and the concept has come in the political agenda of a large number of countries. At present, the term "empowerment" has replaced the erstwhile term "development". It took about twenty-five years for the United Nations to proclaim the year 2001 as the 'International Year for Women's Empowerment' after declaring the 'Women's Decade' in 1975. India also declared the year 2001 as the 'Women's Empowerment Year' (Mandal,2013). Empowerment of women is not only imperative but also crucial for all-round development of society and the nation as a whole. Subsequently, it has also become a major concern of the social scientists, politicians, bureaucrats and researchers (Bhadra, 2001).

If we trace back to the First World Conference on Women held in Mexico in 1975, there were three objectives identified in relation to equality, peace and development for the Decade. The Conference urged Governments to formulate national strategies, targets and priorities. It led to the establishment of the International Research and Training Institute for the Advancement of Women (INSTRAW) and the United Nations Development Fund for Women (UNIFEM), which serve as an institutional framework for research, training and operational activities in the area of women and development. At this Conference, held in Mexico City, women played a highly visible role. Of the 133 delegations from Member States, 113 were headed by women. The Second World Conference on Women held in Copenhagen in 1980 recognized that there was a disparity between women's guaranteed rights and their capacity to exercise them and identified three spheres of equal access to education, employment opportunities, and adequate health care services in which measures were needed. The Third World Conference on Women held in Nairobi in 1985 recognized that gender equality was not an isolated issue, but encompassed all areas of human activity. The Beijing Declaration and Platform for Action were adopted at the Fourth World Conference on Women, held in 1995, by the representatives of 189 countries. The Platform reflects the new international commitment to achieving the goals of equality, development and peace for women throughout the world. It also strengthens the commitments made during the United Nations Decade for Women, 1976-1985, which culminated in the Nairobi Conference, as well as related commitments undertaken during the cycle of United Nations world conferences held in the 1990s (https://www.un.org/en/conferences/women).

Today the digital transformation provides new avenues for the economic empowerment of women and can contribute to greater gender equality. The Internet, digital platforms, mobile phones and digital financial services offer "leapfrog" opportunities for all and can help bridge the divide by giving women the possibility to earn additional income, increase their employment opportunities, and access knowledge and general information. We need to seize this opportunity to foster greater gender equality in the labour market, boost economic growth and build a more inclusive, digital world (OECD, 2018).

Today worldwide some 327 million fewer women than men have a smartphone and can access the mobile Internet. Women are under-represented in ICT jobs, top management and academic careers and as shown in the report prepared by the Organisation for Economic Co-operation and Development (OECD, 2018) men are four times more likely than women to be ICT specialists. At 15 years of age, on average, only 0.5% of girls wish to become ICT professionals, compared to 5% of boys. Women-owned start-ups receive 23% less funding and are 30% less likely to have a positive exit compared to male-owned businesses (OECD, 2018).

The report finds that hurdles to access, affordability, lack of education as well as inherent biases and socio-cultural norms curtail women and girls' ability to benefit from the opportunities offered by the digital transformation. In addition, girls' relatively lower educational enrolment in disciplines that would allow them to perform well in a digital world – such as science, technology, engineering and mathematics, as well as information and communication technologies – coupled with women's and girls' more limited use of digital tools could lead to widening gaps and greater inequality (OECD, 2018).

The reports finds that greater inclusion of women in the digital economy and increased diversity bring value, both social and economic. For instance, inventions arising out of mixed teams are more economically valuable and have higher impact than those in which only men are involved. Co-ordinated policy action can help narrow the digital gender gap. This requires raising awareness and tackling gender stereotypes; enabling enhanced, safer and more affordable access to digital tools; and stronger co-operation across stakeholders to remove barriers to girls and women's full participation in the digital world. Digital technologies provide new opportunities to make progress, but technological fixes cannot address the underlying structural problems that drive the digital gender divide. Concrete policy actions are needed to foster women's and girls' full participation and inclusion in the digital economy, while at the same time addressing stereotypes and social norms that lead to discrimination against women. The digital gender divide needs to be resolved. There is no reason for women to trail behind in the digital transformation. The cost of inaction is high and in the face of sluggish growth, ageing societies and increasing educational attainment of young women, the economic case for digital gender equality is clear. Bridging the gender divide, also in the digital world, can provide new sources of global economic growth, support the implementation of the 2030 Agenda for Sustainable Development and help achieve the G20 goal of strong, sustainable and inclusive growth (Bridging the Digital Gender Divide, Include. Upskill, Innovate, OECD, 2018)

DIGITAL GENDER DIVIDE

According to Curtis Kularski (2012) "the digital divide is composed of a skill gap and a gap of physical access to Information Technology (IT) and the two gaps often contribute to each other in circular causation. Without access to technology, it is difficult to develop technical skill and it is redundant to have access to technology without first having the skill to utilise it".

The digital transformation offers immense opportunities for economies and societies. However, the benefits of the digital transformation are currently not equally balanced between societal groups and genders and access, use and ownership of digital tools are not gender-neutral. The term "digital gender divide" is frequently used to refer to these types of gender differences in resources and capabilities to access and effectively utilise ICTs within and between countries, regions, sectors and socio-economic groups (OECD, 2018).

In recent decades, our society has faced the issue of an undeniably present digital divide. Interactions between members of society and technology have vastly increased in a phenomenon known as the "digital revolution". Access to Information and Communication Technologies (ICTs) has become an essential part of our lives, and a fundamental aspect of our world on all levels, including political, economic, and social. Unfortunately, not everyone has access to this technology; this is where the term "digital divide" comes in. The fact that many females are denied access to ICTs means that they are also denied the potential for change and achievement which these technologies bring with them. Today, 68% of men, compared to 62% of women, regularly use a personal computer and the internet, 33% of men and 18% of women regularly install software on their devices, and 47% of men and 35% of women use online banking. What's more, although women account for more than half of the total number of graduates in the world, women continue to be underrepresented in the science and ICT sectors. (http://fermun.org/wp-content/uploads/2019/11/YA_1_ENGLISH.pdf)

According to Moolman, Primo and Shackleton (2007) the gender digital divide is one of the most significant inequalities amplified by the digital revolution. Of the few studies that have sought to address Internet use specifically, most have found that women in developing countries are significantly less likely to use the Internet than men. Women are estimated to constitute 25% or less of Internet users in Africa, 22% in Asia, 38% in Latin America, and a mere 6% in the Middle East (Hafkin, 2001). Less than 10% of Internet users in Guinea and Djibouti are women, less than 20% in Nepal and less than 25% in India. Only 20% of Internet users in Greece are women and slightly more than 25% in Portugal (Hafkin, 2007). In Africa (where the gender digital divide is thought to be the widest), in 11 of the 13 countries, more men than women use the Internet (Hilbert, 2011).

In a recent study undertaken by Intel (Dugdale, 2013), in which 2200 women and girls from India, Egypt, Mexico and Uganda took part, it was found that 25% of women in developing nations lacked Internet access and this figure was as high as 45% in Sub-Saharan Africa. The report highlights the stubborn gap in women's access to the Internet in Africa, but also in the Middle East and other developing parts of the world. According to Elizabeth Weingarten (2013), there are two critical factors that influence whether or not women can access the Internet: availability and affordability. As such, one of the recommendations outlined in the Intel report was for policymakers and technology companies to make the Internet more accessible and affordable on mobile phones (Heavey, 2013). It is estimated that, in developing nations, an Internet connection can cost up to 40% of annual per capita income, compared to just 1.7% of per capita Gross Net Income in wealthier nations. Weingarten notes that, while these barriers apply to both genders, they hinder women more than men because other cultural obstacles compound the problem (Antonio and Tuffley, 2014).

The digital gender divide has been recognized as a challenge to achieve gender equality for women, particularly as the 4th Industrial Revolution continues to increase the pace of change of information and communication technologies (ICTs). By 2022, 60% of global GDP will be digitized (World Economic Forum, 2018). The extent of this impact on our education needs, our societal structures, our legal frameworks and economic strategies, is still unknown, but urgent action is needed to ensure that the benefits of these transformations are distributed equally. As societies become increasingly dependent on digital technology, women, their broader communities and national economies are at risk of losing out on the positive promise of full participation in digital economies. If the digital gender gap is not addressed, digital technologies may exacerbate gender inequalities rather than help to reduce them. Thus, ICTs are a "double-edged sword". Digital technologies form a vital part of the 2030 Agenda's call for the full development and active participation of women in today's world. One of the targets in the fifth Sustainable Development Goal (SDG5) calls on the international community 'to enhance the use of enabling technology, in particular information and communication technologies (ICTs), to promote women's empowerment.' (W-20, The Digital Gender Gap, 2019).

FACTORS AFFECTING DIGITAL DIVIDE

The digital gap between men and women is not a purely technological problem, but also a complex economic, social and cultural issue, fundamentally linked to the problem of gender inequality at its roots. In developing countries, girls and women struggle to obtain technology and internet access. In addition, socialisation patterns, stereotypes around technology being 'for boys', and fear of discrimination may stop girls from using digital tools (http://fermun.org/wp-content/uploads/2019/11/YA_1_ENGLISH.pdf).

There are a number of root causes of the digital gender divide, including hurdles to access, affordability, education (or lack thereof) and lack of technological literacy, as well as inherent biases and socio-cultural norms that lead to gender-based digital exclusion. Women were found to do 2.6 times the amount of unpaid care and domestic work that men do, which leaves them less times to grow their careers (UN Women, 2018a).

Affordability is a challenge for all but affects disproportionally more women and girls, and remains one of the key hurdles in accessing ICTs. Also, the digital gender divide is found to increase as technological sophistication and functionality grows and with the cost of ownership. A study by Intel and Dalberg (2012) finds that affordability not only represents a barrier for those who are not yet Internet users, but further prevents Internet users from using the World Wide Web to its full extent, if e.g., Internet data allowances increase importantly with the quantity of megabits included in the contract. When it comes to affordability, the cost of accessing the Internet varies across countries and regions and partly depends on the level of development of the country.

Another reason why fewer women than men use digital tools is the lack of awareness of the potential benefits that the Internet may bring. Women are significantly more likely than men to not use the Internet because they think they "do not need it" or they "do not want it" (Fallows, 2005). Intel and Dalberg (2012) find that 25% of the women who do not engage online are generally not interested in using the Internet, and almost all of them believe that accessing the Internet would not bring them any benefit. Evidently, lack of trust in digital devices or the Internet may also play a role, despite women mainly reporting lack of interest or having low expectations about its usefulness and relevance to their local context (i.e., lack of use of local languages).

Illiteracy further hinders women's and girls' ability to access online services. About 83% of women worldwide are literate, compared to 90% of men (UNESCO, 2017), and illiterate women only appear to be using online platform services, such as Skype and YouTube, that are more familiar to them or are easier to access and use. To try and address this hurdle, some search engines, such as Google, have installed voice navigation systems in local languages to make Internet search queries more accessible and inclusive. The digital gender divide is also fuelled by digital illiteracy, which often translates in lack of comfort in using technology and accessing the Internet. Such "technophobia" is often a result of concurrent factors including education, employment status and income level. For instance, Intel and Dalberg's (2012) survey shows that more than half of the women having no formal education said they were not familiar or comfortable with the technology. However, this percentage fell to 15% in the case of women with at least high school education.

Even girls in formal education appear to be less confident in ICTs, maths or science. The OECD ABC of Gender Equality in Education (2015a) report shows that differences in performance in scientific and ICT-related fields do not stem from innate differences in aptitudes, but rather from students' attitudes and confidence in their own capabilities. Girls are less confident in their maths, science and IT abilities, often due to or fuelled by societal and parental biases, and parents' expectations about the future of their 15-year-old boys and girls – independently of performance in mathematics. This ultimately leads to girls' self-censorship and lower engagement in science and ICTs.

Additionally, socio-cultural reasons play an important role in explaining the digital gender divide. In India and Egypt, around one-fifth of women were found to believe that the Internet was not appropriate for them, for a number of cultural reasons. In India, around 12 % of women report not to use the Internet because of the negative social perception associated to its use, and 8% due to the lack of acceptance by family members (Intel and Dalberg, 2012). In the case of women, in fact, family support emerges as a key enabler when it comes to using the Internet. Active female Internet users are three times more likely to have families who are "very supportive" of their Internet use, whereas female non-users are six times more likely to be exposed to family opposition (Intel and Dalberg, 2012). Such family hurdles can range from lack of support to outright discouragement or even prohibition.

Safety-related issues are often a key reason for families' opposition to the use of the Internet or the ownership of a mobile phone for both women and girls in developing and emerging economies. For example, for women in the People's Republic of China and Mexico, harassment is among the top barriers in owning and using a mobile phone (GSMA, 2015a). Women and girls using the Internet can be exposed to additional risks, including cyberstalking, online harassment or even sexual trafficking, and it thus become crucial to develop measures to protect and prevent gender-based violence online.

The European Institute for Gender Equality (EIGE, 2017) estimates that one in ten women have already experienced a form of cyber violence since the age of 15. It further reports the results of a German survey of Internet users aged 10 to 50, which finds that women are significantly more likely than men to have been victims of online sexual harassment and cyber stalking. A 2014 Pew Research Center survey found that women, especially aged 18 to 24, disproportionately experience severe types of cyber harassment, including cyber stalking and online sexual harassment (Pew Research Center, 2014).

If in the developing parts of the world access, literacy and safety are among the greatest barriers to being online and using digital devices, in developed economies women face other types of barriers. Among them, socio-cultural perceptions and biases may prevent women from obtaining senior roles in (digital) companies to the same extent as men. For example, in the mobile industry, women worldwide are 20% less likely to hold a senior leadership position than men. In Africa, the percentage of women holding senior positions in the mobile industry falls to a mere 10% (GSMA and A T Kearny, 2015).

Finally, the ability of women to access and use digital technologies is directly and indirectly affected by market related factors including investment dynamics, regulations, and competition, especially in rural areas. In rural areas, which are often scarcely populated, the investment and installation of infrastructures, such as broadband infrastructures and cell phone towers, is less economically profitable. This can affect disproportionally more women in developing countries as they seem to be more often located in rural areas, whereas working age men tend to be mainly in urban areas (UN Statistics, 2016).

Women and girls in rural areas of developing countries further face persistent structural constraints, including their higher probability to be out of school than boys – their likelihood is twice as high as girls in urban areas. Furthermore, women and girls in rural areas generally work in agriculture, and their work is often unpaid or considered as a contribution to the family. When employed, women in rural areas tend to have shorter term and more precarious jobs and are generally less protected than men in rural areas or people living in urban areas (UN Women Watch, 2018). This ultimately translates in being confined in technology-poor environments where it is difficult if not impossible to use digital technologies, and into having scarce (if any) resources, also financial ones, to be used to go online (Bridging the Digital Gender Divide, Include. Upskill, Innovate, OECD, 2018).

WAY FORWARD

a. Encouraging the education of girls in STEM from an early age and teaching digital literacy to women and girls are the first steps to bridging the gender gap that exists in these fields. Promote education of women in science and technology fields through scholarships, internships and training programs and consider gender quotas for admission into education programs in order to strengthen women participation in decision making positions and leadership within the STEM sector.

b. The internet can be considered a facet of the democratic right to freedom of expression, and attempting to control what citizens can or cannot view is in contradiction to democratic principles. Recently, situations in Iran and China have denied people the ability to access certain websites and share information, or even cut off internet access in certain regions for prolonged periods of time. The internet can be a powerful tool for women to make their voices heard in situations where it is difficult for them to find an audience otherwise. A democratic attitude towards the internet as a tool for free expression and association is essential to benefit from its full potential as an equalising factor between men and women.

c. Facilitating the participation of women in the labour market, while monitoring and ensuring the quality of jobs, and providing support services to enable women to work and pursue a career while being a mother or having a family, could solve a significant part of the problem. It is also important to combine activities related to labour market participation with corresponding activities promoting a better distribution of unpaid childcare and housework, and directing investment towards more targeted lifelong learning programmes

d. Governments around the world need to implement legal and regulatory frameworks that drive ICT adoption. These frameworks must consider that internet as a general-purpose technology and is transversal to all sectors of the economy as well as to the political and social spheres of nations. Policies need to create and strengthen public agencies that coordinate the transversal integration of digital strategies across ministries. Through transversal and integrated policies, government should act as a catalyst for change; promote the active participation of key actors in the promotion and adoption of gender ICT adoption.

e. Inclusive policies must effectively promote useful and meaningful content for women via digital platforms to increase access and use of basic services. Progressive policies would promote technological innovation as driver for social inclusion and economic participation of women. The Pradhan Mantri Jan Dhan Yojana programme is recent governmental initiatives that aims at improving the financial inclusion of women at the national level, including the promotion of mobile wallets, based on mobile transactions through telecom operators, and the development of Cash Out Point centres (PMJDY, 2018).

f. Design and implement capacity building programmes for women that include teaching digital skills and individual mentoring that accompanies women through the learning and adoption process in a case-by-case basis. Restrictions on mobility, for example, often result in women losing access to community internet centres and training facilities. Informal education and lifelong learning spaces are important to impart digital fluency skills to women.

g. The Internet Saathi initiative trains young female digital instructors to show women in rural villages basic digital skills of Google-provided smartphones, including different Internet or chat applications as Google Chrome and WhatsApp (Google, 2018). Internet Saathi has reached more than 2.6 million women in over 60 000 villages. Empowered with basic digital literacy and Internet access, those women were able to access government programmes, including welfare programmes and subsidised meals, and this has increased access to education, and female entrepreneurship. In regions that are less well-connected and have a variable electricity network, women are able to use special "feature-phones" that have more basic functions but extended battery life (OECD, 2018).

h. The "Fightback" app is a mobile application that is contributing to address issues related to sexual harassment, and to improve security for women in India.

The app allows sending global positioning system co-ordinates to pre-selected contacts by pushing an SOS button on the mobile phone. Since its development, it has been downloaded more than a million times (OECD, 2018).

Policies aimed at reducing gender gaps in digital inclusion will further empower women by preventing and reducing gender inequalities on labour markets and improving women's financial inclusion. If existing digital divides are addressed, particularly low and middle-income nations, where the digital gender gaps are the largest, could experience a leapfrogging process towards development. It would enable developing nations to leverage new technologies for long-standing challenges, including effective healthcare, education, political participation, and civil rights, among others. ICTs have the potential of transforming industries, providing opportunities to deliver services in new and efficient ways that can reach the most disadvantaged (Judith Mariscal et al, T-20, Argentina, 2018).

CONCLUSION

If an otherwise capable woman is prevented from progressing beyond the traditional roles of child-rearing and housekeeping, she is unlikely to reach her full potential as a human being. There is strong evidence to suggest that education is a solution. A woman who is educated to at least secondary level acquires both the ability and the desire to engage with the possibilities that Internet technologies offer, whereas a woman who is uneducated is more likely to subscribe to the traditional role of women and not engage with technology, regardless of their access to it. The increasing availability of high quality and often free education on-line is likely to improve this situation in a positive way. The more women engage with technology, the better educated they become and the more likely they will be to engage in activities that benefit themselves, their families, and their communities.

REFERENCES

Antonio & Tuffley. (2014). *Future Internet, The Gender Digital Divide in Developing Countries.* www.mdpi.com/journal/futureinternet

Bhadra, B. (2001). Janani O Prayukti: Lingakaran O Kshamatayaner Sahabastan (Bengali ed.) Yojana.

Bridging The Digital Gender Divide Include. (2018). *Upskill, Innovate.* OECD.

Deborah, F. (2005). *How Women and Men Use the Internet*. Pew Internet & American Life Project.

Dugdale, A. (2013). *One fifth of women in the developing world think Internet use is inappropriate for them*. Available online: http://www.fastcompany.com/3004797/one-fifth-women-developingworld-countries-think-internet-use-inappropriate-them

EIGE (European Institute for Gender Equality). (2017). *Cyber violence against women and girls*. http://eige.europa.eu/rdc/eige-publications/cyber-violence-against-women-and-girls

Google. (2018). *Internet Saathi: Bridging the online gender divide in rural India*. https://www.google.com/about/values-in-action/internet-saathi/

GSMA. (2015). *Accelerating digital literacy: empowering women to use the mobile Internet*. GSMA.

GSMA. (2015a). *Connected Women 2015: Bridging the Gender Gap: Mobile Access and Usage in Low- and Middle-income Countries*. www.gsma.com/mobilefordevelopment/wp-content/uploads/2016/02/ConnectedWomen-Gender-Gap.pdf

GSMA & ATKearny. (2015). *Accelerating the Digital Economy: Gender Diversity in the Telecommunications Sector*. https://www.atkearney.com/documents/10192/5580445/Connected+Women+2015- WDReport.pdf/d3c08b0a-fab6-431c-80c0-0d332b9e882d

Hafkin, N. (2007). Women and gender in ICT statistics and indicators for development. *Information Technologies and International Development*, *4*, 25–41.

Hafkin, N., & Taggart, N. (2001). *Gender, IT and Developing Countries: An Analytic Study*. Center for Education Innovations.

Heavey, S. (2013). *Women in India, Other Developing Countries Lag in Internet Use*. Available online: http://in.reuters.com/article/2013/01/10/internet-access-women-india-developingidINDEE90902820130110

Hilbert, M. (2011). Digital gender divide or technologically empowered women in developing countries? A typical case of lies, damned lies and statistics. *Women's Studies International Forum*, *34*, 479–489.

Intel & Dalberg. (2012). *Women and the Web. Bridging the Internet and Creating New Global Opportunities in Low and Middle Income Countries*. Intel Corporation and Dalberg Global Development Advisors. https://www.intel.com/content/dam/www/public/us/en/documents/pdf/women-and-theweb.pdf

Judith, M., Mayne, G., Aneja, U., & Sorgner, A. (2018). *Gender Economic Equity Bridging the Gender Digital Gap, Kiel Institute for the World Economy & John Cabot University, T-20*. Argentina.

Kularski, C., & Moller, S. (2012). The digital divide as a continuation of traditional systems of inequality. *Sociology, 5151*, 1–23.

Mandal, C. K. (2013). Concept and Types of Women Empowerment. *International Forum of Teaching and Studies, 9*(2).

Moolman, J., Primo, N., & Shackleton, S. (2007). Taking a byte of technology: Women and ICTs. *Empower. Women Gend. Equity, 21*, 4–14.

OECD. (2015a). *The ABC of Gender Equality in Education: Aptitude, Behaviour, Confidence*. OECD Publishing. http://dx.doi.org/10.1787/9789264229945-en

Pew Research Center. (2014). *Online Harassment*. http://assets.pewresearch.org/wpcontent/uploads/sites/14/2014/10/PI_OnlineHarassment_72815.pdf

PMJDY. (2018). *Pradhan Mantri Jan-Dhan Yojana*. https://www.pmjdy.gov.in/scheme

Reiko, K., Lopez, M., Sasaki, J., & Settecase, M. (2019). *W-20, Policy Brief*. The Digital Gender Gap.

Sahay, S. (1998). *Women and Empowerment: Approaches and Strategies*. Discovery Publishing House.

UN Statistics. (2016). Table 7: Population by age, sex and urban/rural residence: latest available year, 2007- 2016. In *Demographic Yearbook – 2016* [database]. United Nations Statistics Division. https://unstats.un.org/unsd/demographic-social/products/dyb/index.cshtml

UN Women. (2005). *Gender Equality and Empowerment of Women through ICT*. UN Division for the Advancement of Women, Department of Economic and Social Affairs of the United Nations Secretariat. www.un.org/womenwatch/daw/public/w2000-09.05-ict-e.pdf

UN Women. (2018a). *Turning promises into action: Gender equality in the 2030 Agenda for sustainable development*. www.unwomen.org/en/digital-library/publications/2018/2/gender-equality-in-the2030-agenda-for-sustainable-development-2018#view

UN Women Watch. (2018). *Facts & figures: Rural women and the millennium development goals*. www.un.org/womenwatch/feature/ruralwomen/facts-figures.html

UNESCO. (2017). *Literacy rates continue to rise from one generation to the next.* Fact Sheet No. 45, September, FS/2017/LIT/45. http://uis.unesco.org/sites/default/files/documents/fs45-literacy-rates-continuerise-generation-to-next-en-2017.pdf

UNESCO EQUALS Skills Coalition. (2019). *I'd blush if I could: closing gender divides in digital skills through education.* Author.

Weingarten, E. (2013). *The Developing World Needs More Female Internet Users.* Available online: http://www.slate.com/articles/technology/technology/2013/01/a_new_report_on_female_internet_ users_from_the_developing_world.html

Women and the Web. (2013). Available online: http://www.intel.com/content/www/us/en/ technology-in-education/women-in-the-web.html

World Economic Forum. (2017, July). *Accelerating Workforce Reskilling for the Fourth Industrial Revolution.* Author.

World Economic Forum. (2018). *Our Shared Digital Future: Building an Inclusive Trustworthy and Sustainable Digital Society.* Author.

Chapter 3
Women in Digital Society and Entrepreneurship in the Republic of Belarus

Albina Sibirskaya
Insitute of Economics, National Academy of Sciencies, Belarus

ABSTRACT

In today's global society, information technologies are actively developing, which provokes the development of business digitalization and the development of new competitive advantages. The leaders of digital technology development show us that it is impossible to develop a digital business without deep transformation, but only through the use of new technologies. The digital transformation of the economy involves a rethinking of how business works and how it interacts with the outside world. The main goal of digitalization development is to increase interaction between consumers and manufacturers, between business representatives and state regulatory and control bodies, and between business entities.

SECTION 1. WOMAN IN A DIGITAL SOCIETY IN THE REPUBLIC OF BELARUS

In today's global society, information technologies are actively developing, which provokes the development of business digitalization and the development of new competitive advantages. The leaders of digital technology development show us that it is impossible to develop a digital business without deep transformation, but only through the use of new technologies. The digital transformation of the economy involves a rethinking of how business works and how it interacts with the outside

DOI: 10.4018/978-1-7998-8594-8.ch003

world. The main goal of digitalization development is to increase interaction between consumers and manufacturers, between business representatives and state regulatory and control bodies, and between business entities.

Section 1.1 General Overview of Digitalization in the Republic of Belarus

The digitalization of society has also affected the Republic of Belarus. To be competitive in global economic relations, business in the country must develop following the requirements of world technologies. Modern digital technologies are gaining a significant role in corporate governance, gradually developing and improving, and capturing all sectors of society one by one. Global changes are taking place: digital technologies are being actively introduced in the economy and social sphere; society is undergoing a digital transformation that requires radical changes in business rules. What is the digitalization of business? It is a change in business strategies, building business processes under the influence of the scientific and technical process, and the introduction of new technologies for commercial activities. Digitalization affects the social sphere of life, introducing new technologies to simplify administrative procedures and improve the comfort and standard of living of the society. It is necessary to distinguish the concept of digitalization of the economy from the automation of economic processes. The difference is that automation is reduced to simplifying a specific process of economic activity, while digitalization covers all business processes. The development of e-government has recently gained the greatest popularity, as the information society is developing in many countries of the world. In the Republic of Belarus, the decree of the President of the Republic of Belarus No. 8 "about the development of the digital economy" was adopted in 2017 in the field of regulating the digital transformation of the economy, the main provisions of which are:

Providing benefits and preferences to participants in relations related to the use of modern technologies. Taking measures aimed at improving the legal protection of participants in relations related to the use of modern financial technologies. Conducting a legal experiment within the high-tech Park to test new legal institutions for the possibility of their implementation in the civil legislation of the Republic of Belarus, etc. In the Republic of Belarus, a significant place in the development of electronic services is occupied by new digital technologies aimed at improving the efficiency of public authorities. To analyze the global assessment of the level of digitalization of the Republic of Belarus, consider the list of indexes.

1. ICT Development Index – IDI.

The information and communication technology (ICT) development index (IDI) is measured annually by the international telecommunication Union – a specialized division of the United Nations. The index consists of 11 statistical indicators that reflect the availability and use of ICTs, and also the practical skills of using ICTs by the population of 190 countries around the world. According to the UNO, by the end of 2019, 53.6% of the world's population, or 4.1 billion people, use the Internet (ITU estimates that at the end of 2019, 53.6 percent of the global population, or 4.1 billion people, are using the Internet). Consider the position of the Republic of Belarus in the digital society according to this rating (figure 1).

Figure 1. Information and Communication Technology Development Index (ICT) of 2017
Source: IDI 2017 Rank

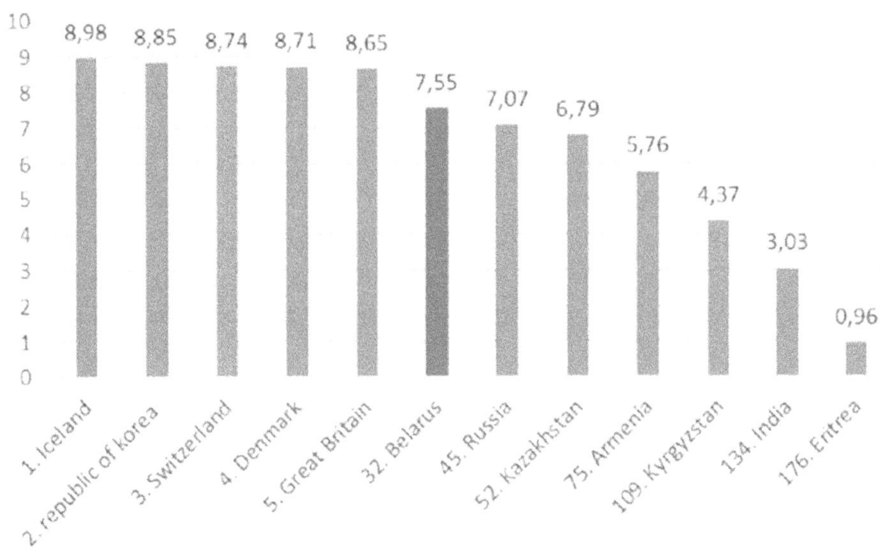

The ICT Access sub-index in 2017 was 7.87. Fixed-telephone subscriptions per 100 inhabitants – 49.01; Mobile-cellular telephone subscriptions per 100 inhabitants – 124.17; International internet bandwidth per Internet user (Bit/s) – 168517.63; Percentage of households with computer – 66.96%; Percentage of households with Internet access-62.46%. The ICT Use Sub-index was 6.54. Percentage of individuals using the Internet – 71.11%; Fixed (wired) – broadband subscriptions

Figure 2. Ranking of countries on the DESI index in 2019
Source: DESI 2019

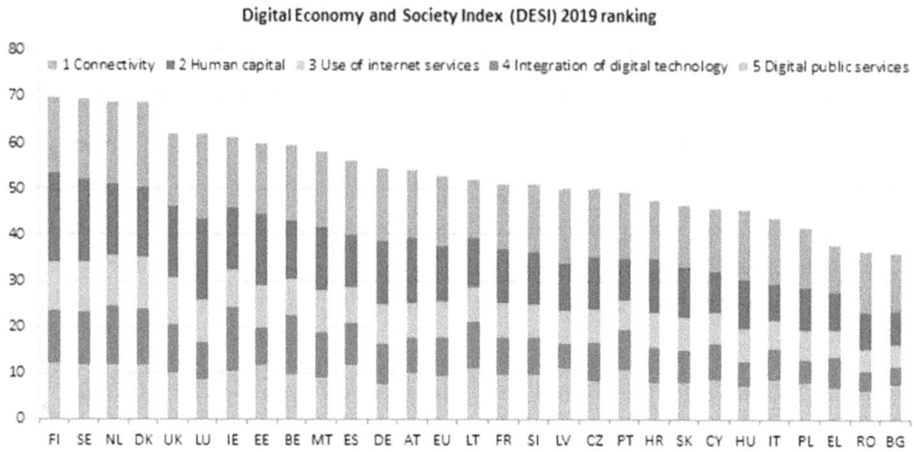

per 100 subscribers-33.30; Active mobile – broadband subscriptions per 100 subscribers-69.49. The ICT Skills Sub-index was 8.93. Mean years of schooling – 12.00; Secondary gross enrollment ratio – 107.12%; Tertiary gross enrollment ratio – 87.94%. Iceland, the Republic of Korea, and Switzerland are in the top three. The Republic of Belarus ranks 32 out of 176, which is a good indicator of the development of information and communication technologies in the country. Among The EEU countries, Belarus is a leader in the rating of ICT: Russia is at a 45 position, Kazakhstan – 52, Armenia – 75, Kyrgyzstan – 109. The last place in this rating is occupied by Eretria.

2. Digital Economy and Society Index — DESI.

The IMD World Digital Competitiveness Ranking 2018 studies 63 economies. This year the majority (29) of countries in the study (29) experienced an improvement in their level of digital competitiveness. About 40% of the sample (26 countries) shows a decline while only eight economies remain in the same position. These changes are not geographically focused. Improvements and declines occur across continents. The objective of the digital competitiveness ranking is to assess the extent to which a country adopts and explores digital technologies leading to transformation in government practices, business models, and society in general.

According to the rating of the digital economy and society, Finland, Sweden, and the Netherlands are in the top three. In the last, 29th place among European countries is Bulgaria. The Republic of Belarus does not participate in the rating.

Figure 3. Ranking of countries on the WDCI index in 2018
Source: WDCI 2018

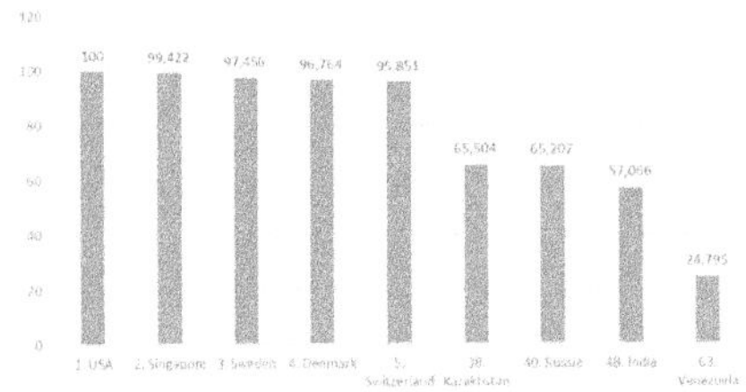

3. IMD World Digital Competitiveness Index — WDCI.

In 2018, the Swiss business school IMD presented its sixth world digital competitiveness Index (WDCI-2018), which reflects the assessment of countries' capabilities and readiness to adapt to the development of digital technologies. WDCI is based on 50 criteria that are aggregated into three sub-indices of the first level (consisting of three sub-indices of the second level): knowledge (talents, education, science); technology (regulation, capital, level of communication development, export); readiness (adaptation, business flexibility, IT-business integration). Criteria from 4 to 6 are first aggregated with equal weights into second-level sub-indexes, with the weights of hard criteria twice as large as the weights of soft criteria measured in points by experts, and then the second-level sub-indexes are aggregated into first-level sub-indexes. Each of the second level sub-indexes in composite WDCI has the same weight approximately 11.1%. The IMD Digital World Competitiveness Ranking presents the 2018 overall ranking for the 63 economies covered by the WCY. The economies are ranked from the most to the least competitive and the results from the previous year's ranking (2017) are shown in brackets. The Scores shown to the left are indices (0 to 100) generated for the unique purpose of constructing charts and graphics.

The US is in first place with an index of 100.00. Singapore and Sweden are in second and third places, respectively. The Republic of Belarus is not in this rating. Of the EEU countries, only Kazakhstan (38th place) and Russia (40th place) were included in the rating. Venezuela is in the last 63rd place (the index is 24.795).

4. Digital Evolution Index – DEI

The Digital Evolution Index analyzes the underlying drivers that govern a country's digitalization: Supply Conditions, Demand Conditions, Institutional Environment, and Innovation and Change. To gain a comprehensive view of digital readiness and competitiveness of countries, the author further divided these drivers into 12

Figure 4. Ranking of countries on the digital evolution index in 2018
Source: DEI 2018

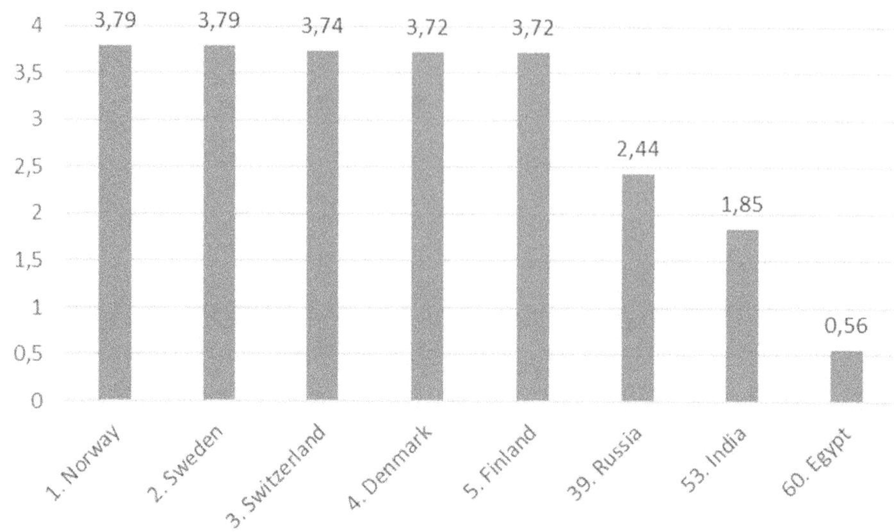

components measured using a total of 108 indicators. The rating takes into account 4 main factors that determine the pace of digitalization:

Offer level (availability of Internet access and degree of infrastructure development);

Consumer demand for digital technologies;

Institutional environment (state policy, legislation, resources);

Innovation climate (investment in R&D and digital startups).

Norway, Sweden, Switzerland, and Denmark are among the five countries with the most developed digital economy according to the rating. But with the rapid spread of innovation and constant changes, the current status of "digital leader" will not ensure primacy in the future. The last place in the ranking of countries for digital evolution is Egypt. The Republic of Belarus is not in this rating. Of the EEU countries, only Russia is in the ranking, which is in 39th place.

5. E-Intensity Index of the Boston Consulting Group

The e-Intensity index is a comprehensive assessment of 28 indicators that are calculated as a weighted average of three sub-indices: infrastructure development, online spending, and user activity. The "infrastructure" sub-index displays the degree of infrastructure development and speed, as well as the quality of Internet access (fixed and mobile). The "online expenses" sub-index includes expenses for e-Commerce

Figure 5. Ranking of countries on the Boston Consulting Group's digitalization of the economy index, 2015
Source: E-Intensity Index 2015

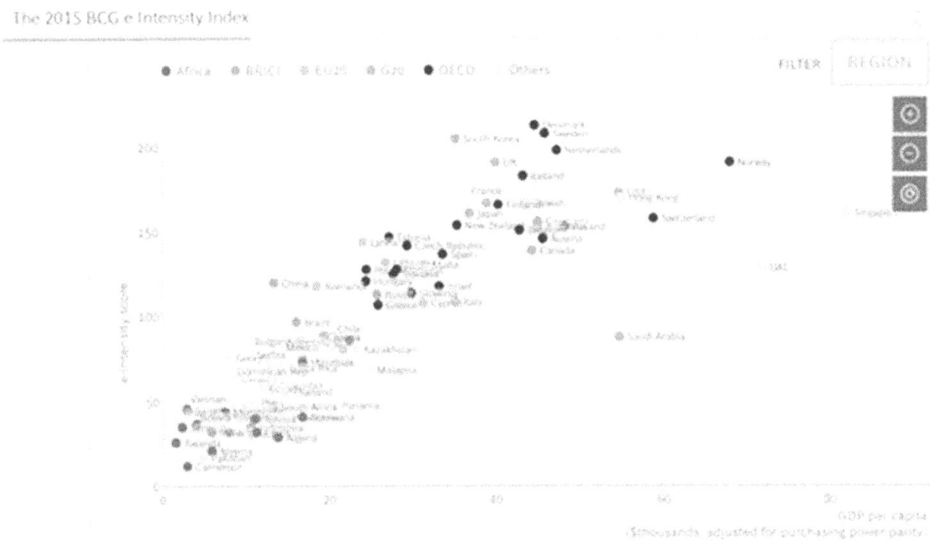

and online advertising. The "user activity" sub-index shows the involvement of the state, citizens, and businesses in using the opportunities of the digital economy and is calculated as a weighted average of three lower-level sub-indexes: company activity, consumer activity, and government activity. All sub-indexes are formed from the weighted average values of several parameters that underlie them.

According to this rating, Denmark, Sweden, the Netherlands, Norway, and the Republic of Korea are the leaders in digitalizing the economy in the last place in Cameroon. The Republic of Belarus does not participate in the rating.

6. Networked Readiness Index — NRI.

Since 2002, the network readiness index (NRI) has been calculated annually jointly by the world economic forum (WEF), the world Bank (WB), and the INSEAD international business school NRI is an assessment of a country's ability to use ICT opportunities for network purposes. First, NRI provides information about the main factors that affect the development of the network economy, to take them into account in public policy. Second, in the long term, this information helps to involve more people, organizations, and communities around the world in the network space. NRI not only assesses a country's readiness to participate in the information world but also shows what lies at the heart of the differences between countries.

Figure 6. Ranking of countries in the network readiness index 2016
Source: NRI 2016

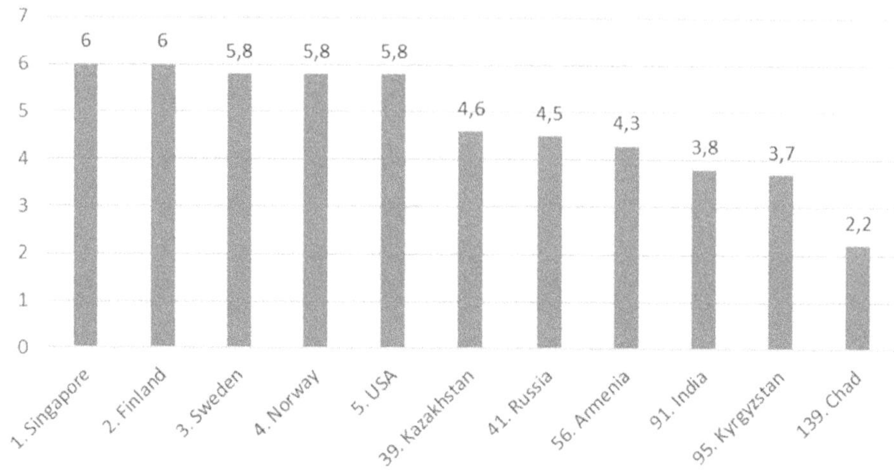

The index measures the level of ICT development in 53 parameters grouped into three main groups:

1. Availability of conditions for the development of ICT – the General state of the business and regulatory environment in terms of ICT, the presence of healthy competition, innovation potential, necessary infrastructure, opportunities for financing new projects, regulatory aspects, and so on.
2. The willingness of citizens, businesses, and public authorities to use ICT — the state's position regarding the development of information technology, the state the cost of development, availability of information technology for business, the level of penetration and accessibility of the Internet, the cost of mobile communication and so on.
3. The level of use of ICT in the public, commercial and public sectors – the number of personal computers, Internet users, mobile subscribers, the availability of existing Internet resources of state organizations, also the total production and consumption of information technologies in the country.

The top five countries for network readiness in 2016 included Singapore, Finland, Sweden, Norway, and the United States. Only the Republic of Belarus is missing from the EEU countries. Russia ranks 41st out of 139, Kazakhstan 39th, Armenia 56th, and Kyrgyzstan 95th. In last place is CHAD.

7. The UN Global E-Government Development Index – EGDI.

The E-Government Development Index presents the state of E-Government Development of the United Nations Member States. Along with an assessment of the website development patterns in a country, the E-Government Development index incorporates the access characteristics, such as the infrastructure and educational levels, to reflect how a country is using information technologies to promote access and inclusion of its people. The EGDI is a composite measure of three important dimensions of e-government, namely: provision of online services, telecommunication connectivity, and human capacity. Belarus transitioned from High-EGDI in 2016 to Very-High-EGDI in 2018. This could be attributed to its National Strategy for Sustainable Social and Economic Development for the period up to 2030 incorporating several initiatives related to ICT development in various sectors of its economy. For example, the Strategy of Informatization of the Republic of Belarus for the period 2016 – 2022 was implemented in 2015 to enhance ICTs in the provision of e-government services. Another initiative, the State Program for the Development of the Digital Economy and the Information Society for 2016-2020 defines the vision for the "digital transformation" of the Belarusian economy and ensures the effective implementation of digital tools. This program was designed to digitalize already existing processes in healthcare, public procurement, education, among others. Presidential decrees and resolutions of the Council of Ministers contribute towards the coherent functioning of e-government services in the Republic of Belarus.

The leaders of the 2018 ranking are Denmark, Australia, and the Republic of Korea. According to the results of the last rating, the Republic of Belarus ranked 38th out of 190. Among the EEU countries, Belarus was second only after Russia, which took the 32nd position. In the last place of the rating is Chad (190th place).

8. E-Participation Index — EPART.

Another component of the assessment of the digital economy is the UNO-published e-participation Index (EPART), an indicator of the development of active communication services between citizens and the state. The EPART index aims to reflect the mechanisms of electronic participation of citizens in government websites. E-participation areas, in turn, are viewed through the lens of participation technologies, which include specialized portals and other Internet sites, social networks, mobile platforms and devices, open government, and data technologies. The E-participation Index measures how useful online services are and how often they are provided to citizens. Its components are:

Figure 7. Ranking of countries for e-government development in 2018
Source: EGDI 2018

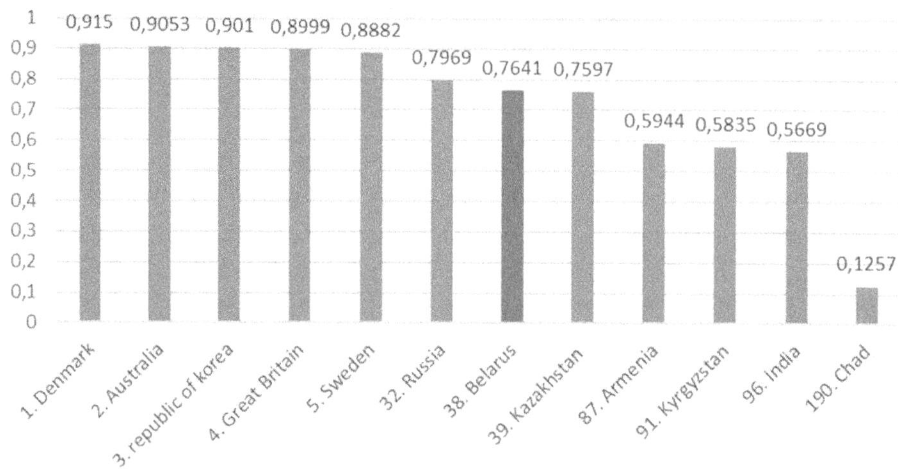

1. E-information of citizens by the government from its website regarding programs, budgets, laws, and everything that is of key importance to society;
2. E-consultation, where visitors to a government website can choose a public policy topic for online discussion;
3. Electronic decision-making with the participation of the country's citizens, while the government provides feedback on the results of solving specific problems.

The top three in the e-participation index are the Republic of Korea, Australia, and Singapore. The Republic of Belarus ranks 55 out of 189. Among the EEU countries, Belarus was ahead of the Republic of Armenia (61 positions) and Kyrgyzstan (101 positions). Chad is in last place in the 2016 e-participation ranking.

9. Global Connectivity Index – GCI, Huawei

In the global networking index for 2018 leaders are a group of highly developed countries on the GCI S-curve that rely on smart networking to accelerate digitalization and search for new opportunities. It is not surprising that in the past 15 years, the growth rate of the global digital economy has been two and a half times faster than the growth of global GDP. Countries with highly developed economies have a better financial position, which allows them to achieve steady progress in the development of ICT infrastructure, and now artificial intelligence, and move up the S-curve of

Figure 8. Ranking of countries on the e-participation index in 2016
Source: EPART 2016

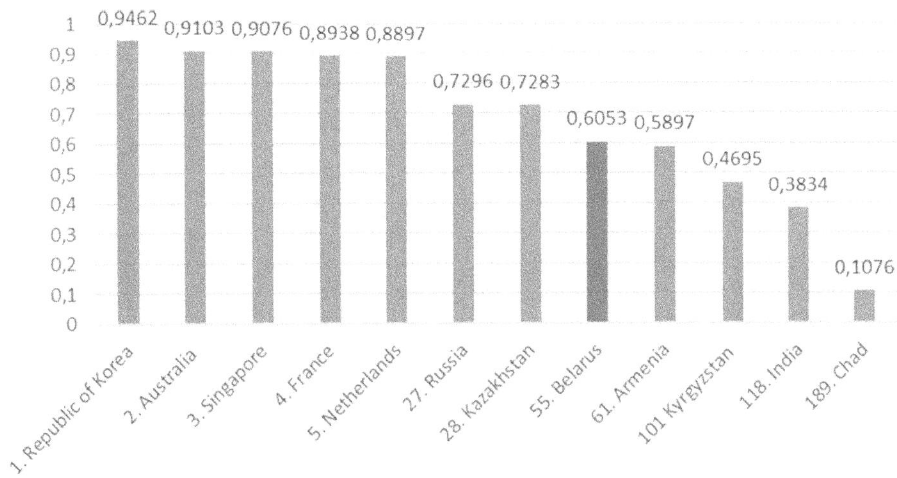

the GCI index, stimulating even greater GDP growth. Against this background, the primary task is to ensure that less developed countries from the "catch-up" and "Newcomers" groups on the GCI scale give preference to investment in ICT to maintain the competitiveness of their economies.

10. The Global Innovation Index – GII.

The index is calculated in 2007 by the French business school INSEAD and Cornell University (USA) with the support of the world intellectual property organization (WIPO). it is the most important indicator of the country's innovative success in the world.

Thus, we can conclude that the Republic of Belarus has an ambiguous position in the world community in the field of digitalization. In some indexes, it is absent at all, in some it is in relatively low positions. However, the development of the digital society in Belarus is active.

Section 1.2. The Availability of Electronic Communications and Information Technology for Women

Digitalization of the economy and the introduction of information and digital means of communication, as the main signs of modern development, affects all areas of modern society, and gender issues are no exception. There is a threat that

Figure 9. Ranking of countries on the global connectivity index in 2018
Source: GCI 2018

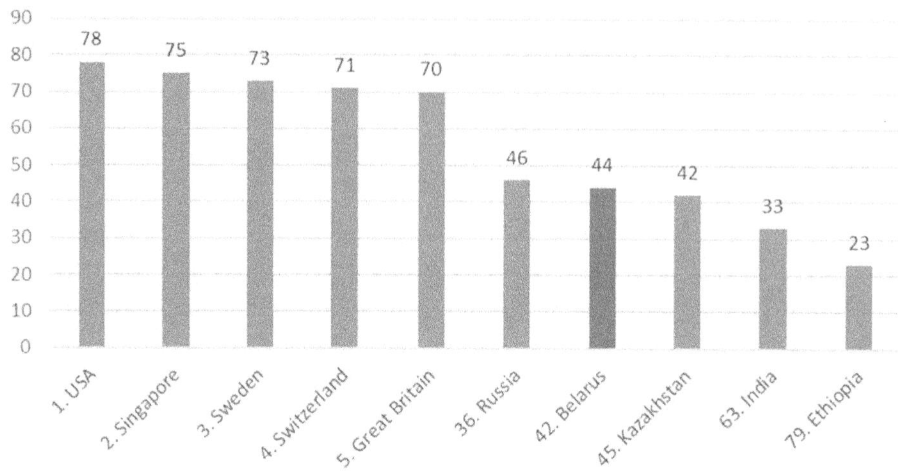

digitalization will not only open up access to new opportunities but also provoke new social challenges and risks. One of the most likely social risks is the emergence of gender inequality in access to new digital resources. For example, in the report of the world economic forum summit in Davos (WEF, 2016), it was noted that the upcoming changes in employment due to the rapidly developing digitalization will

Figure 10. Ranking of Countries on the global innovation index in 2018
Source: GII 2018

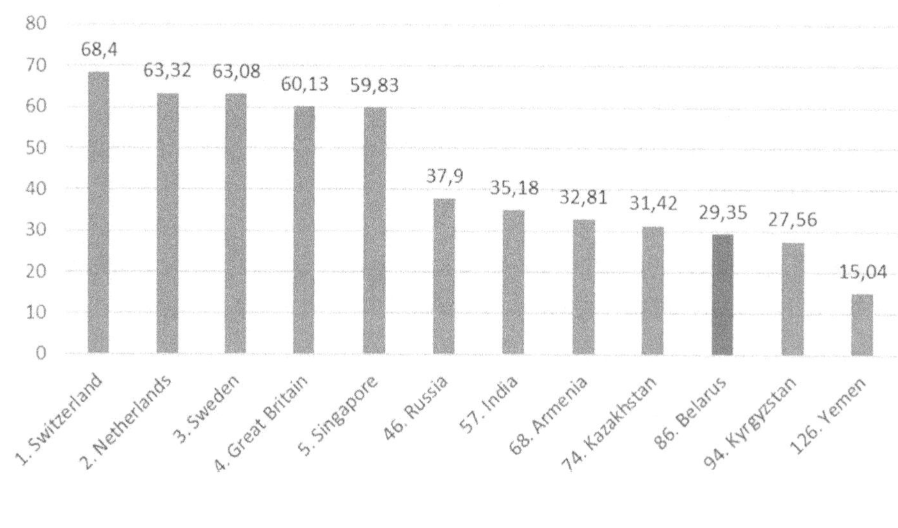

Figure 11. Percentage of Personal Computer Users, % of the total population of the corresponding group
Source: Official Statistics of Republic of Belarus, 2019

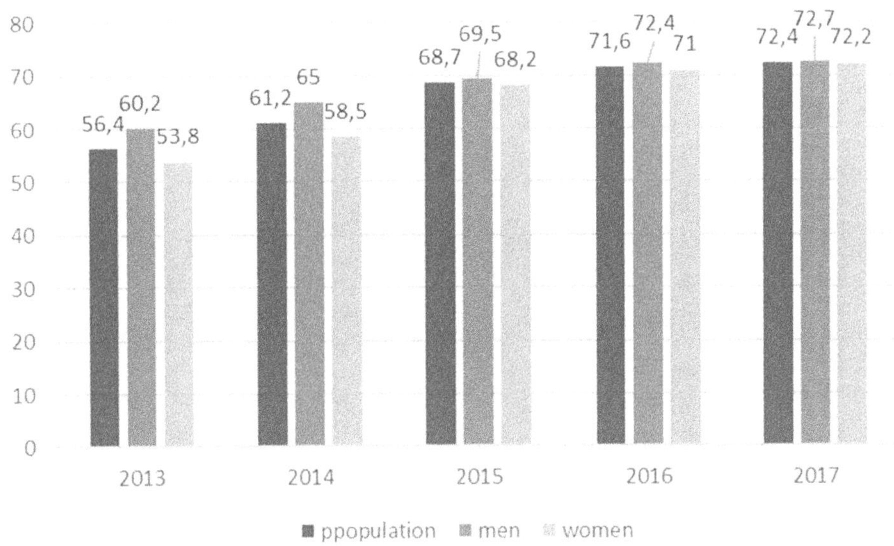

affect women more. "Women's" professions, such as accountants, insurance agents, or librarians, will soon be automated, which will mean a reduction in the number of employees in these areas. At the same time, such "male" areas as engineering, information and communication technologies, computer science, and mathematics are actively developing, which require the involvement of an increasing number of specialists.

Figure 11 shows the dynamics of the share of the population using a personal computer.

The population who use a personal computer has been increasing over the past 5 years. If in 2013-2014 there was a predominant number of male users of a personal computer over women, then by 2017 this indicator was equalized.

In terms of Internet usage, there is a higher percentage of users than the percentage of the population using a personal computer. The Internet is used by the population both through a personal computer and through mobile devices and when visiting computer clubs, cafes, and public points of use.

At the beginning of the analyzed period, the proportion of women Internet users was less than the proportion of men. However, in 2018, these indicators are almost equal. In the Republic of Belarus, about 80% of both men and women are Internet users.

Figure 12. Share of Internet Users, % of the total population of the corresponding group
Source: Official Statistics of Republic of Belarus, 2019

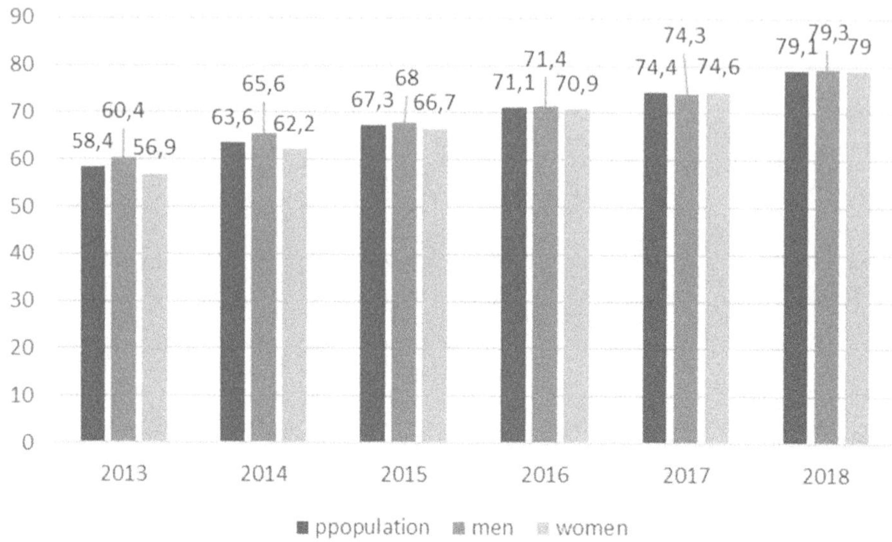

About 95% of all women use the Internet using a wired or Wi-Fi network, and 76.8% of female Internet users also use mobile data to access the Internet.

Most women access the Internet from home. These categories of women mainly include Housewives, mothers on maternity leave. 27.6% of women use it at work. This category of women uses the Internet to solve work tasks.

4.5% of women use the Internet at their place of study. These are mostly female students.

79.2% of the total number of women who use the Internet go online daily, 11.5% - at least once a week, and 9.3% - occasionally. The age structure of women by frequency of Internet access is shown in the figure.

96% of women between the ages of 16 and 24 use the Internet daily. With increasing age, this indicator decreases: 82.8% of women Internet users go out every day between the ages of 25 and 54, 65.1% of women aged 55 to 64, and only 52.9% of women aged 65 to 72. However, the percentage of Internet access increases from time to time. This indicates a decrease in the Internet demand of Belarusian women as their age increases. To explain this trend, consider the goals of women's Internet access.

Figure 13. Structure of Female Internet Users by Location in 2018 (according to a sample survey of households by the standard of living; % of the total number of Internet users in the corresponding group)
Source: Official Statistics of Republic of Belarus, 2019

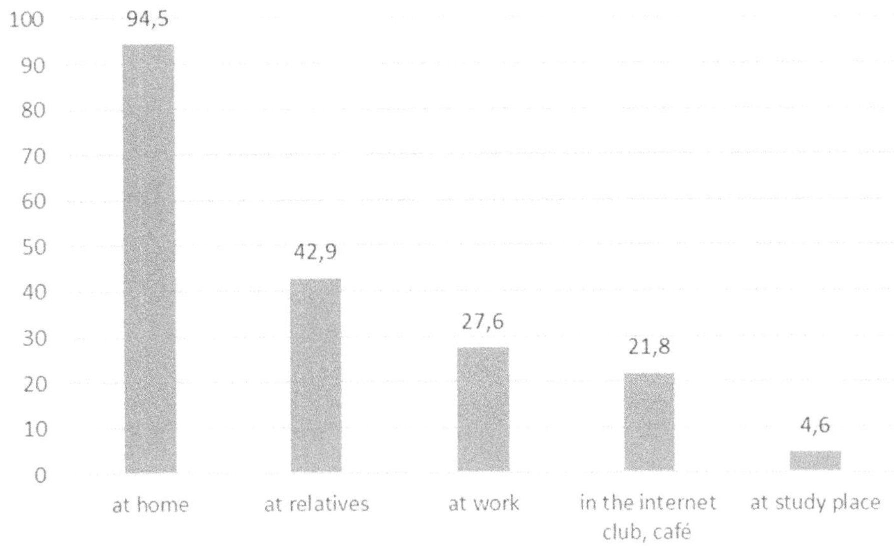

Figure 14. Age Groups of Female Internet Users by Internet Access (% of total)
Source: Official Statistics of Republic of Belarus, 2019

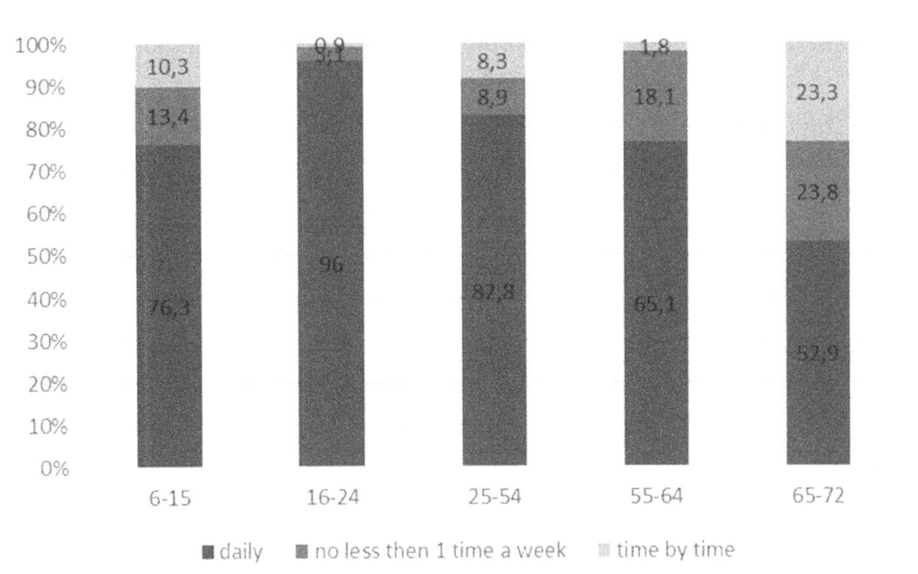

Figure 15. Internet Access Goals for Male and Female Internet Users by Frequency of Access (% of the total number of users in the corresponding group)
Source: Official Statistics of Republic of Belarus, 2019

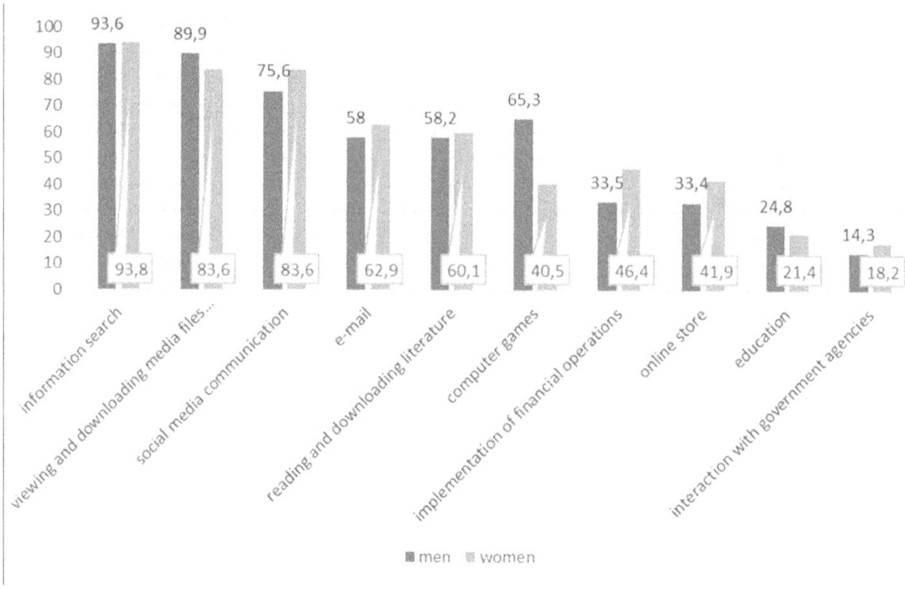

The majority of women use the Internet to search for information (93.8%), with the same number of men in this category. There is a higher number of women than men who use the Internet to communicate in social networks (83.6% of the total number of women Internet users), and women also dominate when using e-mail, performing financial transactions, using online stores, and interacting with government agencies. Men predominate to access the Internet to play computer games.

Interaction with government agencies is mainly limited to electronic appeals, online appointments, etc.

The popularity of financial transactions via the Internet is also increasing. The Non-bank financial institution's "SSIS" payment system allows you to make payments for utilities, pay for loans and use of mobile communications, pay for various paid services, fines, and state duties, which is very time-saving.

The analysis of mobile communication usage also showed that there are no significant gender inequalities in the Republic of Belarus (figure 16).

97.1% of the country's population, including 96.1% of men and 97.8% of women, use mobile communication in the Republic of Belarus. Over the past 6 years, the percentage of the population using mobile phones has grown significantly. Until 2014, more men than women used cell phones. But since 2015, another trend has

Figure 16. Share of Mobile Users, % of the total population of the corresponding group
Source: Official Statistics of Republic of Belarus, 2019

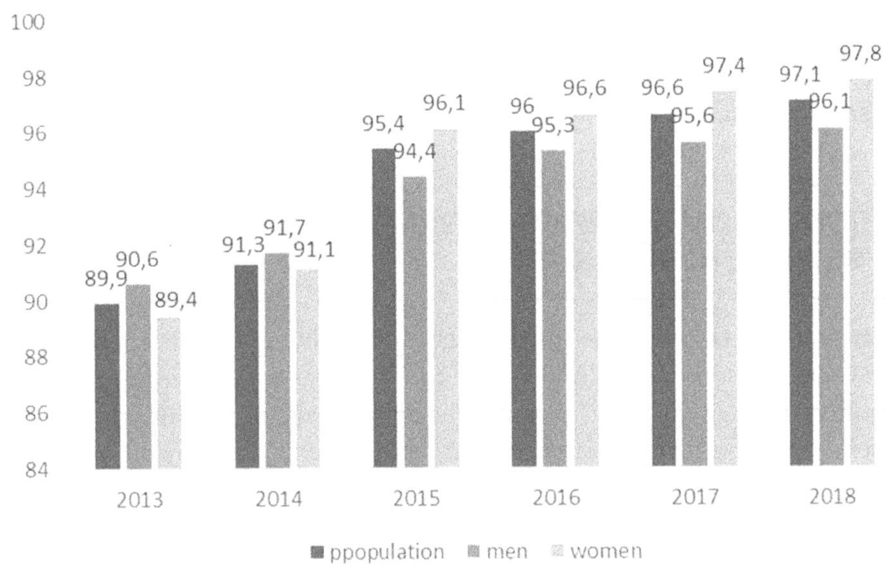

already been observed – the proportion of women who use cellular communication exceeds the proportion of men.

Although there is no gender gap in access to information technology, there are several recommendations that can help increase women's access to digital technologies:

- implementing a coherent and effective economic and social policy that should prioritize countering insecurity and inequality as satellites of technological change;
- bringing labor legislation in line with changes in labor market trends by revising outdated regulations and introducing new ones;
- formation of labor law norms that are symmetrical for women and men;
- improving the level of education, bringing it in line with the trends in the development of modern information and digital technologies;
- development and implementation of national and international programs to attract women to the sphere of "male" professions;

- improving the collection and analysis of gender statistics, paying special attention to the comparability of statistics on women's and men's labor and employment;
- there is an urgent need for information and education on gender equality, aimed at combating gender stereotypes about the role of women in society and the family, and more equitable distribution of household chores and family responsibilities.

SECTION 2. WOMEN IN ENTREPRENEURSHIP AND SCIENCE IN BELARUS

Encouraging women to engage in entrepreneurial activities is a topical issue of gender equality, and is also an important factor in the sustainable development of the economy of the Republic of Belarus. The development of women's businesses helps to expand opportunities for women, reduce the wage gap, and diversify attitudes and new ideas in the market.

Section 2.1. Infrastructure and Legislation for Women's Business

Entrepreneurship in the Republic of Belarus is allowed for both men and women in the following organizational and legal forms:

1.Individual entrepreneur (not a legal entity). This form of business provides for the absence of authorized capital and constituent documents.
2.Legal entity of the firm. This form is carried out through the registration of the following legal entities: open joint-stock company, closed joint-stock company, limited liability company, additional liability company, unitary enterprise. In this form of doing business, the property owners are the founders.
3. Craft activities are non-entrepreneurial activities of individuals engaged in manufacturing and selling goods, performing works, and providing services using manual labor and tools, carried out independently, without involving individuals under labor and (or) civil law contracts, unless otherwise provided by law, and aimed at satisfying the household needs of citizens. The implementation of craft activities is carried out based on the applicant's principle in the tax authorities and the craft fee is paid. Features of this type are that artisans are forbidden to attract individuals as employees; it is forbidden to use automated equipment in their work, except a device, mechanism, machine, or other equipment intended for

> the production of goods (performing works, rendering services), without which it is not possible to carry out craft activities. The legislation of the Republic of Belarus regulating business activities applies to all persons engaged in business, regardless of gender. Restrictions on doing business apply to officials and professionals working in public authorities and management, prosecutors, and courts, also regardless of their gender. In the Republic of Belarus, women are allowed to do business, regardless of their level of education, marital status, and the presence of children.

The country is creating additional favorable business conditions for women. There are several programs for the development of women's businesses. For example, Belinvestbank, together with the European Bank for reconstruction and development, is implementing the project **"I'm Successful"**. The project format is a series of business meetings where women entrepreneurs learn about financial and non-financial opportunities to improve their businesses. The European Bank for reconstruction and development is also implementing the Women in a business project. The program is funded by the EBRD, the European Union under the EU4Business initiative, the Kingdom of Sweden, The Fund for support of countries with transition economies at an early stage of development, and the small business assistance Fund. Belarusian people's Bank, Belinvestbank, and Idea Bank also joined This project. Under the program, the initiators provide access to financing through credit lines opened to local banks, with targeted funding for small and medium-sized businesses headed by women, and at the same time provide business advice to ensure their greater competitiveness. Training, mentoring, and other support programs are also offered so that women entrepreneurs can share experiences and learn from each other as colleagues. The total amount of loan funds allocated under the program in Belarus is 10 million dollars, including about 5.2 million euros allocated by the government of Sweden. More than a hundred women have already participated in the project.

To implement this program, Idea Bank has developed a special project **"Women's Idea**", which includes three different types of lending, as well as special conditions for settlement and cash services. The minimum interest rate for this offer is 11.5%. The loan amount can reach 100 thousand dollars (the minimum amount is 5 thousand dollars). Individual entrepreneurs, unitary enterprises (in which a woman is a founder), legal entities (in which women have a share of ownership or where at least one of the managers and more than 70% of the staff are women) can get access to the credit resource. The joint initiative of EPAM, IFC, and USAID **"Women IT Week"** is a series of events dedicated to women's leadership, business, and IT technologies.

Local government agencies in some regions of the country launched a free project for initiative women "Enterprising landowner". The main goal of the project is to help women find employment, self-employment, and self-realization in agriculture. A center for support and development of women's entrepreneurship was established and operates based on Belinvestbank. The main task of the Center is to stimulate and support women's entrepreneurship, assist in obtaining financial and technical resources, information, methodological, and consulting services for the organization and conduct of business. The work of the Center is organized in several directions. Pre-launch support for women's businesses is designed for those who are just planning to start their own business. It includes courses, educational seminars, and coaching to gain business skills. Assistance to existing businesses is designed for businesswomen who want to develop their own business and bring it to a qualitatively new level. In this area, the Bank provides assistance in obtaining financial and technical resources, organizes networking, cowering, and other training events, and implements special banking products, services, and services for women in business.

Section 2.2. Status and Accessibility of Women in Business

The presence of a sufficient number of women among decision-makers has a positive impact on the level of economic efficiency and innovative development, as well as on the growth of profitability of private and public sector enterprises. In addition, according to the World Bank, the special value of women entrepreneurs is that, unlike men, women are more focused on improving the quality of life and the level of human capital, not only for their children but also for society as a whole (Vanderbrug, 2013). It should be noted that the level of women's presence in business continues to lag behind men's worldwide. According to Global Entrepreneurship Monitor (GEM) estimates, in 2016 the total share of women's business was about 36%, while in 2007 this figure was equal to 30%. Analysis conducted by the Catalyst center (2017) showed that today about 51.5% of managerial and professional positions are occupied by women, but only 5.2% of companies in the S&P 500 index have female CEOS. Thus, there is a narrowing of the gap between the presence of women and men in business, but there is still an inequality in business representation and corporate leadership. In the Republic of Belarus, about 57 thousand women are employed in business (about 1.5% of the total number of women). The ratio of men and women in business is shown in figure 17.

In General, 68.5% of men and 31.5% of women are involved in entrepreneurship in the Republic of Belarus. 66.4% of men and 33.6% of women are individual entrepreneurs. The lowest percentage of women are owners or founders (27.3% vs. 72.7% of men). Most of the women involved in the business are individual entrepreneurs (figure 18).

Owners and craft activities have almost the same share (11.9 and 14.5%, respectively). 25.4% of women entrepreneurs have employees, and 74.6% of women

Figure 17. The ratio of Men and Women in Entrepreneurship, %
Source: Official Statistics of Republic of Belarus, 2019

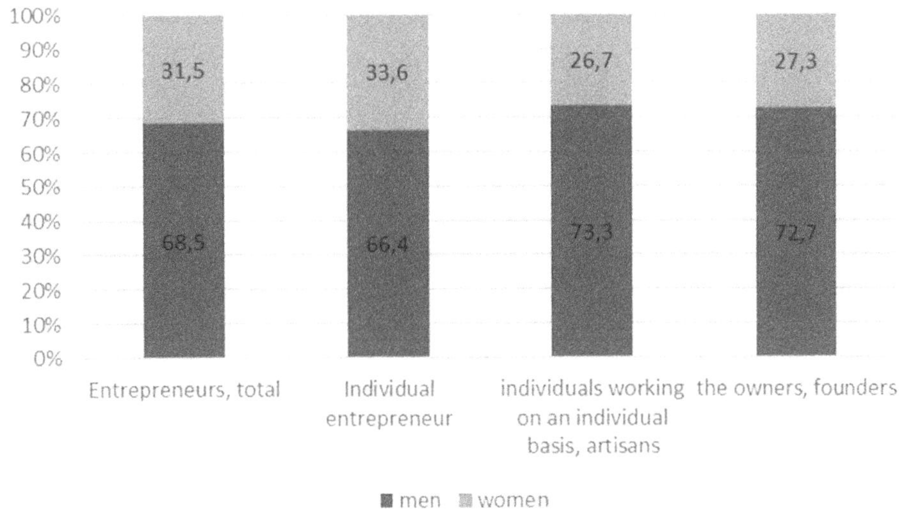

are self-employed (without employees). According to the age classification, it can be noted that women entrepreneurs aged 35 to 39 years prevail (figure 19).

Women aged 40-44 years (17%), 30-34 years (14%), 45-49 years (13%) also have a significant share. The lowest percentage of young women aged 15-24 and 25-29 years (4 and 6%, respectively). This is because a large proportion of women in the Republic of Belarus, after receiving basic and secondary education, continue to study further, receiving higher education and postgraduate (master's and postgraduate). There is also a small percentage of women entrepreneurs of retirement age-55-59 years (6%) and 60-74 years (8%). This is because women entrepreneurs in the country are provided with social guarantees, the same as those employed in the public sector, including pension provision when they reach retirement age and have the necessary work experience. The level of education of 42.3% of women entrepreneurs have higher and postgraduate education, 26.3% have specialized secondary education, 19.9% –professional technical and 11.2% of women entrepreneurs have completed 11 years of school and only 0.3% of women entrepreneurs have only a 9th-grade education. In General, almost half of women entrepreneurs have higher education, and about the same percentage of women entrepreneurs have specialized secondary education for business. A positive note is that the majority of women entrepreneurs in the country have stable family relationships (figure 20).

Figure 18. Structure of Women Entrepreneurs in Belarus, %
Source: Official Statistics of Republic of Belarus, 2019

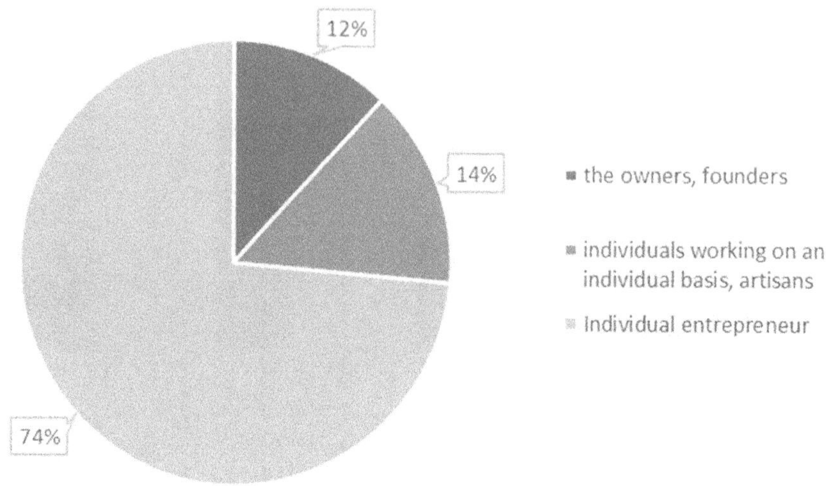

Figure 19. Age Structure of Women Entrepreneurs
Source: Official Statistics of Republic of Belarus, 2019

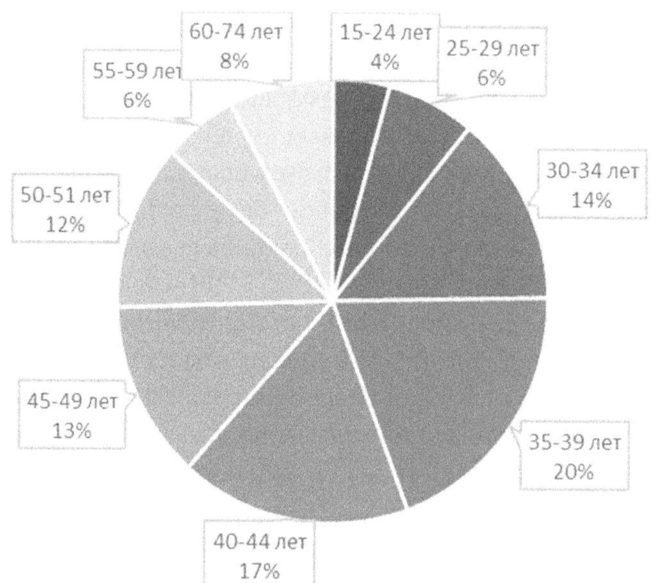

Figure 20. Structure of Women Entrepreneurs by Marital Status
Source: Official Statistics of Republic of Belarus, 2019

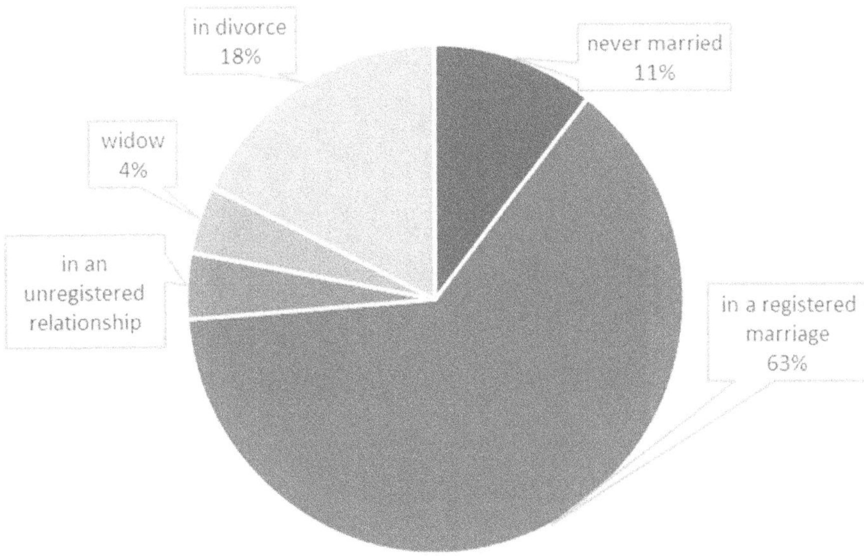

A large percentage of women entrepreneurs are divorced (17.7%). Most women in this group start their businesses because they are supported by minor children who have to be financially supported. In the category of widows (4%), a large proportion of women are engaged in business inherited from a deceased spouse. Half of women entrepreneurs, as noted, have minor dependent children (figure 21).

Half of women entrepreneurs do not have children, and only 4.3% of women entrepreneurs are mothers with many children. Thus, it is clear that the main motivating factor for more than half of women is not the need to provide dependents. Nevertheless, one of the main motives for women to start their own business is dissatisfaction with their financial situation. The average salary of women, which is significantly lower than that of men.

On average, women's wages are 25.4% lower than men's. The gap is particularly large in the field of information and communication (ICT) (by 41.1%), and in the field of culture and sports (by 39.7%). The lowest wage gap is felt in transport and logistics (6.4%), hotel services, and catering (10.1%). In other areas, the gap does not exceed 30%. There is no gender gap concerning accrued pensions. On average, women's pensions are only 1.1% less than men's. And in some regions of Belarus (Vitebsk and Mogilev), the accrued pension of women exceed the pensions of men (by 0.8 and 1.1%, respectively). This causes a small percentage of women entrepreneurs of retirement age and a significant proportion of women entrepreneurs of working age.

Figure 21. Presence of Children in Women Entrepreneurs, %
Source: Official Statistics of Republic of Belarus, 2019

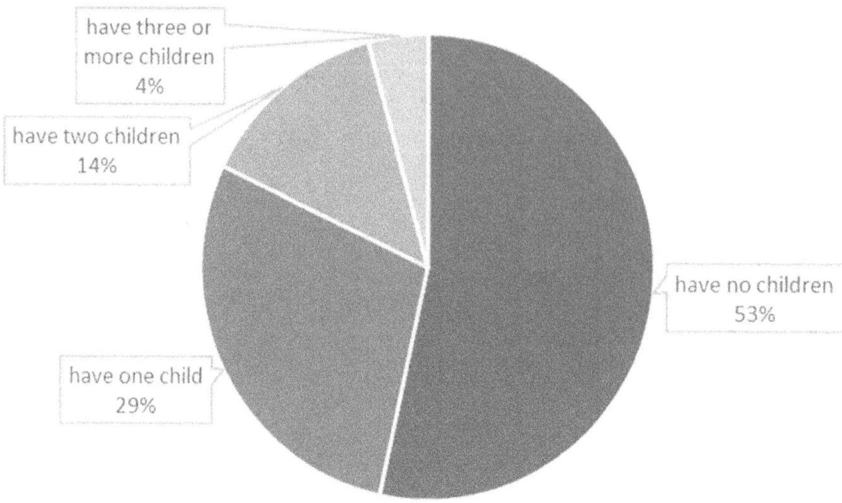

Thus, it can be concluded that women are actively engaged in business. There are no obstacles for women's business in the country. Moreover, the state encourages and promotes women's business. However, there are also several difficulties and barriers for women in business. The main external barriers today are various administrative procedures (certification, licensing, etc.) and issues of legislative variability (about 44.1% of women and 41.1% of male business owners have difficulties with this). This is followed by questions about the tax system: high rates, variability (this problem exists for 33.5% of women and 30.5% of men). In third place is state control, which includes price regulation and currency regulation (32.2% vs. 29.3%).

Almost all barriers were equally mentioned by male and female entrepreneurs, except the issue of corruption. Corruption is the only obstacle identified by more than 50% of women, while only 12% of male owners consider it a problem. One possible explanation for this result is that women are simply afraid to take bold and dangerous actions in business. This hypothesis does not contradict various studies that show that women are less likely to take risks than men. The situation is different in the area of decision-making in the public sector. Here, the percentage of women is very small for most indicators (table 1).

A small percentage of women are among the heads of state bodies subordinate to the Council of Ministers (3.2% in 2017), among the ambassadors of the Republic of Belarus (6.7% in 2017), among the members of the Board of the National Bank

Figure 22. The ratio of Nominal Accrued Average Wages for Women and Men, %
Source: Official Statistics of Republic of Belarus, 2019

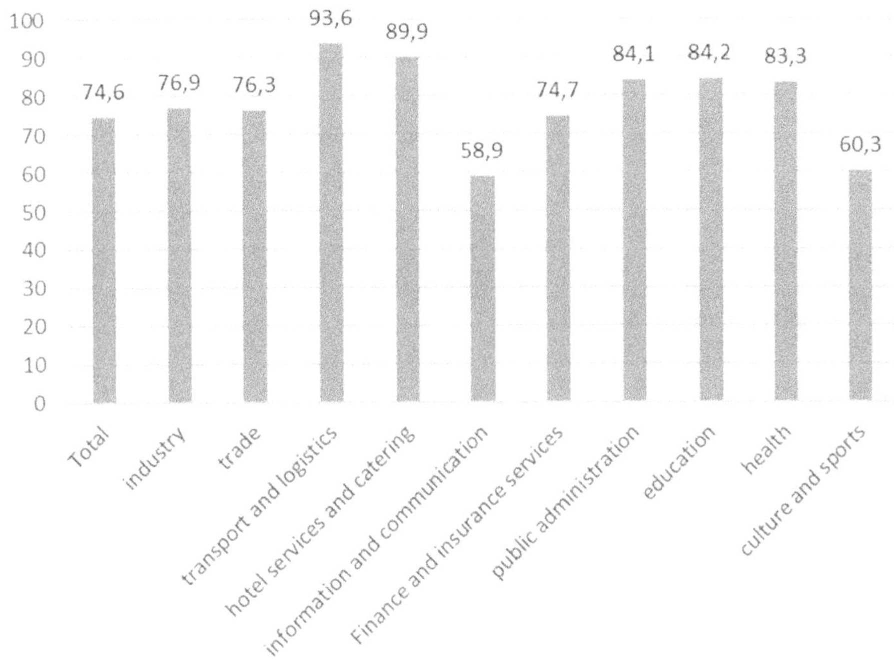

(22.2% in 20107), and among the deputies of the National Assembly (32.9% in 2017). On the other hand, more than half of women are among judges (57.8%) and the heads of rural, town, and city (district subordinated cities) Executive committees and their deputies (57.8% in 2017). According to the Secretariat of the Council of the Republic[2] of the National Assembly of the Republic of Belarus and the Secretariat of the House of Representatives[3] of the National Assembly of the Republic of Belarus, there are significantly fewer women than men (figure 23).

Over the past two years, the share of women in the Council of the Republic has decreased to 29.8%. But we can note a positive trend in the increase in the share of women in the House of Representatives (from 27.3% to 34.5%). It can be concluded that women's entrepreneurship is actively developing in the private sector. The state and other non-governmental organizations actively support and encourage women's business. However, the state structure for women is insignificant, despite the absence of restrictions for women to participate in public administration.

Table 1. Percentage of Women in Public Administration, %

Показатель	2013	2014	2015	2016	2017
Percentage of women ambassadors, %	7,1	5,3	7,0	5,1	6,7
Percentage of women among the Board members of the National Bank, %	18,2	18,2	22,2	22,2	22,2
Percentage of women in the Constitutional court, %	33,3	41,7	41,7	41,7	41,7
Percentage of women among heads of state bodies subordinate to the Council of Ministers of the Republic of Belarus, %	3,2	6,5	6,5	6,5	3,2
Percentage of women among judges, %	56,0	57,7	57,5	58,1	57,8
Percentage of women among the heads of rural, town, and city (district subordinated cities) Executive committees and their deputies, %	70,1	...	68,2	...	68,8
Percentage of women in the National Assembly[1], %	29,7	29,2	29,2	32,9	32,9
Percentage of women among managers at all levels and their deputies, %	...	48,6	47,9	48,2	49,0
Percentage of women among the heads of Republican state bodies and their deputies, %	17,6	...	20,0	...	23,2

Source: Official Statistics of Republic of Belarus, 2019

Figure 23. Distribution of the National Assembly of the Republic of Belarus, %
Source: Official Statistics of Republic of Belarus, 2019

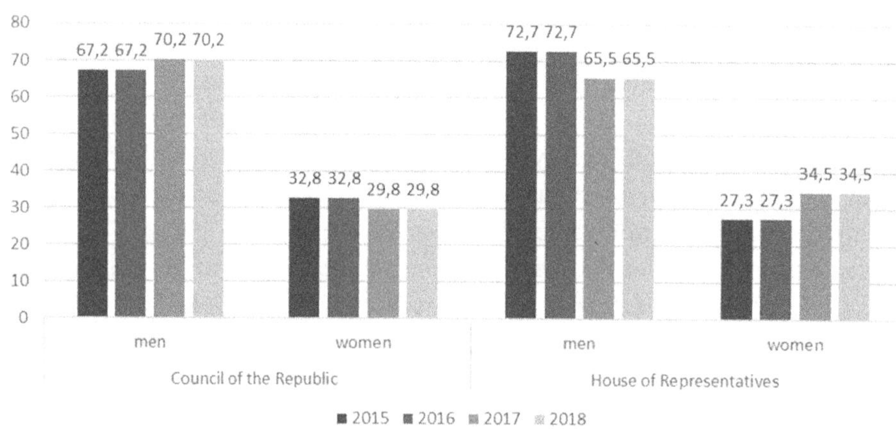

Table 2. Percentage of Women Researchers in the Republic of Belarus, %

	2008	2009	2010	2011	2012	2013	2014	2015	2016	2017
Percentage of women, total	43,9	42,7	42,2	41,7	41,1	41,1	41,2	40,58	39,6	47,7
candidate of Sciences	36,9	36,9	36,8	37,9	38,0	39,2	39,3	40,1	40,5	42,2
doctor of Sciences	16,7	16,8	17,0	16,6	17,1	17,2	17,7	17,7	18,0	18,8

Source: Official Statistics of Republic of Belarus, 2019

Section 2.3. The Position of Women in Science

According to the UNESCO Institute of Statistics, the share of women scientists in the world is less than 30%. Since the fast-growing sectors of science and innovation are particularly important for national economies, and the main role in these conditions is played by the fullest use of the intellectual resources of mankind, it is necessary to achieve a significant increase in the number of women engaged in research activities. As of 01.01.2017, the share of women among the share of Belarus was 39.6% (table 2). The National Academy of Sciences of Belarus has only one female academic and 9 female corresponding members (1% and 6.8% of the total number of academicians and corresponding members, respectively). Among researchers under the age of 35, 52.1% of the total number of young researchers at the National Academy of Sciences of Belarus are women. At the same time, every second of the young scientists has a Ph.D., which is 52.2% of their total number.

The decrease in the proportion of women in the scientific workforce continued throughout the entire period 2000-2016. a large proportion of women who leave science find themselves in business, because, having such qualities as an organization, ability to work, conscientiousness, as well as due to greater flexibility and adaptability, they can produce interesting ideas and compete with men in the business field. By 2017, the total number of women engaged in research and development decreased by 6.6% compared to 2000. at the same time, their share among candidates of science increased by 5.8% during this period, and among doctors of science - by 5.0%. In addition, the analysis of state statistics data on the staff of researchers in certain fields of science shows that women continue to maintain their positions both in the traditionally "female" segments of scientific fields (Humanities, Social Sciences, Medical Sciences) and in the field of natural and agricultural sciences. According to 2016 data, the share of women exceeds the share of men in all fields of science, except natural and technical).

In General, a comparative analysis of statistical data for 2000 and 2016 showed that the share of women employed in the Humanities increased by 8.4%, while in the technical, socio-economic, and social Sciences it decreased by 8.7% and 6.7%, respectively. It should be noted that the largest number of women researchers in Belarus (44.9% of their total number in scientific organizations of the Republic) is concentrated in the field of technical sciences. At the same time, the analysis of the qualification structure of various fields of science has shown that women with the degree of doctor and candidate of Sciences are least provided with the field of technical sciences. So, at the beginning of 2017, their share among doctors and candidates of technical Sciences was 9.3% and 16.7%, while in the field of Medical Sciences – 29.3% and 60.9%, agricultural – 18.4% and 47.5%, natural – 17.8% and 43.4%, socio-economic and social-14.3% and 42.5%, respectively. Thus, when women researchers are concentrated mainly in the field of technical Sciences, the latter's availability of highly qualified women specialists is one of the lowest.

Since in all fields of science, except natural and technical fields, the proportion of women among researchers exceeds the proportion of men, we can talk about the feminization of science. For example, in the fields of medical, agricultural, humanitarian, socio-economic, and social Sciences, more than 56% of researchers are women. The field of technical Sciences remains predominantly "male", where the number of women is 2.3 times lower than the number of men, and their share is 29.9%. On thc onc hand, the high proportion of women in research indicates the effectiveness of the state's gender policy in higher education and science. In General, the analysis of statistical data allows us to characterize the position of women in the scientific staff of Belarus in the period 2000-2016 as quite stable, with minor changes in their number in different years. There is a tendency to increase the share of women researchers among specialists of the highest scientific qualification- doctors and candidates of science. Science continues to be attractive to a large part of women, which is greatly facilitated by the measures taken by the state to improve the socio-economic situation of scientists and to consolidate young people in this field. However, the process of structural transformation is slow.

Gender stereotypes can not only serve as an external factor that hinders women's professional growth but also act as an internal demotivator. Accordingly, women scientists who present obvious or perceived difficulties in science (regardless of their actual existence or presence only in consciousness) may refuse to pursue a scientific career and actively participate in scientific activities. However, only 11.5% of young women consider gender stereotypes that determine the role of men and women in society as a factor that hinders promotion. 93.4% and 94.9% of women and 87.1% and 82% of men, respectively, disagree with the statements "a woman is less competent as a scientist" and "science is a male field of activity". Marriage and motherhood are often cited as factors that hinder women's career growth in science. It is assumed that the double burden associated with performing several household tasks and maternal functions takes a long time, which affects the lack of time for research and publication. However, according to only 13.7% of women, the workload of household chores hinders their success in science. However, 57.4% and 50.8% agree with the statement "it is more difficult for a woman to combine professional and family responsibilities compared to a man", while 41.5% and 41.8% of women and men disagree, respectively. Opinion on the impact of marital status and parenthood was almost evenly divided. Women's participation in research activities is socially significant, since it expands the social base of reproduction of scientific personnel, strengthens the human potential of science and the scientific potential of society as a whole.

SECTION 3. PROSPECTS FOR THE DEVELOPMENT OF DIGITALIZATION FOR WOMEN IN THE REPUBLIC OF BELARUS

Today, the average female business lags in size and growth dynamics compared to male competitors. No gender differences were found in the context of innovation activity. The current barriers to women's business in Belarus are not only related to the functioning of the business ecosystem. Existing exogenous barriers, such as excessive control, various contradictory rules, and procedures, and the level of human capital, undoubtedly maltreat quality and dynamics of women's business development.

However, maintaining the traditional division of social roles is equally important. The latter entails an additional burden in the form of performing most of the household duties and caring for children, which, as the results of the survey show, is no longer perceived as the norm for the majority of women owners. At the same time, the results of the work showed the need to take into account the regional factor to increase the effectiveness and relevance of measures aimed at the development and promotion of business initiatives, and support for women involved in business activities. The results obtained confirm the need to include the gender issue in the program of support for small and medium-sized businesses in Belarus, as well as the need to take it into account when determining the effectiveness of various business support programs. This will give impetus to new gender initiatives and contribute to economic growth and innovative prospects for Belarus.

Having studied the factors that influence the digitalization process and applied them in practice, it will be easier for organizations or the country as a whole to make the transition to a new level of work. It is the modern consumer who acts as a certain engine for the movement of digital transformation. This is because almost everyone, in one way or another, uses gadgets and modern digital services, ranging from social networks, television, and entertainment, to public services. The transition to a new level through digitalization will lead to the fact that the business will not be able to work according to the old model and with the same efficiency. In this regard the author recommend the following areas for improving support for the development of women's entrepreneurship:

- provide funding and implement the actual implementation of the provisions of the National action plan for gender equality for 2021-2025, aimed at the development of business and entrepreneurship among women;
- promote the creation of a permanent system of training and consulting for women in the field of business;
- create schools of information and computer literacy and psychological support for beginning entrepreneurs;
- promote the development and implementation of gender education programs for the population and the prevention of domestic violence;
- develop a micro-credit program for women entrepreneurs, take special measures to ensure women's access to loans, loans, and privatization facilities;
- provide for microenterprises to establish special tax regimes, a simplified method of accounting, and special rules for the privatization of premises leased from the state;
- to lease land plots, non-residential buildings, office and production facilities, and equipment to microenterprises at reduced rates;
- promote the development of business incubators to support women's small and medium-sized businesses;
- consider forming a special section on the development of women's and family entrepreneurship in the annual programs of support and development of entrepreneurship;
- promote information campaigns on the socio-economic effects of women's enterprises, including social ones;
- promote the social image of women entrepreneurs and social entrepreneurship in General;
- establish a permanent dialogue between government agencies that regulate business activities and business entities, and lobby for state support for the annual forum of businesswomen;
- collect statistical data on women entrepreneurs and research women's contribution to the country's economic development.

In General, measures are needed to create a favorable climate for the development of entrepreneurship in the Republic of Belarus. At the same time, special solutions are needed relating to the need for the state to comply with the obligations and recommendations of the Convention on the elimination of all forms of discrimination against women, the Beijing platform for action, and the Millennium Declaration, which indicate that entrepreneurship is one of the priorities in the process of achieving gender equality in economic relations. Gender equality is equal access of women and men to economic resources. This is the equivalence of "female" and "male" professions and roles in society. The equal attitude of society to the contribution of both to economic and demographic development. Sustainable development is impossible without the implementation of Goal 5 "Gender equality", among the priorities which the development of women's entrepreneurship contributes not only to the innovative development of society but also to achieve equal terms with men in business.

REFERENCES

CATALYST. (2017). *Women On Corporate Boards Globally*. Author.

Digital Economy and Society Index — DESI. (2019). Retrieved from: https://ec.europa.eu/digital-single-market/en/desi

Digital Evolution Index – DEI. (n.d.). Retrieved from https://newsroom.mastercard.com/eu/files/2014/09/Digital-Evolution-Index_MC-Key-Findings-FINAL.pdf

E-Participation Index — EPART. (n.d.). Retrieved from: https://publicadministration.un.org/publications/content/PDFs/E-Library%20Archives/UN%20E-Government%20Survey%20series/UN%20E-Government%20Survey%202014_Russian.pdf

Global Connectivity Index – GCI. (n.d.). *Huawei*. Retrieved from: https://www.huawei.com/minisite/russia/gci2018rus/materials/gci2018.pdf

IDI 2017 Rank. (2017). Retrieved from https://www.itu.int/net4/ITU-D/idi/2017/index.html

IMD World Digital Competitiveness Index — WDCI. (2018). IMD World Competitiveness Center.

Networked Readiness Index — NRI. (n.d.). Retrieved from: https://www3.weforum.org/docs/GITR2016/WEF_GITR_Chapter1.1_2016.pdf

Official Statistics of Republic of Belarus. (n.d.). Retrieved from www.belstat.gov.by/en/ofitsialnaya-statistika/

Statistical Yearbook. (2019). The National Statistic Committee of the Republic of Belarus.

The Global Innovation Index – GII. (n.d.). Retrieved from https://www.wipo.int/edocs/pubdocs/en/wipo_pub_gii_2018.pdf

The UN Global E-Government Development Index – EGDI. (n.d.). Retrieved from https://publicadministration.un.org/publications/content/PDFs/UN%20E-Government%20Survey%202018%20Russian.pdf

VanderBrug, J. (2013). *The Global Rise of Female Entrepreneurs*. Harvard Business School.

ENDNOTES

1 The National Assembly of the Republic of Belarus is a representative and legislative body of the Republic of Belarus. the National Assembly or Parliament consists of two chambers – the House of representatives and the Council of the Republic.

2 The Council of the Republic is the chamber of territorial representation. Eight members of the Council of the Republic are elected from each region and city of Minsk by secret ballot at meetings of deputies of local Councils of deputies of the basic level of each region and city of Minsk. Eight members of the Council of the Republic are appointed by the President of the Republic of Belarus.

3 The composition of the House of representatives is 110 deputies. The election of deputies to the House of representatives is carried out in accordance with the law on the basis of universal, free, equal, direct suffrage by secret ballot.

Chapter 4
Digital Financial Inclusion Through FinTech

Shashi Bala
V. V. Giri National Labour Institute, India

Puja Singhal
https://orcid.org/0000-0003-1927-5517
National Centre for School Leadership-NIEPA, India

ABSTRACT

For the economic growth of a nation, it is imperative that the financial condition of a country should be strong. Digital financial inclusion can play a very strong role in achieving inclusive growth of a nation as it can provide suitable financial services at a reasonable cost on a timely basis to marginalized groups such as women and girls of rural areas. This chapter is an attempt to explore new digital financial technologies including FinTech which shall transform the lives of women. G20 financial inclusion indicators have been used to explore the prevailing gender dimensions and issues pertaining to digital financial accessibility. This chapter also focuses on how the initiatives taken by the Indian government and banks, and FinTech start-ups are bridging the financial gender gap and attaining the goal of sustainable growth in India.

1. INTRODUCTION

The sustainable development of a nation requires a robust financial ecosystem. Despite this fact it has been observed for ages that it is not inclusive and there is a big financial gender gap in almost all economies. The situation is more critical for

DOI: 10.4018/978-1-7998-8594-8.ch004

women in developing and underdeveloped nations due to the patriarchal mind of the society. A "potent formula" for generating socioeconomic profits, transforming societies, and enhancing the growth rate of developing economies is closing this gender gap in digital financial inclusion. (Women's World Banking. 2016). Although women make up 40% of the world's workforce, they are less likely to have access to formal financial services (World Bank, 2013). Recent studies (Demirgüç-Kunt, et al., 2018) indicate that this gap has not changed over the years despite various financial innovative policies. In low-income communities, it is the women who manage all the scarce resources and are burdened with much of the care work which is generally unpaid. This lowers their labor force participation rate in the market which restricts their ability to save or manage risks and they are forced to use informal financial instruments often of unreliable nature. Fewer savings also restricts the ability to start their own business which is not only hampering the economic growth of women but also impacts the financial statistics of a country (Demirgüç-Kunt, et al., 2017). They save from their meager household incomes and in the future invest money in the education and health of their children. Therefore, to transform the lives of women and families it is imperative to innovate new financial tools which will manage their money better and save their time. The proliferation of mobile banking and other financial sector innovations has accelerated the pace of financial inclusion worldwide.

The financial Gender gap can be reduced with effective financial inclusion and new digital technologies which are revolutionizing the financial industry around the world. Digital financial services appears to offer innovative and low-cost platforms to provide opportunities to bank the unbanked and address the issues of financial exclusion. These services have the potential to overcome geographical limitations and boost transparency and therefore increase faith in financial systems by reducing the informational asymmetries between lenders and borrowers that keep large segments of mostly poor populations excluded from financial systems. Financial autonomy and privacy for users can also be enhanced by these services and potentially lessen the risk of appropriation of these funds by others. Digital technologies not only ease the access of bank accounts, savings mechanisms for women but they also provide liberty in labor market decisions with more choices like about how they use their time, whether for employment, leisure, income-generating activities, or education. This led to gender equality not only in the field of finance but they may have further substantive autonomy over their lives in decisions ranging from employment, marriage, and relationships to whether to use contraception and ultimately financial inclusion act as an important tool to reduce Gender-based Violence. To empower women in all aspects it is important to make them economically strong. Yet untapped opportunities exist to provide a broader array of financial services for the poor and particularly for women. Conventional financial products and services still do not seem to reach the poor and women well. The research study of the International Monetary Fund also indicates that by bridging the gender gap GDP can be raised by an average of 35 percent leading to substantial macroeconomic advantages. Therefore, it is imperative to innovate new ways to resolve the issues of unbanked especially women. This chapter will focus on a new technology known as FinTech, and how it is helpful to reduce the gender gap in financial inclusion, and how it is integrated into Govt policies and programs to change the financial landscape. This chapter also highlights, how these emerging technologies are helpful for women to overcome their socioeconomic barriers.

2. FINTECH CONCEPT

FinTech in the truest sense is the convergence of financial services and Technology (Figure 1.) or it can be defined as **technology-driven financial innovation–which offers** new financial products and services by leveraging digital technologies to generate new business intentions and targeting unreached and underserved sections of the society in an economically feasible manner. To make FinTech a key enabler for financial inclusion in any economy it is required that there must be a right combination of technical skills, capital investments, government policies, regulatory framework, and entrepreneurial and innovative mindset. Innovation and technology have brought about a radical transformation in traditional financial services and universities, research institutions, technology experts, industry consultants, and government agencies are the key enabler for this change. The financial gender gap can be filled by the integrated effort of each market participant because in this digital era none of them can afford to function in isolation.

Fintech Adoption In India

Fintech in India is growing rapidly and is fuelled by abundant FinTech start-ups, accelerators, and incubators over the last few years. With increasing internet and mobile penetration rate, India has a great opportunity for technology startups. The financial services market in India is mostly untapped, according to World Bank's Global Findex Report 2017, the unbanked population in India is 190 million and most of the payments in India are still made by cash. Under such underserved market conditions in India, the Fintech market can increase demand in almost every segment – consumer lending, insurance, trade finance, digital payments, and many more. New financial innovations and solutions in these areas, will help the market to grow significantly.

Figure 1. FinTech Concept

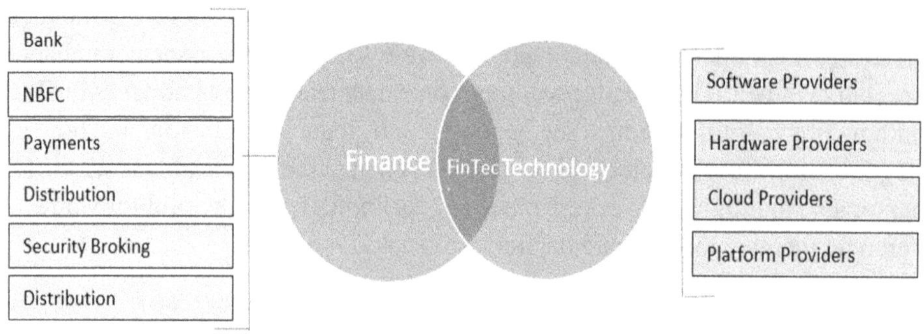

EY's Global FinTech Adoption Index 2019 reckoned that India's fintech adoption has increased exponentially over the last two years from 52% in 2017 to 87% in 2019 which is more than the global average adoption rate that is 64% (2019). Govt.'s policy measures like Aadhar, UPI, Demonetisation and emphasis towards digitalization are the key enablers of this elevation, along with these other factors which are responsible for attracting consumers to use other platforms to access innovative products and ease of onboarding. Within money transfer, adoption is led by peer-to-peer and non-bank money transfers (85%), and in-store mobile phone payments (88%). Demographically, the rate of fintech adoption in the category of payments and transfer is approximately 100% among mid to high-income groups aged between 20-34, Insurance begins with 60% for 18-24 ages, and reaches up to 80% for 25-34-year-old people, and then slashes back to 40-46% for people aged 55-65+ years. But the picture is not all rosy for all the demographic groups including women, consumers in rural areas, and consumers without university degrees. The gender gap persists in the use of savings and investment services which is 27% for women and 40% for men.

Above figure 2 demonstrates that emerging markets like India are leading their way in Fintech adoption. In 2017 the rate of fintech adoption in India was 52% while the global rate was only 33% and the same trend has been observed in 2019, that is India's rate is 87% while the global adoption rate is only 64%. Among all the categories of Fintech, in India most commonly used is a Money transfer and payments with 94%, followed by Insurance at 76%, savings and investment at 67%, financial planning at 63%, and borrowing around 61%. Globally the consumer's first preference is the same that is for Money transfer and payments with 75%, but the next preference is for savings and investment with 48% and is followed by financial planning at 34%, insurance at 29%, and borrowing at 27% in 2019.

Figure 2. Percentage of Population using FinTech services along with Fintech adoption rate from 2017 to 2019 in India and Global
Source: Author's interpretation from Global FinTech Adoption Index 2017 and 2019

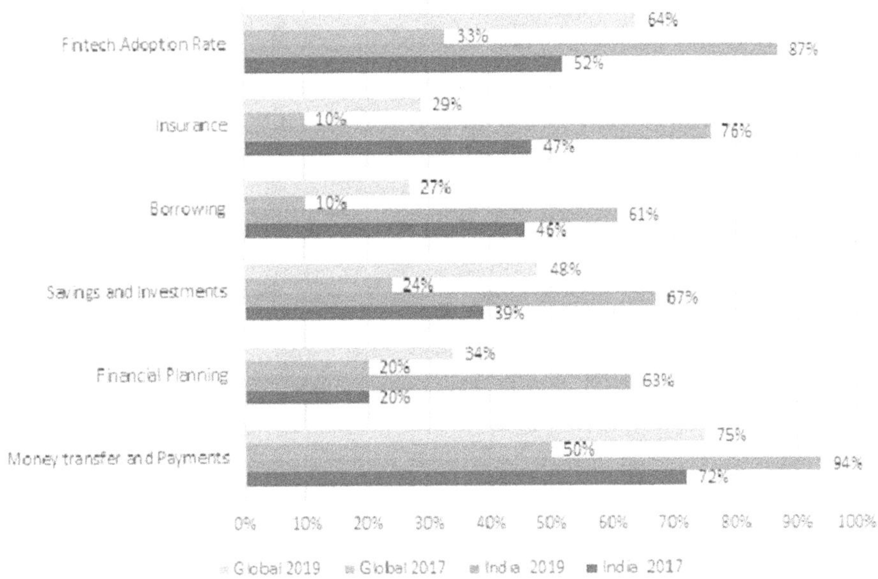

3. GENDER GAP IN DIGITAL FINANCIAL INCLUSION IN INDIA

Due to old customs and patriarchal thinking of society, women are facing poverty more than man which restricts their prospects to own assets, generate income, and capacity to make decisions related to household purchases (UN, 2015). Financial inclusion is crucial for women which enables them to increase their savings and enhances their productive capacity. This creates a ripple effect in their community as they tend to reinvest their money for the improvement of their lives. But, significantly, women must have the knowledge to operate the available financial resources as those resources can support reducing in poverty levels and will impact women's empowerment (Holloway, Rouse, & Niazi, 2017). **Digital financial inclusion is about making financial systems 'women-able' rather than making women 'bankable'. To explore the gender gap in digital financial inclusion** in India, G20 Financial Inclusion indicators have been used in this chapter.

Figure 3. Access to a mobile phone, Internet and its Use for making payments (% age 15+)
Source: Author's interpretation from World Bank Global Findex database

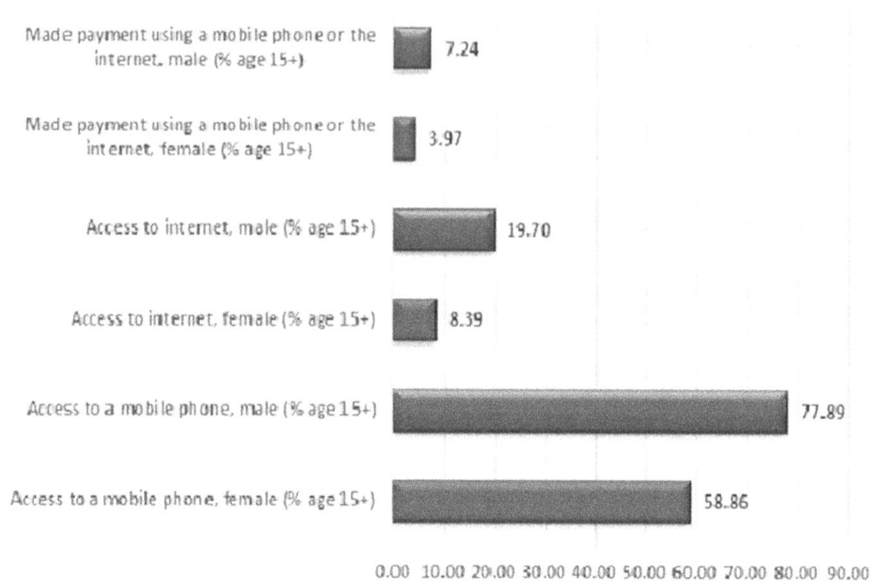

a) Access to Mobile phone, Internet and Its Usage for Making Payments

The above figure demonstrates that there is a disparity in access to a mobile phone by males and females in India, this gap is in double-digit of 19.03, which has its ripple effect in the utilization of mobile-related services. In the case of internet accessibility, both males and females are getting its access below 20% but the situation is more critical for females with a gap of 11.31 which hampers their connectivity to all online services including digital financial services. Due to these gaps, only 3.97 percent of females can use their mobile phones and the internet to make payments. These disparities indicate that there is a need to concentrate on the development of digital infrastructure in India including the availability of broadband services not only in urban areas but also in rural areas which will lead to better connectivity of the internet in remote areas. The next important objective is promoting gender equality through access of technology by changing the patriarchal mindset of families.

Figure 4. Account, Active account, and National Identity card (% age 15+)
Source: Author's interpretation from World Bank Global Findex database

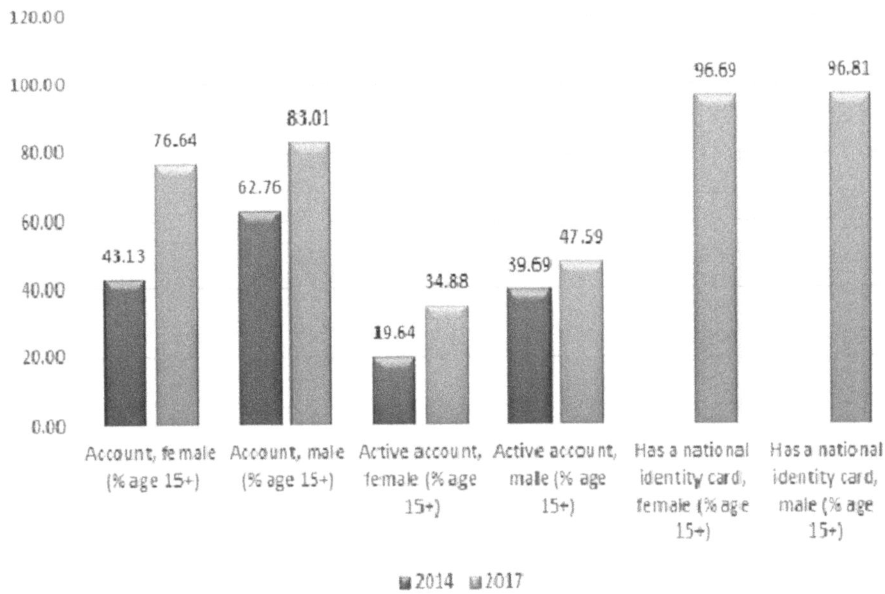

b) Account, Active Account, and National Identity Card

Figure 4 indicate that there is a growth in account opening from 2014 to 2017 for both females and males and the Compounded annual growth rate (CAGR) of account for women is 21% while for male it is 10%. The data also identified the gap between Account opened and Active account and it is more for females (41.76 for the year 2017) in comparison to that of males (35.41 for the year 2017). Social and cultural barriers might restrict women from accessing their accounts regularly. For opening a bank account in India, one of the KYC requirements is the submission of a government-issued identity card. Various research studies have identified that in rural areas most of the females don't have formal government IDs and are usually registered in the names of husbands or sons. But now the situation has been improved by RBI as it allows the use of the Aadhar ID card as a proof of identity to meet the regulatory KYC requirements (Ehrbeck, 2014). Due to Govt. initiatives, there is gender parity in ownership of national ID cards for males and females as reflected in the figure and it makes account opening easier for females.

Figure 5. Savings, borrowings from Financial Institutions, and use of digital devices for receiving and making payment (% age 15+)
Source: Author's interpretation from World Bank Global Findex database

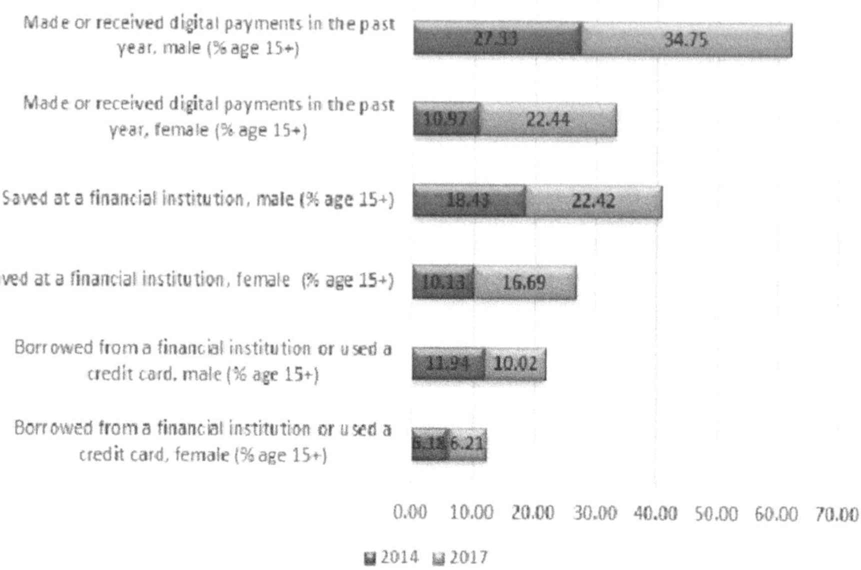

c) Savings, Borrowings From Financial Institutions, and Use of Digital Devices for Receiving and Making Payment

From the above figure 5, it can be observed that borrowings from the financial institutions using a credit card have been increasing from 2014 to 2017 both by males and females but gender inequality does persist in this area also. The same is the case for savings at financial institutions, more males keep their savings at banks or other institutions, but generally, females have fewer savings due to their backward economic conditions, and because of that they are taking less help from financial institutions due to financial illiteracy. The data also indicates that fewer females are making and receiving digital payments, it could be due to and less availability of mobile phones and internet services another reason could be that they consider cash as a safer means of transaction.

4. BRIDGING THE GENDER GAP THROUGH FINTECH

Fintech solutions are more substantive in addressing the digitally financial gender gap as these solutions are more flexible, easier to use, cost-effective, and readily accessible which ultimately increases the formalization of women's transactions. These facilities have a direct impact on women's access to credit, savings account, and other financial products which finally empower them by making them agents of their financial futures. Arun and Kamath (2015) also emphasized that the access of these services should be measured based on their penetration to underserved communities and by the degree to which the products are used.

a) Government Initiatives

Targeted financial policy interventions by governments can play a significant role in leveraging fintech to address the digital gender gap in financial inclusion. GoI is moving forward in this area with the motto of Jandhan to Jansuraksha.

i) Pradhan Mantri Jan Dhan Yojana (PMJDY)

PMJDY is an innovative mission of GoI and was initiated on 15th Aug 2014 to offer universal access to banking facilities with at least one basic bank account to every household, financial literacy, access to credit, insurance, and pension facility. This scheme allows opening an account without the requirement of any minimum balance to support the people not having a savings account. Along with other services beneficiaries also get a RuPay debit card, with an inbuilt accident insurance cover of Rs. 2 lakhs. Census 2011 estimated that out of 24.67 crore households in the country, 14.48 crore (58.7%) had access to banking services and as of 27.3.2019, the number of accounts has grown to 35.27 crores.

ii) Pradhan Mantri Suraksha Bima Yojana (PMSBY)

This risk coverage scheme is applicable for people of the age group of 18 to 70 years with a bank account and Aadhar is the primary KYC for that. The risk coverage under the scheme is Rs. 2 lakh for accidental death and full disability and Rs. 1 lakh for partial disability with a premium of Rs.12 per annum and auto-debit facility. According to the Department of Financial Inclusion, a total of 40,749 Claims were registered under this scheme. These types of schemes can provide a sense of protection among poor and unserved communities including women.

iii) Pradhan Mantri Mudra Yojana

To support the first generation and small entrepreneurs, under this scheme of GoI a loan of up to Rs. 50,000 is given under sub-scheme ‘Shishu’; between Rs. 50,000 to 5.0 Lakhs under sub-scheme ‘Kishore’; and between 5.0 Lakhs to 10.0 Lakhs under sub-scheme ‘Tarun’. This scheme was started on 8th April 2015. One of the important things is that Loans taken do not require collaterals under this scheme. Such types of schemes can enhance the economic empowerment of women also. This scheme benefited 5.99 crore accounts till 31.03.2019 by sanctioning Rs. 3,21,722 crores (DFS, GOI).

iv) Stand Up India Scheme

This scheme of GOI was launched on 5th April 2016 to facilitate bank loans between Rs.10 lakh and Rs.1 crore provided to at least one Scheduled Caste (SC) or Scheduled Tribe (ST) borrower and at least one woman borrower per bank branch for setting up greenfield enterprise which may be in manufacturing, services or the trading sector. The scheme which is being implemented through all Scheduled Commercial Banks is to benefit at least 2.5 lakh borrowers. This scheme is beneficial for those who are facing problems due to lack of inadequate credit and mentorship along with this it also foresees the support the potential borrowers. Till 31st March 2019, this scheme has supported 59,429 women.

V) Pradhan Mantri Vaya Vandana Yojana

GoI has launched this scheme to provide social security to elderly persons aged 60 years and above. This scheme is implemented through LIC and offers a guaranteed payout of pension at a specified rate for 10 years along with this it also offers a death benefit in the form of a return of purchase price to the nominee. Fintech Adoption of FinTech by the Government in various financial inclusion procedures are as follows:

b) Bank Initiatives

Certain initiatives by Indian banks enables and enhances the offerings of Fintech startups with their innovative product and services.

c) Fintech Startups Initiatives

India Fintech Report 2019 reckoned that India is now the world’s second-biggest fintech hub with 2,035 startups functional in the sector. India’s adoption rate for

Table 1. Fintech Adoption by Government

S.No.	FinTech Adoption	Digital Financial Inclusion
1.	Aadhaar-enabled payment systems (AEPS)	Allows online inter-operable financial inclusion transactions at the micro ATM or kiosk banking through Business Correspondents.
2.	Aadhaar Payments Bridge System (APBS)	Enables the transfer of payments from the government to Aadhaar-enabled accounts of beneficiaries at banks and post offices.
3.	Direct Benefit Transfers (DBT) program	Transform service delivery system by speeding up payments, removing leakages and intermediaries, and enhancing financial inclusion and is implemented through the AEP and APB systems.
4.	Modification to existing Bank FinTech App.	Ease the account opening and cash transfer procedure for women. E,g Sukanya Samriddhi Scheme supports parents of girl child for their future education.
5.	Easy cash transfer App	Enhance the Government Social Cash transfer and benefit the underserved and marginalized section of the community.
6.	Enhanced Mobile Banking	Anytime, anywhere financial services can be accessed through this mobile technology.
7.	ATM technology	Allows the customers to access cash anytime.
8.	RuPay Card	Card payment scheme at a lower cost and allowing for more flexibility, and it enables Indian banks and financial institutions to offer electronic payments.
9.	Multiple Guarantee App for agencies /UID for MSME App.	Micro and small enterprises (MSEs) can take advantage of this App. in the area of credit guarantees.
10.	Digitization of land records/ Crop Insurance App	Helpful for Agrarian segments including marginal farmers through Aadhaar linked mechanism
11.	Loan / Payment App.	Support Self Help Groups (SHGs)
12.	Multiple Guarantee App for agencies /UID for MSME App.	To provide credit guarantees in niche areas for micro and small enterprises (MSEs). It would also explore possibilities for counter guarantee and re-insurance Introduction of UID for all MSME borrowers and information from it should be shared with credit bureaus.

fintech products is equivalent to China's i.e. 87%. These startups are accelerating financial innovations and have the potential to bring a transformation in the area of digital financial inclusion in India. Some of the initiatives taken by Fintech Startups are listed in table 3.

5. CONCLUSION

The prevalence of digital technologies and innovations in fintech are permitting economies with large unserved and unbanked populations that formerly relied on cash

Table 2. Bank initiatives

S.No.	Banks	Product	Digital Financial Inclusion
1	ICICI bank	contactless mobile payment system	It could augment NFC payments in India
2	Axis Bank	Invoice to Payment	End-to-end digital invoicing and payment solutions could be enhanced.
3	DBS	First mobile bank	Allows customers to open accounts digitally with their PAN card and Aadhaar card
4	Union Bank	*99# mobile application	Permits basic services like balance inquiry, fund transfers, and mini statements to its customers even when there is no internet.
5	HDFC Bank	phone-based proximity services	To benefit the customer's bank has collaborated with Fintech startup 'Tone Tag'.
6	Yes Bank	sound-based proximity payments	For providing this service, the bank partnered with Ultracash Technologies.
7	State Bank of India	mobile POS	To attain Merchant acquisition, a partnership of bank with Ezetap
8	IDFC	'Bank in a Box' solution	It supports payment processing, card management, e-commerce, and AEPS with the partnership of fintech startup FSS

to experience enhanced financial inclusion. According to World Bank's Global Index Database 2017, the global unbanked population declined to 1.7 billion which was 2.5 billion in 2011. Fintech plays a vital role in bridging the gender gap in financial inclusion. Digital Financial Services are critically significant for women whose needs are not as well administered by traditional banks in the formal sector. Women in developing nations like India are more likely to be illiterate and innumerable. Along with other socioeconomic barriers they also face problems dealing with the male-centric world of banking. In such countries, women are generally more conservative and risk-averse than men and are late adaptors of new technologies. To address these challenges, especially concerning bridging the gender gap in financial inclusion it is critically important to ensure fintech services are tailored to the needs of women, with an increased focus on privacy, reliability, affordability, trust, and education. To facilitate this, there is a need to assess the requirements of the underserved sectors of society, including women. Financial literacy can play a vital role in involving unbanked communities in digital finance which not only provides information on savings and investments but it also shares knowledge about different available digital financial services to save their money. Apart from this, policy interventions by governments play a significant role in leveraging fintech to address the gender gap in financial inclusion. For the diffusion of new technologies, there is a need for robust and broad infrastructures which can be efficiently served by

Table 3. Fintech Startups Initiatives

S.No.	Fintech Company	Category	Digital Financial Inclusion
1	Paytm	M-Wallet/Gateway	Digital wallet company and leverages financial technology to cater into different segments such as payment gateway, payments bank, investments. The company also offered investments and trading platforms through Paytm Money and has also initiated eCommerce with Paytm Mall.
2	PhonePe	UPI-based payments	Renders support online services and enable consumers to send or receive money, make mobile or DTH recharges, pay utility bills from credit cards to insurance premiums, shop through online and offline vendors, or travel. By linking the app to their bank accounts customer can make payments through the unified payments interface (UPI) platform.
3	Mobiwik	Digital wallets	Delivers a digital financial services platform, and also offers its services including digital wallets, wealth management, insurance, etc. Key differentiators are Low customer acquisition cost, inbuilt scoring model, and quick disbursal of loans. The company is first to disburse a loan amount in a matter of 90 seconds.
4	Policybazaar	Insurance aggregator	Expertise in providing transparent and accurate insurance information to consumers. Provides a platform where consumers could compare products and select the utmost viable option.
5	PayU	Digital payments gateway	Competency lies in providing simplifying payments for small and medium merchants by providing technology to fulfill online transactions. A multi-functional mobile app that permits online businesses to receive and process payments. The app is useful for a businessman to regulate their business performance and request payments from customers and vendors.

the Government. Comprehensive regulatory regimes are also important for ensuring the proper working of the Fintech ecosystem.

Finally, the collective effort of the Government, Banking sector, and Startups will significantly increase women's economic participation through digital financial inclusion. With technology continuing its swift advancement G20 Leaders' plan of covering more than 100 million women into the labor force by 2025 which in reality will benefit families, societies, and ultimately the global economy.

REFERENCES

Alliance for Financial Inclusion. (2016). Policy Frameworks to Support Women's Financial Inclusion. Kuala Lumpur: Alliance for Financial Inclusion.

Arun, T., & Kamath, R. (2015). Financial inclusion: Policies and practices. *IIMB Management Review*, *27*(4), 267–287. doi:10.1016/j.iimb.2015.09.004

Deepti, K.C. (n.d.). *Financial Inclusion: Government Promoted Initiatives*. IFMR CMF, Thematic Fact Sheet 8.

Demirguc-Kunt, A., Klapper, L., Singer, D., Ansar, S., & Hess, J. R. (2018). *The Global Findex Database 2017: Measuring Financial Inclusion and the Fintech Revolution*. World Bank Group. doi:10.1596/978-1-4648-1259-0

Demirguc-Kunt, A., Klapper, L., Singer, D., & Van Oudheusden, P. (2015). *The Global Findex Database 2014 - Measuring Financial Inclusion Around the World.* World Bank Policy Research Working Paper No 7255.

Economic Times. (2019). *Fintech startups paving way for a financially smart India with global recognition*. Retrieved from economictimes. indiatimes.com/articleshow/68610868.cms?utm_source=contentofinterest&utm_medium=text&utm_campaign=cppst

Ehrbeck, T. (2014, July 23). Can India Achieve Financial Inclusion within the Next Few Years? *The Huffington Post.*

Global FinTech Adoption Index. (2019). Retrieved from https://www.ey.com/en_gl/ey-global-fintech-adoption-index

Holloway, K., Rouse, R., & Niazi, Z. (2017). *Women's Economic Empowerment Through Financial Inclusion*. Innovations for Poverty Action.

OECD. (2013). *Women and Financial Education: Evidence, Policy Responses, and Guidance, OECD Publishing*. Organization for Economic Co-operation and Development.

Pradhan Mantri Jan-Dhan Yojana. (n.d.). http://www.pmjdy.gov.in/schemedetail.aspx

Toronto Centre. (2018). *Advancing Women's Digital Financial Inclusion.*

Women's World Banking. (2016). Women's Financial Inclusion: A Driver for Global Growth. New York: Women's World Banking.

World Bank Group. (2018). *The Global Findex Database*. Author.

Chapter 5
Addressing Low Female Participation in STEM for an Inclusive Industry 4.0:
Mainstreaming Gender

Sunita Sangar
Independent Researcher, India

ABSTRACT

Increase in enrollment of women in higher education also had an impact on the choice of subjects. Science, technology, engineering, and maths (STEM) subjects also attracted a large number of women as their professional choices. However, employment for women in STEM domain has largely remained inadequate and contributed to the overall declining employment trend for women. There are several socio-cultural barriers seriously impeding women's development as professionals in the field of STEM. The government facilitated re-entry of women in science through dedicated women scientist schemes, but domination of life sciences indicates professional gendered segregation. Women in India are largely employed in the unorganized sectors, and improving women participation in the STEM domain can enable women's participation in the organized industry sector institutions. The emergence of Industry 4.0 provides an opportunity to not contribute further to the widened gender disparities and gender stereotypes. This will be a big leap for the emergence of a gender-inclusive work culture in the industry sectors.

DOI: 10.4018/978-1-7998-8594-8.ch005

BACKGROUND:

The overall increase in enrollment had an impact on access to higher education for women as well as a choice of subjects. Science, Technology, Engineering, and Maths (STEM) subjects also attracted many women as their professional choices (UGC, 2012). However, only a small percentage of women pursuing science can convert their choices into a career in science (INSA, 2004). There are many women engineers, Ph.D. degree holders, and master's degree holders in science who did not end up having a career in science. Women who managed to join the scientific community had to struggle hard for their visibility. Employment for women in the STEM domain has largely remained inadequate and contributed to the overall declining employment trend for women in the country for the past two decades now. Several socio-cultural barriers seriously impede women's development as professionals in the field of STEM as a result increased enrollment of girls in science has not led to an increase in employment for women in science (Sinha & Sinha, 2011, SED's report on status of women Scientists, 2011). Low female participation in STEM studies and consequently STEM careers has been a concern voiced by countries around the globe (UNICEF, 2020).

Science, Technology, and Innovation policy, 2013 (STIP, 2013) envisaged gender parity by addressing mobility challenges and re-entry of women into R&D. Government of India started schemes to facilitate re-entry of women in science through dedicated women scientists Scheme/programs since 2015-161. Women Scientist Scheme-A (WoS-A) is meant to promote women in STEM by granting projects for research in Basic /Applied sciences. There has been an overall increase in several projects in most of the sub-disciplines covered by the scheme but domination of life sciences indicates professional/gendered segregation. Over the years (2015-16, 2016-2017, and 2018-19), the trend of projects in various sub-disciplines has been - life sciences (362 projects), Physical & Mathematics (134 projects), Engineering & Technology (110 projects), and Earth & Atmospheric Sciences (39 projects). The numbers of these projects are low as compared to the need for a large pool of unemployed women qualified in STEM.

With the rapid digital transformation required to meet Industry 4.0 goals, demand for a technologically competent workforce is rising. Research has indicated that STEM-related jobs will grow and play a critical role. India's digital core sectors are expected to create 60 to 65 million jobs by 2025 (McKinsey, 2019), many of which require functional STEM skills. National Education Policy (NEP, 2020), emphasis on flexibility of curriculum and STEM (Science, Technology, Engineering, and Mathematics) courses is a welcome step in this direction. It is time to use this opportunity for inclusive development and meet the goal of inclusive development by increasing the participation of women in this digital transformation. Industry 4.0

has to include gender perspectives by mainstreaming women in various technology-based sectors of the industry.

Women in STEM offer good potential for the generation of highly skilled women workforce (Jain, 2020). Improving the employability of women engaged in STEM by using the opportunities offered by Industry 4.0 can play an important role in ensuring decent and well-paid jobs for women. Efforts in this direction will not only help improve the declining Female labor force participation rate (FLFPR) (Annual Report PLFS 2019-20) but also help us achieve international commitments of United Nation's Sustainable Development Goal 5 (SDG) that includes women's use of enabling technology, including ICTs as a means of achieving economic empowerment and greater agency (UN Sustainable Development Goals(SDGs)2. This will not only help us break the gender stereotypes around STEM and achieve Goal 5 (gender equality) but also ensure the work participation of women for economic empowerment. It is time the industry starts talking about STEM-based carriers for women. A road map for gender-inclusive growth as part of Industry 4.0 should start with increasing girls' enrollment in STEM to plugging the gender gap of women in science.

Enrollment of girls in STEM

There is an increasing number of women participating in science now, for example, highly male-dominated engineering is now occupied by fair numbers of young girls, and many private sector companies are mandated to ensure gender parity. There are drives to recruit women in various companies to maintain the gender balance in the company (McKinsey, 2021). All India Survey of Higher Education (AISHE, 2020) indicates that there has been an increase in Gender Enrolment Ratio in Higher Education (18-23 years) which is 26.3% for males and females it is 26.4%. Out of 382.75 lakh students, there are 186.24 lakh Women Students, constituting 48.65% of the state-wise student's enrolment in Universities & Colleges, and Standalone Institutions during 2019-20. The total enrolment at Undergraduate Level in major discipline/subject based on actual response indicates that Engineering and Technology is one of the key streams with 37.27 lakh student enrolment, where the share of male student enrolled is 70.8% whereas female enrolment is 29.2%. Also, the Science stream has 50936 students enrolled for Ph.D. which is divided into 18 sub-streams such as Mathematics, Chemistry, Physics, and Zoology, etc. Chemistry has the highest number of Ph.D. students which is 9526 with 5554 males and 3972 females. Physics has a total number of 7439 students at the Ph.D. level with 4632 males and 2807 females. There is a total number of 5284 students enrolled in Mathematics for Ph.D. out of which 2924 are male. Mathematics has a higher number of female students. There are 143116 students enrolled in Mathematics which is the highest among all the science streams. Out of the total, 63.9% are female students. Chemistry has an enrolment of 136807 students at PG level with 42.4% male students. Physics has 76382 students and Zoology has 59045 students enrolled at PG level with 72.6% female and 27.4% male respectively indicating gender segregation towards life sciences (Zoology).

Gender Gap for Women in Science

Women's share in the total enrolment has increased as both the number of colleges and universities. The fraction of women in science education has also increased. Women participate in a major way in teaching science and mathematics in schools as well as colleges but the percentage of women on the faculty of the high-profile institutes like TIFR, the IITs, or IISc is only about 10-12%. While there has been an improvement in the number of young girls in STEM but this trend does not commensurate with the number of women as faculty in R&D institutes. Only a limited percentage of women pursuing science can convert it into a career (Godbole & Ramaswamy, 2013). As per the report of the National Task Force for Women in Science, only 15 percent of the Indian research and development workforce are women, while the global average is 30 percent. The imbalance is biggest in fields such as computer science and physics and smallest in life sciences and medicine. Women are underrepresented, underpaid, and often unrecognized for their scientific achievements. Data of women scientists at various faculty positions in selected universities indicates that there are more women at the entry-level such as Assistant Professors and Lecturers but fewer at leadership positions such as Directors /Dean or head/ members of advisory Committees. Even Academies do not have an adequate number of women fellows (DST, 2010). In 2009, out of 744 Indian National Science Academy Fellowships, only 3.2 percent were women awardees. The report highlights that the presence of male-centric selection committees for awards and appointments to research and development positions in government-funded organizations often works against female scientists. There is an uneven playing field for women scientists within research laboratories where they often do give equal outputs but remain low in the hierarchy (Gupta, 2014, SSESS, 2017).

Women in science comprise only a small percentage of the total number of working women in India (NASI, 2016). Although there is no explicit discrimination against women in enrollment and recruitment at the college, university, or faculty levels, attitudinal biases and absence of supportive institutional/social structures have, over the years, operated as powerful forces preventing talented women to reach their full potential in the pursuit of a career in science. There are several stories of women struggling to establish themselves in an area of research such as engineering or mathematics dominated by men. Not only do they have to struggle much more than their male counterparts, but women mathematicians who have made important contributions are still not given their due (Ramdorai, 2017). As per a Global Gender Gap Report, 2014, published by the World Economic Forum 2014, only 14.3% of science researchers in India are women.

It does not appear that there is a societal perception in India of women being incapable of intellectual attainment in science, since women students are not in short supply at the undergraduate and postgraduate levels in science (as discussed in section 2 above). Many of these university women students are gold medalists, and a large fraction enters the Ph.D. programs as well. However, their numbers drop in faculty positions with the increasing level in hierarchy and decision-making. This under-representation of women in science has become a serious cause of concern for women scientists and science-policy planners. The R&D Statistics and Indicators 2019-20, which is based on the national S&T survey 2018 brought out by the National Science and Technology Management Information (NSTMIS) indicates that there were 56,747 women directly engaged in R&D activities at the national level which constitute only 16.6% of the total R&D manpower. Women personnel engaged in R&D activities in the states continued to be very small in number as compared to men. There has been a positive growth of women enrolment faculty wise in higher education from 2001–02 to 2018– 19 and in absolute terms, their number in S&T faculties increased from 9.67 lakh in 2001–02 to 20.20 lakh in 2010–11 and further to 53.27 lakh in 2018–19. Among the women enrolled in S&T faculties 52.7% belonged to pure science, 30.0% to engineering and technology, 15.5% to medicine, 1.7% to agriculture, and 0.2% to veterinary sciences during 2018–19. Thus, the underrepresentation of women in STEM is often due to the availability of limited job opportunities for them. Women in India earned over half of undergraduate degrees in both information technology and computer (50.7%) and science (54.1%) fields but remained underrepresented in engineering and technology undergraduate degrees overall (31.4%) in 2018–19 (AISHE, 2019).

Labour markets continue to exhibit persistent trends towards the segregation of occupations along gender lines. As the deeply entrenched gender stereotypes and gender bias prevalent in society are driving girls and women away from pursuing careers in science-related fields, there is a need to invest in education most relevant to the job market. For instance, only 10.25% of female graduates choose to pursue a science, technology, engineering, and mathematics (STEM) track. Gender gaps are more distinct in jobs requiring higher skills. In India, only 29.2% of technical roles are held by women (WEF, 2021). The lower number of women in STEM fields is often termed as a 'supply problem'. Gendered signals from the labor market—the social experience of learning in STEM classes and working in technology fields shape the men as preferred employees for the future. Present occupational segregation will result in future gender gaps and without opportunities for employment into emerging roles, the share of women in the labor market already showing a declining trend will further deteriorate. Addressing gender gaps in emerging professions may only help in plugging this gap (WEF, 2021).

Government efforts – Schemes & expenditure

Government efforts include the adoption and execution of women component plans and, formulation of gender-specific policies and schemes. Constitution of specific task force/Committee in the institutions for gender mainstreaming were other initiatives in this direction. Report of the working group on Science & Technology Human Resource Development for 12th five-year plan (2012-2017) emphasized the need for expanding scope for careers in S&T, research, innovation, and support services for gainful employment of science graduates/postgraduates including women. It laid stress on the need for specialized technical & skill requirement due to increased automation and sophisticated instrumentation for research, manufacturing, and industrial requirements in future.

Policies have acknowledged that participation of women in STI activities is important, and new and flexible schemes are envisaged to be put in place to address the mobility challenges of employed women scientists and technologists. A broad scope for re-entry of women into R&D and new facilitation mechanisms with special career paths in diverse areas were also envisaged to be made available. The beginning was made through the Science and Technology Policy, 2003 that enunciated its commitment to promote the empowerment of women in all science and technology-based activities to ensure their equal participation. The Department of Science and Technology (DST) adopted the Women Component Plan in 2002 with a separate allocation for compliance and implementation of various government-led programs under gender budgeting. Since then, the DST Technology has been spearheading several pioneering initiatives intending to bring gender parity in science. This has given a much-needed boost to women-oriented initiatives at the national level.

Women scientist's schemes were initiated during 2002-03 with a consideration that women are an important part of the workforce in the science & technology (S&T) domain. Large numbers of well-qualified women do not continue their contribution to S&T activities due to various care-based responsibilities which typically fall on women only. Most often the "break-in career" arises out of motherhood and family responsibilities. This initiative was primarily aimed at providing opportunities to women scientists and technologists between the age group of 27-57 years who had a break in their career but desired to return to the mainstream. Women Scientists Scheme-A (WOS-A) provides a platform to women scientists and technologists for pursuing research in basic or applied sciences in frontier areas of science and engineering. Through this endeavor of the Department, concerted efforts have been made to give women a strong foothold into the scientific profession, help them re-enter the mainstream, and provide a launchpad for further forays into the field of science and technology. This scheme provides a research grant for a well-defined project proposal for a period of a maximum of three years. In addition to fellowship, the cost of small equipment, contingencies, travel, consumables, etc. are also covered through the project.

Projects sanctioned under Women Scientists Scheme –A (WOS-A) through which STEM subjects are covered fall under the broad five disciples of Physical & Mathematical Sciences, Chemical Sciences, Engineering & Technology, Earth & Atmospheric Sciences, and Life science. During the years 2015-16, 2016-17, 2018-19, only 134 and 110 projects have been sanctioned under Physical & Mathematical Sciences and Engineering & Technology respectively. These numbers are low as compared to life Sciences, for which 362 projects have been sanctioned till now indicating gender-based professional segregations prevalent within the science domain in general. Overall, the numbers of STEM-related projects are meager as compared to the need for a large number of unemployed women eligible and having qualifications in STEM subjects. These projects served only as a piecemeal approach, a one-stop service for 2-3 years of temporary employment and not a continuity of stable career. It will, however, be useful to analyze and monitor the career growth of women beneficiaries of these projects to know how it helped them in getting back to mainstream work and the kind of efforts required to meet the growing need of women in STEM.

Ministry of Science & Technology is one of the ministries to adopt gender budgeting as one of many entries points to correct gender gaps, including preparation of gender budget statement (GBS). To prepare GBS, Ministries/ departments share the quantum of public expenditure earmarked for women for the upcoming year. The share of gender budget as a percentage of total budgetary expenditure during FY 2019-20 has been very small (79 crores spent on PART A- schemes only for women and only 0.43 crore on Part B – all the other Schemes of Ministry of S &T) (India Budget, 2021). This trend is true for most of the government Ministries / Departments, over the last 15 years, the size of the gender budget has remained below 5%, with a few exceptions (Mehta, 2020).

The low representation of women in science and technology planning and policymaking is a matter of concern. They are still not getting opportunities in academic institutions R & D laboratories and S&T organizations. The government's acknowledgment of this fact is manifested through a few other efforts such as, DST has been taking steps to facilitate greater representation of women in science through the constitution of a Standing Committee for promoting women in science in 2016 which has been taking proactive measures to identify and correct imbalances that persist and hinder women in S&T. A pilot project Gender Advancement for transforming institutions (GATI) was also initiated in December 2020 by DST to promote interventions promoting gender equity in S&T. GATI[1] pilots have been hailed as a sustainable self-assessment and accreditation model. At the core of the model is the GATI Charter based on ten key principles. These principles explicitly acknowledge gender inequality and articulate a commitment towards overcoming systemic and cultural barriers to women's academic and professional advancement at all levels. GATI aims to nudge institutions of higher education and research towards supporting diversity, inclusion, and the full spectrum of talent for their success and progression. In particular, it aspires to create an enabling environment for equal participation of women in Science, Technology, Engineering, Medicine, and Mathematics (STEMM) disciplines at all levels, addressing deep-rooted problems. Universities, Research institutions (of DST, CSIR, DBT, ICMR, ICAR, etc.), Institutes of National importance, and other autonomous S&T Institutions have participated in this initiative.

To benefit from the changing entrepreneurial landscape and emerging opportunities in India, DST, also set up Science and Technology Entrepreneur's Park (STEP), Technology Business Incubators (TBIs) Innovation, and Entrepreneurship Development Cells (IEDs) in educational institutions to support these young budding entrepreneurs. To nurture women entrepreneurs, DST has developed over 48 STEPs in the country in women-only academic institutes. The initiative will directly involve these women entrepreneurs in the economic development of the country. A scheme, called Consolidation of University Research, Innovation and Excellence (CURIE) was also launched by DST in 2008, to strengthen the R&D infrastructure of women-only universities. Under this scheme, all the six women-only universities in India were supported for enhancing their research facilities. Besides, the DISHA-Science Communicators initiative is for women to have a scientific degree and can contribute to popularizing science and technology among the masses and stimulate a scientific and technological temper among people through S&T communications in different languages. "DISHA" therefore is a holistic approach to address challenges of gender parity in the Indian science sector.

The National Council for Science & Technology Communication (NCSTC) declared the National Science Day, 2020 to be "Women in Science." Several scientists, including women scientists, were awarded on that day. Several women scientists have not only made immense contributions to science but also been honored in India as well as abroad for instance in 2019, the Royal Society of London elected, for the first time, a woman scientist from India as its fellow, and the Indian National Science Academy (INSA) also elected, for the first time, a woman scientist as its president.

Government efforts have managed to acknowledge and address the gender gap in the Indian Science and Technology scenario during the last ten years, but more efforts are required. There is a need to look for opportunities that could help plug the wide gender gap in STEM at the earliest and upcoming Industry 4.0 offers one such opportunity.

Industry 4.0 as an opportunity for women in STEM

The fourth industrial revolution (Industry 4.0) is emerging globally as a powerful force and is being projected as the next revolution of industries (KPMG & AIMA, 2018). However, few deliberations/reports have taken place to discuss the participation of women in the future of work as part of Industry 4.0.(Mehta & Awasthi, 2019, Jadhav *et al*, 2019). Industry 4.0 may offer an excellent opportunity to improve the current dismal work participation of women in decent and high-paying technical jobs (WEF, 2018a, 2018b, 2018c). Women workforce with requisite skills is critical if women need to be put on an equal platform with men for Industry 4.0. Women engaged in STEM are an excellent opportunity to be grabbed by various industries to not only meet requisite gender equality goals, but also opportunities for women to be an equal partner in Industry 4.0.

The emergence of Industry 4.0 offers significant opportunities with the right kind of skill development interventions, this applies specifically to women who largely occupy high-intensity but low-skill and low-paying jobs (IMF, 2018). Skill development interventions for women have been recommended to have a combination of four skill categories – workplace readiness, soft skills, technical expertise, and opportunities for entrepreneurship (Deloitte, 2018, 2019). It would include opportunities for women to skill or upskill in line with evolving industry requirements. Creating a stronger ecosystem for preparing women to participate and benefit from the changing industrial scenarios. For example, Industry 4.0 indicates a transition from simple digitization in the third industrial revolution to disruptive innovation which will require a combination of digital technologies and platforms. These technologies are changing the ways companies will do business across the manufacturing, services, and agriculture sectors. The introduction of disruptive technologies, digitization, the internet of things, and big data will transform the future of work in terms of business models, nature of talent, and type of skills that will be required.

With only 54 % (NFHS, 2019-21) of women having access to mobile technology, digital gender inequalities are evident with a lower number of women demonstrating an understanding of upcoming digital technologies, automation, the internet of things, big data, etc. Women in STEM subjects potentially offer workforce in these future-ready technical skills that can provide chances to women for entry and re-entry to workspaces. Engaging women in STEM can create opportunities for them to enter the organized sector. Lack of adequate skills pushes 120 million Indian women (many of them from rural villages and semi-urban areas) so it is important to impart industry-oriented high-end skills to improve the work participation rate of women in the country (ILO, 2019, WEF, 2018c).

Recommendations -what may be done?

Interventions are required for creating a conducive ecosystem for more and more young girls to study and qualify STEM subjects, which should effectively lead to decent job opportunities for them in STEM-related national and state-level R&D institutions, industry, and entrepreneurial opportunities.

Some of the focused efforts could be:

Enabling ecosystem to plug the persistent gender gap in STEM and changing the mindsets. It will require investments in infrastructure, incentives to students/ schools, awareness about laws to avoid any kind of harassment for girls for breaking gender stereotypes. Breaking the social and cultural gendered notions of intelligence is very critical for more girls to pursue STEM education.

Encouraging girls to STEM education will improve their effective participation in STEM-related jobs of the future. STEM education can open new doors for girls, and give them the required tools to participate in "future jobs" aligned with Industry 4.0. that require the use of high-end technologies including automation, robotics, data science, and Artificial Intelligence. Here, women should get access to some of the highest-paying jobs available in the technology space. STEM education is also critical in fostering state-of-the-art skills such as analytical and conceptual thinking and creative problem-solving. Interventions such as widening the scope for increasing participation of girls in the schemes like Vigyan Jyoti, Inspire – MANAK, Atal Tinkering Labs, and Skill India may be useful in encouraging STEM careers. Incentives through these schemes will positively influence the mindset of parents and teachers alike. The private sector such as industries based on STEM education can invest in girls in STEM as part of their CSR efforts. For example, equipping training labs with newer technologies in consultation with or supported by industry through CSR initiatives (facilitating women entering the workforce with relevant technical skills)

Education systems and schools can play a central role in determining girls' interest in STEM subjects and in providing equal opportunities to access and benefit from quality STEM education (UNESCO, 2015 & 2019). Other innovative efforts like evaluating the existing educational approaches, integration of STEM subjects and humanities for better learning outcomes, interdisciplinary problem-solving approaches are required in future jobs.

Role of a professional association as a catalyst: Academies have played an important role in bridging the gaps and serving as a platform to promote STEM among women. In India, some of the professional Associations such as the Indian National Science Academy (INSA) have already started a few initiatives to promote women in science. These associations can take initiatives to identify technological developments, infrastructure and political needs, sectors, and a road map to promote women's workforce.

STEM and future of work: There is a strong motivation for India to invest in talented women scientists and technologists based in a planned manner, with a mindset of leveraging their potentials and knowledge strength into the developmental processes of the country. Women participation in STEM can foresee a strong opportunity for not only building a strong base in the Science and Technology sector but also in the future opportunities for improving the work participation of women. This will enhance the number of women scientists and also retain them in the S&T domain. Low involvement of women in STEM education leaves women unprepared for future jobs under Industry 4.0. STEM-related qualifications can offer promising participation of women in future jobs.

Skill Development - Findings are indicating that women mostly enroll in skilling trades as per the very obvious socially and culturally approved "gender appropriate" choices instead of adapting to skill sets that would match their aspirations and industry or future-ready skills for job requirements. For equal participation of women in Industry 4.0., there is a need to build capacities of women workforce with a continuous learning cycle involving re-skilling or up-skilling as per the specific industry demand for long term retention in the workforce. Technological skills for women constitute a critical enabler to ensure women are part of this journey through equal opportunity and participation of women in the technology-enabled jobs of the future. Mainstreaming employability for women will only make industry 4.0 more inclusive. For example, India readiness for Industry 4.0 with focus on automotive sector does not even recognize or foresees this opportunity for identification of skill development needs or skilled women workforce (Grant Thorton, 2016).

Entrepreneurial ecosystems for startups- Participation of women in all aspects of S&T from basic sciences to applied aspects through entry or re-entry should be encouraged. It may not be the prerogative of only the Department of Science & Technology to take lead but industry sectors aligned with STEM subjects may invest part of the CSR or through gender-friendly HR policies for skill development and training of women in STEM to getting jobs in the organized industry sector and ensure retention as well. Without these efforts, women may not get to the numbers to have an impact on the dismal work participation rate of women.

Way forward

Declining work force participation of women indicates that women's contribution to the measured economic activity, growth, and well-being is far below its potential in India. This demands inclusion of women in the economy with participation across all the growing sectors of the economy with utmost urgency. International Monetary Fund had projected that GDP in India would expand by 27% if its women participated in the workplace at the same rate as men. Women work force participation in India is mostly composed of primary sector including agriculture & allied activities, and unorganized home-based drudgery-based enterprises. The composition of women workers in various industrial sectors through women engaged in STEM provides a good opportunity for an inclusive development with larger share of women workers in the secondary and tertiary sectors of the economy.

The United Nations Sustainable Development Goals (SDGs) agenda for 2030 underlines that engaging woman in the workforce will be a key factor to meet the needs of future growth. A range of social, economic, and political barriers limit opportunities for women and girls in STEM to have decent employment in various professions related to STEM. The limitations devoid these girls and women from gaining employable skill sets, entering the industry workforce, or establishing an enterprise. Since the women workforce participation is an area of serious concern, investing in women /girls in STEM is one area of hope which can contribute to decent employment for women, as most women/girls in India are currently engaged in the uncertain, drudgery-prone, technologically poor unorganized sector. Largely women in India are employed in the unorganized sectors and improving participation of STEM-related women workforce can enable women participation in the organized industry sector or academic/R&D institutions.

The emergence of Industry 4.0 provides all the sectors an opportunity to bring a gender perspective to encourage women work force participation and not contribute further to the existing gender disparities and gender stereotypes. This will be a big leap for the emergence of gender-inclusive work culture. The launch of new technologies, digitization, and automation should provide an opportunity to employ women in high-skilled and high-paying jobs to add to the workforce.

REFERENCES

AISHE. (2019). *All India Survey on Higher Education, 2018-19*. Department of Higher Education, Ministry of Education, Government of India.

AISHE. (2020). *All India Survey on Higher Education, 2019-20*. Department of Higher Education, Ministry of Education, Government of India.

Bora, S. U., & Sinha, D. (2011). Are India Women Scientists victims of the glass ceiling? *Current Science*, *100*(4), 837–840.

Deloitte. (2018). *Preparing tomorrow's Workforce for the Fourth Industrial Revolution*. Deloitte Touche Tohmatsu Limited. https://www2.deloitte.com/content/dam/Deloitte/global/Documents/About-Deloitte/gx-preparing-tomorrow-workforce-for-4IR.pdf

Deloitte. (2019). *Opportunity or Challenge? Empowering women and girls in India for the Fourth Industrial Revolution*. Deloitte Touche Tohmatsu Limited. https://www2.deloitte.com/content/dam/Deloitte/in/Documents/about-deloitte/UNGCNI_black_final%20v6%20web%20high%20res.pdf

DST. (2010). *Evaluating and enhancing women's participation in scientific and technological research: Indian initiatives. Report of National Task Force for Women in Science*. Ministry of Science and Technology, Department of Science and Technology, Government of India.

Godbole Rohini, M., & Ramakrishna, R. (2013). *Women scientists in India*. The Association of Academies and Societies of Sciences in Asia (AASSA). Annexure 3.

ILO. (2019). *Work for a brighter future – Global Commission on the future of work*. International Labor Organization.

IMF. (2018). *India Country Report, No 18/4*. https://www.imf.org/~/media/Files/Publications/CR/2018/cr1804.ashx

India Budget. (2021). *Expenditure profile 2021-22*. India Budget, 2020-21, Ministry of Finance, Government of India. https://www.indiabudget.gov.in/doc/eb/stat13.pdf

INSA. (2004), Science career for Indian women: an examination of Indian women's access to and retention in scientific careers. The report, Indian National Science Academy (INSA).

Jadhav, V. V., Mahadeokar, R., & Bhoite, S. D. (2019). *The Fourth Industrial Revolution (I4.0) in India: Challenges & Opportunities. International Journal of Trend in Scientific Research and Development*. https://www.ijtsrd.com/papers/ijtsrd23076.pdf

Kapur, M. A. (2020). Union Budget 2020–21: A Critical Analysis from the Gender Perspective. *Economic and Political Weekly*, *55*(16).

KPMG & AIMA. (2018). *Industry 4.0 India INC Gearing up for change.* All India Management Association (AIMA) and KPMG. https://resources.aima.in/presentations/AIMA-KPMG-industry-4-0-report.pdf

McKinsey. (2019). *Digital India: Technology to transform connected nation.* McKinsey Global Institute. https://www.mckinsey.com/~/media/mckinsey/business%20functions/mckinsey%20digital/our%20insights/digital%20india%20technology%20to%20transform%20a%20connected%20nation/digital-india-technology-to-transform-a-connected-nation-full-report.ashx

McKinsey. (2021). *Women in the Workplace, 2021.* https://www.mckinsey.com/featured-insights/diversity-and-inclusion/women-in-the-workplace

Namrata, G. (2014). Uneven playing field: Women scientists in research laboratories. *Current Science, 106*(11).

NASI. (2016). A road map for women in Science & Technology-A vision document, Inter-Academy Panel on "Women in Science" in India. The National Academy of Sciences in India (NASI).

NEP. (2020). National *Educational Policy 2020.* Ministry of human Resource Development, Government of India.

NFHS, (2019-21). *National Family Health Survey (NFHS-5), India Fact Sheet, Compendium of factsheets, India & 14 States/UTs (Phase II).* International Institute for Population Sciences (IIPS).

PLFS Annual Report 2019-20. (n.d.). National Statistical Office, Ministry of Statistics and Program Implementation (MOSPI), Government of India.

SED's Report on Status of Women Scientists in Delhi. (2011). *Status of women scientists in S&T/R&D institutions in Delhi.* Academic Press.

Shruti, J. (2020). STEM and the digital economy for women. *India Matters.* https://www.orfonline.org/expert-speak/stem-and-the-digital-economy-for-women/

Singh, M. B., & Chandra, A. I. (2019). Industry 4.0 and Future of Work in India. *FIB Business Review, 8*(1), 9–16.

SSESS. (2017). *Final Report – Status of women in science among select institutions in India: policy implications.* Society for Socio-Economic Studies and Services (SSESS).

STIP. (2013). *Science, Technology, and Innovation policy, 2013*. Government of India, Ministry of Science & Technology. https://dst.gov.in/sites/default/files/STI%20 Policy%202013-English.pdf

Sujatha, R. (2017). Gender, and Science, A Case for Inclusion and Diversity. *Economic and Political Weekly*, *52*(17).

Thorton, G. (2017). *India's readiness for Industry 4.0- A focus on Automotive sector*. Grant Thorton India. https://www.grantthornton.in/globalassets/1.-member-firms/india/assets/pdfs/indias_readiness_for_industry_4_a_focus_on_automotive_sector.pdf

UGC. (2012). *Annual Report, 2011-12*. University Grants Commission (UGC).

UNESCO. (2015). *UNESCO Science Report–Towards 2030, India*. United Nationals Educational Scientific &Cultural Organization.

UNESCO. (2019). *Women in science, Fact Sheet No. 55 June 2019 FS/2019/SCI/55*. UNESCO Institute for Statistics.

UNICEF. (2020). *Towards an equal future: Reimagining girls' education through STEM*. https://www.unicef.org/media/84046/file/Reimagining-girls-education-through-stem-2020.pdf

WEF. (2018a). *The fourth industrial revolution can smash gender equality-or deepen it*. https://www.weforum.org/agenda/2018/03/the-fourthindustrial-revolution-could-smash-gender-inequality-or-reinforce-it/

WEF. (2018b). *Future of Jobs*. https://www.weforum.org/reports/the-future-of-jobs-report-2018

WEF. (2018c). *Will the fourth industrial revolution be a revolution for Women?* https://www.weforum.org/agenda/2018/01/gender-inequalityand-the-fourth-industrial-revolution/

WEF. (2021). *Global Gender Gap Report 2021*. WEF.

World Bank. (2018). *Labour Force Participation Rate*. https://data.worldbank.org/indicator/SL.TLF.CACT.ZS

ENDNOTES

1 https://dst.gov.in/scientific-programmes/scientific-engineering-research/women-scientists-programs

2 https://www.un.org/sustainabledevelopment/gender-equality/

Section 2
Future of Work and Employability

This section provides information on challenges in access to the digitized labour market from a gender lens. It also discusses issues on leadership through ICT interventions, corporate social responsibility, and mobile wallets in order to mainstream women in the world of work.

Chapter 6
Understanding the Digitised Labour Market Through a Gendered Lens

Astika Sharma
Doordarshan, Prasar Bharati, Ministry of Information, India & Broadcasting, Government of India, India

ABSTRACT

With a view to understanding the changes taking place, studying their impact, and identifying potential opportunities for achieving gender equality, the chapter aims to look at women in the labour market and at the gender digital divide. It discusses the structural change for equality in the information and knowledge society and analyses women's autonomy in the new technology paradigm. It provides four different gendered perspectives to understand women in the labour market in the era of technological development. A gendered perspective on new forms of employment highlights how job markets can be opened up in new and inclusive ways to women. The chapter discusses that if the digital gap is bridged, then it can provide new sources of global economic growth.

INTRODUCTION

Sectors are being transformed through the process of digital adoption, and more recently due to the consequences of the COVID 19. Alongside the need to address the inequalities arising from the evolving patterns of skill requirements that this is prompting, regulation surrounding the employment contract which also requires amendment. The issues relating to the participation of women in the labor market,

DOI: 10.4018/978-1-7998-8594-8.ch006

which has been regarded as one of the important topics revolving around the labor market have not lost their relevance in the digitized labor market. While the process of the digital revolution unfolds, a new form of inequality is added to all the existing forms of discrimination: inequality in the power to communicate and to process information digitally. The term 'digital divide' has been coined to refer to this concept (NTIA, 1995, 1999; OECD, 2001).

Globally, over 42 percent of workers are either own-account or contributing family workers (categories defined as "vulnerable employment") (ILO, 2018a). Thus, it says that there are over 1.4 billion workers who are more likely in informal employment and living in poverty and have limited or no access to social protection systems. The progress in the developing countries in the reduction of vulnerable employment has come to a standstill as the number of self-employed workers and contributing family workers has been on the rise. According to World Employment Social Outlook Report, 2018, the share of workers in these categories of employment in developing and emerging countries is particularly high, reaching 76.4 percent of total employment in developing countries and 46.2 percent in emerging countries in 2018.

Not only are women less likely than men to participate in the labor force, but those who do are also less likely to find employment. As of 2018, according to World Employment Social Outlook Report, 2018, the global unemployment rate of women, at 6 percent, is approximately 0.8 percentage points higher than that of men. This translates into a ratio of female-to-male unemployment rates of 1.2 in 2018. In the coming years, the ratio is projected to remain stable in developed countries, and while it is estimated to increase in both developing and emerging countries, mirroring the deterioration in the relative position of women in terms of global unemployment observed over the past decade. The developing countries show the highest ratio of female-to-male unemployment rates across income groups, at 1.3 in 2018. This largely reflects the fact that unemployment rates among men in these countries are low by international standards, while the rates among women are only slightly above the global average. Such a relatively low unemployment rate, however, is far from being an indication of a healthy labor market, either for men or for women. Indeed, the rate of unemployment is not considered a robust test of labor market performance in developing (and, to some extent, developed) countries. This reflects the complexities of informal employment and the limited access to social protection systems, both of which pressure women and men to take up any employment opportunity, regardless of the working conditions. At the same time, entrenched gender roles and labor market discrimination continue to hamper women's access to decent jobs (ILO, 2016b and 2017a). As per the ILO report (2015), the female unemployment rate is expected to increase further in this group of countries while the rate among men is expected to remain stable, thus increasing the ratio of female-to-male unemployment rates.

Recent reports by the ILO show that, despite women's expressed preferences for paid jobs, socio-economic factors and prevailing social norms continue to obstruct their participation in paid employment, particularly in these regions (ILO, 2017a; Gallup and ILO, 2017). The constraints are often directly linked to the disproportionate burden of unpaid care and household responsibilities that women have to assume, which restricts both the educational and employment opportunities they can access and their ability to participate in the labor market. In contrast, women in developed countries are closer to parity with men in terms of unemployment rates, with a ratio of female to male unemployment rates of 1.1 in 2018, and with no significant changes expected shortly. In certain regions, such as Eastern Europe and Northern America, women even register lower unemployment rates than men. While this reflects the substantial efforts to achieve gender parity in educational attainment and skill qualifications, the success in attaining unemployment rate parity is also attributable to the long-lasting negative effects of the 2008 economic crisis, which have impacted some male-dominated sectors, such as construction, more strongly than the rest of the economy. The progress has slowed since the start of the new millennium, and women's employment status has remained as precarious as ever. It is observed that the women with higher levels of education and more resources to pay for care services have the highest rates of economic participation rather than those with a low level of education and has to devote to the care work at home. The stratification of the women's workforce is exacerbated by the segmentation of the labor market itself. It is interesting that even though women have a significant presence in the labor market, occupational segregation exists. There is a clear divide between what sectors and which jobs are held by men and by women in the market. Occupational segregation can be divided into two dimensions: horizontally and vertically. Horizontal segregation means that women are more often found in certain sectors and certain occupations; with vertical segregation, men and women are distributed unequally across hierarchical levels, and thus reflects the difficulties faced by women in gaining access to more skilled and better-paid jobs or occupying a high position within the organization

Understanding the Digital Divide

The concept of a "digital divide" refers to the gulf between those who have ready access to computers/smartphones (or equivalent) and the internet, and those who do not (Ragnedda and Muschert, 2013; Selwyn, 2004; Rogers, 2001). Adding to this, there is also a notion of a "digital gender divide", which purports that there is a discrepancy between women's and men's access to IT technology (Cooper, 2006;

Cooper and Weaver, 2003; Hilbert, 2011). During the 1990s, researchers were quick to observe that women tend to be latecomers to the digital age (Dholakia, 1994; NTIA, 1999). As a consequence, the new technology was popularly portrayed as a male domain (Badagliacco, 1990). Bimber (2000) concluded that the gap in ICT usage between women and men ——is the product of both socioeconomic differences and some combination of underlying, gender-specific effects. Many researchers claimed that the gender-specific differences had their origins in the women underestimating their actual usage skills, which lead to lower self-efficacy to use ICT (Busch, 1995; Joiner, et.al, 1996; Hargittai and Shafer, 2006), as well as in their general attitudes toward computers (Shashaani, 1994).

The digital divide, once, was a question relating to the access of the Internet, and accordingly, there were exclusion and inclusion based on that accessibility. Today, it has moved beyond the access question. In recent times, Internet coverage is increasing exponentially all over the world. Today, the question of the digital divide has become complex with not only about the accessibility and the internal dynamics like socio- gender and demographic factors but also the intensity and diversity of the usage plays an important role. A recent divide, which is referred to as the second divide, by many scholars concerns the intensity and diversity of use, and it is determined by the capabilities and skills individuals acquire in using new equipment and resources. The 'second digital divide' is particularly important because access (provision of infrastructure, distribution of devices, and introductory learning software) is an easier barrier to overcome than use and skills. The time spent using a computer or the Internet, differences in the way that men and women use these tools require examination (Castaño,2008). The women are disproportionately affected by the 'second digital divide'. It might seem that in several countries in the developed world women and men enjoy equal access to the Internet, which would indicate that the first digital divide is disappearing. But the question arises if that is the case in all sectors of the labor market? If the gaps are reducing also in the labor markets of the developing countries? No, the digital gender divides exist across sectors in the labor market and not decreasing in developing countries. With the 'second digital divide', women are at a clear disadvantage compared with men since their usage is more limited and they perform activities requiring less technological skill (Castaño, 2008). We can trace the differences through the asymmetric power relationships between men and women, which are rooted historically in the hegemonic gender system that is reproduced in the family, at school, and in the working world.

According to a 2018 OECD report, there are many root causes as to why there is gender-based digital exclusion (Borgonovi et al., 2018). The most prominent reasons include restricted access to digital tools in the form of affordability, lack of proficiency and/or education, and deficiencies in technological literacy in addition to inherent gender biases and socio-cultural norms. While connectivity, by and large, is a problem for the developing parts of the world, the aforementioned factors affect women all across the world. Worldwide, there are approximately 327 million more men than women who possess a smartphone and can access mobile internet. On average, women are approximately 26% less likely than men to possess a smartphone. In South Asia and Africa, these proportions are particularly prominent as they stand at 70% and 34%, respectively (Borgonovi et al., 2018).

Women are not currently well placed to take advantage of a growing ICT sector given limitations to their educational orientation, dis-embedded workplace experiences, and relative absence from relevant senior management positions (WEF, 2016). The issue of the inequalities of the newly emerging technological market is two-fold. First, without addressing the growing inequities, the progress towards pay equity will regress. Second, without any diversity in the creation of new technologies, existing intersectional inequalities are likely to become further embedded in the labor market. (Verdin and Jacqueline, 2021)

The issue concerning the digital gender divide is indeed complex and deeply rooted, and it involves many different aspects in various settings. As such, there can be no universal "fix-all" solution for the entire world.

Understanding Women in Digitised World Through Four Different Perspectives

In the late 1960s and early 1970s, critics have pointed out about the policies of modernization and industrialization of producing that industrialization and modernization not produce the expected social and economic improvements rather for many it leads to the reinforcement of earlier inequalities. According to dependency theorists, the conditions in the Third World were deteriorating because of these economies' dependency on the capital, credits, technology, training, and markets of the developed nations. This troubled dependency led many scholars to conclude that the wide-ranging adoption of Western models and technologies might not be the solution to the problems of developing nations (Bourque and Warren, 1987). Another set of questions was raised by scholars exploring the experiences of the marginalized sections by understanding the intersectionality of race, class, and gender in developing societies.

A new dimension, gender, was added to the studies relating to the development and its impact and thus it opened up various debates like impact on lives of women due to dissemination of technology, the sexual divisions of labor, and the gender relationships at home and at work. We need to understand if the newer technologies are improving the lives of women or if so, to what extent their lives are being changed with access to new technologies? How can women gain greater access to contemporary technologies? How can women play great roles in their development due to the dissemination of technology? The issues surrounding the development and dissemination of technology have been widened due to addressing the question relating to the dissemination and accessibility of technology. Now it also includes the cultural and economic complexity of gender relations revolving around dissemination and accessibility of technology in the labor market.

While studying the impact of technology on women and gender and development policies showed that women's status in many third world countries had declined due to technological development. Indeed, the men had also been affected but the crucial differences in the experience of the sexes resulted in more erosion of women's status. Women were denied their customary rights to land, excluded from agricultural development projects, and deprived of access to new tools, techniques, and training on the same terms as men in developing countries. (Lourdes and Sen, 1981). However, the mix of the factors determining the degradation of women varies from region to region.

It is seen that contemporary development advisors and policymakers from the industrialized nations have reinforced the same pattern of gender discrimination while allocating resources or making policy recommendations for labor. As in today's agricultural sector, we see that these advisors cum policymakers have made men the preferred recipients of new seeds, tools, training, and credit, even in areas where women are the primary agriculturalists. It reflects the reinforcement of the legacy of the colonial rulers where they would give land grants to men only. The new so-called development advisors with the colonial patriarchal mindset formulate policies that exclude women in policy benefits thus it led to the lack of presence of women in the technological fields. The development schemes which are directed by the governments of the developing society are characterized by the colonial hungover where they would place women in lower rungs or not consider them while making policies.

It is interesting to note that the local cultural values of the developing countries, reflect the male dominance in community affairs rather than female involvement in productive activities, and thus it leads to the transfer of the new tools and technology and even training to men. Men, as the political leaders of communities, were invited to attend sessions where new tools and techniques were introduced and leaving out wider sections of society, the women. In India and other developing countries, the new machinery displaced women from wage labor and adversely affected the poorest households. In these initial analyses, unequal access was defined as the major issue, and therefore the logical solution seemed to be to equalize it. Women needed the ability to use tools and machines as well as literacy and education.

The women had lost ground in the technological development because of the restricted access and the solution would lie in the availability of the technology to both the men and the women in the labor market. Some considered opening the restricted channels of education and training is considered to be the solution to the inequity. The call to widen access for women has rekindled the debate about technology's desirability. Scholars in both industrialized and developing nations have spoken from four different perspectives. Four approaches, the feminization-of-technology, the appropriate technology, the global economy, and the cultural-political integration approaches, have been talked about to understand the women and technology scenario and how they impact the participation of women in the labor market. (Bourque and Warren, 1987)

Feminization of Technology

The feminization-of-technology perspective argues that women have a nature quite distinct from that of men, two ideas derived from Political philosopher Rousseau's thought of philosophy. The advocates of the feminization of technology argue that women's distinct values, developed through their familial roles, must become part of the public realm if technology is to serve the common good and promote human welfare. Proponents of this view include Hilda Scott, Elise Boulding, and Maria Bergom-Larsson. They argue that technological innovation provides for a masculine world view not only in its development but also in its application thus leading to reinforcement of hierarchy, competition, immediate measurable results, material accumulation, depersonalization, and economic and political expansion. Advocates of this perspective argue about a unique way to incorporate women into the technology paradigm and look at it as a critical tool for orienting society toward more humanistic, egalitarian developments in the labor market scenario. The proponents of the feminization of technology argue that women's values are imprisoned by the separation of home and work. So, there is a need to change the perspective and thus must lead to an expansion of women's sphere. A new political procedure for evaluating technology must be taken into account that involves women in policymaking roles. It should question the impact of new technologies on women and women's culture. (Bourque and Warren, 1987)

Appropriate Technology

Proponents of appropriate technology are a critic of Third World poverty and believe that underdevelopment is due to increasing production in each country without reinforcing the pattern of dependency on the industrialized world. For them, the women in developing societies are caught in the same technological trap that, they argue, has engulfed women in the industrialized world. Marilyn Carr has laid this line of thought out as a field of study and, along with others, argued that appropriate technology would increase women's productivity and give them more time for other obligations and community development. The advocates of this perspective refer to women who have limited resources that restrict their use of the very technologies that might increase their productivity and give them access to credit, education, and land. (Ahmed, 1985) .Also marginalizing the economic position of women makes it very difficult for them to afford to learn new skills unless they receive compensation for the time they take from other work to experiment with new technologies and unless those technologies increase the women's productivity enough to make the new investment pay off. The exponents of appropriate technology criticized the top-down approach and argued that what may appear appropriate at the top, to engineers and development workers, may not be at all appropriate to the people, at the bottom, who are expected to use the new techniques and thus it seems they couldn't cope up with the change in the technology. But the question arises why they are unable to do so. For instance, as cited in Bourque and Warren 1987, the African women found serious drawbacks in the solar cookers, which were designed to be an appropriate fuel-saving technology. These stoves required women to cook during the heat of the day and to continually move the stoves to collect the sun's rays. Since they also could not support family-size pots, the stoves were roundly rejected. Such examples show the need to ask what would make it possible for women to create their technological innovations (Carr,1984)

They think that even with the consultation with the so-called "end users" takes place and designs are consistent with local needs and use patterns, the concept of appropriate technology to lighten women's work may fail. Then why is bound to fail? It is interesting to note that the policies fail because development projects seem to re-create sexual division of labor in terms of technology and women are provided with 'appropriate technology' for domestic work while men become the focus for technology training that generates new employment opportunities. The household responsibilities affect the participation of women in the labor force. However, the history of policy in this area has shown that if the concern is directed to reproduction and domestic roles, those issues are likely to set limits to national policies on women. (Jaquette and Staudt, 1985)

As a result, women become the targets of population programs and welfare projects, or they are integrated into the lowest levels of production as part-time workers. As long as women are conceived of as members of households, there may be a tendency to leave unquestioned their absence from society's significant political, social, and economic institutions. The feminist proponents of the appropriate technology argue for the women to be involved in policy planning so that they can not only influence the use of technology, but also put forward the agenda for research priorities, the choice of government subsidies, and the other policy needs which are otherwise ignored. So, the proponents not only talk about appropriate technology as the form of technology that determines which gender uses it, but rather who controls its development, dissemination, and products.

Global Economy Approach

The advocates of the global-economy approach question using technology with interdependence, economic exploitation, and political domination in the world. They assert that the impacts of technology can be understood by studying the issues of its production and consumption in the context of changing class relations, state policy, and international economics. The global-economy perspective while analyzing the impacts of technology also tries to study the interplay between national governments and international markets in shaping national planning, policy development, and resource allocation.

Of particular concern is the state's creation of labor policy in areas such as employment, migration, education, housing, agriculture, and industrial development They advocate for the change of divisions of labor and the reproduction of the labor force in the household. The proponents argue that the international system of capital accumulation reinforces existing gender inequities in the technology labor market which keep wages at the lowest possible level for the marginalized and women. Thus, the question arises if the women's subordinate position can never be resolved simply by increasing their access and participation? No, as they will most likely be integrated at the lowest level of the hierarchy, where they will remain a secondary, low-paid workforce in the digitized labor market.

Those who work from the perspective of the global economy call into question the tendency to treat women as individuals without other competing identities or to see women as a category with uniform interests and concerns. They argue that we must examine household units by their class position in mixed subsistence, cash-crop, and urban economies. With the changing market conditions, women's domestic responsibilities are also changing. (Agarwal,1985) However socially valued or devalued, women's private household roles are critical for the physical and social reproduction of the labor force. (Bourque and Warren, 1987)

Cultural-Political Integration: A Systems Analysis

This quarter of analysts advocates the integration of cultural and political analysis by using the insights of recent feminist scholarship to identify the limits of access and show the degree to which gender permeates institutions and expectations. Analysts who take this perspective are in the field of development and are concerned with science and education. This approach moves beyond the question of equal access and asks what about institutional cultures, power relations, social values, and stereotypes beyond lifting official or legal barriers that would lead to women's entry. The proponents of this perspective use systems theory to understand the nature of phenomena that accounts for women's low enrolments in fields directly related to technology and also identify obstacles to women's educational and employment achievements, and understand requirements to revise programs to reverse gender asymmetries.

The proponents argue that the linear approach cannot solve the issues relating to gender in access to technology or the consequences of the transfer of technology from one society to another. The only way to widen women's access to technology is to understand the elements of gender in the social and political systems which creates challenges to women's participation in the technical labor market. The acquisition of technical competence and the structural arrangements that reinforce stereotypes are making the scientific fields and expertise advantageous to men and leaving out the section of women. They are advocates of change in the culture and politics of education and the workplace. They argue that it is important to understand the processes that reproduce existing patterns to change gender stereotypes and opportunities. This strand of advocates believes that it is important to understand institutions shape meaning and values as well as how individuals can both internalize and challenge social norms (Bourque and Warren, 1987) In this perspective the school and the workplace become cultural and political environments where rules and norms are perpetuated and legitimated by contemporary ideologies of gender-based exclusion, segregation.

Concerning technology, the challenge, they argue, is to examine the fields in science and engineering in which women have been poorly represented and explore ways to increase women's enrolment in those fields. These analysts see education as a process of structural and ideological tracking. They argue also for widening access as a solution to gender inequality and see institutional change as necessary to alter the structures that constrain choice and equity. Exponents emphasize the perceptual biases revolving around the women's contributions to the household and care work. They argue that the inequality in the treatment of women in the households is widely perceived as legitimate because women's contributions are perceived as marginal or subsidiary and, consequently, their lesser "entitlements" as justified. (Sen,1985-86) Further complicating the issue are employment opportunities, which are shrinking in both the industrialized and the developing world, partly because of the mechanization of labor-intensive processes. Constructing a political agenda to expand women's employment opportunities will be even more difficult where employment opportunities are limited. Proponents of the cultural-political integration approach are alarmed by trends of lower levels of opportunities in the labor market and they focus both on the educational and the employment dilemmas faced by women in the developing world. (Bourque and Warren, 1987)

The advocates of the global-economy perspective, for example, claim that schools perpetuate gender inequality and class difference by regulating access to knowledge and by teaching world views that justify the status quo. The political and cultural integrationists argued that the expansion of educational opportunities for women in the developed world has not eroded unemployment or closed the earning gap between men and women and it is important to see the access and participation, for they will always be integrated at the lowest level, where they will remain a secondary, low-paid, and potentially expendable workforce. Those who argue for the feminization of technology, while limited by their Utopian vision of women's values, lead us to question the consequences of separating the home and the family from political consideration. (Bourque and Warren, 1987). Moreover, advocates of this perspective question the values surrounding technological choice and political life. Those who advocate appropriate technology have emphasized the power relation values of the cultural and political systems in which they are located. Those who advocate appropriate technology have emphasized the power relations operating in the transfer of tools and skills to solve development. If women are provided with low-technology solutions, then this would perpetuate inequity by reimposing a hierarchy of technology. The sexual division of technology does not seem a hopeful route to parity. They emphasize that securing control for the end-user is only meaningful if they are playing a role in decision-making that includes the capacity to develop new technology. Advocates of the global-economy framework have moved neo-Marxist analysis beyond economic reductionism and tried to integrate cultural and ideological constructs into materialist analysis. The inadequacy of class analyses that do not include gender relations and they have an advanced discussion of the politics of the household demonstrating the ties between it and the wider economy and polity. Their analysis demonstrates the limits of assuming a unitary set of interests within the household. When we turn to the cultural and political integration advocates, we can appreciate the complex picture of gender and technology they bring us. (Bourque and Warren, 1987). The household, to which the neo-Marxists have given new significance, can be examined anew to appreciate the conflicting interests within it. Just as the global-economy advocates demonstrate that a simple economic model of "the rational man" cannot adequately explain women's behavior, so the cultural-political integrationists identify the perceptual issues that link the evaluations of household members' contributions to the channels of access. They looked at the blockades to access and their relation to gender, they outline a political agenda that could open up opportunities.

Since advocates of this perspective must think of the policy implications of their analyses, they have been able to demonstrate the greater cost of ignoring gender in national development programs. For us, a combination of insights from the cultural-political systems analysis and the global-economy perspectives is the most promising avenue for change. The cultural-political integration view emphasizes the importance of developing a female technological leadership who can be part of the policy-making process. Thus, this quarter argues that access to technology, education, and employment are not independent solutions to the problems of equity, underdevelopment, and women's continued marginalization but all should be understood as part of economic, institutional, and ideological relations that shape and are shaped by power relations in national and international arenas. It is important to understand that the technology offers answers to women's equity independent of the political and economic contexts in which it operates the context of the production of ideas, skills, tools, and commodities, one realizes how much each factor is a bearer of social relations marked by gender.

Bourque and Warren argue that giving access to education, technology, and employment is not enough to change gender inequality. Thus, the family structures, the decisions are taken within them, and women's access to technology are all linked in an interdependent global economy. Understanding the political, economic, and cultural context of access is the real key to equalizing opportunity in the digitized labor market and increasing in participation of women in the future Industry 4.0 market labor arena.

Women in Labor Market of Developing Sector

Gender inequality in labor markets remains a persistent phenomenon, albeit to varying degrees depending on regional, national, and local contexts. Women still face multiple challenges relating to access to employment, choice of work, working conditions, employment security, wage parity, discrimination, and balancing the burdens of work and family responsibilities. Labor market gender gaps are more pronounced in developing countries than in developed countries. According to Asian Development Bank Report, 2011, the gender gaps are often exacerbated by gendered patterns in occupational segregation, with the majority of women's work concentrated in a narrow range of sectors that are vulnerable and insecure. Women are also migrating in large numbers for work and constitute a large number of migrant workforces. The women are heavily represented in the informal economy where their exposure to the risk of exploitation is usually greatest and they have the least formal protection. The informal economy provides a vital source of livelihood for masses of women and families, including during tough economic times (Asian Development Bank,2011). There has been a veritable educational explosion in the developing countries including in the majority of countries in the African continent. While literacy remains a formidable barrier to improving the status of women in developing countries, it should be noted that there is an increasing number of "school enrolments"' of girls everywhere. At the same time, more girls continue to drop out9 of schools than boys at all levels. The important point, however, to note, is that even where girls manage to cross the first hurdles of primary, secondary, and higher-level schooling, their access to scientific and technical jobs (in fact to all jobs) encounters intangible barriers. Several studies have emphasized that there is an inherent bias in the existing education structure of many countries (including developed countries) which pre-selects women into Arts and Humanities away from scientific and technological subjects. An ILO report pointed out that in most developing countries few girls are enrolled in technical and vocational education (those who are enrolled- led learn sewing, dressmaking, house- crafts, child-care, and embroidery) and few girls are to be found in vocational training outside the school system. The principle is generally conceded that women and men should have the right on the same terms to receive education and training for highly qualified jobs and should enjoy equality of opportunity and treatment for career advancement. However, international data indicate that except for some of the Eastern European countries and the USSR the proportion of women in most countries in the "scientific profession" is particularly low. (Tinker, 1981)

On the whole, women are employed in research rather than in productions and management, in specialist and advisory posts rather than in positions of authority, and the public rather than the private sector. Outside the formal schooling system and in 'the agricultural extension programs, projects, and training schemes, the inequalities of access of women to learning continue. On this point, the existing information is unequivocal. "In nearly all countries, agricultural training at low, middle, and high levels is given to men only. This of course produces exclusively male instructors - instructors who, in turn, address themselves to the male farmers, overlooking and disregarding women, even in cases where the wives, daughters and hired female labor are doing the work". (Carr, 1984). The reasons for this neglect seem to lie in attitudes and beliefs that agriculture with female labor is backward and that female labor will be replaced by male labor due to "modernization" of agriculture. For instance, in Africa, where women account for a large share of the labor force in agriculture, the failure to teach modern farming methods to women results in adverse effects on agricultural productivity and rural incomes. This patriarchal mindset is pushing women to the world of inequality and discrimination where it is not only becoming difficult for them to leave behind already persisting inequalities in the market, home and society and thus hampering their possibilities to engage in the new digital world of opportunities.

Turning to the modem sector, it can be seen that the profile of women workers does not change fundamentally. In this sector as well, the introduction of mechanization or digitization has produced similar results. The studies and reports that had been written a decade ago and those published recently point to the same direction of inequality of employment opportunities and also facing discrimination in the digitized labor market. That technological progress has the dual effect of widening women's employment opportunities and at the same time pushing them into less skilled and less mechanized occupations. This was recognized by the ILO Panel of Consultants on the Problem of Women Workers as early as 1957. (Briscoe and Pfafflin, 1979)The Panel underlined the positive features of technological developments which reduced the physical effort in a great many jobs, but also noted that wherever employment opportunities for all workers were in short supply, women workers were more likely to suffer the adverse consequences in the transitional period. In 1967 when, at the request of the UN Commission on the Status of Women, the ILO undertook a preliminary survey to analyze the impact of scientific and technological progress on the employment and conditions of work of women in selected, industries, the conclusions were again similar. The analysis of various industries such as metal trades, textiles, clothing, leather and footwear, food and drink, and printing and allied trades indicated that there is a consistent pattern in the employment of women. The new industries tended to displace women workers from previously held jobs to low productivity and low wage occupations.

Based on a comparative analysis of many countries on the employment of women in postal and telecommunication services, an ILO report states that rationalization measures made possible by the introduction of new technical equipment often entail the abolition of temporary or part-time posts which are occupied by the women. For instance, the automation in the telecommunication sector has led to do away with operators' jobs; computers eliminate much clerical or book-keeping work. "Such posts are frequently occupied by women, it is the female staff who are the most affected by the adoption of new techniques...". (Hacker,1986)There is no empirical evidence on measuring the actual technological gap between men and women's jobs ad it appears that through various stages of the introduction of advanced or sophisticated technology, the wage differentiates between men and women have also disproportionately widened. Women workers are generally less skilled than men, and technical skill qualifications are lower than men, from which it is concluded that women are not able to carry out highly complex and technical tasks in the technological market scenario.

Structural Change in the Information and Knowledge Society

Production structures in the South Asian, Latin American, and Caribbean countries and other developing countries need reforms. They are heterogeneous and the knowledge-intensive sectors make up only a form a minuscule portion. This knowledge-intensive sector reinforces social inequality. Many argue that the structural heterogeneity is one reason for the region's deeply rooted social inequality since productivity gaps reflect and at the same time determine capacities to integrate technical progress, bargaining power, access to social safety nets, and options for upward occupational mobility (ECLAC, 2013b).

It is important to note that women encounter more difficulties than men at the same socioeconomic level. Structural changes carry within them models that perpetuate the entrenched inequalities in gender labor relations that assign hierarchical roles and more advantageous places or jobs to men. Thus, the unequal structural changes go beyond the sustained efforts in training, professionalization and autonomy made by women in the developing regions. Many suggest that the development strategies which are based on structural change can be an option that would enable countries to join the information and knowledge society in a more advantageous position but then we need to be cautious if those development strategies are reinforcing colonial, patriarchal age-old inequalities that already exist in the labor market. The digitized labor market should be an arena where information and knowledge society equally integrates men and women at equal positions.

Women's Autonomy in the New Technology Paradigm

The burden of unpaid work and the sexual division of labor carried out by women lead to their inability for full incorporation into the process of structural change in the economy. So, in the era of digital transformation of the market, women are unable to fully participate in the process. It is important to put special focus on aspects that could underscore the concept of structural change with equality, specifically gender equality, opening opportunities for men and women alike and thus creating an equal digitized labor market.

Economic, technology and social policies that aim at structural change can either promote gender equality or take a neutral approach leads to the reinforcement of inequalities. It is significant to understand that in each stage of production policy development, from design and implementation to subsequent monitoring and evaluation, it becomes important to continuously measure its impact on the lives of women and men.

The subject of women's autonomy in the new technology paradigm can be understood into two levels of analysis. Firstly, it stresses possible strategic links between the information and knowledge society and the gender equality agenda are discussed. Secondly, it focuses on tools that the gender equality agenda could exploit to meet its objectives.

The WEF claims the 4IR may provide opportunities to shift gendered roles, through developments such as improved workplace flexibilities and the increasing automation of household work (WEF, 2016). Evidence shows improved workplace flexibilities have a positive impact on gender pay gaps (GEO, 2018), and lead to higher rates of maternal employment (OECD, 2017). Utilizing innovations and new flexibilities as a way to reimagine gendered identities may, in turn, enable changed approaches to care across the generations (Howcroft and Rubery, 2019). However, caution is to be noted as greater flexibility may further institutionalize and embed women's roles as carers (Grönlund and Magnusson, 2016). So, the flexibilities have to be available and utilized by both men and women to begin to reimagine approaches to care work and thus understand its role in the participation rate in the economy. Only then there can be better employment policies relating to the future market economy.

A gendered perspective on new forms of employment highlights how job markets can be opened up in new and inclusive ways to women, beyond the importance of flexibility. Barriers that may have prevented women from accessing labor markets and limitations in accessing entrepreneurial funding, such as inherent bias and cultural stereotypes, can be offset (WEF, 2019). Platform work can bypass national and cultural barriers. Equally, there is potential for greater financial and entrepreneurial inclusion as women can access financial services in new and different ways (Mariscal et al., 2019; Ruehl and Kynge, 2019). Understanding the myriad of ways that women may be limited from participating in the labor market, helps expose the opportunities that the 4IR may afford to re-navigate these trends.

CONCLUSION

Policies on development cannot be neutral. They must take account of inequalities between countries and economies and various strata of society and should try to unmask and demolish the supposition that men and women shed their social and cultural roles when they enter the labor market. They need to understand that getting women into paid work under equal conditions with men will take policies of structural change that take account of the differences and inequalities between women and men in terms of their position in society, the labor market, and the family.

The chapter emphasizes that many girls and young women in the developing regions have the capacities and the talent to become highly skilled scientists and engineers, participate in technological innovation and contribute to the development and general well-being but as there are only a few opportunities and incentives in the field education and information for women in developing countries to pursue a career in science and technology. It is also seen that those who work in this field dominated by male roles, images, and stereotypes are less likely to be promoted, and as women are more concentrated in positions at the lower end of the occupational hierarchy in national systems of science and technology (UNESCO, 2007).

Governments should also ensure that measures prompted by Covid are not merely focused on the short-term crisis but address the wider workplace changes and future of work. Evidence from the financial crisis and previous recessions shows that increased spending trends through periods of economic decline are typically withdrawn as economies recover (Chote et al., 2015: 25-26; Lohr, 2020). The investments for the training need to maintain relevance beyond the economic crisis. The prerequisite to a gender mainstreaming approach to these policy programs is to address the barriers that women, and those with other intersectional inequalities faced by the women, be while pursuing STEM qualifications or occupations (Queisser et al., 2020).

Policy recommendation

The policy is needed for the successful adoption of the new digital age opportunities by women. From a gender perspective, the challenge for public policies for the information society is two types. Firstly, it is to maximize the opportunities offered by the digital revolution and secondly to minimize the risk of women falling behind. Christiane Krieger-Boden and Alina Sorgner (2018) argue that this is not only a technological but also a political challenge for the policy-making quarters. To overcome this challenge, it is needed to adopt gender-mainstreamed digital strategies and to tap new possibilities offered by ICTs with gender equality agenda. For any future gains to women from digitalization, it is important for policymakers to reduce the well-known traditional gender gaps in tertiary education and STEM occupations. Simultaneously, the policies should provide universal, affordable, secure and open broadband internet access; foster female digital literacy; facilitate web-based female entrepreneurship, and empower women financially through innovative digital finance tools and e-government. These suggestions are not new and have already been proposed in previous studies on women's inclusion as a G20-based country solution. The study by Sorgner et al. (2017), while also including the recommendations of the earlier studies, suggests that more attention should be paid to the five following areas:

A. ***The design and implementation of national digital*** **strategies** that actively aim at closing the gender digital access, adoption and use gaps, and enhancing the affordability of digital technologies at the same time as increasing online safety. The national digital strategies should include targets (both numbers and dates) for closing the digital gender divide across at least four dimensions, namely:
   (1) Extend networks and digital access (e.g., through satellite) to rural areas
   (2) Promote access to and affordability and use of connected digital devices (Example: smartphones, tablets, laptops), especially for low-income individuals and women.

(3) To boost availability and promotion of e-banking and mobile money, especially to women and other disadvantaged categories

(4) Increase online safety.

B. ***Establishing an early warning system for potential adverse effects of digitalization on gender equality*** - The G20 should continuously monitor changes that takes place in female employment prospects that accompany digitalization developments and this cross-country initiative will help to spark an early warning system, which will trigger timely policy responses. The G20 should not confine its focus to digitalization impacts for the female workforce in developed countries only but to developing countries where there is a majority of the population who is vulnerable to the impact of digitization.

C. **Help women complement their social skills with higher education and advanced digital skills in all G20 countries.** The G20 should foster female participation in higher education, research and should focus on the acquisition of advanced digital skills by women. Many argue that digitalization is likely to promote jobs that strongly rely on complementarities between social and emotional intelligence and abstract skills that can be acquired through higher education, such as creativity and critical thinking. Also, high proficiency in digital skills is likely to become a core requirement in the digital age. Since many women are found to possess stronger social skills and empathy than their male peers (Petrides and Furnham 2000, Pohl et al. 2005), they could benefit from exploring these complementarities. But the current gender gaps in higher education and digital literacy are particularly strong in emerging economies may deprive women of these opportunities, and thus they won't be able to occupy those high-profile jobs in management, STEM occupations, or entrepreneurship that are expected to flourish best in the digital age. Many of the G20 countries have introduced various initiatives to promote advanced digital literacy and to increase interest in STEM fields among girls and young women, for instance, in form of hackathons, coding workshops, or mentoring programs. These programs should not be only restricted to women of younger age but also be extended to women of older age, as it is likely that digitalization will affect people who have been already employed for some time.

D. ***Use digital tools to foster women's entrepreneurial skills*** - The G20 should make use of digital opportunities in the enhancement of women's entrepreneurial skills. Those can be developed and supported, using high-quality online platforms which will provide training to female entrepreneurs and facilitate knowledge exchanges with experienced female entrepreneurs. Digitalization is likely to create new opportunities for entrepreneurship. Entrepreneurship-relevant human capital can be acquired utilizing higher education and work experience, particularly in STEM fields, through frequent interactions with entrepreneurial peers and thus this will empower the women in the digitized labor market. High-quality online training and mentoring platforms for female entrepreneurs should prove particularly beneficial for women in regions with few entrepreneurial role models or who face restrictions in access to these role models.

E. ***Popularize innovative web-based instruments that improve female entrepreneurs' access to financial capital*** - The countries should promote innovative web-based instruments for women-led businesses to raise financial capital for their ventures and also popularize high-quality digital platforms for angel investors, venture capital investors and equity crowdfunding. This will then bring together female entrepreneurs and female investors of all sections and various fields. It should also promote innovative ways of risk assessment that rely on transaction histories and other Big Data, in addition to traditional forms of securities. In addition to less-developed entrepreneurial skills, female entrepreneurs face difficulties in accessing the necessary financial capital to set up and grow their businesses. Such difficulties are due to the reason that many women lack the necessary collateral required by traditional financial institutions. The promotion of female participation in financial sectors utilizing web-based platforms by providing training programs and mentoring for the female investors by their more experienced peers are crucial to overcoming this obstacle for better financial inclusion of women.

F. ***Foster evidence-based gender-related actions by collecting gender-disaggregated data*** - It is important to add a gender dimension to data already collected by National Statistical Offices which at present are not declined by gender (e.g. related to entrepreneurship, innovation, etc.) and to design and implement the collection and publication in periodical reports (e.g. education and employment-related reports) of gender-related statistics, also linked to the targets mentioned above and thus it can further help to collect the evidence available in support of policy assessment and or monitoring and benchmarking of signs of progress made.

G. **Asian Development Bank Report (2011)** recommends addressing both economic and social vulnerability through interventions that are not only "protective" (providing relief), "preventive" (averting deprivation), and "promotive" (enhancing incomes and capabilities) but also "transformative" (addressing concerns of social equity and exclusion): "Many of the difficulties involved in the provision of social protection for women relates to socio-cultural values that leave women in vulnerable positions. Social protection instruments designed for many categories of women must include a substantial 'transformative' element, in the sense that power relations between men and women become more balanced" (Devereux and Wheeler 2004)

The 12th Regional Conference on Women in Latin America and the Caribbean (2013) pointed out that there is no doubt the development of gender proposals within digital agendas for the promotion of equality, is not a task for a single State actor but it is rather a representation of convergence of efforts, resources and sensitivities from the various public stakeholders involved in issues such as innovation, ICTs, equality, education, health and employment. The ultimate goal is to help to bridge the gap between men and women in the construction of and participation in the information and knowledge society; to this end, the gender perspective must be effectively mainstreamed into digital strategies both in terms of their overall and sectoral objectives and about the different lines of action and the indicators necessary for monitoring them.

REFERENCES

Agarwal, B. (1985). Women and Technological Change in Agriculture: The Asian and African Experience. *Technology and Rural Women*, 67-114.

Ahmed, I. (1985). *Technology and rural women*. Academic Press.

Asian Development Bank. (2011). Women and labor markets in Asia: Rebalancing towards gender equality in labor markets in Asia. ILO Regional Office for Asia and the Pacific. Bangkok: ILO.

Badagliacco, J. M. (1990). Gender and Race Differences in Computing Attitudes and Experience. *Social Science Computer Review*, *8*(1), 42–63. doi:10.1177/089443939000800105

Beneria, L., &Sen, G. (1981). *Accumulation, Reproduction and Women's Role in Economic Development: Boserup Revisited in Signs*. Academic Press.

Bimber, B. (2000). Measuring the gender gap on the internet. *Social Science Quarterly*, *81*(3), 868–876.

Boden, C. K., & Sorgner, A. (2018). Labor market opportunities for women in the digital age. *Economics: The Open-Access, Open-Assessment E-Journal, 12*, 1–8. doi:10.5018/economics-ejournal.ja.2018-28

Borgonovi, F., Centurelli, R., Dernis, H., Grundke, R., Horvát, P., Jamet, S., Keese, M., Liebender, A. S., Marcolin, L., Rosenfeld, D., & Squicciarini, M. (2018). *Bridging the Digital Gender Divide: Include, Upskill, Innovate*. OECD.

Bourque, S. C., & Warren, R E. (1987). Technology, Gender, and Development. *Learning about Women: Gender, Politics, and Power,* 173-197. https://www.jstor.org/stable/20025130

Bourque & Warren. (1987). Technology, Gender, and Development. *Daedalus, 116*(4). https://www.jstor.org/stable/20025130

Briscoe, A., & Pfafflin, S. (1979). *Expanding the Role of Women in the Sciences. Expanding the Role of Women in the Sciences.* New York Academy of Sciences, Association for Women in Science.

Busch, T. (1995). Gender differences in self-efficacy and attitudes toward computers. *Journal of Educational Computing Research, 12*(2), 147–158. doi:10.2190/H7E1-XMM7-GU9B-3HWR

Carr, M. (1984). *Technologies Appropriate for Women.* Intermediate Technology Publications.

Castaño, C. (2008). *La segunda brecha digital.* Ediciones Cátedra.

Chote, R., Nickell, S., & Parker, G. (2015). *Welfare trends report responsibility.* Office of Budget Responsibility. London: HMSO. https://obr.uk/wtr/welfaretrends-report-june-2015

Cooper, J. (2006). The digital divide: The special case of gender. *Journal of Computer Assisted Learning, 22*(5), 320–334. doi:10.1111/j.1365-2729.2006.00185.x

Cooper, J., & Weaver, K. D. (2003). *Gender and Computers: Understanding the Digital Divide.* Lawrence Erlbaum Associates, Inc. doi:10.4324/9781410608932

Devereux, S., & Wheeler, S. R. (2004). *Transformative social protection.* Working Paper No. 232. Brighton, UK: Institute of Development Studies.

Dholakia, R. R., Dholakia, N., & Pedersen, B. (1994). Putting a byte in the gender gap. *American Demographics, 16*(12), 20.

Economic Commission for Latin America and the Caribbean (ECLAC). (2013b). Economía digital para el cambio estructural y la igualdad (LC/L.3602). Author.

Gallup; International Labor Office (ILO). (2017). *Towards a better future for women and work: Voices of women and men.* ILO.

GEO. (2018). *Reducing the gender pay gap and improving gender equality in organisations: Evidence-based actions for employers.* London: HMSO. gender-pay-gap.service.gov.uk

Grönlund, A., & Magnusson, C. (2016). Family-friendly policies and women's wages - is there a trade-off? Skill investments, occupational segregation and the gender pay gap in Germany, Sweden and the UK. *European Societies*, *18*(1), 91–113. doi :10.1080/14616696.2015.1124904

Hacker, A. (1986). Women and Work. *The New York Review of Books*, 26–32.

Hargittai, E., & Shafer, S. (2006). Differences in Actual and Perceived Online Skills: The Role of Gender. *Social Science Quarterly*, *87*(2), 432–448. doi:10.1111/j.1540-6237.2006.00389.x

Hilbert, M. (2011). Digital gender divide or technologically empowered women in developing countries? A typical case of lies, damned lies, and statistics. *Women's Studies International Forum, 34*(6), 479-489. doi:10.1016/j.wsif.2011.07.00

Howcroft, D., & Rubery, J. (2018). Gender equality prospects and the fourth industrial revolution. In M. Neufeind, J. O'Reilly, & F. Ranft (Eds.), *Work in the Digital Age: Challenges of the fourth industrial revolution*. Rowman & Littlefield.

ILO. (2016a). Global Wage Report 2016/17. ILO.

ILO. (2016b). Women at Work: Trends 2016. ILO.

ILO. (2017a). World Employment and Social Outlook: Trends for women 2017. ILO.

ILO. (2017b). *World Social Protection Report 2017–19: Universal social protection to achieve the Sustainable Development Goals*. ILO.

ILO. (2018a). World Employment and Social Outlook: Trends 2018. ILO.

ILO. (2018b). *Women and men in the informal economy: A statistical picture* (3rd ed.). ILO.

International Labor Office (ILO). (2015). Women in business and management: Gaining momentum. Global report. ILO.

Jaquette, J., & Staudt, K. (1985). *Women 'At Risk' Reproducers: Biology, Science, and Population in U.S. Foreign Policy. In Women, Biology and Public Policy*. Sage Publication.

Joiner, R., Messer, D., Littleton, K., & Light, P. (1996). Gender, computer experience and computer-based problem solving. *Computers & Education*, *26*(1-3), 179–187. doi:10.1016/0360-1315(96)00008-5

Larsson, A & Viitaoja, Y. (2020). *Identifying the digital gender divide: How digitalization may affect the future working conditions for women.* doi:10.4324/9780429317866-142018a

Lohr, S. (2020, July 13). The Pandemic Has Accelerated Demands for a More Skilled Work Force. *The New York Times.*

Mariscal, J., Mayne, G., Aneja, U., & Sorgner, A. (2019). Bridging the Gender Digital Gap. *Economics, 13*(1), 1–12. doi:10.5018/economics-ejournal.ja.2019-9

NTIA (National Telecommunications and Information Administration). (1995). *Falling through the Net: A Survey of the "Have Nots" in Rural and Urban America.* Retrieved August 2, 2009, from https://www.ntia.doc.gov/ntiahome/fallingthru.html

NTIA (National Telecommunications and Information Administration). (1999). *Falling through the Net: Defining the Digital Divide. A Report on the Telecommunications and Information Technology Gap in America. Revised.* U.S. Government Printing Office, Superintendent of Documents. https://www.ntia.doc.gov/ntiahome/fttn99/contents.html

OECD. (2001). Understanding the Digital Divide. Paris, France: OECD (Organization for Economic Co-operation and Development).

OECD. (2017). Going Digital: Thc future of work for women. The pursuit gender equality: an uphill battle. Paris: OECD Publishing.

Petrides, K. V., & Furnham, A. (2000). Gender Differences in Measured and Self-Estimated Trait Emotional Intelligence. *Sex Roles, 42*(5/6), 449–461. doi:10.1023/A:1007006523133

Pohl, R. F., Bender, M., & Lachmann, G. (2005). Autobiographical Memory and Social Skills of Men and Women. *Applied Cognitive Psychology, 19*(6), 745–759. doi:10.1002/acp.1104

Queisser, M., Adema, W. & Clarke, C. (2020). *COVID-19, employment and women in OECD countries.* London: VoxEU.

Ragnedda, M., & Muschert, G. W. (2013). Introduction. In M. Ragnedda & G. W. Muschert (Eds.), *The Digital Divide: The Internet and Social Inequality in International Perspective* (pp. 1–14). Routledge.

Rogers, E. M. (2001). The digital divide. *Convergence, 7*(4), 96–111. doi:10.1177/135485650100700406

Ruehl, M., & Kynge, J. (2019, Dec. 12). Fintech: the rise of the Asian 'super app'. *Financial Times*.

Selwyn, N. (2004). Reconsidering political and popular understandings of the digital divide. *New Media & Society*, *6*(3), 341–362. doi:10.1177/1461444804042519

Sen A. (1985-86). *Women, Technology and Sexual Divisions*. Trade and Development, United Nations.

Shashaani, L. (1994). Gender-differences in computer experience and its influence on computer attitudes. *Journal of Educational Computing Research*, *11*(4), 347–367. doi:10.2190/64MD-HTKW-PDXV-RD62

Sorgner, A., Bode, E., & Krieger-Boden, C. (2017). *The Effects of Digitalization for Gender Equality in the G20 Economies, Women 20 study*. https://www.ifw-kiel.de/pub/e-books/digital_women-final_report.pdf

Tinker, I. (1981). New Technologies for Food-Related Activities. Academic Press.

UNESCO. (2007). Science, Technology and Gender: An International Report. UNESCO.

Verdin, R., & Jacqueline O.R. (2021). *A gender agenda for the future of work in a digital age of pandemics: Jobs, skills and contracts.* WSI Study, No. 24. HansBöckler-Stiftung, Wirtschafts- und Sozialwissenschaftliches Institut (WSI).

WEF. (2016). *The Future of Jobs: Employment, Skills and Workforce Strategy for the Fourth Industrial Revolution.* Global Challenges Insight Report. Geneva: World Economic Forum.

WEF. (2019). *Global Gender Gap Report 2020.* Insight Report. Geneva: World Economic Forum. Available at: https://www3.weforum.org/docs/WEF_GGGR_2020.pdf

World Employment and Social Outlook. (2018). *Trends for Women Global snapshot.* International Labor Office.

Chapter 7
Issues, Challenges, and Impact on Women Employment in Industry 4.0

Nisha Saini
Independent Researcher, India

ABSTRACT

Industry 4.0 will not only change the way we work, but it will also change the process and management of work. This will impact all the dimensions of the labour market. If we are enhancing the industry on one hand, we also need to think about upskilling of labour on the other hand. What kind of employment opportunities will it generate for the labour force? Will it solve the problem of unemployment of the people present in the developing and developed worlds? As purchasing power parity of people is equally important along with the production of goods, to what extents will Industry 4.0 be sustainable? The other factors we need to consider with these issues are cyber security, data protection, climate change, impact on women empowerment, and achieving gender balance in this sector of economy. This is what is explored in this chapter.

INTRODUCTION

Everything into this world has its own advantages and disadvantages. Technology on one hand is improving and providing us with wide-range of services but on the other hand it is going to affect the employment opportunities of existing people. The effect on employment will vary from country to country as the world resources are divided into developed and developing world. Industry 4.0 is a boon for industrial

DOI: 10.4018/978-1-7998-8594-8.ch007

Figure 1.
Source: - *https://www.tibco.com/reference-center/what-is-industry-4.0*,**(2021)**

development no doubt but for labour market it is going to discard position of certain skill set and further this will result in wider gender gap in workforce than at present. Therefore upskilling of labour force is very important for the development of the economy and country. Upskilling will not only give employment to labour but also make them work ready for the industry 4.0.

Similarly, upgradation of women into skills which accommodate the industry 4.0 becomes more crucial to maintain gender balance in the industry. As gender equality is goal number five in Sustainable development goals. It (Gender equality) is not only a fundamental human right, but a necessary foundation for a pacifying, flourishing and ecologically composed world. For achieving this goal there are many programs and schemes run by the government, Ngo's, international organizations and regional self-help groups of women. But definite women empowerment and equality can be achieved in real sense when women gender gap in employment is reduced. There has been progress in development of women and girls then again challenges are present which need to be conquered yet.

The result of this progress has led to women taking lead roles as entrepreneurs in many sector of the economy. It is well said by the United Nation Industrial Development Organization (UNIDO) that "there is requirement of creating encouraging environment for women growth. Even though they are already participating in e-commerce, STEM-areas, and digital innovations but there is need to introduce women to technological literacy for reducing the gender gap in industry 4.0". The pillars of this industry rely on internet of things and artificial intelligence which does needs human intervention for assessing and controlling the automation of the machines. Already there is practically less percentage of women who are engaged as professionals in artificial intelligence area. Sudden change will widen the gender gap. So to reduce this we need to maintain balance between the females' employment and upgradation of industrial revolution 4.0.

Here figure below shows the stages of industrial revolution.

The industrialization began from first revolution in 1760 which was the age of mechanical production where water / steam mechanization was only engine to manufacture goods and services. This economic activity gave employment to many people. After completion of 110 years new evolution took place in this sector that is age of science and mass production began with the addition of electric engines in the technology. The transition from second phase to third phase took place less than century that is 80 years to transform the industry itself to this phase which is also known as digital age. In this the electronic automation and its information technology is utilised on each step of production. From here onwards after mere 61 years third became fourth industrial revolution which is also known as the age of technology. It is also known as cyber physical system (hardware, software and biology).

Therefore we can analyse that from the first phase to fourth phase gradually the time span of modification from one technology to another has decreased. Due to enhancement of expertise, equipment's, know-how, interconnectivity among developing and developed countries, exchange information communication technology and open "political economy".

Beside all this there are various issues and challenges which confront the establishment of industry 4.0. Let's have a glance on them one by one.

ISSUES AND CHALLENGES

These issues and challenges are at every level of industry 4.0. They are as follows:-

- **Establishment of Industry 4.0**

The term Industry 4.0 was first publicly introduced in 2011 as "Industrie 4.0" by a group of representatives from different fields (such as business, politics, and academia) under an initiative to enhance the German competitiveness in the manufacturing industry. The most simplified definition of the industry 4.0 would be the application of technologies such as the internet of things (IoT), industrial internet of things (IIoT),cyber-physical systems (CPS),smart manufacture, smart factories, cloud computing, cognitive computing, artificial intelligence. It is a combination of physical to digital also digital to digital. With Industry 4.0, the manufacturing process becomes rapid and more competent than in the past, due to evaluating a huge amount of production data.

Now let's have a look at the challenges on the establishment of this industry. Fact is fully automation of industry has to go through many stages itself. For every business it is going to be a new industry concept to adopt and implement. To bring out the maximum production in their respective business model, efficient working of machine and affordable, healthy end product for consumers. Need of artificial intelligence trained labour market. Upskilling the existing labour force will be major tasks in front of the industry. When this industry will be established each department will be connected with internet which has continuous data transmission system this will change the manufacturing, computing and other industries too. For the successful functioning of these industries one has to be assertive and understand the power of whole structure to take right decisions. With establishment of industry comes the cyber security.

- **Cyber Security**

As stated by (Anderson, 2020, para. 2), the challenge of cyber security will be a concern to safeguard data from theft from unknown sources. Cyber-attack on artificial intelligence can impact the functioning of the any system if not protected. As industry 4.0 will be fully automated and will depend on internet, artificial intelligence. There will be issues regarding day-to-day functioning to major network or process disorders due to misconfigurations, inaccurate instructions, software faults or device failures. Network misconfiguration can include unstable and broken links which do not reach destinations will affect the production of goods. To protect the data one needs not only cyber security laws but efficient set of cyber security professional who can keep the data safe. As we all know that cyber-attack is an area which is a threat to the online transaction and data available today. In coming future bringing down industrial sector of the economy of another country through cyber-attack is going to be another task to be taken into consideration. Similarly, data management challenge is another area to focus.

- **Data Management Challenge**

As per (Khan and Turowski, 2016a, p.445), the automation of industries will generate different types of data such as product data, quality data, plant data, logistics data, data from partners, and infrastructure data. As data will be generated and collected from different machines sensors in industry 4.0. The data management will be major task to manage. This data will need additional technologies and methodologies to store and apply while accomplishing any task. Special data engineers will be required to manage the process of this industry to understand and function smoothly. Absence of standardize method is still missing in data supervision this leads to data redundancy. Further decisions made on this data will not incur profit. Another point is sharing data can be problematic at times as passing of data can lead to delay in transmission this can affect the production of goods and services. Along with all these issues sustainability and industry 4.0 must be addressed too for meeting not only SDG goals but to be environment friendly industry to make a relevant difference in the way human and its activity exist at present.

- **Sustainability and Industry 4.0**

According to (Anonymous, 2020, para. 1), Sustainability means that manufacturing and designing of products without affecting environment and 100% ecological produces. In sustainable development environment, society and economy are regarded as three major pillars. All these pillars are managed by the political system of the particular country. To further give boost to sustainability in the industrial sector, Industry experts and researchers are working on the environmental challenges such as climate change, resource deterioration, and environmental protection will be addressed with industry 4.0 technologies. This brings a novel perspective to industry 4.0, which was conventionally looked at digitizing procedures and acquiring profits. Sustainability is important for not only keeping environment safe but also the energy and resources we utilize have limitation. To utilise those resources well and efficiently at some place technology is required. Therefore industry 4.0 can help in creating such technologies to support environment. Another point is three R's which play a significant role they are Reduce, Recycle and Reuse. So, the human activity which disturbs the balance of environment can be controlled to some extent without harming the atmosphere. The table one below explains about how industry 4.0 can support in sustainable manufacturing: -

The information in the table above reflects that how each module of industry 4.0 technology will contribute in sustainable development. The first segment explain that Internet of things and industrial internet of things equip with sensor and automatic devices will support in saving time, monitor energy consumption and operate safely by providing cautions whenever required. Secondly, the autonomous robots and cobots make the task of employees easy by sharing their work load at the work station. The work station due to automation will become smart easily accessible by the customers. Thirdly, virtual system that will take into account improvement in procedures while functioning, utilising the amount of energy which is required by the production system. Another point is system integration which will help in transparency and communication of system with other necessary coordination. Similarly, visualization assists in maintenance, training and cost reduction of the industry 4.0. Also manufacturing with industry 4.0 reduce waste production and rise customization of products.

Hence it can be stated that industry 4.0 will keep up with the balance of the environment which is prime importance along with the development. As climate change is going to be very devastating if small steps are not taken with utmost care as sustainable development.

At the same time, with sustainability comes the employment too which is the talk of every department in industry 4.0. Even the researcher and academicians in this field are pondering on this issue.

Table 1. How technology will help in sustainability

Technology	Description	Benefits of Sustainable Manufacturing	Dimension of Sustainable Manufacturing
IoT and IIoT	Connection of production areas with sensors and devices, which communicate with each other	• Prevention of unwanted manufacturing steps • Waste and inventory management • Monitoring and management of energy consumption • Improves equipment and operator safety by providing real-time warnings	• Economic • Environmental • Societal (as it improves employee safety)
Autonomous Robots and COBOTS	Mechanical device that operates with high degree of autonomy along side humans	• Workload reduction of employees • Development of smart workshops near to client location	• Economic • Environmental
Simulation Systems	Virtual replication of process or service	• Reduction in energy consumption • Process improvement • Preventive and predictive maintenance	• Economic
System Integration	Extended value network by integrating value chain (both horizontal and vertical integration)	• Increases transparency and reduces waste • Seamless communication between stakeholders	• Economic
Virtualization	Building mixed reality with digital content and real-world industrial content	• Remote maintenance and remote training • Cost reduction (by managing maintenance activities remotely)	• Economic • Societal
Additive Manufacturing	Successive deposition of different types of materials to develop a product or prototype	• Reduction in waste generation • Increased customization of products • Reduced product development time	• Economic • Societal • Environmental

Source: Future Bridge, n.d.

• Employment in Industry 4.0

According to (Anonymous,2017, para. 3), the technology is advancing the employment opportunities are also changing for instance in the tourism industry increase in online flight link sites has considerably reduced the number of physical travel agents and progressions in mobile technology has made many operators outdated. On the other hand, technological developments have also led to the establishment of new job titles like app developers, social media marketers, and digital marketing plus data scientists. According to the McKinsey Global Institute reports that roughly one-fifth of the global workforce will be impacted by the adoption of AI and automation. About 50% of companies believe that automation will decrease their numbers of full-time staff and by 2030; robots will replace 800 million workers across the world. The study done earlier shows that there will be reduction of jobs in manufacturing, agriculture, food preparation, construction, driving, sales, healthcare, business administration, information technology, recruiting managers and retail management. By analysing above statement, we can say that technology in industry 4.0 will impact every profession in some or the other way as and when this concept is implemented. If its implementation is done in phased manner it will support the labour force to gain and understand the system of this technology. On the aspect of employment in various sectors the changes induced by industry 4.0 must be taken judiciously. As it will lead to new age of work but if it is not managed well then it will lead to skill gap, greater inequality and broader polarization. This area can be further divided into employment ratio among men and women in industry 4.0 that is in short gender gap.

- **Gender Gap in Employment**

(Briony Harris, 2017, para. 2) Generally gender gap is the difference between women and men as reflected in social, political, intellectual, cultural, or economic attainments or attitudes. The Global Gender Gap Index aims to measure this gap in four key areas: health, education, economics and politics. This concept has another dimension of gender pay gap between men and women. The gender pay gap happens due to many factors such as unequal social environment, gender based roles, orthodox thinking and socio- economic barriers. On the other hand I consider the point that job opportunities are also less as compared to population. Most of the places are male dominated and women have low key roles to play in an organization. Very few women get the opportunity to reach at the top.

At the same time there is already a gender gap but with the introduction of industry 4.0 it will increase more as very limited percentage of women opt for artificial intelligence and technology based work. According to the World Economic Forum's (WEF) Future of Jobs report, "65 percent of children entering primary school today could ultimately end up working in completely new job types which do not exist today or at present. Mostly the jobs are expected to be created in science, technology, engineering, mathematics (STEM), and IT in developed countries who will adopt industry 4.0. Most of the women tend to avoid STEM jobs and opt for office, administration and supervision jobs, which are most susceptible to displacement by robots but every country scenario will be different in this context as all do not have same resources and amenities. Therefore gender gap will be there in future as well if necessary measures are not taken on time. The table two below shows the gender-gap in particular category of job:-

This data from world economic forum report in 2016 reveals the future of jobs with the enhancement of industry 4.0 and the share of women, gender wage gap, current trend and year 2020. According to the report worst hit area is installation and maintenance where women percentage is about 8%. Other sectors **such** as Arts, Design, Entertainment, Sports and Media here the gender wage gap is about 12%

Table 2. Gender gap in particular job area along with other details.

Job category	Share of women	Gender wage gap	Current	2020
Architecture and Engineering	11%	27%	–1.18	–0.27
Arts, Design, Entertainment, Sports and Media	48%	12%	–0.21	0.07
Business and Financial Operations	43%	30%	–0.42	–0.16
Computer and Mathematical	23%	28%	–0.91	–0.13
Construction and Extraction	10%	48%	–1.48	–0.64
Installation and Maintenance	8%	24%	–1.43	–0.20
Management	25%	34%	–0.84	–0.03
Manufacturing and Production	20%	32%	–0.99	–0.12
Office and Administrative	54%	36%	0.21	0.31
Sales and Related	41%	35%	–0.42	–0.03

Source: World Economic Forum, 2016

which is less than all other wage gaps. The scenario for the year 2020 explains that sales and related areas will be poorest in terms of gender gap followed by management, construction and extraction, Computer, mathematical, manufacturing and production. If we analyse the complete table, it can be said that there will be impact of new technology at every level in all professions to some extent. The difference would be somewhere it will be more and anywhere it will be less this depends on the induction of industry 4.0 technology. Only upgradation of technology won't support the development of the country. It is crucial to introduce re-skilling and up skilling of the labour force for both men and women to maintain equal ratio of workforce. To eliminate gender gap women empowerment and working conditions must be congenial for them to work. This must be promoted and implemented for maintaining gender balance.

After the gender gap, I would like to bring in notice training of labour force though it's not an issue but a challenge to meet up the goals of this fourth industrial revolution.

- **Training of Labour Force**

(Khan and Turowski, 2016b, p 446), with the upgradation of industrial system arises the need of training of labour force. The manufacturing joints have a huge task of upgrading the existing staff with digital skills and select the tech savvy talent for their firms. An extremely technical progressive environment means more employee assistances revolving around technology, digital and artificial intelligence role. Frequent training sessions, updated learning and development sessions will take into account the learning gaps of existing workforce.

The training programs have to be more accessible, modified, and flexible to adjust to the vibrant requirements of the Industry 4.0.To execute efficiently with Industry 4.0, workforces will have to apply a diversity of hard skills. They have to combine know-how related to a particular job or process, such as methods for working with robots or altering tools on machines, with IT proficiencies that range from basic technology that is (using spreadsheets and accessing interfaces) to advanced (applying advanced programming and analytic skills). The necessity for multiple hard skills and the extraordinary scope of modifications on the workshop level means that "soft" skills will become more important than ever before. Teams will have to be more open to conversion, possess better flexibility to adjust with new roles in the working environment and get habituated to continual interdisciplinary knowledge and learning of industry 4.0. Next issue and challenge to cope with is climate change that is one of the important aspects to be discussed before keeping the base of this fourth industrial revolution.

- **Climate Change on the Fourth Revolution on Industry**

As per (Josefsson, 2019, para.2), with the introduction of 5G technology and industry 4.0 climate changes can be controlled to some extent if the resources and energy is used wisely. Collected data from the manufacture procedure give a clearer indication of material and energy movements and the use of production volume. This can help develop new understandings into resource and energy use in the production method itself. The technology used here can support in reducing the time between abnormalities and reaction or even revealing emissions that could have otherwise gone unobserved. For example:- by tracking of methane emissions, which are often caused by oil, gas and other heavy industries all over the globe can be observed by the technologies of fourth revolution industry. This industry can reduce resource usage such as water and energy, minimise waste, and reduce carbon dioxide emissions at early manufacturing stages also it can help detect the stock of natural resources and action can be taken on time to protect for climate change if needed. Therefore many advanced features can help in maintain balance of environment and achieve sustainable development goals. After discussing the issues and challenges so far another significant characteristic is impact on women empowerment.

- **Impact on Women Empowerment**

Women empowerment means women elevation from all those factors which supress her being herself and making her economically self-dependent to take decisions for her betterment. It is important aspect for the development of female and generations to come. As stated by (Suen, 2013, para. 1), the old African proverb "If you educate a man you educate an individual, but if you educate a woman you educate a family (nation)" was a pioneer in its time for recognising the importance of women's education and now I would emphasis on women empowerment as well. Women contribution in development of country is immense through her paid and unpaid work. If any change takes place in professional, social, laws and family front it impact women the first.

Similarly, the jobs and professions which have empowered some women today will be vanished by upgradation of industry 4.0 due to automation. New opportunities will rise up but in the sector of artificial intelligence. At present very few women have skill pertaining AI and IOT. To combat this situation upskilling of women in this sector will be mandatory to reduce gender gap and generate employment for women. Impact on women empowerment will be both positive and negative.

Positive impact would be usage of digital platforms make available women with a greater access to markets, knowledge and more flexible working schedules, generates opportunities for women faster than ever before. Negative impact would be automation will take away low skill and routine jobs in information technology and it will be occupied by Industry 4.0 .Women is more likely than men to leave the tech field. The most common reasons are workplace conditions, a lack of access to key creative roles and a sense of 'feeling stalled in their career'. The work does not involve any creativity. It will increase gender gap and women employment will be at risk in most countries due to robotics.

Hence we can say that impact of industry 4.0 on employment of women will be both advantageous and disadvantageous. Women need to upgrade her with the information technology to remain in job market also to take on 50 percent position in the industrial sector. Despite all these challenges and issues there are successful case studies of industry 4.0 as it is going to be the future in the coming years. All the case studies are taking support of leading providers of risk, financial and business advisory firms.

CASE STUDY-1 OF RENAULT COMPANY

According to (Scherer, 2020, para.2), Case study of industry 4.0 Renault, it is officially known as Groupe Renault. This company is a 119-year-old French multinational automobile manufacturing conglomerate. Renault began its journey of automation in 2015 with a plan whose next stage of strategic planning began on 2017-2022 that included with it full transformation. Before implementation they went through analytical phases to change their business model. The problem which was coming in front of them was of related to a lack of digital skills and rigid governance. It was crucial to change all of this. On January 1, 2017, Renault Group decided to set up Renault Digital, an independent, but fully owned supplementary with the objective of supporting the labour or group to achieve its digital transformation objectives. At present it consists of more than 350 employees, with skills and knowledge in agile methodologies, UX Design, DevOps and Data Science. To work on each project they separate into two phases where team of digital skill experts, subject matter experts take the necessary decision. Due to this they can work as new start up and employ new talent whenever required. Similarly, the persons employed earlier from head office or other business units after incubation of 4 to 5 months can move to their offices, with a new mind-set, they effectively become change agents in the digital transformation.

At the same time by introducing Wi-Fi connectivity and by developing a bespoke mobile office solution for their unit managers they allowed them to save 45min/Day of ineffective timed. The digital methodologies not only increased productivity and job satisfaction but now business unit managers' can work around with their mobile office tablets and have access to real-time product data whenever they need it. Even by connecting machines and robots also allowed them to create value in other areas. To reduce machine failure Renault has put more than 2000 sensors in place to collect data from their equipment.

Similarly, in manufacturing plants, robots and automation are of course essential, but human intervention is often needed to ensure quality. By staying connected with its customers Renault expects more sales lead generated through digital, providing better opportunities to achieve its growth ambitions. By staying connected with its customers through mobile app Renault expects more sales lead generated through digital, providing better opportunities to achieve its growth ambitions. Now human resource has to transform itself and give more power to employees to manage their careers and make Renault a company as remarkable employer where digital aptitude is still limited in the world for now. Let's have a glance at second case study on conversion of another automobile company to industry 4.0.

CASE STUDY -2 OF LAMBORGHINI COMPANY

(Souchet, 2021a), case study of Lamborghini Company which transformed its business model to industry 4.0 its journey began while keeping in focus the customer centric market. After analysing every aspect KPMG supported in setting up the information technology platforms that manages manufacturing operations that take care of manufacturing operations in the industry along with new modular design, utilizing digital sensors to analyse data and robotics to perform various functions. At Lamborghini there is merging of two domains that is artificial intelligence with the production unit workers.

Here every car model in the production process is placed on the appropriate location for further development through or via automatic guided vehicles (AGVs) technology. Due to the advancement of mechanism electronic monitoring, data collection and reporting from all links of the factory are accessible directly and workers can control each feature of production process on site, remotely from any position using tablets that entirely abolish dependence on paper documents or work. This characteristic put the company on sustainable path. In this project they focused on understanding value and performance before technology was applied to their business at every stage. Similarly, in third case study we will have look at how industry 4.0 will be applied in pharmaceuticals.

CASE STUDY -3 OF TRANSFORMING A PHARMACEUTICAL GIANT

(Souchet, 2021b), for any industry to transform itself into industry 4.0 is not easy task. It requires a lot of analyses, investment, study of previous mechanism and manufacturing techniques. All this evaluation is crucial for the application of new technology which will not only enhance the production but also change the method of working entirely. Same goes for this multinational pharmaceutical company who tried digital transformation for about one year but due to insufficient return on investment. The management board postponed the idea and put for revision. They approached KPMG who advised them to adopt performance over technology and not getting on to the decisions too early. Their strategy here was to highlight and prioritize where digital technology would help the most to achieve the company's business approach. Then the top quality initiatives were purposefully selected and arranged in a manner that enhanced returns for the company. There journey for industry 3.0 to advance 4.0 is in progress with entire board consent for beneficial and lucrative expectation of this automated version of industry. To understand it in more better way let's know the industry 4.0 application on agriculture.

CASE STUDY-4 SMART FARMING BLOOMS IN SOUTH KOREA

(Souchet, 2021c), this case study is about South Korean Agriculture Company producing 23 kilogram of mushroom yearly. Due to three factors this company decided to change into industry 4.0. They were changing the unstable structure of company, raising cost of labours and global market competition. For support, advisory, assistance for their establishment they took advice from KPMG. Data of production is collected through internet of things technology, digital sensors and state of the art data analytics platform. Other tasks such as farming, sorting and packing ecosystem were automated by adding equipment's and robots. This farming company took roadmap from heavy manual labour to a digital platform of artificial intelligence.

The result of this conversion has brought a fresh manufacturing aspect which has improved crop yield in there farming through data that examines the fertilizer-to-soil ratios to be used in mushroom farming creating a significant 30 percent growth in harvest. The company has reorganized its factory design, boosting productivity and lowering labour costs. This approach has improved its value, performance and competitiveness in terms of productivity, efficiency and quality for this agriculture firm. It is a bright change in future prospects for success in the digital economy.

CASE STUDY 5 OF SCANIA A TRANSPORT FIRM IN SWEDEN

(Watzlawek, 2018, pp1-5), Scania is a global transport and its services provider in Sweden. It is wholly owned subsidiary of the Volkswagen Group. The company vision is to provide sustainable transport solution and value to its stakeholders such as their employees, suppliers, owners and lenders. To achieve this they introduced electric trucks and investments for better services. But to implement industry 4.0 it went step by step. First step is standardized process about the manufacturing of trucks and busses. The production facility works with identical machines and connected through IOT with sensors to gather data. Other steps involve connected technology, data gathering, data analysis, predictable future and action to be taken accordingly.

All the methodologies of industry 4.0 are handled by this company for its smooth functioning. They have work stations where human and robot work together. Here labour force is given smart clothing to wear while working which takes care of their health and bad posture if any. Scania Company and experts are currently working on AGV that is automated guided vehicles to transport necessary material from logistics rooms to assembly rooms. Along with this they are also working on usage of multiplayer virtual reality to support factory layout design. Due to this feature creating and recreating of various models have become beneficial as new machine plans are sent in a 3D model by the supplier. By adopting this method error which was not detectable earlier was now visible. Similarly, they have involved digitalization in their purchasing process which saves time, faster and partly automatic. By transforming into industry 4.0 this firm has become more efficient and sustainable.

CASE STUDY 6 OF TEXMO INDUSTRIES

In accordance with (Venketesh, 2020, para 7), A Texmo industry is a manufacturing hub which was established in year 1956. It works on domestic, agricultural and industrial sector. Produces agricultural pumps in India wanted elaborated value stream mapping. The supreme task was to improve the forecasting precision. Texmo wanted to develop its supply assurances through flexible and agile manufacturing structures to support the right products and their availability at the right locations at any specified point of time.

Bosch supported this industry began by applying a smart manufacturing simulation. Man, machine, and materials were interconnected through HMIs, adapters, and RFID technologies. The automatic solutions controlled the entire material flow in the factory. On the other hand, continuous amalgamation of information and messages helped connect the shop floor with the top floor. The solutions helped to assimilate key manufacturing functions like production, maintenance, stores, and quality. Role-based manufacturing control panel with significant KPIs were installed to upturn competences.

CONCLUSION

To conclude industry 4.0 is a blessing and blight both. The upgradation of industry has huge task ahead of adding skillset to its employees and recruiting new with industry 4.0 skill set. If the necessary measures are not taken on time industry 4.0 will have effects which will make suffer the industrial sector, labour force, economy and consumers. Male and female participation of both genders in workforce is important to maintain the gender balance.

On the other hand, retaining women in the work force is equally significant as female labour force contribution is a substantial part for its outcome of growth and development in any economy. Women in developing world participate in workforce because of different factors such as poverty, to support household budgets, power to have choices of their own and to support themselves. Various studies have revealed that women are paid less then male for the same work, maternity benefits are consider as burden by some companies, female are given low grade work and few are promoted to higher posts.

At the same time, according to the report of PricewaterhouseCoopers Company "the challenges cannot be handled alone by the industry it needs the support of governments, industrial associations, trade unions and employer associations". Further it states that this industry 4.0 need excessive investment and profits are still not clear for everyone. Secondly, lack of ethics, guidelines and forms of documentations. Thirdly, sub-standard levels of development for the machinery or technologies. Fourthly too slow expansion of basic technologies and inadequate strength of network plus data backup. I hope such kind of issues are dealt and solved before adopting industry 4.0 model. This model of industry must become female inclusive.

Beside all these issues and challenges there are various successful case studies in India and abroad which shows that if proper study of technology application along with deep analyses is made and implemented step by step according to the requirement of particular industry. Industry 4.0 will turn into successful venture which will generate new employment opportunities in future and upgrade or elevate existing work force in there technical skills. At the same time, optimistically, eliminate gender gap for purposeful, meaningful, competitive growth of economy, polity, social and technical structure for women as balanced labour force for industry and world in existence.

REFERENCES

Anderson, E. (2020). *3 Challenges of Industry 4.0 and how to address them*. https://www.forescout.com/blog/3-challenges-of-industry-4-0-and-how-to-address-them/

Anonymous. (2017). *How will the fourth industrial revolution impact the future of work?* Change. https://www.changerecruitmentgroup.com/knowledge-centre/how-will-the-fourth-industrial-revolution-impact-the-future-of-work

Anonymous. (2020). *Industry 4.0 and sustainable manufacturing*. Future Bridge. https://www.futurebridge.com/industry/perspectives-mobility/industry-4-0-and-sustainable-manufacturing

Future Bridge. (n.d.). *Industry 4.0 and Sustainable Manufacturing*. Future Bridge. Retrieved from https://www.futurebridge.com/industry/perspectives-mobility/industry-4-0-and-sustainable-manufacturing/

Harris, B. (2017). *What is gender gap and why it is getting wider?* World Economic Forum. https://www.weforum.org/agenda/2017/11/the-gender-gap-actually-got-worse-in-2017/

Josefsson, E. (2019). *Industry 4.0 can be game changer for climate action*. https://www.ericsson.com/en/blog/2019/9/industry-4.0-can-be-a-game-changer-for-climate-action

Khan, A., & Turowski, K. (2016a). *A Perspective on Industry 4.0: From Challenges to Opportunities in Production Systems*. University of Magdeburg. https://www.scitepress.org/Papers/2016/59297/59297.pdf

Khan, A., & Turowski, K. (2016b). A *Perspective on Industry 4.0: From Challenges to Opportunities in Production Systems*. University of Magdeburg. https://www.scitepress.org/Papers/2016/59297/59297.pdf

Scherer, J. L. (2020). *The Digital Transformation People:- Renault-an Industry 4.0 case study*. https://www.thedigitaltransformationpeople.com/channels/the-case-for-digital-transformation/renault-an-industry-4-0-case-study/

Souchet, S. (2021a). *Industry 4.0 case study: - Lamborghini shifts gears into smart manufacturing's fast lane*. KPMG. https://home.kpmg/xx/en/home/insights/2018/11/industry-4-0-case-studies.html

Souchet, S. (2021b). *Industry 4.0 case study: Transforming a pharmaceutical giant*. KPMG. https://home.kpmg/xx/en/home/insights/2018/11/industry-4-0-case-studies.html

Souchet, S. (2021c). *Industry 4.0 case study: Smart farming blooms in South Korea*. KPMG. https://home.kpmg/xx/en/home/insights/2018/11/industry-4-0-case-studies.html

Suen, S. (2013). *The education of women as a tool in development: Challenging the African maxim*. http://journals.ed.ac.uk/hydra/article/view/720

UNIDO. (2019). *UNIDO addresses the need for enhanced women's inclusion in Industry 4.0*. https://www.unido.org/news/unido-addresses-need-enhanced-womens-inclusion-industry-40

Venkatesh, D. (2020). *India Manufacturing Seeing Innovations*. ARC Advisory Group. https://www.arcweb.com/industry-best-practices/india-manufacturing-seeing-innovations

Watzlawek, L. M. (2018). *Implementation of Industrie 4.0 in Purchasing: A Case Study*. University of Twente, The Faculty of Behavioural, Management and Social Sciences. https://essay.utwente.nl/75246/6/watzlawek_BA_BMS.pdf

World Economic Forum. (2016). *Women and Work in the Fourth Industrial Revolution.* https://reports.weforum.org/future-of-jobs-2016/women-and-work-in-the-fourth-industrial-revolution/

World Economic Forum. (2016). *The Industry Gender Gap Women and Work in the Fourth Industrial Revolution.* Retrieved from https://www3.weforum.org/docs/WEF_FOJ_Executive_Summary_GenderGap.pdf

Chapter 8
Gender, Leadership, and ICT

Shashi Bala
V. V. Giri National Labour Institute, India

Nimra Khan
Indian Institute of Management, Amritsar, India

ABSTRACT

Mainstreaming women has been an agenda of the policymakers for long. The Beijing platform for action initiated this in 1995. Still, across the world, women have been denied expressing their potential in various forums. Though the glass ceiling has been crossed in many developing countries, we don't know at what social cost that glass ceiling has been crossed. Technology has played a vital role in effective communication to reach out to target groups, but it has also created a digital divide among the users for men and women. In this chapter, the authors analyze the significance of positive leadership in motivating inclusive growth and sustainable development. They present various case studies on leadership styles being adopted in various organizations that motivated women to be a part of the active labour market without facing any discrimination on the grounds of sex. They explore flexible working hours and the provision of institutes and infrastructure for a conducive working environment in this chapter.

INTRODUCTION

It can be said that women have been left out from leadership roles and the difference in wages and occupations are noticeable between men and women. The patriarchal status in many organizations have left women out of leadership roles as it is believed that women cannot hold a position of responsibility. In today's world, where the

DOI: 10.4018/978-1-7998-8594-8.ch008

glass ceiling of such statements have been crossed, we do not know whether they are practically implied in the organizations or not. An eye-opening statistic has been reported that women make up less than ten percent of national leaders across the world. There is a pattern of unequal access to the power behind this statistic (Gilliard and Iweala, 2021).

We generally focus on output, performances purely on those measurement standards which are quantitative. It is essential to understand and capture the social cost through qualitative analysis and in-depth understanding of this issue. Behavioral science has gained momentum to capture this through various exercises and models. This has planted seeds of inequality in access to Technology. We look forward to the role of action-oriented leadership in mainstreaming these issues. The achievements of women are extraordinary in every field, but they need to take hold of positions and lead by example in many areas. Although women have been making major decisions in family for long but that has not been explicit in the public sphere which would have strengthened their position in their community, nations etc. Women in every field should play a proactive role. Existing decision-making structures and processes should be changed and should be more inclusive. Women affected by the development interventions must be engaged in the decision-making process, which should be more democratic and participatory. Through this, woman will be able to shape the objectives, priorities, and strategies of development (Jahan & Mumtaz, 1996).

The graph in today's workplace needed to be filled in a holistic manner that ensures that a diverse group of people creates the Technology of the future. It is critical to assess how Technology is affected by humans, how it affects humans, and how it affects women at the workplace (Jivani A, 2020). Technology in women's life plays an important role.

Because of Job segregation, women might be exposed to several work hazards than their male counterparts (Haw, 1982). To overcome such work hazards, a women-friendly work environment should be built. Women's empowerment emphasizes the creation of such an environment that promotes equality between men and women (Salgaonkar & Salgaonkar, 2009). This environment of equal values supports women's empowerment and development in the right way.

Women in today's world are not only employed in labor markets. The majority of women wage earners in India are self-employed. Women entrepreneurs are indirect and direct leaders in their communities in developing countries (Bullough et al., 2015). No arguments can be made with the effort to expand women's employment opportunities (Redefining Women's Work, 2000). Women's employment opportunities in both the employment and self–employment market contribute to increasing their representation in the world of work and supports workplace diversity.

It is still perceived that work-life balance is a personal issue, not societal (Loretto & Vickerstaff, 2015). Despite developments and ambitions, women still face formidable obstacles for leadership, such as household and childcare responsibilities, lack of family-friendly workplace policies, stereotypes of gender, and laws and practices denying women education or opportunities in some parts of the world. It is believed by some observers that only a few women aim to hold significant, demanding leadership posts. But, the increasing prominence of women in leadership positions is one of the most prominent changes of recent decades. Women have been largely absent from the formal authority positions. With exceptions, such posts are primarily held by men. Therefore women have lacked opportunities to exercise leadership in the most visible public settings. And both as cause and consequence of this fact, leadership is closely associated with masculinity. In multiple contexts and different parts of the world, today, many women are becoming much comfortable exerting authority and holding power and are openly ambitious to do so (Keohane, 2020). Hence, there is a requirement to understand the challenges faced by women employees and leaders not only at the workplace but in their life.

This chapter notes the kind of leadership women have routinely provided and lists factors that explain the dramatic changes. It also lists the obstacles that blocked, and skill breaks the path of women in leadership. It also includes several case studies defining Technology and its help in the leadership of women. The purpose of this chapter is to build existing literature to highlight the struggle of women in achieving & pursuing leadership roles and the use of ICT in this process. This chapter analyzes the portrayal of women's role and the consistent changes in the environment around it. Hence, a thorough literature review on gender and its role in leadership and ICT is made in this chapter.

In this chapter, first, we sketch the background providing information regarding the growth of women in the world of work, primarily focusing on the leadership and the use of ICT in this process, then it is followed by covering all the aspects that a woman has to face in the process of achieving the leadership position. The chapter first aims to focus on the pay differences between women and their male counterparts. Second, it follows the role of Technology in the career of women and its effect on her leadership role, Third; it explores the relationship between Gender and Leadership, which is further divided by highlighting the different Leadership styles used by women and the traits of leadership; both these aspects aims to explain the relationship between the women and her leadership journey. Fourth, it is further described how a woman grows at the workplace, especially highlighting the obstacles she faces and the opportunities to be achieved. The fifth section underlines the number of challenges in the path of Women leaders. This section includes workplace flexibility, which is undoubtedly very important in the career of women. The sixth section defines the leadership of women in the trade unions. The seventh section talks about the importance of favorable workplace Infrastructure in women's careers. The eighth section takes a note of positions led by women at the Grass-Root level of India. In the end, the chapter includes several case studies from different well-established organizations around the world defining the support and growth they provided to their women employees and leaders to achieve great heights in their careers. The chapter then concludes with a discussion to define the future paths for the women leaders and also underlines the future research aspects related to the topic.

BACKGROUND

Organizations often overlook women's traditionally defined feminine skills that can be proved to be strengthening today's economy. They have social structures and policies misfit women's different roles and preferences (Markel K., 2016). Despite narratives of women's equality at the workplace, the reality is disappointing. Leave policies, equality in leadership, and behavioral shifts in mindsets are variables that tell another story. Although there have been many positive changes that provide women more opportunities, progress has been made very little in such a long period. It is required to bring a more balanced workforce (Jivani A, 2020). Women experience gender-specific problems in the workplacc.

At first, women face many challenges besides workplace problems such as childcare, elderly care, household responsibilities, and pressure to complete a full day's work. Second, women have to lack progress towards the upper-leadership of organizations. Does the question arise whether women encounter a glass ceiling that blocks their progress at any point? This may come in the form of discrimination, sexual harassment, being labeled as the weaker sex and not as capable as men (Barney Erasmus, 1997). There are many dimensions of gender discrimination such as sexual violence, child marriage, human trafficking, denial of reproductive rights, honor killing, etc (Gilliard and Iweala, 2021). Women's work and the nature of work are continuously being transformed in the face of changing patterns of childbearing, marriage, divorce, family structures, reducing fertility rates, and demographic transitions. The majority of women in this world play multiple roles, including child care, maintaining the house, market work, agriculture work, wage employment, and social support. By analyzing women's roles, many complexities and multiple- dimensionality can be uncovered with each of the roles women tend to have (Such as mother, wife/partner, and employee). Women's work is problematic to classify because it does not reflect her skills, training, or full potential. In terms of public policy, the patriarchal, dominant, market-driven conceptualization of work has resulted in the women's marginalization and devaluation of their work. In the establishing process of legal systems and policy developing decisions, the voices of women have been hidden and inaudible, and consequently, these systems rarely integrate the unique characteristics of the work of women. Women's work emerges within different social, cultural, emotional, structural, and environmental contexts. The women's works in these contexts are prone to overlap. Women's work properties include activity, energy, space, time, results, resources, values, and meanings (Deanne K. et al., 1997). A major social transformation has gone through the role of women in the labor market. Though women represent the small number of leadership roles across the globe during the global pandemic of Covid-19, women leaders were featured because of their skillful navigation of an unknown and invisible threat (Soares & Sidun, 2021).

Along with the social developments of society, the sheer number of working women has steadily climbed each year. Women have become an essential element for the community's productive capacity, whereas the employers also have become majorly dependent on the women workforce to achieve their production goals. Women's proportion is several of the non-traditional occupations that have increased in recent years (Norwood, 1992). In the broader phenomena of leadership, women tend to have a strong interest. For many decades, women have played a role in conceptualizing and critiquing bureaucracy, organization, management, and leadership. Attention to the leadership of women is welcome on many levels (Sinclair, 2014). Women from the higher education sector in India remain restricted to middle-ranking posts and hardly reach higher ranking posts. It is a sector that traditionally attracts women of India as their preferred choice of career, the lack of an adequate talent pool is not the answer to fewer women in a higher position in the industry (Gandhi and Sen, 2020).

Women and the Pay Gap

The Gender pay gap plays an important role in the acquisition of Leadership positions by women. Although women have recently been trained for some higher-paying professions but they are still concentrated in the lower pay levels of the occupations. Some scholars believe that the pay difference between their counterparts decline as women move up in their careers. Another school of thought is convinced that the supply and demand factors play a role in keeping them from achieving full parity (Deanne K. et al., 1997).

In the figure above we can analyze the average hourly earnings of men and women who are managers in their respective organizations in the year 2020 from some nations around the world. We can notice that Belize is the only nation that provides equal pay to both men and women. Whereas, there is a huge pay gap in Czechia between both sexes. It should also be noticed that in both Thailand and Afghanistan women are receiving more pay than their male counterparts. Aggregation of sex

Figure 1. Average hourly earnings of employees by sex, 2020(Local currency)
Source: **International Labour Organization. (2020). ILOSTAT database**

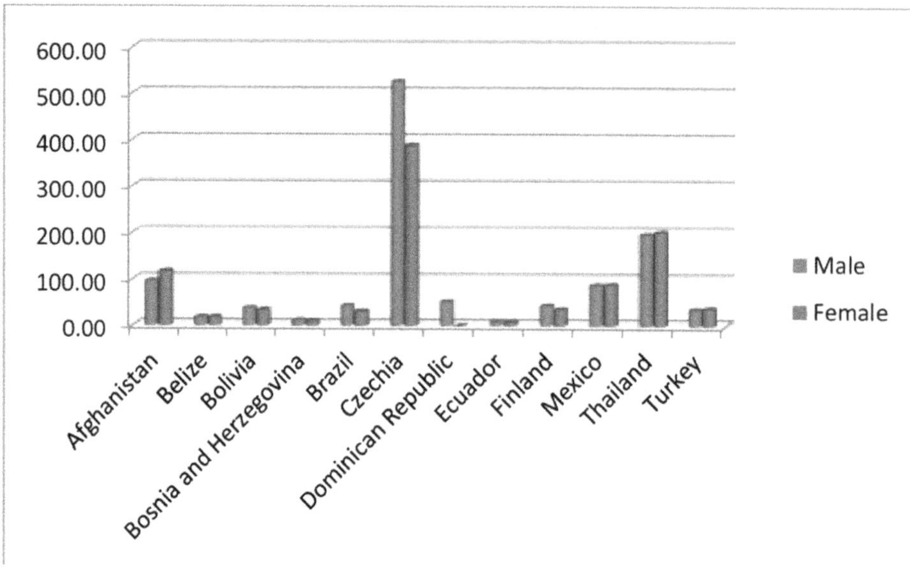

is pervasive, and the majority of women work in a low-paying female-dominated profession. Gender pay inequalities are less pronounced when women are in leading positions (Hultin and Szulkin 2003; Cohen and Huffman 2007).

Women and Technology

The relation between women and Technology affects their position in the organization, the process of their decision-making, and empowerment. It can be said that the dissemination of technological knowledge is different among males and females, which leads to further gender discrimination. Women's access to Technology is challenging in nature. Despite women's increasing entry into managerial and professional jobs, women are underrepresented at more senior levels of management (Baral, R, 2016). Venkatesh & Morris (2000) focused on the differences between women and men regarding their decision-making process and regarding the acceptance and use of Technology. While adopting Technology, men consider only productivity-related factors, and women feed inputs from several sources, including productivity assessments. Gender plays a crucial role in shaping decisions regarding technology adoption in today's era. Marked differences are there regarding physical ICT facilities accessing, which depends on gender in terms of training, management, and institutional support. There is a requirement for several ways to disseminate ICT

Figure 2. The Circle of the relationship between Gender, ICT, and Leadership at the workplace for women

policies and information so that it can reach both males and Females effectively. It can be said that ICT access will contribute to women's empowerment (Madanda et al., 2007).

The conceptual framework above describes how events are connected between Gender, ICT, and leadership at a workplace for women. Women are provided with fewer opportunities provided to access and learn about technology at the workplace. This forces her to make slow decisions and further reduces her chances to get promoted and represent themselves at the senior level management. In the end, the empowerment of women at the organization slows and leads to further gender discrimination. Again this gender discrimination gives birth to the same cycle of fewer technological opportunities offered to women and the women at workplace find no rescue from this process.

New technology does not always replace the worker's skills and deskills them, but it often requires upgrading skills. The new technologies introduction might also increase skills and income differences among the women- predominant jobs. Acker (1989) said women's careers are often perceived by managers, male colleagues, and women workers themselves that they require fewer skills than men's jobs when accessed by different job evaluation methods. Hence, new technologies might facilitate up-gradation of skills but not necessarily recognize nor reward. E.g., according to Acker, Computerization has resulted in reskilling as well as deskilling. Kuhn & Bluestone 1987; Sweeney & Nussbaum 1989 predicts that women's jobs are becoming increasingly polarized into the routine, Low-pay, highly controlled and non-routine, and relatively autonomous. Many lower-level jobs of women that cannot be automated still demand high skill and responsibility, but they are devalued in our society and broadly under-rewarded. The skills required for caring work which should be learned through experience rather than using technical method or classroom training (Acker, 1992).

Women and Leadership

We know what position a women leader holds in an organization, but we don't know under what circumstances she has achieved this position. Leadership roles attained by women in an organization are essential to understanding the climate of the organization. It can be said that it is a different experience for every woman to achieve a position of responsibility in other organizations. Women's access to these positions is affected by various factors. The struggle of women to attain this position and the after-effects of this process is worth discussing.

The glass cliff theory advocates that a woman gets into a leadership position where the organization is in a period of crisis, and the risk of failure is high. Also, when a woman is in a leading role in an organization, the number of women in lower-ranking positions is more significant. Women are underrepresented in leadership positions, but only in a certain kind of organization (Smith, A., 2015). The glass cliff is said to be a documental phenomenon in which the organizations reach out and embrace the leadership of women especially when they are in trouble (Gilliard and Iweala, 2021).

Access to women to leadership positions is hindered by stereotypes and discrimination. Historically, good leadership had been associated with characteristics related to masculinity (Cheryl de la Rey, 2005). It is an urgent task to have an equal number of women leaders in comparison to men leaders in both business and politics around the globe (Gilliard and Iweala, 2021). Ladders of promotion are truncated as higher-level jobs require more training; the employer will be looking for trained personnel from fresh graduates rather than promoting senior personnel from lower levels of their organizations (Acker, 1992). It is a matter of concern that the women at Higher Education Institutions aspiring for leadership positions often face prejudice, glass cliffs, and unfavorable responses from peers, seniors, and society (Gandhi and Sen, 2020). Women achieve leadership roles often through entrepreneurial endeavors. As an entrepreneur leader, her direct reports include her employees and other subordinates in the organization. Still, she also influences the behavior and attitudes of less obvious constituents, e.g., external business associates, community observers, potential protégé's, and family. Women Entrepreneurs are often able to influence important community members and even in public policy affecting positions (Bullough et al., 2015).

Sinclair claims that leadership can be exercised by the individuals located in the middle or bottom of the organization by those who do not own formal authority as much as by a CEO or prime minister. It is not only a way a leader performs a job or activity, but rather a series of ways of talking and understanding, prefigured by the reactions of knowledge and power. It is also shown that often leadership is done in resistance and refusal from the margins of society rather than from positions of the top, as is mentioned in the latter section of the chapter. Leadership celebrates women's way of diversity and richness that is often blocked with sexism, and patriarchal rules having found a way to resist and change the schedule of public and mobilization and empowerment of others (Sinclair, 2014).

It can be seen that in many nations the participation of women has crossed 40% but it should also be noticed that none of the nations was able to make the participation till 50%. It means that no nation across the globe has achieved the equality of women participating in the Senior and Middle-level managerial positions across the world.

It can be seen that the proportion of women across the globe since 2009-2018 in the junior managerial positions specifically has not increased much. It can be then said that it is difficult for women to even move towards junior managerial positions. Leaders can mobilize the employees' energy in ways that range from subtle, quiet persuasion to coercion. Some measures of power are present in all leaders to determine and influence priorities for other individuals. Leadership cannot always be a synonym of holding power (Keohane, 2020). It is at most times representing working from within the group and with the group members.

Figure 3. Proportion of Women in Middle and Senior Level Management positions, 2020 (%)
Source: **International Labour Organization. (2020). ILOSTAT database**

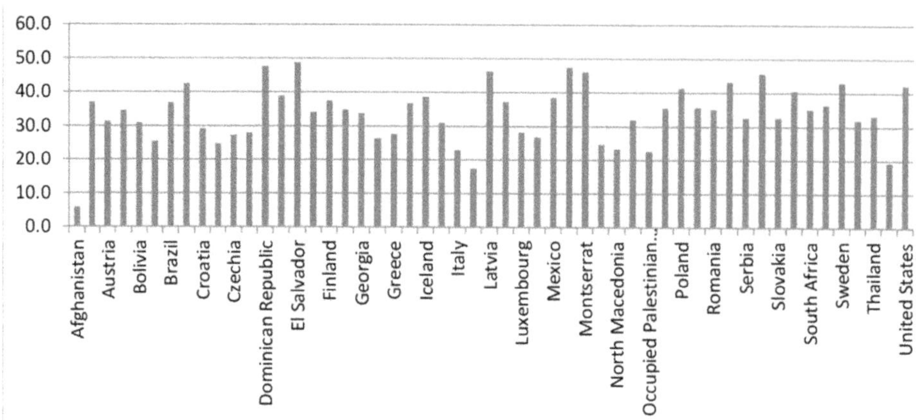

Leadership Style of Women

The Government and organizational policies have helped integrate gender inequality measures to change women's status in the workplace. Leadership is about the organizations it is present in, such as Panchayat, self-help groups, households, corporate organizations, etc. The style of leadership adopted by women is different from its male counterparts. Men's leadership styles are perceived as autocratic

Figure 4. Proportion of Women in a managerial position, 2009-18 (%)
Source: **International Labour Organization. (2020). ILOSTAT database**

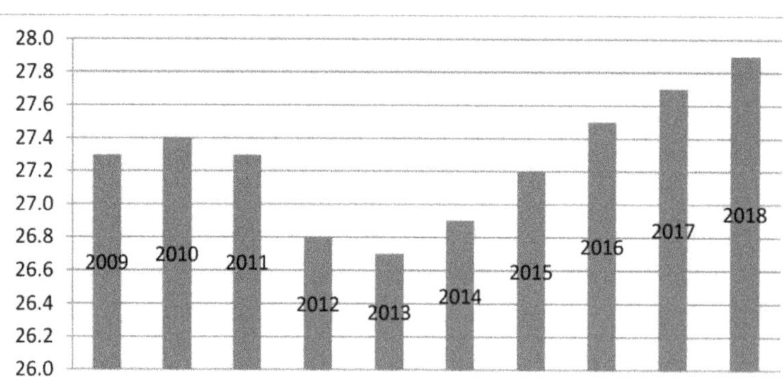

and assertive, whereas women's leadership styles are perceived as flexible and accommodating administrative (Bhatti & Ali, 2021).

This difference contributes to the women's status at the workplace and the productivity of its team members. We can see a glimpse of women's leadership styles not only in the corporate organizations but also in other grass-root level participatory bodies. The leadership styles of women are affected by the use of ICT. It is likely that more than men, women use a transformational style of leadership. They motivate others by transforming their interests into organizational goals. Women use their power based on charisma and contacts, whereas men extensively use the power of position, reward, and punishment. Women who rely majorly on their feminine characteristics tend to enjoy more significant support than those who use the masculine management style (Barney, 1997).

(Premuzic and Gallop, 2020) women's leadership styles or their traits have been defined such as their styles of leadership are more competent rather than confident, they are self-aware of their traits and understands their limitations, they are more likely to lead through the transformational style of leadership which is linked to a higher level of team engagement, performance, and productivity; They put people/ employees ahead of themselves instead of adopting a self-centered style of leadership; they don't command instead empathize and create emotional connections with their followers; they are more likely to coach and mentor as they serve as a true talent agent who uses feedback & directions to help employees grow and elevate and women leaders tend to be more humble than their male counterparts.

Traits of Leadership

Women's leadership is said to be including different and unique traits from its male counterparts. The leadership traits of women are said to be nurturing includes more interpersonal communication than male leaders and their style of leadership is interpersonal, which enhances their leadership position. Women are more like to care for the collective work and they step in when they see a gap or ambiguity in work (Cullian, 2018). The ideology of women's scarcity at the top level makes it more difficult to propose and advocate new policies that shape the emerging new world of work.

Growth of Women at the Workplace

(Kelan, 2012) the organization plays a vital role in the current leadership development of women. To leverage the capabilities of millennial women, organizations need to support women's career progress by making conscious changes. It also needs to recognize that women should articulate their talent within the workplace. The current organizational practices such as leadership should be reconsidered by throwing light on the distinct abilities of women leaders. The different skills, abilities, and preferences of women leaders are necessary for the advancement of leadership development. However, organizations and leadership development programs are designed while keeping men in mind. Women's will be more successful at the workplace by creating better ways to navigate existing systems and to embrace their feminine characteristics. She recommended that today's women require new role models and a performance feedback system that focuses on motivating women at the workplace.

The complexity in the management of new technological innovations corresponds with the power and the influence of women in the workplace. Technology (social media and the internet) plays a channel to elevate women's voices, but secondary consequences need to be unfolded. Women are proven to have less formal time and engagement with senior management than their male counterparts. This lack of access prevents them from receiving the opportunities males can achieve (Jivani, 2020). The theoretical basis of achieving technological skills is dominated by computer science and engineering, and women represent a tiny percentage of participants in these programs. This directly influences the number of women holding STEM (Science, technology, engineering, and math) jobs. Acquiring a new set of skills is a challenge for both genders. Still, women face more disadvantages in their ability to respond to it efficiently, such as off-hour training, financial investment to acquire skill, non-engagement due to child-rearing, caring for parents, and other societal responsibilities which women are bonded by at majority. This can lead to a poorly skilled segment of the workforce. Organizations' ability to customize experiences for women by introducing real-life applications that build confidence in themselves and expose themselves to like-minded communities. These settings help them to overcome barriers. Providing women the ability and skills to craft skills and Technology by themselves which helps to develop a new future.

It is required to invest strategically in teaching women the technical and non-technical skills needed to succeed in this era and supporting them with mentor and apprenticeship opportunities. It will serve women with increased opportunities at all events. Flexible working is centered on parents, especially mothers and those trying to juggle paid work and care (Child, elderly, household, etc.). Several women, significantly less affluent, have spoken about flexible working conditions throughout their lives just to fill in paid work while meeting their domestic commitments. When such conditions are not provided, they retire completely from their paid work. In theory, flexible working offers a way to combine employment and caring needs, but in reality, there is a mismatch between the employee and employer's needs. (Loretto & Vickerstaff, 2015). Women tend to develop different psychological contracts than a man in the organization. They tend to become more committed and satisfied with work when they perceive that their organizational policies are consonant with their family role than men. Scandura and Lankau, 1997 in their study indicated that it might be possible that women are more sensitive to the attitudinal effects of their organization providing family responsive policies, e.g., flexible working hours.

Part-time work among women has become one of the primary reasons for the gender pay gap. This gap is an acute problem for lower waged women, but it widens as the level of responsibility increases. It is recommended to focus on implementing equal pay receives in the organization. Flexible and part-time working is assumed to impact pay and promotion negatively, and men are susceptible to this; a gender-neutral rise of flexible working is more likely to increase the gender pay gap (Smithson et al., 2004). Flexible jobs have become increasingly available. To resolve time conflicts between paid work and family responsibilities, women with families are turning towards them (Silver & Goldscheider 1994).

For several women, part-time work proves to be a good solution for combining unpaid and paid responsibilities (Acker, 1992). Glauber. R (2011) claims, women are more flexible when working in large establishments, whereas men are more flexible when working in small establishments. He added that numerous studies prove that as the proportion of women in a worker's, occupation or job increases, their accessibility of flexible work arrangements also increases (Goodstein 1994; Osterman 1995; Davis and Kalleberg 2006; Lowen and Sicilian 2009). There are many types of workplace flexibility, such as place flexibility, where the work can be conducted from various locations. Other is time flexibility, where ones amount of time spent at work in a given period may vary. Another is scheduling flexibility when one can initiate and end their workday at different times. Part-time workers are tending to have greater job flexibility than full-time workers. There are many reasons for the employment to facilitate their employees with scheduling flexibility. It includes an increase in profits, increases in worker morale, productivity & recruitment, and reduction in turnover and job absenteeism (Glass and Fujimoto 1995; Osterman 1995; Glass and Riley 1998; Baughman, Di Nardi, and Holtz Eakin 2003; Davis and Kalleberg 2006).

It is also proposed that employees adopt these policies only when they expand their organization and have increased institutional pressure. Although women use flexible work benefits more than men, there is no agreement on gender differences in flexible scheduling access. It is also stated that female-dominated jobs provide greater accessibility to scheduling flexibility. The reasons include women's continuous shouldering of children burden pressures employer and in the female-dominated job women receive more support and sympathy to their work-family concerns from their supervisors, especially if they are women. Women are working in female-domination occupations are more likely to work part-time than most. Women working in integrated or male-dominated professions have absenteeism (Glass and Fujimoto 1995; Glass and Estes 2007; Davis and Kalle berg 2006). It is also discovered in his study that flexible working access of men increases when the percent of women in their occupation increases alongside. Flexible working is positively associated with the education and labor market experience.

Workplace Challenges for Women Leaders

O. Folke et al. (2020) Claim in their article that women supervisors are more prevalent to be sexually harassed than women employees. The harassment risk is high for lower and middle levels of women leaders when their subordinates are male. It is also claimed that the women supervisor faces more professional and social retaliation despite they are more likely taking action against the abuser. The power in the workplace increases the risk of women. Folke et al. named it a paradox of power. It can be the reason for women's scarcity on the higher levels of the organizational hierarchy. It increases their responsibilities and damages their psychology, productivity, and sense of belongings in the workplace. Another reason for such harassment can be interpreted as a result of women's leadership in male-dominated workplaces such as Information Technology, Construction, and Finance. They serve as a threat to male identity and receive challenges and harassment as a result. The women leaders are more likely to report the events and are aware of the harassment because of their educational and responsible qualities. The harassment at some times rises from status equalization. Sexual harassment at the workplace increases the challenges in women's careers to pursue ambitions and become leaders, which creates gender gaps in status, income, and voice. According to Erasmus B., 1997, Women face stress, pay, and benefits at their workplace, where stress is regarded as their primary problem.

Women's Leadership in Trade Unions

This section discusses the invisibility of women as leaders of trade unions. The unions follow dominant patriarchal attitudes; in the past, women were taken as unsuitable for providing any kind of leadership. The union's men demonstrated their power to women's subordination by compromising the leadership of women. (Tshoaedi, 2012). The trade unions mainly bargain with working conditions & wages and give less importance to issues relating to women, such as Maternity leave, Equal pay of both genders, and sex discrimination. Fewer union organizations contribute to low wages because, without the help of union organizations, the relatively powerless women have no mechanism that can push for pay levels (Acker, 1992).

2016-17 defines the percentage share of women in Trade Unions in selected countries across the globe. It is analyzed that the membership of women in Trade unions is slowly increasing as nations like Croatia, Ireland, New Zealand, and the

Figure 5. Percentage shares of female union members, 2016-17
Source: J. Visser, ICTWSS Database. version 6.1. Amsterdam: Amsterdam Institute for Advanced Labour Studies (AIAS), University of Amsterdam.

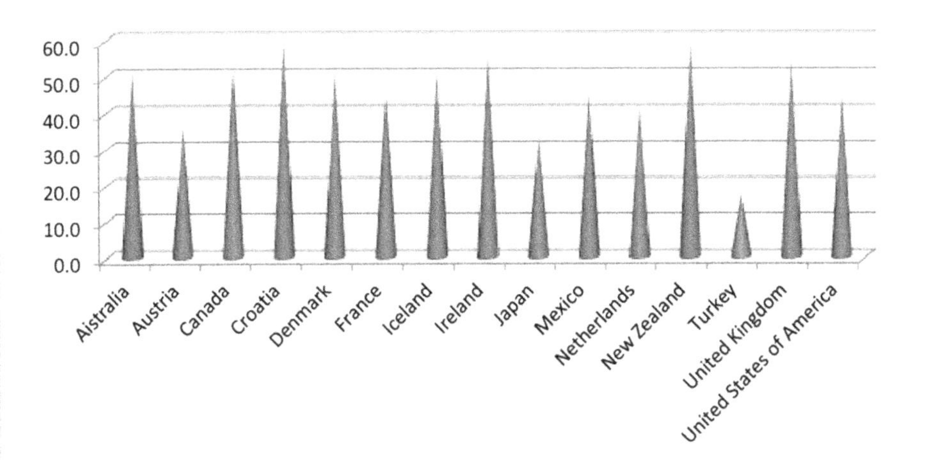

United Kingdom have the participation of women more than 50%. It is critically important that women are facilitated with equal opportunities to engage and assume leadership positions in trade unions and collective bargaining processes (ILO, 2020). It is important to unionize women's labor force and train them. It is also crucial to see more women being promoted to leadership roles. But in our country, India where the patriarchy is deep-rooted, it becomes difficult to induct women into trade unions and promote them as future leaders. When a woman is elected to be a trade union it demonstrates the seriousness of the union. The women leaders are required to be engaged in a dialogue process, negotiations, collective bargaining, and settlement with employers. Women should be provided with the opportunities to get trained at labor institutions and to be present and contribute to negotiation processes; this will help them to become future union leaders (ILO, 2018).

(Basistha and Pathak, 2020) in their study found that mostly Assam Chah Mazdoor Sangha (ACMS), which is affiliated with the Indian Trade Union Congress (INTUC). The number of members in the union ranges from 9-70 which majorly includes male members. The female members present in the union have a very minimum participation level and serve only as a representation purpose. When it comes to raising voices and proving opinions these female members take a backseat. The study also provides the reason for low participation of women in trade unions such as their perception of the trade union as a male-dominated zone and hence they don't feel comfortable to join, they know that they will be a part of it for the representation purpose only, they are always burdened with double workload while managing both household and professional activities, and when working along with the males in the union they fear of being stigmatized as bad women.

Infrastructure for Women

The Government's provision of infrastructure on growth impacts women's allocation of time, cumulating of human capital, and the strength of congestion effects. The access to improved infrastructure induces women to reallocate their time away from home production activities and productive uses, including market work and spending time to care for themselves and their children (Agénor & Agénor 2014).

Grass Root Level Leadership

The leadership is not just performed at the highest levels or the board rooms of the giant corporates. It is also be performed at the most basic level of society. In this section, with the perspective of Salgaonkar & Salgaonkar (2009), we will try to understand the leadership of women at the Grass-root level of India. Institutions of panchayats raj in India serve as the grassroots unit of self- Government. They prove to be the instruments of decentralization and participatory democracy at the grassroots level. The constitution has guaranteed equality and demands active political participation by women at these institutions, which is essential for women's progress—by reserving one-third of women's seats, further reserved for S.C. and S.T. women, and one-third reserve seats at offices at the chairpersons at each level, which led to introduction to many women leaders at the grassroots level. Women's entry into the village political system ensures the changes in the political system of the village, familial and social perception of the role of women, and most importantly, development of grassroots level leadership among women. It is desired that women should become beneficiaries through it and become contributory in this process. The institutions of Panchayati raj include women SHG (Self Help Groups) and Panchayat itself. SHG is micro- cooperative which aims to help alternative development. It functions on the principle, that poverty can be eliminated by making the member more independent and confident. It shows the features of informality, transparency, and participatory management. They serve as a tool for empowering the poor and promoting opportunities among its members for exposure and unearth hidden talents. Women self-help groups mobilize women towards micro-credit. It paves the way for the participation of women and increases their economic independence. It is a means of empowerment to them. It also increases their access and control over resources. There is evidence where WSHGs are evident to become the springboards for promoting members in panchayat elections. It suggests that their increased numbers at Panchayat Raj Institution will offer them equally increased opportunities to influence the local decision-making. WSHGs can also act as a pressure group to convince their member to bring issues affecting women and children of their village in public.

Conducive Working Environment for Women

With increasing occupational mobility developed by women, maybe they are exposed to the similar physical and emotional harm of the workplace environment as men and perhaps exposed to the pressures created by the multiple roles women have to play and its demands and even the expectations of conflicting roles (Haw, 1982). Teleworking being promoted can serve as a magic wand to 'free' women for 'productive' work. Telework provides an opportunity even for a small portion of educated, middle-class women. It gives the advantage of a regular wage, allows women to take care of their household and children. It eliminates communication to work, saves quality time as well as wear and tear (Redefining Women's Work. 2000).

Case Studies of Women in Leadership

Gay, G. (2020) Women are a progression in the workplace and breaking glass ceilings in the presence of numerous challenges. Many organizations aim to detangle these challenges to support women's mobility, access to resources, involvement, equality, and other concerns. Following are the cases of some companies that took a step in the direction of developing and supporting women at their workplaces.

It can be summarized from the number of case studies above that it is essential to improve the number and representation of women in the world of work. Different organizations in different cases use several tools and techniques to generate more opportunities for women in the organization. All the programs aim to provide career direction, progression, development, advancement, training, etc., with the help of mentoring, sponsoring, and developing networks. Women are provided mentoring to strengthen and grow their careers. It is essential to create employee networks within the workforce so that diversity can be reflected. It also increases women's access to career development tools. Training, networking, and mentoring are valuable social capital for women leaders (Bhatti & Ali, 2021).

FUTURE RESEARCH DIRECTION

This chapter focuses on the role of gender in leadership and the use of ICT that affects both gender and leadership. The future research can highlight the advantages and challenges in using ICT for decision making, understanding the whole process

Table 1.

Affirm
A financial, technological company believes that their biggest goal in growing is to achieve parity in the women's representation in the traditionally male-dominated industries such as Technology and finance. To proportionally increase the representation of women in this industry, it is working and examining the recruiting and hiring process to infuse more diversity, particularly with recent graduates in engineering.
American Express
A multinational financial service corporation claims that 20% of its Board Directors are women, and women represent 40% of its Executive Committee. The organization conducts a bi-annual Global Women's Conference, which aims to bring together senior women and men allies from all around the globe to discuss leadership, culture, ambition, elevation, and empowerment of women across the organization. It also creates an employee's network of its workforce that reflects its diversity. Out of which, Women's Interest Network and Women in Technology Network represents women in workforce diversity.
Blackstone
A leading investment firm designed a Blackstone Women's Network (BWN) to recruit, develop, and retain talented women and create a solid professional community within the organization. It directs to create a platform globally for women employees who help them connect and increase their access to career development tools. Another innovative program named BX WIN was specially designed for analysts and associates level professional women across the globe, focusing on creating a critical network across the organization. Each group is partnered with senior leaders and sponsors who continually meet with the participants throughout the year. Each spring, a program named Future Women's Leaders Program ushers a high-achieving group of second-year college women to its offices to provide their early exposure to business and finance by using interactive and informational seminars, networking, and critical skill-building sessions.
Paypal
A digital payment platform states that its affinity group consisting of women and men works together to generate more opportunities for women in the organization. It also focuses on gender equality and balance. It set its sight on helping women thrive, producing growth opportunities for women, and assisting the next generation in exploring the world of Technology.
Wells Fargo
A financial services company states that in 2018, 57% of its U.S. workforce was women. It has ten Team Member Networks which includes one Women's Team Member Network. The organization recognizes the fact that businesses owned by women are among the fastest-growing segments of small businesses. It runs a one-year business development program named Million Women Mentors Entrepreneurship Initiative Mentor Program in partnership with STEM Connector. It lines up women owners of well-established small businesses with its executives. Those Executives serve as mentors and help the women CEOs to strengthen and grow their businesses.
Fifth Third Bank
The diversified financial services company headquartered in Cincinnati has established a program named Women in Leadership (WIL) to provide integrated development and experience for high-performing women leaders of the bank. All the women enrolled in this program are actively guided for career direction and facilitated with progression. A traditional mentoring relationship is formed to increase the representation of women at high levels. Apart from leadership support, the bank has launched a groundbreaking maternity concierge program that aims to help women during pregnancy, after Childbirth, and in case of a mother's return to work.
Ernst & Young
One of the big four accounting firms aims for the development and advancement of women by engaging both men and women in open dialogues/discussions on critical issues and experiences, initiation of mentoring & sponsoring, and development of networks.
Bank of America
A multinational investment bank initiated a women's Executive Development Program in 2007, empowering women to make meaningful contributions to the company and the communities. Another program named Diverse Leadership Sponsorship targets top–performances in diverse talent to help accelerate their advocacy development and visibility in 10 months and increase their chances of promotion at the bank. Its Global Ambassador Program connects the women entrepreneurs to senior women executives for skill-building and monitoring.
J.P. Morgan Chase and Co.
A global financial service firm established a global initiative to empower women stakeholders to build their careers, grow their businesses and support their financial health. The organization promises to support women in leadership positions by providing adequate growth culture, opportunities, training, policies, benefits, etc. It also aims at expanding women-run businesses from startups to global enterprises by providing access to critical resources, expertise, and networking. It focuses on women's financial health & future and celebrates Women on the move Leadership day in September.
Source: Women of Color Magazine, Vol. 19, No. 1 & 20, No. 1.

of decision making with the help of ICT, the different challenges faced by the genders in the organization, success stories of women leaders in the organization, etc. Future research could examine the outcome associated with working from home and leadership. In future research, we intend to extend the findings on temporary leadership roles performed by both of the Genders.

DISCUSSION

The skills and abilities brought by women to the workplace and support structures contribute to leadership development (Markel, 2016). Career progression worries serve as a significant barrier to flexible working arrangements by both men and women. There is a need for an approach that focuses on concerns about promotion and pay. This can be assisted by senior board members and especially senior men (Smithson et al. 2004). In an extended period, physiological, affective, and behavioral responses to work-related stress that are not normal which might lead to outcomes involving permanent structure and functional damages. Trends in women's workplace participation indicate that work outside the home will be an increasingly important part of their lives (Haw, 1982). The stakeholders should answer women's immediate needs by granting them access to opportunities that they have been denied so far some of which are earning better wages, making decisions at the top levels and enabling them to compete with an equal footing with their male counterparts. All of this can be counted as women's special gender needs. Empowerment of women is increasingly becoming a portmanteau concept carrying a lot of wanted baggage, and in the process, severe attempts towards women's development are derailed (Redefining Women's Work, 2000). Sinclair (2014) suggested ways to bring the following to attention: 1. to pay attention to the power and privilege proved in the leadership process. 2. In research towards individualism and universalism of leadership, one should not collide with the stereotypes. 3. Be more reflective of works on leadership. Women workers can reasonably be satisfied at their workplace if they are provided with essential maintenance aspects such as pay leave benefits and more. As women are more likely to use a transformational style of leadership, it is a factor of crucial importance that can prove to provide success to the organization in the next millennium. The positive women's psychology is an invite to new management qualities and styles at workplace. Women must be a part of any organization's board members to ensure workforce diversity is managed effectively (Barney, 1997).

CONCLUSION

The motive of this chapter is to increase insights into and understanding of the relationship between gender, leadership, and ICT. The conclusions from this chapter are familiar to many who work in the area of gender studies. Leadership, Gender, and ICT are three variables that affect the organization, and all three are interrelated. These three variables play a significant role in the growth of the organization. In this chapter, we tried to understand the role of various factors in the women's leadership span and the barriers to attaining the position. It can be concluded that the policies at a workplace do not protect women from harassment. Women leaders should break gender norms and pursue their jobs. The assertive and dominant characteristics of leadership may clash with the stereotypical perception of women in the mind of society. The continuous advancement of women, especially in the leadership roles in the labor market, acts as a necessary pathway that connects men and women's economic equality (Folke et al., 2020).

Wright, P.(2011) Said that the women holding the leadership positions should be willing to seize the moment and take risks. They should know that they will be criticized and scrutinized more vigorously than their male counterparts. Finally, they should understand that the feminine style of leadership has its extraordinary advantage, which deserves to be honored and used for leading. The attribution of power and influence does not confirm the dominant stereotypes about women being perceived as the weaker sex. To reduce the barriers at the workplace faced by women leaders, the importance of feminine attributes should be recognized by the workplace structure. Women's involvement in trade union activities describes the differences in the identities of workers and the diversity in their issues (Tshoaedi, 2012). Hence, involving women in the Trade unions will support workplace diversity and growth.

To maintain a high level of productivity and growth, organizations must make concerted efforts in the direction of upskilling women. This upskilling will support women to attain new jobs that are required for today's workplace. Women's ability to stay and grow in an organization depends on their position in the larger working ecosystem. To retain women at the job, it is critical to foster the actual quality of the ecosystem and the relationships with them (Jivani, 2020). Active upskilling on the job should be incorporated, especially for women. It should be ensured that bias is not being built into technologies. Women are required to work on a higher level and with more flexible skills. Equipping women with flexible working policies may reduce absenteeism and turnover. Scandura & Lankau, (1997) suggest that these policies may increase levels of commitment and overall satisfaction for both genders. Still, women are more affected by it as well as individuals with responsibilities and multiple obligations. If employees with caring responsibilities are permitted to adjust their schedules for days, weeks, or years or sometimes allow them to work from home, then they will be able to balance their household work well (Silver &Goldscheider 1994). Access to work flexibility might prove as a great advantage for working in integrated occupations as these occupations are located disproportionally in managerial and professional sectors of the labor market (Glauber, 2011).

Whereas, at the grassroot level, Women's self-help groups are receptive to new ideas, technologies, training, employment, and secular social concerns for others. New leadership can emerge from these grassroots level institutions, which are expected to administer financial resources reasonably and promote innovative thinking and decision-making at the village level. A synergy between WSHGs and PRIs can prove to go a long way for the empowerment of women in rural areas (Glauber, 2011). The stakeholders of women's health must consider the health status, health behavior, and health care needs of women in their daily lives and work (Deanne et al., 1997). Women are here to contribute in the world of work in large scale participation. They are enriched with skills and productive capacity that are required to support the nation's economic growth. Women have shown a great deal of progress in the economy, but there is still a long- way to go (Norwood, 1992). Despite the stubborn linkage between leadership and masculinity, women from every society have proven their solid and significant leadership capacity (Keohane, 2020). We cannot reach the most peaceful and prosperous version of our planet without including women for the better (Gilliard and Iweala, 2021).

In the case of self-employed and entrepreneur women leaders, Effective Entrepreneurship Education and Training (EET) can assist them in their business and leadership goals (Bullough, 2021). This chapter will be appealing to academician, practitioners, and even policymakers concerned with understanding how leadership is affected by gender and ICT. Overall, this chapter emphasizes the importance of making explicit, not just to academician but also to a broader audience, and the link between Gender, Leadership, and ICT.

REFERENCES

Acker, J. (1992). The Future of Women and Work: Ending the Twentieth Century. *Sociological Perspectives*, *35*(1), 53–68. doi:10.2307/1389368

Acker, J. (1989). *Doing Comparable Worth*. Temple University Press.

Agénor, P., & Agénor, M. (2014). Infrastructure, women's time allocation, and economic development. *Journal of Economics*, *113*(1), 1–30. doi:10.100700712-013-0358-0

Baral, R. (2016). Women Managers & Professionals: Work-Family Conflict & Job Satisfaction. *Indian Journal of Industrial Relations*, *51*(3), 432–446.

Erasmus, B. (1997). Women Power: Aspects of Work-Life. *Agenda: Empowering Women for Gender Equity*, *13*(35), 35–44. doi:10.2307/4066087

Basistha, S., & Pathak, D. M. (2020). Participation of Women in the Emerging Trade Union Activities in the Tea-Gardens of Assam. *International Journal of Research and Innovation in Social Science*, *4*(3), 321–324.

Baughman, R., DiNardi, D., & Holtz-Eakin, D. (2003). Productivity and Wage Effects of family-Friendly' Fringe Benefits. *International Journal of Manpower*, *24*(3), 247–259. doi:10.1108/01437720310479723

Bhatti, A., & Ali, R. (2021). Women constructing leadership identities in academia: Intersection of gender and culture. *Issues in Educational Research*, *31*(1), 1–18.

Bullough, A., De Luque, M., Abdelzaher, D., & Heim, W. (2015). Developing Women Leaders through Entrepreneurship Education and Training. *The Academy of Management Perspectives*, *29*(2), 250–270. doi:10.5465/amp.2012.0169

de la Rey, C. (2005). Gender, Women, and Leadership. Agenda. *Empowering Women for Gender Equity*, (65), 4–11.

Cohen, P. N., & Huffman, M. L. (2007). Working for the Woman? Female Managers and the Gender Wage Gap.'. *American Sociological Review*, *72*(5), 681–687. doi:10.1177/000312240707200502

Cullian, R. (2018). In Collaborative Work Cultures, Women Carry More of the Weight. *Harvard Business Review*. https://hbr.org/2018/07/in-collaborative-work-cultures-women-carry-more-of-the-weight

Davis, A. E., & Kalleberg, A. L. (2006). Family-Friendly Organizations? Work and Family Programs in the 1990s. *Work and Occupations*, *33*(2), 191–22. doi:10.1177/0730888405280446

Deanne, K., Hilfinger, M., Im, E., Page, A., Regev, H., Spiers, J., Yoder, L., & Meleis, A. (1997). Defining and Redefining Work: Implications for Women's Health. Gender and Society, 11(3), 296-323.

Kelan, E., & Stars, R. (2012). Developing Millennial Women as Leaders. Palgrave Macmillan.

Folke, O., Rickne, J., Tanaka, S., & Tateishi, Y. (2020). Sexual Harassment of Women Leaders. *Daedalus*, *149*(1), 180–197. doi:10.1162/daed_a_01781

Gandhi, M., & Sen, K. (2021). Missing women in Indian university leadership: Barriers and facilitators. *Educational Management Administration & Leadership, 49*(2), 352–369. doi:10.1177/1741143219896048

Gay, G. (2019). Best Practices in Diversity: Companies Keeping Advancement of Women a Priority. *Women of Color Magazine, 19*(1), 32–36.

Gay, G. (2020). Supporting Women in the Workplace: A Priority For Companies Large And Small. *Women of Color Magazine, 20*(1), 28–31.

Gilliard, J., & Iweala, O. N. (2021). *Women and Leadership: Real Lives, Real Lessons*. The MIT Press.

Glass, J., & Fujimoto, T. (1995). Employer Characteristics and the Provision of Family Responsive Policies. *Work and Occupations, 22*, 380–384.

Glass, J., & Riley, L. (1998). Family Responsive Policies and Employee Retention Following Childbirth. *Social Forces, 76*, 1401–1435. doi:10.2307/3005840

Glass, J., & Estes, S. B. (2007). Do Flexible Work Practices Influence Time Spent in Domestic Labor? *Journal of Family Issues, 28*, 263–288. doi:10.1177/0192513X06292703

Glauber, R. (2011). Limited access: Gender, Occupational Composition, and Flexible Work Scheduling. *The Sociological Quarterly, 52*(3), 472–494. doi:10.1111/j.1533-8525.2011.01215.x PMID:22081800

Goodstein, J. D. (1994). Institutional Pressures and Strategic Responsiveness: Employer Involvement in Work-Family Issues. *Academy of Management Journal, 37*(2), 350–382.

Haw, M. (1982). Women, Work, and Stress: A Review and Agenda for the Future. *Journal of Health and Social Behavior, 23*(2), 132–144. doi:10.2307/2136510 PMID:7108179

Hultin, M., & Szulkin, R. (2003). Mechanisms of Inequality: Unequal Access to Organizational Power and the Gender Wage Gap. *European Sociological Review*.

ILO. (2018). *Trade Unions Need To Strategize To Reach Youth and Vulnerable Workers*. https://www.ilo.org/newdelhi/info/public/fs/WCMS_649893/lang--en/index.htm

International Labour Organization. (2020). *Empowering Women at Work- Trade Union Policies and Practices for Gender Equality*. ILO.

Jahan, R., & Mumtaz, S. (1996). The Elusive Agenda: Mainstreaming Women in Development. *Pakistan Development Review, 35*(4), 825–834. doi:10.30541/v35i4IIpp.825-834 PMID:12294613

Jivani, A. (2020). Gender Lens to the Future of Work. *Daedalus, 149*(1), 134–143. doi:10.1162/daed_a_01778

Keohane, N. (2020). Women, Power & Leadership. *Daedalus, 149*(1), 236–250. doi:10.1162/daed_a_01785

Kuhn, S., & Bluestone, B. (1987). Economic Restructuring and the Female Labor Market: The Impact of Industrial Change on Women. In L. Beneria & C. R. Stimpson (Eds.), *Women, Households, and the Economy* (pp. 3–32). Rutgers University Press.

Loretto, W., & Vickerstaff, S. (2015). Gender, age, and flexible working in later life. *Work, Employment and Society, 29*(2), 233–249. doi:10.1177/0950017014545267

Lowen, A., & Sicilian, P. (2009). Family-Friendly Fringe Benefits and the Gender Wage Gap. *Journal of Labor Research, 30*(2), 10. doi:10.100712122-008-9046-1

Madanda, A., Kabonesa, C., & Bantebya-Kyomuhendo, G. (2007). Challenges to Women's Empowerment through ICTs: The Case of Makerere University. Agenda. *Empowering Women for Gender Equity*, (71), 81–88.

Markel, K. (2016). Options and opportunities for women's workplace engagement. *Work, Employment and Society, 30*(1), 192–197. doi:10.1177/0950017015590342

Norwood, J. (1992). Working Women: Where Have We Been? Where Are We Going? *Population and Environment, 14*(1), 95–103. doi:10.1007/BF01254609

Osterman, P. (1995). Work-Family Programs and the Employment Relationship. *Administrative Science Quarterly, 40*(4), 681–687. doi:10.2307/2393758

Premuzic, T., & Gallop, C. (2020). 7 Leadership Lessons Men Can Learn From Women. *Harvard Business Review*. https://hbr.org/2020/04/7-leadership-lessons-men-can-learn-from-women

Redefining Women's Work. (2000). *Economic and Political Weekly, 35*(52/53), 4591–4592.

Salgaonkar, S., & Salgaonkar, P. (2009). Panchayats and Women Self Help Groups: Understanding the Symbiosis. *Indian Journal of Poultry Science, 70*(2), 481–494.

Scandura, T., & Lankau, M. (1997). Relationships of Gender, Family Responsibility and Flexible Work Hours to Organizational Commitment and Job Satisfaction. *Journal of Organizational Behavior*, *18*(4), 377–391. doi:10.1002/(SICI)1099-1379(199707)18:4<377::AID-JOB807>3.0.CO;2-1

Silver, H., & Goldscheider, F. (1994). Flexible Work and Housework: Work and Family Constraints on Women's Domestic Labor. *Social Forces*, *72*(4), 1103–1119. doi:10.2307/2580294

Sinclair, A. (2014). A feminist case for leadership. In J. Damousi, K. Rubenstein, & M. Tomsic (Eds.), *Diversity in Leadership: Australian women, past and present* (pp. 17–36). ANU Press. doi:10.22459/DL.11.2014.01

Smith, A. (2015). On The Edge of a Glass Cliff: Women in Leadership in Public Organizations. *Public Administration Quarterly*, *39*(3), 484–517.

Smithson, J., Lewis, S., Cooper, C., & Dyer, J. (2004). Flexible working and the gender pay gap in the accountancy profession. *Work, Employment and Society*, *18*(1), 115–135. doi:10.1177/0950017004040765

Soares, S. E., & Sidun, N. M. (2021). Women leaders during a global crisis: Challenges, characteristics, and strengths. *International Perspectives in Psychology: Research, Practice, Consultation*, *10*(3), 130–137. doi:10.1027/2157-3891/a000020

Sweeney, J. J., & Nussbaum, K. (1989). *Solutions for the New Work Force*. Seven Locks Press.

Tshoaedi, M. (2012). Women in the Forefront of Workplace Struggles in South Africa: From Invisibility to Mobilization. Labour, Capital and Society / Travail. *Capital EtSociété*, *45*(2), 58–83.

Venkatesh, V., & Morris, M. (2000). Why Don't Men Ever Stop to Ask for Directions? Gender, Social Influence, and Their Role in Technology Acceptance and Usage Behavior. *Management Information Systems Quarterly*, *24*(1), 115–139. doi:10.2307/3250981

Wright, P. (2011). Women and Leadership Style. *Group*, *35*(3), 247–253.

Chapter 9
Gender Diversity on the Board and Corporate Social Responsibility Disclosure in the Digitalisation Era:
A Study of the Indian Service Sector Industry

Bhoomika Batra
https://orcid.org/0000-0003-3747-9812
EdBhoomi, India

Rajesh Sannegadu
University of Mauritius, Mauritius

Kamakshi Mehta
Amity University, Gurgaon, India

ABSTRACT

The purpose of this chapter is to examine how gender diversity affects corporate social responsibility disclosure. Considering the socio-economic impact of the deployment of the fourth industry revolution (Industry 4.0), firms have a moral obligation to disclose information on how different stakeholders may be affected by the extensive use of smart technologies in their value-adding activities. The study used multiple regression analysis with 176 publicly traded Indian service sector organizations for the financial year 2020-21. The findings revealed that GD has a negligible impact on CSR filings. By focusing on Indian public firms in the service sector, this study fills a vacuum in the literature. It is the first study to evaluate the impact of women on boards on the scope of CSR reporting in an Indian context. The findings of this study have crucial implications for future board composition as they show that women's representation on boards did not affect CSR disclosures.

DOI: 10.4018/978-1-7998-8594-8.ch009

INTRODUCTION

The role of Gender Diversity (GD) in the business corporate world has been a hotly debated topic for ages. Past researches have posited that Gender Diversity (GD) on the boards of corporates has led to an innovative thought process of the investors to believe that these corporates are competently governed. Governance has been a major subject of interest for both public and private corporates. It is the company's BOD who is responsible to ensure good governance of their companies. According to the report from Fenwick – Bloomberg Law Silicon Valley 150 List as of March 31st, 2021, California law is mandating the Gender Diversity (GD) standards for companies to include more women in the board composition. The preamble of the Indian Constitution has laid stress on the Fundamental Rights and Duties, Directive Principles, and the grants permitted to women's rights. The government has also encouraged society to embrace measures in favor of the upliftment of women. Post-Five-year plans, there has been a drastic change in the focus for women's welfare and their development. The measures included the control of female infanticide, domestic violence against women, equality in terms of social, health, monetary and occupational aspects. The Ministry of Women and Child Development has emphasized the companies in collecting data and publicize the benefits and programs which are gender-specific. CSR implies Social Accountability including individual, societal, environmental, and economic aspects. Based on Schedule VII (Section-135) of Companies Act, activities that were mandated to be included in CSR reporting are the encouragement of healthcare, education, gender equality, environmental sustainability, art & culture, sports activities, contribution to PM relief fund, rural and slum area developments, elimination of poverty and sanitation.

Based on smart technologies (including Digitalisation, Artificial Intelligence (AI), robotics, Internet of Things (IoT), and Augmented Reality (AR) among others), the fourth industrial revolution (Industry 4.0) has significantly transformed the way value is created, exchanged and distributed. Several benefits are associated with the digitalization of operations including increased flexibility/agility in the supply chain, ease of personalizing the products/services, and improved operational efficiency. On the other hand, this radical transformation is also having profound implications on businesses as well as many aspects of human life. In addition to the creation of market opportunities and efficient business models, smart technologies are also creating social inequalities through the laying off of lower-skilled employees. Indeed, the disruptive potential of technological advancement has since the second industrial revolution created a lot of insecurities in particular among the poorest and most vulnerable group of people. Other jobs that are repetitive such as telemarketers, accounts clerks, loan officers, credit analysts and human resource coordinators amongst others have around 98-99 percent chance of being automated through a machine learning algorithm. In this respect, Pollitzer (2017) warns that as with precedent industrial revolutions, Industry 4.0 is also likely to be "gender-blind" and "poor-blind". From the business perspective, the firm's reputation is at stake due to the laying off of employees.

On the other hand, as CSR extends beyond the sole interest of shareholders, firms are increasingly disclosing their information on the contribution of Industry 4.0 on the financial performance and the strategies to manage their stakeholders ethically and responsibly. Such disclosures in the context of Industry 4.0 include strategies and operation plans intended to (i) develop networking with key partners, (ii) develop future skills and talent and (iii) maintain sustainable growth amongst others. Existing literature has demonstrated that many aspects of a system tend to be humanized through the presence of women in board rooms. In light of the disruptive nature of digitalization, the question is whether women directorship can improve the quality of CSR disclosure, in particular the strategies set in place to limit the socio-economic impact of smart technologies. To answer this question, the authors attempted to determine if a relationship exists between the presence of women on boards and CSR reporting.

The present study concentrates on how gender diversification influences the disclosures of CSR expenditures among corporates operating in the Indian service sector. As a dominant contributor to India's GDP, the services sector has been considered the backbone of the Indian economy. The sector has proved as a powerful engine of growth of the Indian economy by generating large-scale employment, attracting Foreign Direct Investment (FDI), and generating foreign exchange through its significant contribution to the export market. The sector constitutes a wide variety of activities including real estate, hotels, and restaurants, construction, leasing, financing, and insurance amongst others. In 2019-2020, the service sector's Gross Value Added (GVA) totalled to a whopping figure of 100.46 lakh crore INR and contributed 27.5% to India's Gross Domestic Product (GDP). However, Majmudar, Rana, and Sanan (2015) note that firms operating in the Indian service sector spend a relatively lower percentage of their profits in CSR compared to their counterparts in the manufacturing sector.

The Indian services sector has been left devastated by the deadly blow suffered during the COVID-19 pandemic owing to the lockdown and social distancing measures taken by the government with the motive of containing the infection (Chaudhary, Sodani, & Das, 2020). However, the service industry is expected to take off in the aftermath of the COVID-19 pandemic. The outsourcing service market is likely to grow by 6-8% between 2021-2024 (India Brand Equity Foundation, 2021). The 8-year period from 2004 to 2014 has witnessed a consistent increase in the ratio of working women in the service sector of the Indian economy. India has bagged the third rank in Grant Thornton's report on leadership positions held by women. The involvement of women in a leadership position is expected to elevate the quality of board decisions and also shall contribute to higher CSR disclosures. Against this backdrop, the study aims at confirming whether a higher female presence on corporate boards indicates a higher commitment to CSR performance and disclosures.

The study contributes to the ongoing debate on gender representation and CSR disclosures. By investigating the relationship between women's presence on boards and the quality of CSR disclosure from a new perspective (i.e., the Indian service sector and the Digital era), this study provides new insights and builds on the current work of other researchers and scholars. On the practical side, the findings of the study are relevant to company managers who are interested in improving CSR reporting through the introduction of gender quotas. The change in the board composition to include more women also represents a giant leap in applying the Sustainable Development Goal (SDG) 5 "Gender Equality and women's Empowerment". Moreover, the study can help in creating a sustainable Industry 4.0 by disclosing relevant information on the social, economic, and environmental impact of Industry 4.0. Finally, the findings can also be used by the government to formulate evidence-based strategies to reinforce the presence of women on boards.

RELATED STUDIES

Corporate Social Responsibility

CSR has often been subjected to misunderstanding, misinterpretation, and cynicism due to the lack of a widely agreed definition of the concept. For example, Van Marrewijk (2003) notes that owing to an absence of an "all-embracing definition", CSR is frequently regarded as the solution that is intended to solve economic, social, and environmental issues. These issues include degradation of the environment, global poverty, and social inclusion. According to Van Marrewijk (2003), the following three approaches have been used to answer the question *"To whom an organization has a responsibility?"*:

1. *The shareholder approach* is based on the premise that increasing profits is the social responsibility of business. Under this approach, business enterprises are primarily driven by the need to increase shareholders' funds.
2. *The stakeholder approach* indicates that business enterprises should give due consideration to an array of stakeholders who can influence or be influenced by the activities of the organization.
3. *The societal approach* posits that companies are responsible for society since they form an integral part of it.

Drawing from the ongoing academic debates on CSR and business practices, it can be concluded that CSR implies "*the need to serve appropriate stakeholders*". Previously driven by profit motives, managers gradually started to realize the importance of serving the interests of all other stakeholders in pursuing organizational goals. In simple terms, (Masum et al., 2020) relate the concept of CSR as conducting the business in an ethical manner that is not only beneficial to society but is also advantageous to the development of the community. Over the years, CSR emerged as a crucial element to the survival and growth of many companies across the globe as it is likely to improve future cash flows. Furthermore, (Tuokuu & Amponsah-Tawiah, 2016) note that considerations given to the demand and expectations of various stakeholders contribute significantly to the enhancement of the business's corporate image which in turn attracts more investors. The present-day socially responsible investors strongly believe that both financial and CSR criteria are equally important as compared to the traditional investors whose decisions were primarily influenced by the firm's financial performance. Other economic benefits of CSR include sales growth and returns on sales as well as improved profitability resulting from the implementation of "eco-efficiency" measures. Furthermore, socially responsible behaviour improves environmental risk management by proactively avoiding the cost related to lawsuits (due to non-compliance of environmental norms), clean-up costs, and fines. Nevertheless, some empirical studies have not established a significant relationship between the performance of the corporates and their CSR expenditures and disclosures.

On the other hand, the implementation of CSR activities carries its loads of challenges. These challenges are well documented in the literature and include among others cost, commitment of stakeholders and loss of management's interest. For example, (Azman & Mustapha, 2018:215) identified cost, complexity of implementation and excessive time consumed as major challenges to the implementation of CSR activities among Malaysian firms. Moreover, the inability and unwillingness of other stakeholders (such as supplier of raw materials and distributors) to follow the firm's moves throughout the length of the supply chain do not contribute to the overarching aim of creating economic, social and environmental value for the society (Setthasakko, 2009). Another factor influencing the success of CSR activities is the cultural diversity since people having different beliefs and values about CSR may find it difficult to work together. Furthermore, (Sundström, Hyder & Chowdhury, 2020:775) found that SMEs fails to initiate CSR policies due to a lack of knowledge regarding the implementation CSR activities. In the Indian context, Tandon and Gupta (2019) identified a lack of transparency, an absence of clarity of CSR objectives, limited communication between stakeholders and the companies initiating the CSR activities, a shortage of trained personnel to implement effectively the CSR initiatives and difficulty to reach out rural areas as major challenges for the implementation of CSR activities.

Albeit being a fairly new concept in India, CSR emerged as a fundamental business practice focusing on the alignment of disclosures and the social value system with the corporate business strategies and operations. Recognised as a means of charity in the earlier days, CSR is presently considered an integral part of corporate strategy by Indian firms across several industries (Rahman & Singh, 2019). According to (Tandon & Gupta, 2019), CSR activities in India were initially confined to one time financial aids while neglecting the stakeholders' need. Nowadays, Indian businesses are engaged in myriad CSR activities including environmental CSR, community-based CSR, and philanthropy. These engagements take the form of the introduction of the latest techniques and processes to reduce waste and pollution and encourage the adoption of processes that are not only environment friendly but also contribute to social and educational upliftment. The legal framework regulating CSR in India has been a major driver for the implementation of CSR activities. For example, CSR became more apparent with the enactment of the Companies Act (2013) which aimed at promoting greater transparency and disclosure of CSR activities. Section 135 of the Companies Act provides that any company registered and functioning as a corporate unit in India should offer 2% of its total profit while Schedule 7 of the Act makes provisions for the mandatory responsibility of the company towards the community and the environment (both ecological and social). According to Shira (2021), CSR spending by Indian firms significantly increased following the applicability of mandatory CSR provisions in 2014. For instance, in 2018, a 47% increase (US$1 billion) was registered in the corporates' contribution to CSR initiatives compared to the year 2014-2015 (Shira, 2021). Moreover, in 2019, 76% of the companies spent 2% or more on CSR activities while the number of firms having a CSR foundation has increased from 6 in the year 2014-2015 to 18 in the 2018-2019 (KPMG, 2020).

In India, several studies have been carried before and after the insertion of Section 135 in the Companies Act to assess the impact of CSR on corporate performance. For example, before the amendment brought in the Companies Act, a study by (Mishra & Suar, 2010) on the Indian stock-listed companies showed that a favorable perception of managers existed towards CSR's positively significant impact on the corporates' financial performance. However, empirical studies conducted after the amendments of the Companies Act revealed mixed results. (Garg, 2016) concluded that the relationship between CSR performance and corporate performance of Indian firms was positively significant. (Aggarwal, 2021), on the contrary, concluded that mandatory CSR expenditure negatively impacts companies' profitability.

Industrial Revolution- From Water and Steam-Powered Mechanical Manufacturing to Digitalization (Industry 4.0)

Alongside human development, technological and technical advancements in the methods of production have evolved rapidly over the last decades. Starting from the first industrial revolution in the 18th century (with the introduction of water and steam-powered mechanical manufacturing facilities) till the 21st century, methods of production have continuously evolved intelligently. For example, the second industrial revolution (at the beginning of the 20th century) has witnessed the replacement of steam-powered mechanical manufacturing by electrically powered production together with the intensive application of division of labour. The integration of IT and electronics into production in the 1970s has been another important milestone in the development of production techniques which was subsequently named the third industrial revolution. Later, the need to have smart factories that optimize resources through smart production techniques led to the creation of Industry 4.0. The industry 4.0 concept which was first coined in Germany in 2011, radically transformed production systems by integrating sophisticated technologies such as robotics, Artificial Intelligence (AI), Augmented Reality (AR)/Virtual Reality (VR), 5G mobile communication, Internet of Things (IT), big data analytics, simulation, and sensors. The integration of these advanced technology into the production systems has proved to be highly beneficial to the firm in terms of improved flexibility, reduction in costs and the possibility to offer customized products (Mohamed, 2018:256)

Industry 4.0 and CSR Disclosure

According to (Caputo, Paiano & Foltynowicz, 2019:152), there is a close link between Industry 4.0 and CSR which opens up scope for thought and actions to reduce the negative impact of corporate activities on the firm's long-term performance and trust building with stakeholders. Although these technologies are likely to contribute to the achievement of the 17 Sustainable Development Goals (SDGs) through sustainable use of both the human and national resources, many developing countries fear that their attractiveness (low-cost status) may be threatened. This is so because firms will no longer rely on the low labour cost countries to increase their competitive power. Moreover, the introduction of these smart technologies will also have an impact on the livelihood of many unskilled people as Industry 4.0 will create jobs that require IT-based skills. Moreover, the introduction of innovation technology will lead to a situation where the workforce will represent a smaller proportion of the total cost. The situation is more daunting for India where labour, in particular, unskilled women in both rural and urban, are more likely to be replaced by an ICT-based system. For example, sensor-based IoT technologies in the agricultural sector will lead to the lay-off of many people. Similarly, other processes in the manufacturing sector such as packaging and inventory management will be replaced by technology-driven devices. Although Industry 4.0 is perceived to bring economic benefits to the firms, other stakeholders opine that this industrial transformation will worsen the unemployment situation due to the increase in the world's population.

It is apparent that from a sustainability and stakeholders' standpoint, firms should not narrow down their focus solely to the economic benefits of their activities while ignoring the social and environmental impact. As firms are becoming increasingly responsible towards society, they are integrating social reports into financial statements. Social reports generally include information on employment, social relations, and the environment. As women will be more vulnerable to the introduction of robotics at the workplace, it is deemed appropriate for firms to disclose information on the (i) impact of Industry 4.0 on employment and livelihood of women and (ii) the accompanying measures to mitigate the negative impact on their lives. On the other hand, given that female directors are generally more sensitive to women's distress, there is a high probability that their presence in board rooms improves the board's decision and social disclosures, in particular, the impact of Industry 4.0 on women participation in the workforce. However, the question of whether "Female directors influence board room decisions or CSR disclosure?" has been subject to much debate.

Gender Balance in Corporate Directorship and its Impact on Firm's Financial Performance

Female representation in board rooms has received the attention of many researchers over the years. Much of the studies aimed at investigating the impact of women on board inputs and firm outcomes. Board diversity (as determined by the members' age, gender, work experience, ethnicity, and nationality among others) enhances the quality of the board (Osariemen *et al.*, 2018). It is widely accepted that a heterogeneous group of people on board (i) improves decision making, (ii) ensures that stakeholders' rights are safeguarded (through multiple diversity dynamism), and (iii) encourages voluntary disclosure. Among the different board members' demographic variables that can potentially influence a firm's financial performance, gender has received considerable attention from researchers, policymakers, and professionals. Existing literature posits the fact that the quality of boards' decisions is likely to elevate with the presence of women in top-level management. For instance, (Adams and Ferreira, 2009) consider that organizational success is largely dependent on the active role played by female directors in monitoring performance. They further consider that female director represents a reservoir of skills, knowledge, and competencies which is completely different from male directors. On the other hand, some studies have concluded that diversity may not always yield positive outcomes, in particular when the person does not believe in the functioning and effectiveness of a diverse workgroup.

Policy decisions to increase the ratio of female directors on the company boards vary from country to country. In some countries, myriad non-binding policies have been introduced by the government to increase the number of females (Pucheta-Martínez, Bel-Oms, & Olcina-Sempere, 2018) while in countries such as Spain, Australia, Japan, and the UK, gender quota law has been enacted to regulate women's participation on boards. Further many firms around the world have voluntarily changed board composition to achieve gender representation on corporate boards (Yarram & Adapa, 2021). The Institute of Chartered Accountants of England and Wales in 2017 enumerates the reasons leading to the importance of GD: (i) effectiveness of the management is eyed with doubt in case of uneven GD on the board, (ii) governance is easily accepted by the society and (iii) diversity enables a sound understanding of the working of the business and enhances the rigor. On the other hand, the issue of board diversity has, over the years, triggered the attention of academics and researchers in the field of corporate governance (Rao & Tilt, 2015).

The initiatives undertaken by the top management to increase the female ratio on the board's directorships have grabbed the attention of many scholars over the years. Several studies have been conducted to analyze the impact of board GD on (i) enhanced adoption of CSR (Rafique, Al-Mamun); (ii) CSR reporting and firm's value (Issa *et al.*, 2019) amongst others. Existing literature shows that the mere presence of women on boards improves the board's consistency, promotes board strategic control, and lessens conflicts (Benkraiem *et al.*, 2017). Other business areas that have been enhanced by board diversity include financial performance, innovation, and governance quality.

Empirical studies have further demonstrated that board GD positively influenced the value of Kuwaiti firms (Issa *et al.*, 2019) and the performance of Turkish firms (Karamahmutoğlu & Kuzey, 2016) and Singaporean firms (Duppati, Rao, Matlani, Scrimgeour, & Patnaik, 2020). In a similar vein, (Bae & Skaggs, 2019) associate the productivity of Korean firms to GD in management. In a similar vein, (Beji, Yousfi, Loukil, & Omri, 2020) note that women, in general, tend to bring new vision and perceptions on issues related to CSR in particular human rights.

Nevertheless, the presence of females onboard has not always led to expected results in a few cases. (Bøhren & Staubo, 2014) found that mandatory gender balance in Norway led to either inefficient organizational forms or inefficient boards. Another study by (Gallego-Álvarez, García-Sánchez, & Rodríguez-Dominguez, 2010) among Spanish listed firms revealed that GD did not influence corporate performance be it in terms of marketing or accounting measures. Moreover, several studies have shown that improved female's board representation did not contribute to the financial performance of (i) Italian corporates (Provasi & Harasheh, 2021) (ii) Indonesian listed companies (Satria, Mahadwartha, & Ernawati, 2020), and (iii) Dutch firms (Marinova, Plantenga, & Remery, 2016)

Female Directors and CSR Reporting

On average, the female directors are involved in more diverse roles in organizational setups as compared to men as they work in both corporate and social organizations such as NGOs, while men tend to specialize in a narrow field of expertise. They tend to be more inclined towards the social aspects such as CSR when compared to men. Some authors noted that the paths of women leaders are usually longer and more arduous as compared to their male colleagues, and this notion is also backed by various authors. The main limitations in this respect are mostly with the cultural norms and gender discrimination. Physical traits such as appearance and type dressing are also scrutinized when they appear for higher job positions. They usually face discrimination, as many roles are considered to be only for men, which leads them to develop more sympathy towards social considerations such as fair treatment, transparency of systems, and social activities, which benefits a wide range of stakeholders such type of actions also strengthens the CSR performance of the organizations in which they work. The presence of women in power positions such as the board of directors also allows them to be more objective towards the existing CSR activities of the organization and they tend to be more scrutinizing towards the general CSR activities, and thus they are better able to root out any negative CSR activities. Thus, the improvement in GD may improve not only the level of CSR activities but also improve the overall positive impact of such activities

Gender Diversity in CSR Committees in the Indian Context

Before 2013, women who are constituting approx. 27% of the labour force and are holding more than 45% of university degrees were not even holding a mere 5% of the directorships in India. Intending to enhance and encourage female participation on board, the Indian government introduced a mandate which required a minimum of one woman on the BOD of listed and certain other companies. The Companies Act (2013) was accordingly amended to give effect to the government's decisions. Subsequently, as a response to the mandate, nearly 600 companies announced the appointments of women directors. KPMG (2020) notes that the percentage of women in CSR committees has increased by 9% in 2020 compared to the financial year 2016-2017. Moreover, in 2020 the percentage of women as Chairperson of CSR committees has registered a slight increase (1%) to reach 38% compared to the year 2016-2017. Although these figures are encouraging in showcasing a paradigm shift towards the inclusion of women on boards, the corporate world, post-2013, has experienced a surge in the debate on the number of women participating in the corporate boards as well as their contribution to board decisions.

CSR disclosure

The Board report remains an important means of communication by the BOD of a company with its stakeholders. The board report provides key information on the performance of the firm, changes in the management structure, future orientation, committees composition, and the distribution of profits amongst others. These disclosures aim at building and enhancing the trust between the corporates, their key stakeholders, and the communities. Disclosure of non-financial information, in particular, CSR disclosures has, over the years, received increased attention as a result of the growing demand for information on the businesses' activities within the economic, environmental and social spheres. CSR disclosure has, indeed, emerged as an important tool to interact with the stakeholders including society. Standard CSR disclosures include information on the societal, economic, and environmental implications of the organization's strategy. According to (Cho, Kang, Lee, & Park, 2020), CSR disclosure aims at providing non-financials information on the governance, environmental activities, relationship with employees, and other social activities to both the internal and external stakeholders. Although CSR disclosure is voluntary in many countries, extant literature widely accepts a significant relationship of CSR disclosure of the corporate and its financial performance. Several studies have confirmed that the firm sends a positive signal to investors when it voluntarily discloses its CSR activities. This is so because CSR disclosure practices not only provide information on how transparent the firm is but also demonstrates the firm's commitment to CSR performance. According to (Lawal, May, & Stahl, 2017), CSR disclosure provides a competitive edge and complements the company's goodwill and intangible asset contributing significantly to the sustainability of the company.

In India, CSR disclosures have been made mandatory by the government of India by the amendment of the Companies Act (2013) and inclusion of Section 134 which requires the companies to disclose details about all CSR activities which have been undertaken during the financial year. According to KPMG (2020), the number of companies disclosing details of CSR initiatives has increased by 325% following the amendments to the Companies Act. KPMG (2020) further reports that one in every three companies has already aligned their annual disclosure on CSR to SDGs.

Board Diversity and CSR Disclosure

The BOD plays an indispensable role in an organization. (Nicholson & Newton, 2010) categorized the roles of the board into four, namely (i) the control role (i.e., supervising management and protecting shareholders), (ii) the service role (counselling and advising executives), (iii) strategy role (approval, monitoring, and reviewing strategy) and (iv) access to resource role (providing the company with access to resources). Several connotations have been used to determine the effectiveness of the board such as "adding value to the organization", "assisting the company to move closer to its goals" and "working in the interest of the shareholders/stakeholders". Moreover, the board of directors is considered as a strategic resource in improving the firms' relationships with relevant stakeholders through CSR disclosure.

The impact of GD on disclosures of CSR activities has been widely discussed in the literature. Several studies such as (Harjoto & Rossi, 2019) and (Khan, Khan, & Asim Afridi, 2021) have concluded and strongly confirmed a positively significant influence exerted by women on corporate boards on CSR disclosure. For example, Widyasari and Ayunda (2020) found that female directors having a financial expertise tend to report objectively the firms' CSR activities. In a similar vein, (Tapver, Laidroo, & Gurvitš-Suits, 2020) have advocated a notion that the presence of women on board broadens the horizons of the company's diversity and discussion as they tend to implement their family values and sentiments as a wife and mother to the corporates otherwise very professional environment. Extant literature posits that a highly diversified board is witnessed to be all the more eager and willing to engage in social practices and CSR reporting. Empirical studies have also found that countries exhibiting a higher proportion of diversified boards of directors exhibited higher levels of CSR reporting. The stakeholder theory posits that companies have a high responsibility to the stakeholders, both internal and external. According to the Encyclopaedia of 2013 CSR reporting "refers to a company's systematic disclosure of information on its social performance. The term social performance is understood in a broad sense and refers to social, environmental, and governance issues that are typically not covered by financial performance metrics". According to (Tapver, Laidroo, & Gurvitš-Suits, 2020), corporates having a highly female-centric board composition would be more inclined towards CSR towards specific stakeholders and shall also engage in extensive CSR disclosure. They further note that gender-diverse boards tend to develop stronger relationships with shareholders, communities, and other stakeholders through their active contribution to issues. However, (Vinnicombe *et al.* 2008) note that corporate governance may not be achieved when women are persistently underrepresented on boards or when they are serving the boards in token number. A similar conclusion was drawn by (Rupley, Brown, & Marshall, 2012b) who averred that the presence of only one woman on the board limits her willingness to express freely her opinion on social, environmental, and ethical issues. Moreover, (Gallén & Peraita, 2017) posit that an increased number of women on board leads to better dissemination of information about environmental and ethical issues.

The on-board diversity and its influence on the disclosures of CSR activities have been tested empirically in different contexts. (Hoang, Abeysekera, & Ma, 2018) have found a significant positive impact of GD-on-the boards and CSR disclosure among Vietnamese firms. Similar findings were noted among Pakistani firms (Khan, Khan & Şentürk, 2019) and Australian (Rao & Tilt, 2016). However, a negative association has been found between female directorship and CSR disclosures amongst Bangladeshi firms (Muttakin, Khan & Subramaniam, 2015). Given that the results of existing studies are mixed and indecisive, (Rao & Tilt, 2016) commend further studies to analyze the influence of GD on CSR reporting.

Although extant literature widely acknowledges the relationship between the presence of women on boards and improved CSR (CSR) disclosure, little is known about this relationship in the Indian context. In this study, the author analyses the impact of GD on CSR disclosure. Section 149 of the Companies Act (2013) provides that there shall be at least one woman director on its board for a certain class of companies as prescribed. Since literature widely accepts the positive relationship between CSR reporting and GD, the following hypothesis has been formulated in this study:

Ho: There is an insignificant relationship between GD and CSR reporting.

H1: There is a positive significant relationship between GD and CSR reporting.

RESEARCH METHODOLOGY

Sample Selection and Data Collection

To test the hypothesis of this study, 200 Indian publicly traded companies in the service sector are chosen from the list of 500 companies compiled by the Fortune India 500, using the Simple Random Sampling approach. The study covered the financial years 2020-21 and data on the disclosure of CSR activities and gender representation is retrieved from the annual reports of the said period. During the data collection process, two out of the 200 companies did not have a website, and 17 companies did not have any women on board. Content analysis has been used to acquire secondary data for 176 companies.

Measures

Dependent Variable: The current study's dependent variable is CSR disclosures, which is measured using an index that includes factors such as the Business Responsibility Report, CSR Policy, Corporate Sustainable Report, Special CSR page, CSR Contact Details, Quality Policy, and Environmental Health and Safety Policy/Report. A value of 0 is assigned if a company disclosed/reported the CSR activities, and a value of 1 is assigned if the company did not disclose/report its CSR activities.

Explanatory Variables: The authors considered the percentage of women on boards to the total number of directors (GD) and board size (total number of directors on board) following prior studies. On the one hand, boards with a high number of directors are more likely to have agency issues and be less interested in information transparency. More board members, on the other hand, would result in a wider exchange of ideas and experiences, and hence better counsel.

Control Variables: Firm Size is defined by the total number of assets of a corporation (Marquis & Lee, 2013).

Statistical technique

Using IBM SPSS vs. 22, multiple regression is used in this investigation to find the best-suited variables.

DATA ANALYSIS

Table 1 shows the industries in which the sampled companies operate. As the companies were drawn randomly from the pre-defined list of companies compiled by Fortune India 500, it is evident that they are operating in different industries of the Indian economy. Companies operating in diverse industries (Iron & Steel, Industrial Equipment, Wholesale Trade, Ports & Logistics, Power, Retail Trade, Storage Batteries, Basic Materials, Auto Ancillaries, Gems & Jewellery, Sugar, etc) have been clustered under "Others" and represent the majority of the sample (N=73, 46%).

The central tendency and dispersion statistics are presented in table 2. Table 3 shows the Pearson correlation among the study's measures, which shows a negative and negligible association of CSR with GD (-0.32;0.561) and Firm Size (-0.64;0.251), as well as a positive and significant association with Board Size (-0.64;0.251). (0.141;0.011).

Table 1. Distribution of sample firms by type of industries

Sectors	Frequency (N)	%
Capital Goods	9	5.11
Iron & Steel	3	1.70
Banking	19	10.80
Pharma	12	6.82
Cement	3	1.70
NBFC	2	1.14
FMCG	15	8.52
Telecom	4	2.27
Construction	5	2.84
Chemicals	7	3.98
Food	3	1.70
HealthCare	3	1.70
Infotech	5	2.84
Infra Development	3	1.70
Auto	10	5.68
Others	73	41.48
Total	**176**	**100.00**

Source: SPSS

Table 2. Descriptive Statistics

Variables	Minimum	Maximum	Mean	Std. Deviation
GD	6.67	66.67	16.4	8.2
Board Size	3.0	18.0	9.781	2.7
CSR	5.00	10.00	8.9347	.98

Source: SPSS

Table 3. Correlations

		CSR	GD	Board Size	Firm Size
CSR	Pearson Correlation	1	-.032	.141*	-.064
	Sig. (2-tailed)		.561	.011	.251

Source: SPSS

Table 4. Multiple Regression Analysis

Model		B	t-value	Sig. value
	Intercept	17.005	.612	.541
	GD	.002	.223	.824
	Board Size	.060	2.833	.005
	Firm Size	-.110	-1.297	.195
R^2			0.210	

Source: SPSS

Table 4 shows the regression value or coefficient of determination (R^2) is 0.210 which implies that only 21% of variance has been explained by each independent variable in the present model and the GD (sig. = 0.824) has a positive but insignificant influence on CSR Disclosures, whereas Board Size (sig.= 0.005) has a substantial and favourable impact on CSR Disclosures, and Firm Size (sig. = 0.195) has a negative and negligible impact.

CONCLUSION

As Industry 4.0 will directly impact women's employment across several industries in India, in particular labour-intensive industries, firms should provide the right accompanying measures (training and compensation) to them as part of their social responsibility. It is believed that being a wife and mother, female directors are more likely to safeguard the rights the women at the workplace and in society. However, this can only be achieved if their voices are heard in the board rooms. This study aimed at analyzing the impact of female directorship on CSR disclosures. Drawing from existing literature, the authors hypothesized that the presence of women will improve CSR disclosure. Contrary to our expectations, the findings revealed that female directorship did not have a significant impact on the firms' CSR disclosure. This finding is consistent with (Muttakin *et al.*, 2015) study. It can be further concluded from the findings that men tend to overlook the contribution of women in board rooms.

Although these findings do not add to the current study on the causal effect of GD on CSR disclosures, they do contribute to the current literature on the impact of board size on CSR disclosures. During the data collection, it is discovered that all of the 200 listed sample companies have only met the bare minimum of having one woman on board as prescribed by Section 149 of the Companies Act (2013). There were fewer companies with more than two women on the board. As a result, the authors concluded that board size (total number of directors) has a strong link with CSR disclosures, but not with GD. According to a recent report from "The HINDU" dated April 26th, 2021, the government said that every firm must join hands to empower women to boost GDP. In addition, the survey indicated that women make up 22 percent of the workforce in India, compared to 50 percent in other countries. By 2029, if MNCs and small businesses join forces with women in the market, economic growth (GDP) will be in the billions. In comparison, companies with more women gained 22% greater productivity, 40% greater customer retention, and 27% more revenues.

Another pertinent finding of the study is the substantial and favorable impact of Board Size (sig.= 0.005) on CSR Disclosures. This finding is consistent with existing studies which suggest that a higher number of directors in board rooms tends to improve the quality of discussions and decision-making on several strategic issues including CSR reporting. Moreover, larger boards are recognized to exercise more control and to adopt a multi stakeholder's approach in decision-making. However, deciding on the appropriate board size to ensure effective decisions has been subject to much debate for several years. A smaller size board is perceived to be more effective due to better coordination and improved communications among members. On the other hand, larger boards often face the problems associated with free riding, communication, and conflicts which reduce the efficiency of the board.

PRACTICAL IMPLICATIONS

Several studies have demonstrated that GD on boards contributes to the improvement of a firm's financial and non-financial reporting. Therefore, to enhance the level of CSR reporting practices among Indian firms in the industry 4.0 context, the government should further amend the Company Act to provide for a higher proportion of women on the corporate board presently Section 149 of the Companies Act (2013) provides for at least one woman director on boards. Several studies have demonstrated that women's performance is harshly judged when they are underrepresented on boards. For example, (Rupley *et al.*, 2012) found that conditions of openness and inclusion are faded when the number of women in boardrooms is inferior to men. According to (Vinnicombe *et al.*, 2008), a minimum of three women on board can positively contribute to the board's decisions and governance. In a similar vein, (Rao and Tilt, 2015) found that CSR is favourably considered by a board that comprises of three or more three female directors while other studies have demonstrated that an increased number of women on board influences both financial performance and reporting.

At the firm's level, it is recommended that firms honestly disclose the economic, social, and environmental impact that the transition to IT-based solutions may have on the livelihood of the people. The community will, thus, be morally prepared to face the new challenges in the technological era. Information on the accompanying measures should also be disclosed as part of the moral obligations towards stakeholders affected by Industry 4.0. Furthermore, firms should also voluntarily take initiatives to enhance board diversity to (i) promote a higher level of CSR disclosure as well as to (ii) enhance the quality of the firm's strategic decision. The authors consider that the firms are likely to meet the expectations of different stakeholders through a fair representation of women on boards. Moreover, a gender-balanced representation on boards may ensure that decision-making is not dominated by an individual or a small group of individuals. Besides, the appointment of women in different committees including the audit and governance committees can empower them to make the right decisions while gauging their influence on the board. Another way of empowering women on board is to break the glass ceiling which is prevalent in Indian society. Moreover, since the board of directors represents a pool of social capital and the quality of the decisions resides on the competency of the member, it is recommended that the appointment of board members, including female directors, is solely based on the merit (qualifications and experience). This will ensure that independent, innovative, and credible decisions are taken by women directors. Similarly, some decisions require a higher level of intellectual ability and advanced technical skills that can be found in highly qualified board members. A study by (Smith *et al.*, 2006) found that the qualifications of female directors positively contribute to the firm performance. Finally, on their appointment, women directors should understand that they have a key role in safeguarding stakeholders' interests rather than just complying with the legal provisions of the Companies Act.

LIMITATIONS OF THE STUDY

Like all studies, this study also suffers from certain limitations. The first limitation pertains to the time frame of the study. Since our analysis covers a specific period i.e.,2021, it is not deemed appropriate to extrapolate the findings over other periods. It is, therefore, recommended that future studies use a longitudinal approach to cover a longer time frame. These studies should, inter alia, assess the evolution of the women directorship in Indian firms and analyze such evolution on CSR disclosure. The second limitation relates to the scope of the study. Since this study relates to the service sector, the authors consider that generalization of the findings across other industries may not be appropriate. Hence, future studies can consider firms from different industries to determine if significant differences exist across industries concerning GD and CSR disclosures. Moreover, the authors believe that since a fair representation of women on boards may not always guarantee CSR disclosures due to the differences in the personal characteristics of board members, it is recommended that future studies explore the extent to which the characteristics of women directors (age, education level, and experience) influence CSR reporting and other strategic decisions.

REFERENCES

Adams, R. B., & Ferreira, D. (2009). Women in the Boardroom and their Impact on Governance and Performance. *Journal of Financial Economics*, *94*(2), 291–309. doi:10.1016/j.jfineco.2008.10.007

Aggarwal, P. (2021). Impact of mandatory corporate social responsibility on corporate financial performance: The Indian experience. *Social Responsibility Journal*. Advance online publication. doi:10.1108/SRJ-09-2020-0394

Azman, H., & Mustapha, M. (2018). Benefits and challenges of corporate social responsibility implementations: Evidence from manufacturing sector in Malaysia. *International Journal of Engineering & Technology, 7*, 215-218.

Bae, K. B., & Skaggs, S. (2019). The impact of gender diversity on performance: The moderating role of industry, alliance network, and family-friendly policies – Evidence from Korea. *Journal of Management & Organization*, *25*(6), 896–913. doi:10.1017/jmo.2017.45

Beji, R., Yousfi, O., Loukil, N., & Omri, A. (2020). Board diversity and corporate social responsibility: Empirical evidence from France. *Journal of Business Ethics*. Advance online publication. doi:10.100710551-020-04522-4

Benkraiem, R., Hamrouni, A., Lakhal, F., & Toumi, N. (2017). Board independence, gender diversity, and CEO compensation. Corporate Governance: The International. *Journal of Business and Society*, *17*(5), 845–860.

Bøhren, Ø., & Staubo, S. (2014). Does mandatory gender balance work? Changing organizational form to avoid board upheaval. *Journal of Corporate Finance*, *28*, 152–168. doi:10.1016/j.jcorpfin.2013.12.005

Caputo, D., Paiano, A., & Foltynowicz, Z. (2019). Corporate social responsibility for industry 4.0. the case study of the Italian company operating in Poland. *Proceedings from the Basiq International Conference "New Trends in Sustainable Business and Consumption."*

Chaudhary, M., Sodani, P. R., & Das, S. (2020). Effect of COVID-19 on the economy in India: Some reflections for policy and programme. *Journal of Health Management, 22*(2), 169–180. doi:10.1177/0972063420935541

Cho, S. Y., Kang, P. K., Lee, C., & Park, C. K. (2020). Financial reporting conservatism and voluntary CSR disclosure. SSRN *Electronic Journal*. doi:10.2139/ssrn.3556255

Companies Act 2013. (n.d.). http://ebook.mca.gov.in/Actpagedisplay.aspx?PAGENAME=17923

Duppati, G., Rao, N. V., Matlani, N., Scrimgeour, F., & Patnaik, D. (2020). Gender diversity and firm performance: Evidence from India and Singapore. *Applied Economics, 52*(14), 1553–1565. doi:10.1080/00036846.2019.1676872

Encyclopedia of Corporate Social Responsibility. (2013). *Definition of CSR reporting*. Retrieved from https://linkF.springer.com/referenceworkentry/10.1007%2F978-3-642-28036-8_145

Gallego-Álvarez, I., García-Sánchez, I. M., & Rodríguez-Dominguez, L. (2010). The influence of gender diversity on corporate performance. *Revista de Contabilidad, 13*(1), 53–88. doi:10.1016/S1138-4891(10)70012-1

Gallén, M. L., & Peraita, C. (2017). The relationship between femininity and sustainability reporting: Femininity and sustainability reporting. *Corporate Social Responsibility and Environmental Management, 24*(6), 496–508. doi:10.1002/csr.1423

Garg, P. (2016). CSR and corporate performance: Evidence from India. *Decision (Washington, D.C.), 43*(4), 333–349.

Gender Diversity Survey – 2020 Proxy Season Results. (n.d.). *Fenwick & West LLP*. https://www.fenwick.com/insights/publications/gender-diversity-survey-2020-proxy-season-results

Harjoto, M. A., & Rossi, F. (2019). Religiosity, female directors, and corporate social responsibility for Italian listed companies. *Journal of Business Research, 95*, 338–346. doi:10.1016/j.jbusres.2018.08.013

Hoang, T. C., Abeysekera, I., & Ma, S. (2018). Board diversity and corporate social disclosure: Evidence from Vietnam. *Journal of Business Ethics, 151*(3), 833–852. doi:10.100710551-016-3260-1

India Brand Equity Foundation. (2021). *Services Sector in India*. Retrieved on 8 July 2021 from https://www.ibef.org/industry/services.aspx

Issa, A., Hanaysha, J., Elfeky, M., & Ullah, I. (2019). The Impact of Board Gender Diversity on Firm Value: Evidence from Kuwait. *International Journal of Applied Science and Research*, *2*(1), 1–21.

Karamahmutoğlu, M. L., & Kuzey, C. (2016). The effect of board gender diversity on firm performance: Evidence from Turkey. *Gender in Management*, *31*(7), 434–455. doi:10.1108/GM-10-2015-0088

Keeping the gender diversity conversation going – Women. (n.d.). https://www.hotelierindia.com/business/13878-keeping-the-gender-diversity-conversation-going

Khan, I., Khan, I., & Asim Afridi, M. (2021). Does board diversity matter for the quality of CSR disclosure? Evidence from the financial sector of Pakistan. *Review of Business Management*, 104–126.

Khan, I., Khan, I., & Şentürk, I. (2019). Board diversity and quality of CSR disclosure: evidence from Pakistan. In *Corporate Governance*. Emerald Publishing Limited.

KPMG. (2020). *Towards gender-balanced boards*. Retrieved from http://www.kpmg.com/IN

Lawal, E., May, G., & Stahl, B. (2017). The significance of corporate social disclosure for high-tech manufacturing companies: Focus on employee and community aspects of sustainable development: Significance of corporate social disclosure for high-tech companies. *Corporate Social Responsibility and Environmental Management*, *24*(4), 295–311. doi:10.1002/csr.1397

Majmudar, U., Rana, N., & Sanan, N. (2015). *India's Top Companies for CSR & Sustainability*. Indian Institute of Management, Udaipur. Retrieved from https://www.iimu.ac.in/upload_data/main_containts/about/SocialResponsibility/IIMU_CSR_REPORT.pdf

Marinova, J., Plantenga, J., & Remery, C. (2016). Gender diversity and firm performance: Evidence from Dutch and Danish boardrooms. *International Journal of Human Resource Management*, *27*(15), 1777–1790. doi:10.1080/09585192.2015.1079229

Marquis, C., & Lee, M. (2013). Who is governing whom? Executives, governance, and the structure of generosity in large US firms. *Strategic Management Journal*, *34*(4), 483–497. doi:10.1002mj.2028

Masum, A., Abdul Aziz, H. H. H. A., & Ahmad, M. H. (2020). Corporate Social Responsibility and its Effect on Community Development: An Overview. *IOSR Journal of Business and Management, 22*(1).

Mishra, S., & Saur, D. (2010). Does Corporate Social Responsibility Influence Firm Performance of Indian Companies? *Journal of Business Ethics*, *95*(4), 571–601. doi:10.100710551-010-0441-1

Mohamed, M. (2018). Challenges and Benefits of Industry 4.0: An overview. *International Journal of Supply and Operations Management*, *5*(3), 256–265.

Muttakin, M. B., Khan, A., & Subramaniam, N. (2015). Firm characteristics, board diversity and corporate social responsibility: Evidence from Bangladesh. *Pacific Accounting Review*, *27*(3), 353–372. doi:10.1108/PAR-01-2013-0007

NationalC. S. R. Portal. (n.d.). https://csr.gov.in/index20.php

Nicholson, G., & Newton, C. (2010). The role of the board of directors: Perceptions of managerial elites. *Journal of Management & Organization*, *16*(2), 204–218. doi:10.5172/jmo.16.2.204

Osariemen, A., Edosa, J. A., Uwuigbe, U., & Uwuigbe, O. R. (2018). Audit committee attributes and audit quality: A benchmark analysis. *Business: Theory and Practice*, *19*(0), 37–48. doi:10.3846/btp.2018.05

Pollitzer, E. (2017). *Will the '4th Industrial Revolution' be gender-blind?* Elsevier. Retrieved on July 7, 2020, from https://www.elsevier.com/connect/will-the-4th-industrial-revolution-be-gender-blind

Provasi, R., & Harasheh, M. (2021). Gender diversity and corporate performance: Emphasis on sustainability performance. *Corporate Social Responsibility and Environmental Management*, *28*(1), 127–137. doi:10.1002/csr.2037

Pucheta-Martínez, M. C., Bel-Oms, I., & Olcina-Sempere, G. (2018). The association between board gender diversity and financial reporting quality, corporate performance and corporate social responsibility disclosure: A literature review. *Academia (Caracas)*, *31*(1), 177–194. doi:10.1108/ARLA-04-2017-0110

Rafique, Q., Al-Mamun, A., & Ahmed, I. (2017). Corporate Social Responsibility and Gender Diversity: Insights from the Asia Pacific: Gender Diversity, Corporate Social Responsibility. *Corporate Social Responsibility and Environmental Management*, *24*(3), 210–221. Advance online publication. doi:10.1002/csr.1400

Rahman, D., & Singh, R. (2019). An overview of CSR taken by TATA Group. *International Journal of Developmental Research*, *9*(1).

Rao, K., & Tilt, C. (2016). Board diversity and CSR reporting: An Australian study. *Meditari Accountancy Research*, *24*(2), 182–210. doi:10.1108/MEDAR-08-2015-0052

Rupley, K. H., Brown, D., & Marshall, R. S. (2012a). Governance, media, and the quality of environmental disclosure. *Journal of Accounting and Public Policy*, *31*(6), 610–640. doi:10.1016/j.jaccpubpol.2012.09.002

Satria, Y., Mahadwartha, P. A., & Ernawati, E. (2020). The effect of gender diversity on company financial performance. In *Proceedings of the 17 Th International Symposium on Management (INSYMA 2020)*. Paris, France: Atlantis Press. 10.2991/aebmr.k.200127.094

Setthasakko, W. (2009, July 24). Barriers to implementing corporate environmental responsibility in Thailand. *The International Journal of Organizational Analysis*, *17*(3), 69–83. doi:10.1108/19348830910974905

Sharma, R., & Aggarwal, P. (2021). Impact of mandatory corporate social responsibility on corporate financial performance: The Indian experience. *Social Responsibility Journal*. doi:10.1108/SRJ-09-2020-0394

Shira, D. (2021). *Corporate Social Responsibility in India*. Retrieved on 7 July 2021 from https://www.india-briefing.com/news/corporate-social-responsibility-india-5511.html/

Smith, N., Smith, V., & Verner, M. (2006). Do Women in Top Management Affect Firm Performance? A Panel Study of 2,500 Danish Firms. *International Journal of Productivity and Performance Management*, *55*(5), 569–593. doi:10.1108/17410400610702160

Sundström, A., Hyder, A. S., & Chowdhury, E. H. (2020). Market-oriented CSR implementation in SMEs with sustainable innovations: An action research approach. *Baltic Journal of Management*, *15*(5), 775–795. doi:10.1108/BJM-03-2020-0091

Tandon, J., & Gupta, H. (2019). *A study of Corporate Social Responsibility (CSR) practices in select Indian companies with special reference to environmental aspects*. Paper presented at the National Conference on "Achieving excellence through sustainability and innovation" organized by Delhi Institute of Advanced Studies.

Tapver, T., Laidroo, L., & Gurvitš-Suits, N. A. (2020). Banks' CSR reporting – Do women have a say? *Corporate Governance*, *20*(4), 639–651. doi:10.1108/CG-11-2019-0338

Top 100 stocks by Market Capitalization: BSE Listed stocks Market Capitalization. (n.d.). https://www.bseindia.com/markets/equity/eqreports/topmarketcapitalization.aspx.com/markets/equity/eqreports/topmarketcapitalization.aspx

Tuokuu, F. X. D., & Dartey-Baah, A. (2016). Corporate social responsibility: Is it an alternative to the government? *Journal of Global Responsibility*, *7*(1), 26–38. doi:10.1108/JGR-05-2015-0007

Van Marrewijk, M. (2003). Concepts and definitions of CSR and corporate sustainability: Between agency and communion. *Journal of Business Ethics*, *44*(2), 95–105. doi:10.1023/A:1023331212247

Vinnicombe, S., Singh V., Burke, R.J., Bilimonia, D., & Huse, M. (2008). Women on Corporate Board of Directors. In *International Research and Practice*. Edward Elgar Publishing Ltd UK.

Widyasari, P. A., & Ayunda, N. F. (2020). CSR Reporting: Perspective of Female Audit Committee Having Financial Expertise. In *Proceedings of the 17th International Symposium on Management (INSYMA 2020)*. Atlantis Press.

Yarram, S. R., & Adapa, S. (2021). Board gender diversity and corporate social responsibility: Is there a case for critical mass? *Journal of Cleaner Production*, *278*, 123319. doi:10.1016/j.jclepro.2020.123319

Chapter 10
Cashless Society and Development of Gender-Friendly Services Through Mobile Wallet

Chammika Mallawaarachchi
General Sir John Kotelawala Defence University, Sri Lanka

ABSTRACT

In the recent past, the idea of mobile wallets was very new to the world, but it is now becoming popular due to the expansion and development of smartphones with robust and sophisticated facilities. However, the literature on mobile wallets does not deeply identify and discuss how gender is significant in the business world with the power of mobile wallets and how it is helping to adopt the best strategies to incorporate it into the business through e-commerce activities. Therefore, this research contributes to knowledge by exploring mobile wallet users in Sri Lanka from a gender perspective and their significance in business development. The research adopts a qualitative research method to gather the primary data with a case study strategy. So, the case study found that mobile wallet has many inhibitions constraining its adoption and diffusion about gender. Also, it found that mobile wallets provided many social benefits that contributed to overcoming most of the gender-exclusive activities in e-commerce.

DOI: 10.4018/978-1-7998-8594-8.ch010

INTRODUCTION

The era of the digital revolution has penetrated almost every aspect of human life and we are experiencing the 4th Industrial revolution which is evolving at an exponential rate. The development of the Internet and the emergence of e-commerce have a significant impact on online as well as offline shopping. It leads to a change in the traditional economic theory and practice. The era of the digital revolution has penetrated almost every aspect of human life. Similarly, ICT contributes significantly to the expansion of globalization. One of the simplest examples is the invention of mobile technology which offers much more than just being one of the primary sources of communication. At the same time, different ICT tools with mobile devices led to the inception of smartphones which has given the potential of managing various additional tasks apart from offering connectivity.

At its peak, Web 2.0 has created greater interactivity between multiple users while building numerous opportunities, especially for business. As a result, it brought new forms of communication among the business customers where they were able to exchange messages amongst one another quickly. It also created a pool of knowledge sharing and trading online. So, it was a convergence between the physical and virtual space where virtual is gradually overcoming the challenges which the physical tend to offer. Trading over the Internet is usually referred to as e-commerce which involves making financial transactions over the Internet, Web, and mobile applications in exchange for products or services (Qin, et.al 2014; Jackson, 2015; Mallawaarachchi, 2019). E-commerce also brought the idea of market-at-doorstep which allows the consumers to select from multiple varieties of online stores offering a diverse range of products through a single window of operation is a big game-changer for the existing markets all across the globe. Now the consumer is no longer limited to the geographical boundaries rather they are exposed to such a space where knowledge on any kind of commodity situated anywhere across the globe, could be accessed at any point in time via ICT. So, technology and standards of data transfer over the Internet have become a universal medium of business information exchange and in many ways have defined business principles in the field of e-commerce. Therefore, in a broad sense, electronic commerce is an entrepreneurial activity that implements commercial transactions with the use of electronic means of data exchange.

In addition, e-commerce covers commercial transactions carried out with the help of information networks to transfer rights to use a product or service (Laudon & Traver, 2007; Mallawaarachchi, 2014). However, Information technology is a reality of the modern economy, and entrepreneurship is inconceivable without electronic trading methods, without sales promotion on the Internet. The use of the Internet radically transforms the processes of economic cooperation between the companies and their customers, partners, suppliers, and even competitors. Methods and means of carrying out commercial transactions in e-commerce are somewhat different from those carried out in the real economy (Albadr, 2003).

Therefore, the idea of mobile-based payments is introduced as a new platform for the global markets as a means of exchange of goods and services and also as a payment method. Man has sought to evolve the means of exchange to such a progressive stage where the sale and purchase of goods and services have been made as easy and convenient as possible. From the traditional modes of barter system to the gradual shift to minted coins and later on to gold and currency and plastic cards are some of the clear indicators on how man has utilized the knowledge in making different kinds of exchange of commodities and services within domestic and beyond, possible with lesser complications.

However, in today-world, Smartphone has become an important part of everyday life. As it has become more affordable, the number of Smartphone users has increased dramatically. The quantity of Smartphone consumers surpassed 1 billion in 2012 (eMarketer, 2014). Along with Smartphone production, plenty of services have been created to utilize the possible functions of Smartphone. Not only Smartphone is used as communication devices but also be used as socialized tools, entertainment tools, Internet access tools, and even payment tools (Rajgopal, 2012; Mallawaarachchi, 2015). With this development, mobile users can nowadays use their smartphones to make money transactions or payments by using applications installed on the phone. Besides payment, people can also store receipts, coupons, business cards, the bill on their smartphones.

A smartphone can function as a leather wallet due to the rise of mobile-based payment which is the revolutionary step in the expansion of business. Mobile phones, from being an instrument for communication to a tool to allow monetary exchange, complement the idea of a global wallet. Now individuals are no longer dependent upon the physical forms of money. Today, the consumer can at any point of time access currency of any value and any region as quickly and conveniently as one can imagine. Mobile-based transactions, such as mobile banking, remote purchases, person-to-person transfer, and point-of-scale transactions are some of the important features accessible to the individual in today's age.

However, the finance sector in the digital environment is experiencing a digital divide higher than predicted by digital marketers. Also, there is a persistent gender gap in access to basic accounts in the financial system, where 72% of men have access to an account while only 65% of women have an account; this gender gap is unchanged since 2011 (Global Banking Alliance for Women, 2018). Further, the study shows that closing the gender gap in financial inclusion could have positive effects on various activities in businesses. Such activities are ample from consumption to facilitating new business opportunities. Therefore, equal gender inclusion may especially contribute to their growth not only by building businesses but also by better managing their financial resources. In short, closing the gender gap in financial inclusion can act as an enabler of countries' development, economic growth, inequality reduction, business evolution, and social inclusion.

Therefore, this chapter aims to discuss how important is the inclusion of gender in mobile payments and also how the concept of digital wallet transforms the exclusive society in services of e-banking with an agenda of gender equality.

DESIGN/ METHODOLOGY/APPROACH

The research is based on a qualitative analysis, therefore, the study is strongly supported by survey results that reveal the trends in digital payments influencing the paying behavior of gender. The survey also highlights the factors affecting the credibility and growth of digital Payments.

LITERATURE REVIEW

E-Commerce

As the Internet has been evolved robustly in society, it has brought new forms of communication for users to exchange ideas instantly with one another. So, the Internet and other ICT-based communication tools and platforms have also created a pool of knowledge sharing and trading online. As a result, trading over the Internet is possible and most people usually referred it as Electronic Commerce or e-commerce. Therefore, e-commerce involves making financial transactions through the Internet, the Web, and other mobile applications in exchange for products and services (Qin et al., 2014; Jackson, 2015).

However, it has been reflected in the literature that the meaning of e-commerce is vast therefore, there is no universal definition of e-commerce regardless of their efforts (Piris, 2004). As a result, Jackson (2015) defines e-commerce as "the type of business that delivers services and products over electronic-based systems through marketing, distribution, buying, and selling". But, Qin et al. (2014) define e-commerce as "the process whereby traditional trade is carried out by electronic methods. So, electronic methods in e-commerce have been used in a broader way which refers to electronic technologies, tools, equipment, and systems, including telephone, telegram, television, facsimile, e-mail, electronic data interchange, computer, the communication network, credit card, electronic money, and the Internet, etc". Zwass (1996) defined e-commerce as "the sharing of business information, maintaining business relationships, and conducting business transactions utilizing Internet-based technology".

However, in general, e-commerce can be classified into many categories. First, there is a business-to-customer (B2C) category where online consumers shop on the Web. Second, there is the business-to-business (B2B) category where transactions are conducted online on the Web between different businesses. The third category, customer-to-customer (C2C), includes transactions between customers such as in auction websites (Schneider, 2014). As e-commerce evolved, new types of e-commerce emerged such as social commerce and mobile commerce (m-commerce). Social commerce is enabled through social media while m-commerce is used to be carried out with the help of mobile devices (Laudon & Traver, 2015).

Mobile Wallet or E-wallet

Physical wallets are typically used to store things of value. Wallets date back to Ancient Greece and Rome, were used to hold food. During the Renaissance, period wallets were used as a leather sack with a drawstring to hold paper currency, coins, and miscellaneous paperwork. In the 1690s when paper currency was introduced, they began making a wallet out of leather and included a place to store calling cards and other forms of identification. By the 1800s, American workers began to attach leather pouches to their belts. These leather pouches would become the prototype wallet until the mid-20th century when the leather billfold was introduced.

So, the contents of a personal wallet represent the person's behavior and gender. Therefore, the things stored in a wallet can judge patterns of social life based on gender representation. And, in terms of personal perspective, it may represent financial security to certain gender or people, along with purchasing power and prosperity. A belief is that the bigger a woman's purse, the more she will cram into it, and the same goes for her wallet. She may keep her membership cards, coupons, receipts, business cards, credit and bank cards, photos, metro transit cards, and anything else she can fit, into her wallet.

However, it seems that digital commerce has transformed the concept of a mobile wallet. Unlike a physical wallet, there is no standard definition of a "mobile wallet" (Mckinsey & Co, 2019). But, a mobile wallet is a software application that enables users to digitally store money, payments credentials, and more, to implement various types of cashless transactions. Therefore, a mobile wallet or e-wallet has been described as a way to pay for something with a device such as a computer or mobile phone. It can take the functions of a physical wallet, with all of its contents and behaviors, and integrate it into the digital device.

As a result, the "digitized valuables" stored in a mobile wallet can be represented in many different forms (Fundinger, 2019). They may take the form of a number (like on a credit card or a password), a digital certificate, a mobile phone readable bar code referred to as a Quick Response Code (QR Code), an image of the owner, or something else. These representations are linked to the mobile wallet owner's sensitive personal information. Mobile wallets provide valuable access to this information but may require stronger protection and security.

Further, the same or similar objects kept in a physical wallet may be more neatly stored and grouped on a mobile wallet, eliminating the clutter. A mobile wallet may be able to provide additional functions and benefits such as virtually unlimited storage, location, awareness, and quick sorting or searching of its contents (IBM, 2019). Doing away with the paper receipts, business cards, and other paper artifacts, and the potential for optimizing or eliminating trips even benefit the environment.

However, the literature reveals that the mobile wallet is developed from a concept called "Digital Wallet". It dated back to 1996 when the founder of Digital Wallet, Sam Pitroda, filed the patent in the United States. He "professed that a digital wallet would consist of a liquid crystal display not much bigger than a regular plastic bank card, which preferably a touch-sensitive screen and simple user interface that lets the user flip through the digital wallet in the same manner he/she flips through a leather wallet" (Pitroda S., Desai M., 2010). So far, there has not been yet a proper definition for the word "Mobile Wallet" written by specific scholars. In the Non-Confidential GSMA White Paper, the mobile wallet was defined as "a software application on a mobile handset that functions as a digital container for payment cards, tickets, loyalty cards, receipts, vouchers and other items that might be found in a conventional wallet. The mobile wallet enables the user to manage a broad portfolio of mobile NFC [Near Field Communication] services from many different companies" (GSMA, 2012). In other words, mobile wallet is "formed" when Smartphone functions as a leather wallet: it can have digital coupons, digital money (transaction), digital cards, and digital receipts, etc. all in personal Smartphone. This means, there is a need to install the application that is created by some companies such as Google Inc., Apple Inc., or PayPal on the phone, and use those applications to pay directly for the products that have been purchased online or offline.

Further, there may be trade-offs to using a mobile wallet. Unlike a physical wallet, a mobile wallet owner may have the perception of autonomy over his/her wallet, but it is maintained and controlled by a third party. Highly personal information is entrusted to an unknown entity. A physical wallet owner is responsible for protecting his/her identity. With a mobile wallet, the owner's risk profile is different. Consumers may not be fully aware of the protections needed, nor do they anticipate the problems, and incorporate appropriate risk mitigation tools (Boston, 2012).

As a result, it can seem that nowadays most countries have experienced significant advancements in financial inclusion by using mobile payment services (Raj, 2015). Mobile payment is an important application of mobile commerce. Mobile commerce

Figure 1. Payment Development Process into the Digital Wallet

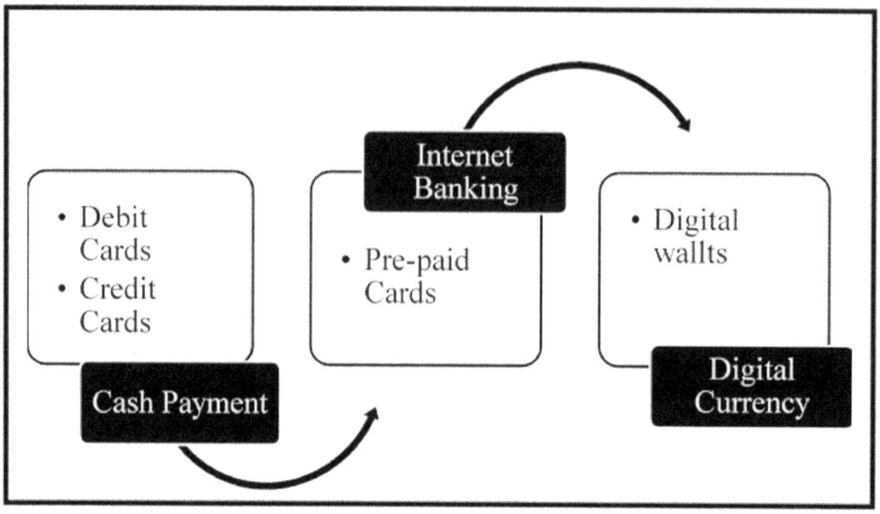

is a broader term encompassing the application of mobile devices and wireless networks to conduct commercial transactions over the web-based system (Nilashi, et.al, 2015). So, Digital wallet or E-wallet refers to an electronic, internet based payment module which stores financial value as well as personal identity related information. It is a feature that allows an individual to make transactions over Internet. This includes online shopping and making payments using Smartphone or a computer. The wallet allows to stock a number of credit, debit and prepaid cards and bank account numbers in a secured environment to facilitate payments. A mobile wallet is a combination of both, software and information component. Security and Encryption of the personal data and the actual transaction is done by customized software. These wallets are stored on the client site and are easily maintained. They are also fully compatible with most e-payment websites. An E-wallet is considered to be a component of the payment module, which includes the systems that enable various operations like a credit card, debit card, smart card, money transfer, or any other similar operations. For example; Fast food giant Pizza Hut, which is famous for manufacturing pizzas, was the first to open a system for online payments. Then after the security of the payment systems were more intensified, more companies started coming up with the initiative like Amazon and E-bay in 1995. As e-commerce and online shopping gained popularity, payment methods also had to be modified and simplified with wider coverage of consumers. Payment Development Process into the Digital Wallet is shown in figure 1.

As the concept is ever-evolving, a wide variety of names are used interchangeably for such transactions as e-money, digital money, micro-payments, etc. Both, 'terminology' and 'technology' for the operation of the wallet are continuously evolving. So, Samsung Galaxy Series and the Google Nexus series running on Google's AOS and Apple Inc. Iphone6 and 6+ are exploring smartphones with NFC digital wallet capability.

It has been seen in the marketing world that e-wallet systems facilitate the widespread use of mobile wallet transactions between various retail vendors in the form of mobile payments systems and digital wallet applications. As a result, the emergence of the E-world and the rise of E-commerce invented a new payment mechanism. Without monetary exchanges there can be no business and E-commerce wouldn't survive without proper and effective means of value exchange. Most of the payment mechanisms that exist today have remained in one shape or another. The barriers and requirements of the electronic world enable both sophisticated and simplified ways of value exchange.

Types of Digital Wallets

Four types of e-wallets are accepted and recognized all around the globe are Open Wallets, Semi-Open Wallets, Closed Wallets, and Semi-Closed Wallets.

Open Wallets can be used for purchasing goods and services, including financial transactions such as fund transfer at merchant locations or point-of-sale terminals that accept cards, and also cash withdrawals at automated teller machines or business correspondents. Only banks issue such wallets. Whereas Semi-Open Wallets are used to purchase goods and avail services at any merchant outlet. A gift card is one such instrument. These, can't be used to withdraw cash.

Closed Wallets is one that a business house issues to its customers for in-house goods and services only. These instruments do not provide the leverage of cash withdrawal or redemption. However, a Semi-Closed Wallet can be used for goods and services, including financial transactions, at selected merchant locations or establishments. They get into a contract with the issuing company to accept these payment instruments. These wallets do not permit cash withdrawal or redemption by the holder as well.

In addition, the following authentication and payment methods can be commonly seen all these types of e-wallets in table 1.1

Table 1. Authentication and payment methods in mobile wallets

Methods of authentication	Description
Name	Names have always been a convenient way to the identification of individuals. An individual's name has been linked with reputation and it acted as a bond while entering transactions. When dealing with people outside of the community using names became a problem. This led to uncertainties and duplication.
Seals	Affixation of a seal to an envelope lends certainty that the contents were confidential and the information it carried was directly from the sender. Seals eliminated the duplication of a name but were vulnerable to themselves being copied.
Fingerprint	Fingerprints are unique identification for every individual. They are very difficult to be impersonated. They have widespread use in criminal cases and passport issuance. But, they are very complex to be compared and need to be checked individually.
Signature	Signatures are considered an effective means of identification in today's world. They are unique and easily identifiable. They have certain drawbacks as well like they require physical presence, being an imprint on a paper renders them unsuitable for use as online identification.
Username and Password (PIN)	Emails to E-banking they accept the Username and password. These passwords do not require physical presence at the point of sale. They too have certain drawbacks like remembering multiple passwords and their security is dependent on the individual.
Digital Certificate	These certificates were specially designed for online identification. They are effective in a closed system. These certificates are issued to a physical hardware device which makes them non-transferable to different Internet points of access. They are also difficult to maintain and take care of as they need to be periodically followed up. The value of a digital certificate is determined by the credibility of the holder.
Biometric, Retinal Scan, Voice Recognition	Biological measurements are the new identification techniques. Fingerprint and retina scanning has already been deployed into various industries. Other biological measurements are currently not readily available and in excess use. These require expensive hardware devices to record and function which makes them unviable for extensive usage.

Mobile Wallet Technologies

Direct Carrier Billing

This has been the traditional technique for decades. "It is also called direct operator billing or mobile content billing, which lets the users purchase their phones from merchants without entering credit card data" (PCMag).

QR and Bar Codes

"QR codes are the square bar codes that empower many cloud-based advertising and payment apps" (Webster, 2012). The optional confirmation code can be required for security purposes.

Near Field Communication

Near Field Communication is also known as NFC that is any device that is installed this technology can communicate and exchange information as well as data within a few centimeter's distances (GSMA, 2012). To make it function, both devices are required to have NFC (Webster, 2012).

Cloud-based Solution

The cloud-based solution is also known as cloud computing which is defined as "a model for enabling ubiquitous, convenient, on-demand network access to a shared pool of configurable computing resources (e.g., networks, servers, storage, applications, and services) that can be rapidly provisioned and released with minimal management effort or service provider interaction" (Peter Mell, Timothy Grance, 2011). For example, PayPal is trying to let its users make transactions just by typing their mobile phone number and PIN code at physical POS (Webster, 2012).

The Future of E-wallets

The E-wallet is on the track of becoming a personalized portal for every Individual. The following are some of the benefits individuals can expect from their E-wallet as shown in the figure 1.2

The component of the Online Shopping in E-wallet facilitates buying from smartphones and PDAs. Issues of user input via keypad were considered as a barrier to e-commerce. The E-wallet minimizes the number of key clicks required to shop from these devices by automating the online purchasing process. It is now possible for a consumer to compare services and prices on a mobile device while shopping at a physical location. This enables price transparency and consumer control. Bill Payments facilities indicate that the E-wallet can make bill payments on behalf of the user. This includes payment scheduling for electronic bills and invoices and receiving bills. However, Loyalty Rewards is that to provide real-time points tracking, accumulated over time by shopping, recharges, etc. Personal Information Access indicates that the Electronic wallet can hold all your personal information at a single registered account. It can include medical, motor vehicle, Insurance, Investment reporting, mortgage, and superannuation. It will act as a personal financial portal. This information aggregation can also extend to online gaming and

Figure 2. Future of e-wallets

auction monitoring. But, Virtual Personal Organizer in the E-wallet can store users' Calendars, Contacts, to-do lists, and tasks allowing it to be accessed on any system for updates or changes. Further, the component of Wireless purchasing at physical stores allows purchasing at stores when the wallet is supported by Bluetooth or an Infra-Red device. The wallet will have the capability of retrieving the User's credit card number from the pre-stored account details and then transmitting the credit card number to the point of purchase. Whereas, Pre-emptive Buying is allowing purchases to also record their transactional history. It will analyze your purchasing patterns and remind you about making a purchase. Furthermore, Device to Device and Person Person money transfer will change how the world looks today at the money exchange. Once installed on a device it will be possible to transfer payments from one person to person without much hassle.

Also, the components of Mobile Wallets and its Eco-system (Stringer, 2014) are very important. So, such components are consumers, card controllers, merchants, device manufacturers, etc. For any business, it is undeniable that consumers are the most important factor. The great and "cool" technology is not forceful enough to trigger the consumers to use a mobile wallet. Thus, it is very crucial to gain adoption from consumers. The interesting thing is that paying by the mobile device does not have much attraction toward consumers. Approximately ten million customers pay with the app and more than five million transactions per week are taking place in the USA (Bertoni, 2014). Card controllers are defined as "those that own the card or account data " (Stringer, 2014). Those companies for instance are: Visa, Master Card, American Express, Discover, Wal-Mart, Apple, Google, Amazon, PayPal, Facebook etc. They are simply categorized into three groups like Card Network: Visa, Master Card, American Express; Card-on-file Merchants: Google, Apple, PayPal, Starbucks, Wal-Mart and Digital Assets Companies with their strengths and weaknesses to influence the mobile wallet market.

However, the physical stores are called merchant or point of sale (POS), for example, a retail outlet or a restaurant. "A successful mobile wallet must have a large merchant base that accepts the wallet" (Carrington, 2014). Due to this fact consumers would like to have alternative payments, merchants have to adapt in the mobile wallet market. They should change from cash-based system into other alternative payments. The main focus of merchants is to sell the products faster and cheaper (Stringer, 2014). Therefore, the change is a necessary action for the merchant. Carriers are the Mobile Service Providers. Different countries will have different carriers. So, in many countries, the carriers often control what software or hardware on the mobile devices that connect to their network (Stringer, 2014). For instance, AT&T Inc., T-Mobile, and Verizon Wireless are the 3 biggest mobile service providers in the USA. In Japan, the biggest carrier is NTT DoCoMo and TeliaSonera in Finland.

In addition, device manufactures are the companies who create the smartphones, Apple, Google, Samsung, HTC, Microsoft, etc. are the most known manufacturers. They are considered to be "the only ones that can really get consumers to pick their mobile device over their leather wallet" (Stringer, 2014). In other words, they have a large market adoption with embedded mobile payment application in their products (Carr, 2008). Most of these companies have tried to develop their own mobile devices so that they can acquire a big amount of consumers. For instance, Google has successfully developed Nexus Smartphone; Amazon also had the intention to create its phone, even Facebook had the same plan too (Bilton, 2012).

E-wallets and Gender

It is reflected that most of the business success or failure depends on how does its services and products acceptable by all genders. Therefore, the mobile wallet is also the concept of gender. So, much research on mobile wallets has analyzed that gender is one of the significant factors for its success and development (Wynn, 2009; Mallawaarachchi, 2016). So, many studies showed that behavioral differences in online purchasing and purchase orientations among users, according to their gender are very high. Traditionally, men were more willing to engage in e-commerce than women; men have a greater tendency to make planned purchases (e-hardware), while women were more prone to buy other types of products or to make less planned purchases (food and drinks) (Van Slyke et al., 2002). Further, the role of gender in the original TAM has been analyzed since the end of the 1990s. Gefen and Straub (1997) pointed out that gender has generally been avoided in behavioral research in the IT field. Not only that but the moderating effect of gender has also been demonstrated in the loyalty of internet operators (Sanchez-Francoet al., 2009), the adoption of e-commerce (Hwang, 2010).

It has been seen that there is a persistent gender gap in access to basic accounts in the financial system, where 72% of men have access to an account while only 65% of women have an account; this gender gap remains unchanged since 2011. In terms of use, recent research based on 18 countries states that, at a global level, men represent 65% of customers, they handle 80% of loan volume and 75% of deposits (Global Banking Alliance for Women, 2018). Women face multiple barriers that limit their access to and use of financial services. These include lack of an ID to prove identity, insufficient traditionally required collateral, mobility constraints, and limited financial literacy, amongst others. Evidence shows that different measures can be used to overcome these barriers, and financial institutions must take these measures into account when developing inclusive financial services. Positive measures include gathering sex-disaggregated data to develop customized value propositions tailored to women's needs and gender-smart products, training employees to provide expertise and design-friendly ecosystems, providing financial training and education to women, improving women's networks. Financial institutions and policymakers can push forward regulations that promote the use of tiered to know your customer and anti-money laundering, simplified accounts, the development of alternative collateral registries, and support the development of fintech companies that could create new mechanisms to serve women's financial needs. The broad nature of the hurdles faced by women requires the direct action of the financial sector, regulators, and policymakers.

Financial inclusion is important for women to access loans, credit and to make transactions, but it is also essential to save money and build assets in a safe place, which can, in turn, help them move out of poverty. Savings interventions increase women's business earnings. Women seek savings vehicles and use personal savings to invest in their businesses (Aldana and Boyd, 2015). Women's ability to save has effects on other aspects of their lives, as evidence shows that saving can positively impact women's empowerment (Holloway, et al. 2017; Trivelli and de Los Rios, 2014) and household welfare (Karlan et al. 2016). Studies also show that even poor women are eager to save if given appealing interest rates, conveniently located financial facilities, and flexible accounts—with bankers in Indonesia, rural Mexico (Morduch, J., 1999), and South Asia finding that convenience generally beats interest rates (Trivelli & Montenegro 2011).

The new alternative forms of digital finance open a new set of services, channels, and value opportunities for women, both the financially excluded and the already financially included but underserved. Digital channels and innovative product designs have the potential to offer new and better value propositions for women (W20 Argentina, 2018). Improving and increasing the outreach of such solutions will allow women to use more convenient financial services. Fintechs and new digital financial service providers should be seen as key partners of regulators for closing the financial gender gap.

Finally, regulators, financial sector businesses, and fintech need to improve the presence of women in leadership positions. More women CEOs, more women board members, more decision-making positions in women's hands are required to close the gender gap. As new market entrants, Fin techs should be encouraged to take a lead in this area.

RECOMMENDATIONS

It has been seen that many women have fewer opportunities to hold mobile wallets due to various reasons, among them lack of computer and ICT literacy are the major reasons. However, the survey showed that they do online shopping similar to men but still they are interested in cash payments. Fees paid to access public services and payments for public utilities are steadily increasing but women are still made mostly in cash, however, the facility of digital payment through electronic means is available for all but not only for men. For example, 74% of digitized payment systems of government services exist in developed economies however only 55% in middle-income countries are in the same situation and 39% in low-income economies use accounts (World Bank, 2017). However, some government, as well as private banks in Sri Lanka, have designed mobile wallet account which use mobile phones in rural areas as a transaction point to make deposits and withdrawals. With the help of mobile artificial intelligent platforms, clients can open an account in ten minutes from any location. And because the product conveys information simply and visually, the customer does not need to be literate to use the service systems.

So, digital service providers should support the creation of women's active participation in digital business activities to raise their voice and visibility if gender exclusion is practiced. Supporting to build women's business associations would be one of the possibilities to educate and promote gender equality and equality. Because it allows them to involve in decision-making powers. Further, using tax incentives, providing capacity-building resources, or just creating seats for representatives of such associations could resolve the problems of women in business. For these two examples can be taken from the Women Impacting Public Policy (WIPP) in the US and the incentive program in Argentina. In addition, some professional women associations in the world have shown the power of their voice to call an action to treat equally for women as well as to enjoy benefits that are given to men. This phenomenon is very much important in the digital products and services offering environment because it is affecting their career development too.

It is widely shown that men-led businesses, as well as women-led businesses, grow faster in mobile environments. However, women face greater difficulties than men in gaining funding for their businesses and funders tend to believe that men are more entrepreneurial and growth-minded than women (Eddleston et al., 2016; Mallawaarachchi, 2019). There are gendered differences in the ways men and women deal with risk and experience institutions, which can, in turn, translate into differences in the types of financial products that men and women prefer. But research findings showed that women are cautious and more risk-averse than their male counterparts, and that is partly due to women's trust in institutions. Further, gender differences in risk perceptions and risk aversion can be seen (Akter et al.,2016).

However, the lack of traditional collateral, the prevalence of discriminatory property rights, and insufficient financial information are at the center of the capital and credit shortages that women face. As they lack these resources, it is hard for them to scale up their activities and increase their productivity, which would be necessary for them to enter value chains and procurement processes. Businesses run by women tend to be small and medium enterprises and to be underrepresented in the business associations, limiting their voice and bargaining power. Consequently, they tend to participate to a lesser extent in international trade (ITC, 2015; Mallawaarachchi, 2019).

Women led-businesses need to be strengthened through better financial services. Not only to allow them to realize their value but also to diversify the business sector, to open new opportunities for women, and to add gender diversity to the leading companies. And similarly, action has to be taken to address some of the other existing barriers women face with the heavy usage patterns in mobile wallets. Some of them can be identified as lack of traditional gender security; lack of financial information; lack in financial literacy and numeracy; differentiated preferences between men and women in terms of risk and growth appetite; and lack of voice to interact with public policy and to talk to the financial services providers.

CONCLUSION

It has been seen that paper cash was a mode of payment in history but due to the tremendous expansion of the ICT and the Internet its role has been changed significantly. As a result, many economies in the world are moving from cash-based to cashless electronic payment systems. Cashless electronic payment systems help in various ways to businesses by reducing currency management costs and easy tracking transactions including enhancing financial inclusion and integrating the parallel economy with the mainstream of digital transactions. So, as a new payment method mobile wallet came into practice and their usage expand the boundaries of all economies of the world. Similarly, many online and offline e-commerce shoppers are started to offer discounts on mobile wallets. And also, not only giants in e-commerce but also individual buyers have shown interest to have their e-wallets. As a result, mobile wallets have emerged as the most significant contributor in pushing cashless and electronic payments in the marketing world.

REFERENCES

Akter, S., Krupnik, T., Rossi, F., & Khanam, F. (2016). The Influence of Gender and Product Design on Farmers' Preferences for Weather-Indexed Crop Insurance. *Global Environmental Change*, *38*, 217–229. doi:10.1016/j.gloenvcha.2016.03.010 PMID:27212804

Albadr, B. (2003). E-commerce. *Science and Technology*, *65*, 14–19.

Argentina, W. (2018). *Digital inclusion communique*. Retrieved from w20argentina.com/wp-content/uploads/2018/07/comm_digital_inclusion_2.pdf

Bertoni, S. (n.d.). *How do we win the mobile wallet war? be like Starbucks*. Retrieved July 28, 2017, from https://www.forbes.com/sites/stevenbertoni/2014/02/21/how-do-you-win-the-mobile-wallet-warbe-like-starbucks/

Bilton, N. (2014). Facebook tries, tries again on a smartphone. *The New York Times*.

Boston, F. R. (2012). *Mobile Phone Technology: smarter than we thought*. Retrieved 2019, from https://www.bostonfed.org/bankinfo/payment-strategies/publications/2012/mobile-phone-technology.htm

Boston, F. R. (2017). *Mobile phone technology: smarter than we thought*. Retrieved from https://www.bostonfed.org/bankinfo/payment-strategies/publications/2012/mobile-phone-technology.htm

Carr, M. (2008). *Mobile payment systems and services: an introduction*. Retrieved from http://venturewoods.org/wp-content/uploads/2008/06/mobile-payment-systems-and-services.pdf

Carrington, D. (2018). *Merchants will decide the fate of Apple's mobile wallet*. Retrieved from http://blogs.forrester.com/denee_carrington/14-09-04-merchants_will_decide_the_fate_of_apples_mobile_wallet

Centre for Information Technology. (2015). *Unlocking markets for women to trade*. Retrieved from https://www.intracen.org/uploadedFiles/intracenorg/Content/Publications/women_in_trade_web.pdf

Fundinger, D. (2015). *What is a mobile wallet and how does it work?* Retrieved from http://asmarterplanet.com/mobile-enterprise/blog/2015/01/what-is-a-mobilewallet.html

Fundinger, D. (2019). *What is a Mobile Wallet and How does it work?* Retrieved from http://asmarterplanet.com/mobile-enterprise/blog/2015/01/what-is-a-mobilewallet.html

Gauging the disruptive potential of digital wallets. (2019). Retrieved from www.mckinsey.com

Gefen, D., & Straub, D. (1997). Gender differences in perception and adoption of e-mail: An extension to the technology acceptance model. *Management Information Systems Quarterly*, *21*(4), 389–400. doi:10.2307/249720

Global Banking Alliance for Women. (2018). *The mobile wallet version 1-0*. GSM Association.

Gulati, S., Nadeau, M.-C. N., & Rajgopal, K. (2015). *Gauging the disruptive potential of digital wallets*. McKinsey.

Hwang, Y. (2010). The moderating effects of gender on e-commerce systems adoption factors: An empirical investigation. *Computers in Human Behavior*, *26*(6), 1753–1760. doi:10.1016/j.chb.2010.07.002

IBM. (2019). *Toward a mobile digital wallet*. Retrieved from https://domino.watson.ibm.com/library/CyberDig.nsf/1e4115aea78b6e7c85256b30066f0

Jackson, E. (2015). Global Information Technology Strategy. *Journal of Information Technology*, *1*(2), 6–9.

Jackson, E. (2015). Global Information Technology Strategy. *Jackson Journal of Information Technology*, *1*(2), 6–9.

Karlan, D., & Kendall, J. (2016). *Research and impacts of digital financial services*. National Bureau of Economic Research. (Original work published 2016) doi:10.3386/w22633

Laudon, K., & Traver, C. (2007). *E-commerce: business, technology, society*. Pearson Prentice Hall.

Mallawaarachchi, C. (2014). Significant of Information Rich Contents in Technology-based marketing communication channels to reach knowledge savvy customers. *International Journal of Scientific and Research Publications*, *4*(10), 1–5.

Mallawaarachchi, C. (2015). Impacts of media literacy to enhance right to know and access to information: Democracy perspective. *International Journal of Scientific and Research Publications*, *5*(11), 257–261.

Mallawaarachchi, C. (2016). Universal responsibilities and challenges towards changing the landscape of knowledge access in higher education. *International Journal of Scientific and Research Publications*, *6*(10), 343–350.

Mallawaarachchi, C. (2019). The Application of artificial intelligence and interactive voice recognition in the banking industry in Sri Lanka. *Journal of Modern Accounting and Auditing*, *15*(8), 315–321. doi:10.17265/1548-6583/2019.06.004

Mallawaarachchi, C. (2019). Significant Influences of digital literacy to promote gender equity and equality in education: Digital Literacy perspective. In Gender Issues in Technical and Vocational Education Programs. Academic Press.

Mell, P., & Grance, T. (2011). The NIST definition of Cloud Computing. *Computers & Security*, 2.

Nilashi, M., Ibrahim, O., Mirabi, V. R., Ebrahimi, L., & Zare, M. (2015). The role of security, design, and content factors on customer trust in Mobile commerce. *Journal of Retailing and Consumer Services*, *26*, 57–68. doi:10.1016/j.jretconser.2015.05.002

PCMag. (2014). *Definition of Direct Carrier Billing*. Retrieved from www.pcmag.com: http://www.pcmag.com/encyclopedia/term/63496/direct-carrier-billing

Pitroda, S., & Desai, M. (2010). The march of mobile money: the future of lifestyle management. *The Mobile Wallet*, 127-155.

Qin, Z., Chang, Y., Li, S., & Li, F. (2014). *E-commerce strategy*. Springer Berlin. doi:10.1007/978-3-642-39414-0

Raj, S. (2015). Financial Inclusiveness: The role of mobile money and digital financial services. *Socrates*, *3*(1), 95–112.

Rajgopal, K. (2012). *McKinsey on payments: Payment wave, commerce ocean.* Academic Press.

Sa'nchez-Franco, M., Villarejo, A., & Martı'n, F. (2009). The moderating effect of gender on relationship quality and loyalty toward internet service providers. *Information & Management*, *46*(3), 196–202. doi:10.1016/j.im.2009.02.001

Schneider, G. (2014). *Electronic Commerce*. Cengage Learning.

Slyke, V., Comunale, C., & Belangr, F. (2002). Gender differences in perceptions of web-based shopping. *Communications of the ACM*, *45*(7), 82–86. doi:10.1145/545151.545155

Smartphone users worldwide will total 1.75 billion in 2014. (2014). Retrieved from http://www.emarketer.com: http://www.emarketer.com/Article/Smartphone-Users-Worldwide-Will-Total-175-Billion-2014/1010536#sthash.UnbdaSGM.dpuf

Trivelli, C., & De Los, R. (2014). *Creating Financial Assets: the case for Saving Accounts as means for Economic Independence and Empowerment for Women.* Proyecto.

Webster, K. (2018). *How to make it in mobile commerce.* Retrieved from www.humnwallet.com/article/-the-evolution-of-the-wallet-ancient-to-modern-times

World Bank. (2017). *The Global Findex Database.* Retrieved from worldbank.org/curated/en/332881525873182837/The-Global-FindexDatabase-2017-Measuring-Financial-Inclusion-and-the-Fintech-Revolution

Wynn, A. (2009). *An investigation of the contributions of gender, shopping orientation, online experience and website's interactive features to consumers' intentions to engage in apparel e-commerce shopping*. Nova South-Eastern University.

Chapter 11
Gender Bias in Science and Technology: A Medico's Perspectives

Sunita Nayak
All India Institute of Medical Sciences, Patna, India

ABSTRACT

This chapter is a medico's perspective on the impact of gender bias on science and technology. It is entirely about what a female doctor feels about the society and the struggles a female faces in her journey, the lacunae in our system, how we should deal with the people and the system for the betterment of humanity in general. Her experiences in the medical college as a student, as a doctor, as a researcher, and as a teacher have been shared. How to maintain a perfect work-life balance and still be happy and content in life without being stressed.

INTRODUCTION

In European culture, females are only considered, "sex objects," but our Indian culture considers females as "Goddesses" because they possess certain divine qualities. A man is considered, "complete" only if he is married. To comply with the Hindu rituals, both the partners need to sit in front of the "Havan-Kund". But in the name of modernization, we are following western culture because the west has shown us the value of the industry. During industrialization, the females in the west felt that they are not being treated well and they started the "Gender Equality" movement. In India, women started following them although it was not necessary. In the name of "Gender Equality" or "Women's Liberation Movement", our ladies fought for the

DOI: 10.4018/978-1-7998-8594-8.ch011

"Right to wear Jeans, consume liquor, cigarettes, and go for night parties as men do". Our Indian ladies started downgrading themselves. Taking care of the family and rearing children were considered less prestigious as they did not contribute to the economy directly. As men were the sole bread earner, women felt oppressed asking for money. In this process, they forgot that the divine had bestowed upon them the natural hormones of care & nurture i.e., oxytocin and prolactin. Giving birth to the young one and then nurturing the next generation with all the necessary values and virtues is the greatest contribution to the nation. In other words, a mother has a huge contribution to nation-building. But our society and especially the younger females forgot that. This was the worst impact of Industrialization on the feminine gender.

Our males have grown up seeing women playing the role of a caregiver at home. They are not ready to accept a female boss at the workplace or industry. So, the workplace is a bit difficult and different for women especially if she is the boss. In medical colleges or other scientific institutes, peons, lab attendants, or other class 3 or class 4 male workers look at women just as they look at their mothers or wife or sisters. It is difficult for them to accept ladies in the higher post as heads (Weidekamm & Willer, 2012). They cannot accept a female as a person under whom they must work as they are the rulers and kings at their homes, taught to dominate the females, can make all mistakes in life and can be forgiven, can be lazy, sit and do nothing and still be proud as they are men. Who can change their views? Lack of education plus how they are brought up must be kept in mind while dealing with them. How can they tolerate a female shouting at them, telling them to work, telling them the mistakes they make and how far can they accept those? Very difficult to change the attitude of men even if they are educated as they see women first as mothers, wives, or daughters and not as co-workers or heads. Females also sometimes let us down by not working up to the expectation, taking advantage of being females, and avoiding work on a day-to-day basis. It's a double-edged sword. Playing the "victim-card" by the females will not give them the due respect they deserve.

Women in the government sector must go through the proper channel because they are expected to follow all rules and regulations whereas men can decide what to do. Women are not given the freedom to take any decision, be it on any divisional matter. Women who do speak their minds are silenced by some sensitive comments. In other words, they are not allowed to show their positivity. The majority of the males show male authoritativeness. Even if they commit blunders, they don't apologize as their "male ego" comes into the picture. They have a problem obeying a senior lady officer. They just talk about women's empowerment but no major decision-taking jobs are ever assigned to a woman. Laws and gazettes are there at their place. Practically what women face is different.

It's very common thinking that female employees are less competent as compared to their male counterparts when it comes to the division of tasks or duties. A lack of empathy towards the female colleague by a male colleague is always seen. Unless the highest authority is a female, even clean, tidy toilets for females are not considered important. The ladies' toilets are usually dirty with no dust bins for pad disposal. Considering a lady's common room with a resting couch is still considered a luxury in the workplace but nobody understands that they desperately need it during their periods. Every mother would be deeply indebted if there is an attached creche for toddlers or nursing of the infants.

Females Are Great Leaders

A mother is close to the child as she knows the child's mood, taste, likes, and dislikes. She can talk to the child in the child's language and come down to the child's level of understanding. As a result, it becomes easier for the child to follow the mother. In due course, the mother can mold the child as per her wish and requirement. So, females are great leaders when they are given the opportunity. The best parts of human nature like empathy, creativity, and stewardship are found in abundance in females which is needed to be channelized in the right direction. The emotional and sensitive side of a female leads to decisions and behaviors that yield innovative, ethical, and rigorous research.

Women leaders struggle a lot to maintain a work-life balance (Hua, D., et al., 2018). Their sensible and empathetic nature makes them understand the personal problems of the subordinates. They are great listeners and strong communicators. Multitasking and nurturing are like their inborn talent, so they handle crises very well. This holistic approach can be taken as an opportunity to serve society. They have high emotional intelligence, and they lead by example. As they dream big, they get motivated by challenges and have intrinsic motivation to excel. As a single mother in a single kitchen can take care of all the needs of the entire family, a female leader focuses on teamwork, checks on her ego, usually is not arrogant.

There are certain mistakes to be avoided by female leaders. One needs to understand that we need to grow up with our job and we can't be the same always. We need to be more visionary, and plan & think ahead. New responsibilities will come, we need to accept them gracefully. Trying to play safe every time is not going to help. Although women know that they are great managers, they don't try to reach the top. Being a 'female' is their only fear. They must be pro-active (initiative-taking) and learn all skills whether it is to deal with the subordinates or fix the budget. Managing finances at home is easier for a female but in big firms or offices, they feel can't manage well. Knowledge is either true or known, there should not be any gap between preaching and practicing. Managers do things rightly, there should not be any ambiguity in goal settings. Appreciating our subordinates and being open to them will not make us less impactful. Limited accessibility to resources should not be our complaint as we are brought up in an environment where we are taught to 'adjust'.

Biggest Challenges Faced by a Female

Being treated equally at the workplace in India is a goal that is yet to be achieved. Females who are already on top should not be gender biased and should empower each other. Lack of sisterhood and leg-pulling in society ultimately harms the progress of a female which proves that females are the biggest enemies of females. Decisions should be taken when there are no wrinkles in heart or mind i.e., by not being sentimental or judgemental. Dealing with negative thoughts and comments by being confident and speaking up in the meetings. Building an alliance with the policymakers and generating revenues or getting money for projects is an uphill battle for females. Developing such friends who will be your advocates and prepare in such a manner that your presence is counted is rarely seen in the female community. We need to grow up but not grow old while cramming for success. We need to remain ethical, trust our voice yet try for excellence and not perfectionism.

Even in technical colleges, a female student is expected to be more obedient and well behaved, she should answer well, her apron should be clean enough. A female student is commented on these things even in the viva-voce examinations. Whereas a male will be excused for not answering well because he can learn later in his life. But when will a female learn as she is immediately going to marry, and take care of the in-laws family, bear children, etcetera?

Impostor Phenomenon is usually seen in high achieving women because of the continuous backstabbing at the workplace. Impostor syndrome is a psychological disturbance where one is good but is confident that he or she is not good. Even if a woman is highly successful in her professional carrier, she is not given due respect at her own home. The male counterpart may not be even as half of the caliber as his wife but will be accepted as the "boss" of the house. Women are getting more and more educated and professionally skilled as industrialization and technology are advancing. We are teaching our girl children to be highly competent but not our boys how to accept them. The result is unhappy marriages and broken families. The age-old tradition that the female will sacrifice her carrier and not take promotional transfer for the sake of her family is still there in the mindset of the males. The problem lies in upbringing. We must teach our male child also to take care of the household chores and nurture the children because cooking, cleaning, and nurturing is no more a domain of the female only.

Solution

Management depends on the leader be it a male or a female. If a female is accommodating everyone with a cordial feeling so that the department does not suffer, taking ownership of the department, working beyond hours if needed, is assertive or aggressive depending on the need then she can do wonders. If management takes due care of the safety and security of the females during night duties, then she won't hesitate to work at night. Generally, men feel insecure when women are equally qualified and accomplished. Especially in discussions, they try to put the females down by ridiculing their idea or their view in a subtle manner. This is also seen in female colleagues to some extent too. The males sometimes forget that ladies are sensitive, so react immediately and hence counseling is needed sometimes to prevent dropouts. Because of industrialization and the use of high-end technology, stamina or physical strength is no more required to be the boss. If she is given the freedom of taking big decisions, she will leave her dependent mentality and understand the situation better with her patience and perseverance. She won't call her husband or others before making any decisions as is usually seen in many offices. There should be no room for sexual harassment of females and if Government policies, law & order situations for the females are stringent enough, she would travel freely in this country and perform her duties without any fear or prejudices. People should know that a female is not a spineless creature who is always dependent on male support. Let her feel a human first, a woman second. Showing that you care is more important than showing that you are perfect.

Impact of Technology and Industrialization

The age-old tradition and culture that a female must take care of the house and the male will go out for work is gradually vanishing as machines are taking up all the heavy work. Gone are the days when muscle power and stamina were needed to do the outside work. Science and technology have advanced so much that with the touch of a button, the entire planet can be destroyed. The need now is that human beings should behave like "humans". "Being human" should not be a brand or a charitable trust. Rather should manifest in everybody's behavior. Every human being should behave sensibly so that they do not harm the nature of the ecosystem. To save our mother nature, the feminine or soft corner of every individual should be cultivated. Be a human first, a scientist second whenever you are doing any kind of research on animals or humans.

Except for a few specializations like Orthopaedics, where muscle power and stamina are required during the operative procedures, females are dominating in almost all branches of science where intelligence and patience are required. Even the machines have become so advanced that females are not hesitating to take "Orthopaedics" as their area of specialization. There is no branch in science now where females cannot excel. Even the Indian Army has approved the entry of women officers because of the impact of technology. The enemies can be blown away by machine guns and other artilleries.

The only thing which is creating an obstacle in a female's carrier in science is her "Biological Clock" which has an inverse relation. Both (biological clock and carrier) are at their peak at a given time when a female must choose one of them i.e., either carrier or family. If she chooses her carrier, she misses her childbearing age and then must face many complications of late pregnancy. Science has given a solution to that too…she can freeze her ovum (egg) and use them later or use a surrogate mother. But this means playing with mother nature and her rules. This again has its complications like maternal, paternal rights, ethics, monetary conflicts, privacy, and many complications which have recently come up in the law of jurisdiction.

Lessons Learned in the Covid Era

As far as the impact of technology on mainstreaming of female employment is concerned, this was very helpful to both genders during the work-from-home scenario during the recent pandemic. But it also put an extra burden on several female employees to cope up with looking after children and carrying out household jobs along with online work and no outside help. During the lock-down, both males and females had to work from home. During this time, the majority of males complained of lack of privacy and work environment at home, but females complained that their work doubled because when they were in the office, they were doing only the official work but now, they must do both together. The biggest advantage of Covid and lockdown was that everybody has become tech-savvy. People used many innovative techniques to be in touch with their loved ones. Company owners and bosses found out many new ideas for getting their work done. Many people who were staying alone learned many new life-saving skills. Everybody tried to become "aatmanirbhar" or "self-sufficient" as there was no other choice. No maids, no helpers, no drivers were allowed to maintain social distancing. The stereotypical roles of males and females like cooking, driving, gardening, stitching, decorating, nurturing vanished. Indirectly, the Coronavirus helped in bringing down the gender bias slightly.

Kitchen as a Scientific Laboratory

There are a lot of equipment and gadgets in a modern kitchen due to industrialization. The role of a mother has increased many folds now as she plays the role of mother "Durga" with many hands. Experimenting with the ingredients and the available resources, adding a personal touch of her love and affection, a mother creates many wonders in the kitchen daily. Multitasking and time management skills are a necessity in the kitchen. It is in the kitchen that many ideas are born as was evident in the movie, “Mission Mangal”.

LGBTQ community

Before 6th September 2018, people were not usually seen talking about their sexual orientation in public. Even medical students didn’t have complete knowledge about this community. A girl who is sexually attracted towards a girl is a ‘Lesbian’ and a boy who is sexually attracted towards a boy is a ‘Gay’ was the basic knowledge. With the annulment of article 377 on 6th September 2018 and with the release of many Bollywood movies, people could understand that there is another category that is sexually oriented towards both the sexes known as the ‘Bisexual’. ‘Transgenders’ are the ones whose sense of personal identity and gender does not correspond with their birth sex. Now, these terms were creating so many confusions that the teenagers now had a different identity crisis. The ones who had questions or doubts in their minds about their sexual orientation were now grouped under the ‘Queer’ group.

What was the need for so much of ‘Halla-Gulla’ about sexual orientation and gender identity? The sex of a person should only be considered only in their private spaces like their bathrooms and their bedrooms. Screaming about the rights for sex in public spaces is so disgraceful to human society. Where are we heading as humans? Aren’t animals more civilized than us? Although they are not as intelligent as human beings are, their behavior is so eco-friendly, unlike the humans!!!

The Tiara Syndrome

Females think that they do a lot for their family and the society which they do! But their work remains unacknowledged, they are never given the due credit. What to do? Should they wait for society to acknowledge them and put that “Tiara” on their head? The answer is an absolute, ‘NO’. We must put on that ‘imaginary tiara’ on our heads and celebrate life as such. We must face all the balls that life throws at us.

According to writer Craige Chappelow, the issue is really of control. One needs to take control of one’s own life instead of waiting for circumstances to get better or for someone else to do it. Need better preparation and a realization that there will be ups and downs. No ideal solutions that can be applied to bring about balance. Individual needs differ. Taking control and choosing to work on relationships, taking accountability for one’s work and personal life, and learning to say “NO” to things that are of low significance is one way to being in control.

More than half of Indian working professionals rate their current work-life balance, 'average to terrible' says, the 'Understanding Work-Life Balance' survey of 2,000 working professionals by Monster.com. Significantly, as much as 45% of the respondents were from non-metro cities where work-life balance is supposedly a lesser issue. Collectively, 67% of India's working professionals either sometimes, often, or always think about work when not at work.

Life is not divided into compartments called work and life – neither is it lived that way. There is a "no one size fits all" approach in dealing with work-life balance issues. Creating a vision for all aspects of life – setting realistic goals and evaluating the work to be done against those goals can help prioritize what needs to be done and what can be dropped (Jones, Burke, 2013).

The Relationship is the Key to Success!

Rapport building: Knowing your people personally – likes-dislikes, challenges, aspirations, hobbies, and interests); Knowing your people professionally too– job description and job specification. While managing others ask specific questions like, "What do my people need to accomplish? What is the level of knowledge, skills, attitude, and aptitude that they possess? What is needed to accomplish the task? What are some other skills that they possess for crisis management, leadership, decision making, problem-solving, should they be proactive, or do-as directed, etc.? What drives them? Is there any need for affiliation, achievement, recognition, or power?

The Role as a Subordinate

Realize that Boss has a wider vision. Devote time as per organizational objectives and your goals. Go to the Boss after doing your homework. Manage the problems which can be tackled at your level.

Five core values of diversity management like Compassion, Fairness, Honesty, Responsibility & Respect for others are the key to success.

WHO ARE YOU DOES MAKES A DIFFERENCE!

CONCLUSION

Irrespective of any factor, there is a gender bias because the gender bias lies not in these factors but the mind of the male-dominated society. The age-long deprivation of all these self-respect and autonomy of the feminine gender. It is rather a psychosocial human behavior through ages yet certain factors like industrialization and technology have multiple impacts. The age-old, constricted mind of the males is somewhat broadened and becomes more towards equality although it is not in full measure. The slightest paltry or scope offered to the feminine gender becomes a powerful tool in their hands and they start excelling. The time has proved it through the last few decades, and they seek autonomy as well as equality in different capacities and all fields including the Indian Army. Technology, industrialization and women empowerment seems to proceed parallel in a proportionate manner. So, one is fascinated to think that there is a positive direct impact of the new trend in the world i.e., industrialization, etc. to coax the mind of the male-dominated society, to provide more autonomy and freedom to the females. This is just an observation. Yet, it needs further broadening of the mind of the males to accept it wholeheartedly and give true equality to females or the feminine gender.

However, the real key lies in the hands of the females themselves contrary to the popular belief that it lies in the hands of the males. The solution lies along with the problem always. Therefore, the key to true emancipation of the females lies in the hands of the females only. They should wake up not for a fight or tussle but for enhancing their skill, education, entrepreneurship. Their faith in their capabilities. Shed off their age-long complex of begging for autonomy and all that. They should wake and walk up to their true capability and quality of work. Above all, to develop a sense of security in them and self-respect because autonomy given, or freely given cannot be sustained with a minimized self-respect. Self-respect is never given, it is earned and it is never obtained by fight but by enhancing the dignified caliber. Many times, the ladies play a victim card. That should stop immediately.

There should be sufficient fraternal feeling that must replace jealousy and leg-pulling. Irrespective of gender, one should be honest enough to give value to the true caliber instead of getting biased by the gender. There should be a holistic approach because, after a certain stage, this sort of lowliness doesn't work. In the other jobs, it is different but in science at the higher level, the quality must matter. Where quality counts, automatically the gender bias should evaporate. If evaporation or nullification of gender bias is the aim, it seems that only the urge for quality will bridge the necessary solution.

REFERENCES

Chappelow, C. T. (2004). 360-degree feedback. In C.D. McCauley & E.Van Velsor (Eds.), The Centre for Creative Leadership handbook of leadership development (2nd ed., pp.58-84). Jossey-Bass.

Hua, D., Mahmood, N., Zakaria, W., Lin, L., & Yang, X. (2018). The relationship between work-life balance and women leadership performance: The mediation effect of organizational culture. *IACSIT International Journal of Engineering and Technology*, *7*(4.9), 8–13. doi:10.14419/ijet.v7i4.9.20608

Jones, F., Burke, R. J., & Westman, M. (2013). *Work-life balance: A psychological perspective*. Psychology Press.

Schueller-Weidekamm, C., & Kautzky-Willer, A. (2012). Challenges of work–life balance for women physicians/mothers working in leadership positions. *Gender Medicine*, *9*(4), 244–250.

Section 3

Mainstreaming Women Through Good Governance in the Digital Era

This section explores the impacts of positive governance and discusses judicial diversity, a case study of construction sector, and the impacts of the financial literacy for inclusive sustainable development in the digital era.

Chapter 12
Judicial Diversity in India:
A Strategic Imperative

Vaishali Trivedi
St. Kabir Institute of Professional Studies, India

Vikas Trivedi
Institute of Law, Nirma University, India

ABSTRACT

As the businesses across the world are all set to enter the Fourth Industrial Revolution, agile work practices and diverse work teams have become new survival strategies. Experts say to be smart in real sense, this digi-revolution needs to be more inclusive. From the educational institutions to sports, politics, governance, corporates, military, and parliament, the institutions of all kinds are facing the challenges of ensuring greater gender inclusiveness. Along similar lines, the judiciary cannot be an exception either. . In a country like India wherein the women constitute 50% of the population and where there are already good number of women members in bar available to be elevated, the presence of only a handful women in the judiciary raises multiple questions. This chapter reflects on the underrepresentation of women in the Indian judiciary. It uncovers the existence of a glass ceiling in the Indian judiciary and advocates the case for judicial diversity.

INTRODUCTION

From times immemorial, the roles played by men and women have been well defined in the social setup. It was the men who performed the role of bread earner for the family and women's role was always secondary and limited to being a homemaker

DOI: 10.4018/978-1-7998-8594-8.ch012

and performing day-to-day chores at home. This model of living has been deeply rooted since primitive times. However, like in all walks of life, this too has gone a sea-change over the years. Globalization has led to a structural change in the very status of women. Women have made it big and have got themselves counted at all prominent positions of public life. There has been remarkable participation of women in the workplace.

As businesses across the world are all set to enter the Fourth Industrial Revolution, agile work practices and diverse work teams have become new survival strategies. The representation of women in the workplace across the sectors thus is seeing an increasing trend. However, their contribution has largely been undervalued by the organizations. Under the emerging turbulent and disruptive environment, gender diversity has become extremely critical to the success of any business. In the age of talent crunch, businesses have begun their talent hunt by tapping these unique talent pools. From the educational institutions to sports, politics, governance, corporates, the military, and Parliament, institutions of all kinds are facing the challenges of ensuring greater gender inclusiveness. Along similar lines, Judiciary cannot be an exception either. The Indian judiciary is one of the prominent fields where women's representation is seen to be predominantly lopsided. It is a universally accepted fact that judicial diversity in a country like India is not only the need of the hour but also a herculean task. The representation of women in the Indian legal system needs to be improved given the numerous advantages it offers to improve the delivery of justice and sustainable development.

THE GLASS CEILING IN INDIAN JUDICIARY: AN OVERVIEW

Out of the total 247 judges appointed so far, the Indian apex court has witnessed only eight women judges since Independence (More women judges needed in judiciary, 2021)

The first female judge of the Supreme Court of India was *Justice Fatima Beevi* in 1989. She served as a judge in Kerala High Court before her appointment in Supreme Court. *Justice Ruma Pal* was preceded by *Justice Sujata Manohar* to become the longest-serving Women judge in Indian history. She was serving as judge of the Calcutta High Court before her appointment in the Supreme Court of India. *Justice Gyan Sudha Misra* was the next woman judge appointed in the Supreme Court who got appointed after a long gap of four years post-Justice Pal's retirement. It was around the same time, *Justice Ranjana Desai* also got appointed as Supreme Court judge and history was created by both of them as they held an all-women bench for a day in the year 2013. *Justice R Banumathi* was appointed as Supreme Court judge in the year 2014, *Justice Indu Malhotra* in 2018. Currently

Table 1. Women judges in Supreme Court of India - A Timeline

S No	Name	Date of Appointment	Date of retirement
1	Fathima Beevi	6 October 1989	29 April 1992
2	Sujata Manohar	8 November 1994	27 August 1999
3	Ruma Pal	28 January 2000	2 June 2006
4	Gyan Sudha Misra	30 April 2010	27 April 2014
5	Ranjana Desai	13 September 2011	29 October 2014
6	R. Banumathi	13 August 2014	19 July 2020
7	Indu Malhotra	27 April 2018	13 March 2021
8	Indira Banerjee	7 August 2018	23 September 2022

Source: www.thequint.com

out of 27 judges, the Supreme Court of India has only one-woman judge - *Justice Indira Banerjee* (Representation of Women in Judiciary,2020)

Table 1 presents the data on Women judges in the Supreme Court of India.

There has been a glass ceiling for women in the Indian judiciary which is evident from table 2 The share of women judges in High Courts increased from 11 to 13 percent and in Subordinate Courts from 28 to 30 percent. Despite the percentage share of women judges improving across courts consistently for the last two years, the prevalence of glass ceiling can be seen from the very fact that while one in every three judges happens to be a woman at subordinate courts, in High Courts one in every nine judges happen to be a woman. The state-wise data shows that Sikkim (33.3%) has the highest number of women judges in High Courts, followed by Andhra Pradesh (19%), Haryana -Punjab (18.2%), and Tamil Nadu (16.7%). While the states of Bihar, Uttarakhand, Meghalaya, and Tripura have no women judges in the High Courts. As far as Representation of Women in Subordinate Courts is concerned, Goa leads with 72% Women judges, followed by Meghalaya (50%)Telangana (46.2%), Andhra Pradesh (43.6%) (Gender Gap and Sensitisation in Judiciary,2020)

ARGUMENTS FOR WOMEN IN THE JUDICIARY

Women's safety is fast becoming a matter of grave concern in India. The pathetic state of women's safety is evident from the fact that a survey from Thomson Reuters Foundation rated India as the most dangerous country for women in the year 2018. (Target judicial patriarchy, not the judge, 2021) Added to this, the data from the National Crime Records Bureau report suggests that in the year 2019, 32,032 rape cases were reported which means on an average 88 rapes per day. As per the data by

Table 2. Women representation across states

States	High Court Judges	Subordinate Court Judges
Andhra Pradesh	19.0	43.6
Bihar	0.0	14.5
Chhattisgarh	14.3	37.4
Gujarat	14.8	16.8
Haryana	18.2	34.6
Jharkhand	5.9	12.1
Karnataka	10.9	30.7
Kerala	13.5	37.9
Madhya Pradesh	9.7	27.2
Maharashtra	13.4	28.4
Odisha	6.3	40.2
Punjab	18.2	40.9
Rajasthan	8.0	34.5
Tamil Nadu	16.7	36.8
Telangana	7.1	46.2
Uttar Pradesh	5.1	25.2
Uttarakhand	0	37.3
West Bengal	13.2	36.4
Arunachal Pradesh	4.8	NA
Goa	13.4	72
Himachal Pradesh	11.1	29.1
Meghalaya	0.00	50
Mizoram	4.8	33.3
Sikkim	33.3	28.6
Tripura	0.0	31.6

Source: India Justice Report 2020

United Nations Women across 39 different countries, the presence of women police is positively correlated to the reporting of crimes related to sexual assault which itself proves that having women in the judiciary is extremely vital for establishing a gender-responsive justice system. It is said that worsening women's security in India is attributed to the lack of gender sensitivity on the part of the judiciary. The dire need for improving women's representation in the judiciary is evident from the judgment by The Sujata Manohar in the case *Vishaka v. State of Rajasthan (1997)*, when for the first time in Indian history legal provisions related to sexual harassment at the workplace were made actionable.(Nishith Desai, 2020)

Recently, research was carried out at National Law University, Delhi to identify the tendency of the court to perpetuate gendered opinions and to determine whether the court stereotypically evaluated rape victims- as to the behavior of accused and victim post-rape incident. It was observed that judges often have a stereotypical image of a rape victim. (Gender of Justice, 2018) In many cases, the study revealed an unfortunate state of affairs. There were quite a few judgments where insensitive comments were made that trivialized such heinous offenses. The case of *Raja v. State of Karnataka* (2016) relates to the rape of a domestic worker in Bengaluru. The trial court had convicted the three accused involved in the case. However, the same was overturned in appeal on the defense argued that this was a case of false accusation and the victim was a prostitute. The court observed: *"(the victim's) post-incident conduct and movements are noticeably unusual. Instead of hurrying back home in a distressed, humiliated, and devastated state, she stayed back in and around the place of occurrence, enquired about the same from persons whom she claims to have met in the late hours of the night. Her confident movements alone past midnight, in that state, are also out of the ordinary. The medical opinion that she was accustomed to sexual intercourse when admittedly she was living separately from her husband for a year-and-a-half before the incident also has its implication."* *Sudhanshu Sekhar v. State of Orissa* (2002) again was a case where the judges did not trust the version of the victim and passed an order of acquittal of the accused and held "*though the past conduct of the prosecutrix is an irrelevant matter, in the instant case, (the prosecutrix) asserted that she was a virgin until the alleged incident, but the evidence supported by her physical features revealed that she was habituated to sex. All factors cast serious doubt on the prosecution case*". At times, judges inadvertently undermine the seriousness of a traumatic incident.

Another shocking remark came up in the case of *Vinod Kumar v. State of Kerala* (2014). The court again passed an order of acquittal to a married man who was being tried for raping a 20-year-old girl on the pretext of marrying her. The court hoped that "*his wife would find in herself the fortitude to forgive so that their family may be united again and may rediscover happiness*". All in all, the victims of an offense e as heinous as Rape are subjected to *institutional sexism* from all male-dominated quarters-police, advocates, and judges too. There are hugely prevalent notions of victim-blaming which leads to the accused wrongfully getting acquitted. Recently, a High Court imposed the bail condition on the accused of a case of sexual assault to tie Rakhi to the victim, as a condition for bail. (Her Lordship, 2021)

The Supreme Court in *Aparna Bhat v. State of Madhya Pradesh (2021)* took upon the issue seriously and noted:

"Using rakhi tying as a condition for bail, transforms a molester into a brother, by a judicial mandate. This is wholly unacceptable and has the effect of diluting and eroding the offense of sexual harassment. The act perpetrated on the survivor constitutes an offense in law and is not a minor transgression that can be remedied by way of an apology, rendering community service, tying a rakhi, or presenting a gift to the survivor, or even promising to marry her, as the case may be. The law criminalizes outraging the modesty of a woman"

It has been seen that putting more women in influential positions leads to increased reporting of crimes against women and faster delivery of justice (Dubochet Lucy, 2014) The biases in the judgments would increase in the absence of women judges. The presence of women in the judiciary reflects a representative character of society. This is because judges are always very much part of the social set up and including women in the judicial circles presents a much better picture than the one without a women representation. A bench with women gestures the state of equality of opportunity in the legal arena. This surely exhibits that the appointments to the judiciary are fair, merit-based, and devoid of discrimination. An important aspect of women's participation in judicial offices will be that it will send a very powerful message to women in the law profession. It will be a big boost to those aspiring judicial services thereby also enabling gender balance.

The Judges do bring with them their own experiences while deciding cases. On this ground, the presence of female judges gives a sense of empathy, especially to female litigants. In this way, it does guarantee a better courtroom experience, than their male counterparts. The litigants, in this case, are more assured that gender bias that prevails even from the bench is negated considerably. Benches with women likely keep a check on the sexist mindset. This will ensure adequate gender sensitization right from the judiciary and the male colleagues too will be ensuring that stereotyping doesn't go unnoticed and any such instances won't be played down. It is quite natural for the judges to bring their own life experiences to the judgment table. On this approach, the women judge will surely bring a lot more to the desk on account of her similar life stages- education, marriage, the times of pregnancy, childbirth, and others. (Hunter R, 2015) The male-dominated benches fail to portray the true picture and women judges will bring in fresh perspectives on the upcoming laws. The equal opportunity for women is surely fundamental for the very institution that is tasked with safeguarding the said democratic values.(Tilting the Scale, Gender Imbalance in Lower Judiciary,2018)

A Judge speaks his mind through judgments. The judges must display utmost care and choose a progressive vocabulary while writing judgments. Even one instance of a casual gender stereotype will badly hit the fair justice aspect of the constitution. It is also critical that judges should avoid using any gender-specific stereotypes as to portraying women as weak-physically, mentally, or emotionally and incapable of taking prudent decisions. The instances of judges holding women victims responsible for the sexual assault cases as provoking through their western outfits are killing the messenger. It is imperative for the judges not to pre-judge such cases.

SUSTAINABLE DEVELOPMENT GOALS AND JUDICIAL DIVERSITY

Sustainable Development Goals as prescribed by the United Nations, especially SDG 5 and SDG 16 very strongly advocate the need to establish gender equality and women's representation in public institutions such as the judiciary through SDG 5 and SDG 16. Discrimination against women is an age-old taboo. It is woven deep into our social fabrics which are leading to huge wastage of human potential. Equality to Women will benefit the world tremendously across social, economic, and political fronts. SDG 5 aims to eradicate all forms of discrimination against women by eliminating violence and harmful practices; recognizing and valuing unpaid care and domestic work; ensuring full participation of women in social, economic, and public spheres; access to sexual and reproductive health and reproductive rights; initiating reforms to provide women equal rights to economic resources, using ICT for women empowerment; Adopting& enforcing the legislation that promotes gender justice at all levels. SDG 16 aims at promoting peaceful and inclusive societies for sustainable development, creating the provisions for access to justice for all, and building effective, accountable institutions at all levels.

None of the global sustainable development agenda for 2030 can be fulfilled without adequately safeguarding the human rights of the individuals who have been devoid of the same. Women in India have been one of such vulnerable cohorts. India was in the bottom 20% of ranked countries when its Gender Inequality Index stood at 0.524 in the year 2017.

Crime against women in India largely goes unreported because many expressions of violence against women are not even considered as a crime in the first place. Having more women in the judiciary can go a long way in ensuring truly inclusive and representative decision-making. *Women judges add a more empathetic edge to the judgments by putting their own real-life experiences into action.*

SDG 5 AND SDG 16 are seen to have a mutually reinforcing impact on the law. The law of land plays a critical role in recognizing and implementing women's rights. Ample evidence exists to suggest that on many occasions, legal machinery has failed to protect the rights of women be it social, economic, or cultural front. To address this challenge SDG 16 holds great relevance as it advocates the establishment of a robust legal and justice environment as a necessary precondition for achieving gender justice. (United Nations and Rule of Law)

The Chief Justice of India has also vouched for greater social dioversity for judicial appointments. (Judicial appointments should reflect social diversity, 2021)

THE FEMALE JUDGES: MEMORABLE JUDGEMENTS

Women judges have been known for bringing in a holistic perspective to the issue at hand. Here are some of the noteworthy interventions by the women judges in the past which justify the need for their presence in the judiciary.

Justice Indu Malhotra

Sabarimala Temple at Kerala is devoted to Lord Ayyappa. The temple is of great ancient times. As per the traditional belief, it strictly prohibits women in the menstruating years (age group 10-50 years) This practice has existed since times immemorial and women. As per the Hindu traditions, women are considered impure while menstruating therefore the temple authorities have placed complete restrictions on the entry of women to preserve the temple's sanctity. This age-old practice was recently challenged by Indian Young Lawyers Association by filing public interest litigation before the Supreme Court of India. The two major arguments raised by the petitioners were the violation of the Right to Equality (Article 14) and Freedom of Religion (Article 25) of the Constitution of India. The apex court held the practice of restricting women to be unconstitutional by 4:1 majority in *Indian Young Lawyers Association v. State of Kerala, (2018)* Most ironically, the dissent came from the only woman judge on the bench- *Justice Indu Malhotra*. On the challenges to religious practices through PIL's, she opined that it is setting up a dangerous precedent and could be detrimental to the secular feature of our constitution. Ours is a country that comprises people of diverse faiths and beliefs and that need to be respected. On the right to equality, she stated that it cannot be the only criterion to test religious practices. Concerning the aspect of gender equality, she observed that there are 1000 other temples of Lord Ayyappa, where the entry isn't denied to women for the reason, he hasn't manifested himself in the form of a 'Naishtik Brahmachari. She holds the distinction of being the first woman advocate to be directly elevated as a Judge to the Supreme Court of India. (Shankar*, U., & Chowdhury, S. (2019).

The Beauty of Dissent:

The majority has its way, but the minority has its say. One of the most fascinating aspects of a dissenting judgment is that it ensures that the constitution is not a lifeless document, but a living one. If one judge is convinced today, it lays a foundation for other judges to be convinced as well. Dissent is thus a great tool for evolution of law. (The Value of Dissent in Supreme Court Judgments, 2020) Thus, we must respect, cherish and celebrate the dissenting opinions to flourish. It is in this backdrop that the dissenting judgment of Justice Indu Malhotra assumes great significance. There are many times when unanimity of opinion may not exist among judges. Law isn't an exact science and difference of opinion needs to be respected. It depends on a variety of factors- education, social setup, culture, and overall environment. The presence of women on the bench will bring fresh perspectives on issues of the day. This will matter even more in the case of the most important cases brought before the courts. This seems to be well recognized by Mr. Justice Caton in Swift v. Castle, 23 Ill. 209, 340, where he said:

"We find, upon many of the most important questions affecting human rights, parallel lines of conflicting decisions running down through a long course of years, kept up and maintained by the accidental circumstance that the judges upon whom the duty of deciding devolved, in the various courts and different ages, entertained different views as to what would best promote the ends of justice and the public go"

Justice Indu Malhotra was also part of another noteworthy judgment relating to decriminalizing Section 497 of the Indian Penal Code, 1860. Adultery finds its base in the deeply rooted patriarchal setup in Indian society.

"Whoever has sexual intercourse with a person who is and whom he knows or has reason to believe to be the wife of another man, without the consent or connivance of that man, such sexual intercourse not amounting to the offense of rape, is guilty of the offense of adultery and shall be punished with imprisonment of either description for a term which may extend to five years, or with fine or with both. In such a case, the wife shall not be punishable as an abettor". Section- 497 IPC.

In the case, it was held that hitherto existing Section 497 of Indian Penal Code, restricted various fundamental rights- "*Right to sexual autonomy as provided under Article 21(Right to life), Right to sexual expression as provided under Article 19(Right to freedom), Right to equality as provided under Article 14(Right to equality), Right against discrimination as provided under Article 15(Right against discrimination)"* of the constitution.

Justice Indu Malhotra holding in her judgment stated,

"A legislation that perpetuates such stereotypes in relationships, and institutionalizes discrimination is a clear violation of the fundamental rights guaranteed by Part III of the Constitution. There is, therefore, no justification for the continuance of Section 497 of the IPC as framed in 1860, to remain on the statute book."

Justice R. Bhanumati

16 December 2012 is the day that shocked the concise of the entire nation in *Mukesh v. State For Nct Of Delhi, (2017)* The case is popularly known as "Nirbhaya"- the referred pseudonym for the rape victim. The victim and her friend were coming back from a movie theatre. While looking for the bus, the culprits convinced them to get into the empty bus wherein the victim was brutally raped by six men, one of whom was a minor. She later succumbed to her injuries. The brutality of the incident led to a huge social outrage in the country and people demanded the death penalty for the rapists. On the legal side, this incident led to the coming up of The *Criminal Law (Amendment) Act, 2013* which gave a broadened definition of 'rape'. In this case, Justice R Bhanumati was one of the judges on the bench. In her judgment, she advocated for the need for gender sensitization in the early formative years of a child. And rightly stated that only having the related legislations will never be enough. The offense of rape is to be evaluated not just in terms of its physical part. It is the exertion of force on the overall personality of women. She placed the need for a change of mindset of the society which largely resonated with a psychological view. On the offenses against women, it assumes another dimension to be coming from a woman judging herself. She observed:

"Persisting notion that the testimony of victim has to be corroborated by other evidence must be removed. To equate a rape victim to an accomplice is to add insult to womanhood...Where the victims are helpless women, children, or old persons and the accused displayed depraved mentality, diabolically committing a crime, the accused should be shown no remorse, and the death penalty should be awarded"

Justice Sujata Manohar

Gyan Sudha Misra J. in an interview said, "*I guess lack of faith and belief in the abilities of women is still rooted in society and more so in the male psyche and we prefer to have their token presence, especially in the higher judiciary, more for the sake of symbol rather than their equal participation*" The courts should refrain from getting swayed by minor discrepancies, rather should appraise the broader possibilities in a case.

Medha Kotwal Lele v. Union of India

The Supreme Court of India has issued guidelines popularly known as Vishaka Guidelines. However, despite the required mandatory compliance with these guidelines, the implementation remained a very challenging task. They weren't being complied with at many places. Dr. Medha Kotwal of Aalochana (an NGO) wrote a letter highlighting several individual isolated instances where the Vishaka Guidelines weren't being complied with. (*Medha Kotwal Lele v. Union of India, 2012*) As in many other cases, the apex court converted this letter into a writ petition and directed the respective state governments to emphasize the implementation of these stated guidelines. It has strongly directed the states to ensure that there is an adequate and effective mechanism placed for the effective implementation of the guidelines. It has also gone to the extent of asserting that in case of non-adherence to these guidelines, the aggrieved persons can directly approach the High courts of respective states.

Dr. Punita K Sodhi v. Union of India Case

The definition of Sexual Harassment under Section 2 and 3 of the POSH Act are very elaborate. Also, many times it depends on the interpretation of actions of the respondent. Thus, the interpretation of actions of the respondent by the Internal Complaints Committee assumes great significance. In the case of *Dr. Punita K Sodhi v. Union of India,(2010)* the Delhi High Court has held the view that Sexual harassment is a very subjective element. *A complete understanding of the complainant's view requires "harmless social interactions to which only overly-sensitive women would object. The characteristically male view depicts sexual harassment as comparatively harmless amusement... Men, who are rarely victims of sexual assault, may view sexual conduct in a vacuum without a full appreciation of the social setting or the underlying threat of violence that a woman may perceive."*

REASONS FOR LEAKING JUDICIAL FUNNEL

The reservation policy in many states offering reservations to women in lower levels of the judiciary is seen to be absent in the case of higher-order courts in the country which is also one of the reasons why the number of women at Higher-order courts remains below. At certain High Courts, one of the criteria to be designated as a senior counsel is the income limit. The women lawyers are hit hard on this aspect too with difficulty in finding well-paying clients. They face discrimination from all quarters-clients, seniors, judges as well. Thc clicnts in criminal cases generally prefer male lawyers to represent their cases. Also, the road is even tougher for a first-generation women lawyer. Getting the cases independently gets very difficult in many cases, and thus they have to restrict themselves as juniors to someone else's (male) who can source cases. Even in that position, women lawyers are mostly sent to seek routine adjournments or at the admission stage. Moreover, clients in criminal cases feel prefer male lawyers. The reason is that the clients tend to socialize well with the male layers. It is seen that more women have been entering the lower levels of the judiciary since the recruitment happens through an entrance exam. However, the prevalence of the collegium system lacks transparency and hence possesses the scope for biases for the movement of women to the higher levels of the judiciary.

SECURING JUDICIAL INCLUSIVITY FOR WOMEN THE BALANCING ACT

The *Supreme Court of India* is entrusted with the interpretation of the Constitution. It shapes the political, economic and social, and legal landscape of the nation. During the last 70 years, it has made the most remarkable contributions on a wide range of subjects- equality, due process of law, human rights, environmental protection, freedom of speech and expression, freedom of speech and expression, privacy, sexual autonomy, and many others. Most recently, it has made the judicial intervention in some of the most controversial and contemporary issues- Sexual Harassment at the workplace, Sabrimala Temple entry, Same-sex marriage, Right to Privacy, Marital Rape, etc. It continues to be the battleground for negotiations between patriarchal society and the newfound thought leaders. The fact that women are hugely unrepresented in this arena gives unfair veto power to an all-men elite.

All judges must be provided with gender sensitization training. (Skewed justice, 2020)The law schools in the country must run a compulsory course on Gender Sensitization. Steps must be taken to bar the sexist remarks from the judgments and consequently from judicial language. TAs far as the appointment of district judges is concerned lawyers need to have an experience of seven continuous years of service. This is the age when women are pushed to marry. Added to this, long working hours in the field of law while handling household responsibilities well further induce the women to drop out from the profession. Thus, there is a need for complete reorientation on the part of the societies' attitude towards women and their responsibilities in managing the house. There is a need to diversify the process of judicial appointment by the collegium to address this prevalent gender gap in the judiciary (ForumIAS,2021). A distinguished Women jurist can be appointed to Supreme Court as per Article 124. Initiatives need to be taken on the part of the government and Bar Council of India to encourage more women to take up law as their profession. The Supreme Court of India should come out with the vision document to address the long-prevailing gender gap in the judiciary to achieve women's representation in the judiciary at least up to 50%. All lawyers must be mandated to undergo gender sensitization training.

It makes a lot of sense to sensitize judges on gender education. As part of the foundation training, there can be a separate module on gender sensitization. This will go a long way in ensuring judges that judges display ample sensitivity. The role of judges as thought leaders in promoting and protecting equality and fairness in society is critical. The National Judicial Academy (NJA) is also required to come up with concrete training along with adequate awareness programs and avoid biases that have been deeply rooted. Regulatory bodies like the *Bar Council of India* (BCI) also need to step in as they have a good opportunity to make a meaningful contribution to the issue of gender sensitization. The subject should be made a compulsory part of the curriculum at colleges/universities at the UG/PG level. The same should also form part of the syllabus of the All India Bar Examination (AIBE). Judiciary is believed to be the ultimate guardian of the language of law and therefore, it must set the tone of dignity and equality. The onus is more on the judiciary as is the last bastion of hope for the common man. It must set the benchmark for the ideal legal and political discourse that takes place.

Concluding Remarks:

As per Attorney General *K K Venugopal*, having more women in the judiciary would lead to a more empathetic outlook in the cases related to sexual violence. It's important that judges need to put themselves into the victim's shoes while delivering the judgments especially in cases involving sexual violence. Though the number of women in the legal profession is improving since 1990, still it remains much lower as compared to men. The presence of Women judges not only strengthens the judiciary but also improves the public's trust. In times when the crime against women is rising at an alarming rate, women are a must-have in the judiciary to improve the quality of justice to their cohort. The symbol of justice may be a blindfolded woman, but no self-respecting citizen will ever settle just for tokenism or symbols. (Jaisingh, I 2019).

REFERENCES

Aparna Bhat v. State of Madhya Pradesh, Supreme Court of India (2021) https://www.livelaw.in/pdf_upload/aparna-bhat-v-state-of-mp-168-390769.pdf

Bajpai, G. (2018). Gender of justice. *The Indian Express*. Retrieved 19 July 2021, from https://indianexpress.com/article/opinion/columns/gender-of-justice-appointment-of-female-judges-5452591/

Dr. Punita K. Sodhi v. Union Of India, Delhi High Court (2010) https://indiankanoon.org/doc/87321004/

Dubochet. (2014). Why India Needs the Women's, Reservation Bill (No10).

Gender and law synergies between SDG 5 and 16. (n.d.). https://www.idlo.int/fr/news/highlights/gender-and-rule-law-synergies-between-sdg-5-and-16

Gender equality in decision-making positions. (2017). https://www.intereconomics.eu/contents/year/2017/number/1/article/gender-equality-in-decision-making-positions-the-efficiency-gains.html

Gender equality in decision-making positions. (n.d.). https://www.intereconomics.eu/contents/year/2017/number/1/article/gender-equality-in-decision-making-positions-the-efficiency-gains.html

Gender gap and sensitization in judiciary. (n.d.). https://www.drishtiias.com/daily-updates/daily-news-analysis/gender-gap-and-sensitisation-in-judiciary

Her Lordship. (2021). *The Indian Express*. Retrieved 28 July 2021, from https://indianexpress.com/article/opinion/editorials/her-lordship-indian-judiciary-supreme-court-women-lawyers-association-7276985/

How many women judges in supreme court and high court. (n.d.). https://www.thequint.com/voices/women/how-many-women-judges-in-supreme-court-and-high-court

Hunter, R. (2015). *More than Just a Different Face? Judicial Diversity and Decision-making*. Academic Press.

Indian Young Lawyers Association v. State of Kerala, Supreme Court of India (2018) https://indiankanoon.org/doc/163639357/

Issue of gender gap in judiciary explained pointwise. (n.d.). https://blog.forumias.com/issue-of-gender-gap-in-judiciary-explained-pointwise/

Jaisingh, I. (2019). An Open Letter From Indira Jaising to the Chief Justice of India on Women's Day. *The Wire*. Retrieved 10 July 2021, from https://thewire.in/law/open-letter-indira-jaising-to-cji-womens-day

Judicial appointments should reflect social diversity: CJI. (2021). *The Hindu*. Retrieved 4 July 2021, from https://www.thehindu.com/news/national/judicial-appointments-should-reflect-social-diversity-cji/article34730621.ece

Medha Kotwal Lele v. Union of India, Supreme Court of India (2012) https://indiankanoon.org/doc/48293767/

More women judges need in judiciary. (n.d.). https://www.hindustantimes.com/cities/chandigarh-news/more-women-judges-needed-in-judiciary-101623059014130.html

Mukesh v. State For Nct Of Delhi, Supreme Court of India (2017) https://indiankanoon.org/doc/68696327/

Prevention of Sexual Harassment at the Workplace (POSH). (2020). Retrieved from https://www.nishithdesai.com/fileadmin/user_upload/pdfs/Research%20Papers/Prevention_of_Sexual_Harassment_at_Workplace.pdf

Raja v. State of Karnataka, Supreme Court of India (2016) https://indiankanoon.org/doc/134419727/

Shankar, U., & Chowdhury, S. (2019). Representative judiciary in India: An argument for gender diversity in the appointment of judges in the supreme court. *ILI Law Review*. Retrieved from https://www.ili.ac.in/pdf/uss.pdf

Shekhara, R., & Raza, R. (2020). *The Value of Dissent in Supreme Court Judgments*. Retrieved 17 July 2021, from https://www.theleaflet.in/dissent-judgments-supreme-court/

Skewed justice. (2020). *The Indian Express*. Retrieved 30 July 2021, from https://indianexpress.com/article/opinion/editorials/supreme-court-women-judges-kk-venugopal-7088348/

Sudhansu Sekhar Sahoo v. State Of Orissa, Supreme Court of India (2002) https://indiankanoon.org/doc/76278/

Swift v. Castle, 23 Ill. 209, Illinois Supreme Court (1859) https://cite.case.law/ill/23/209/

Target judicial patriarchy, not the judge. (2021). *The Hindu*. Retrieved 18 July 2021, from https://www.thehindu.com/opinion/lead/target-judicial-patriarchy-not-the-judge/article34030694.ece

Tata Trusts. (2020). *India Justice Report 2020*. Retrieved from https://www.tatatrusts.org/Upload/pdf/ijr-2020-overall-report-january-26.pdf

Tilting the Scale: Gender Imbalance in the Lower Judiciary. (2018). *Vidhi Centre for Legal Policy*. Retrieved 20 July 2021, from https://vidhilegalpolicy.in/research/report-on-gender-imbalance-in-the-lower-judiciary/

Vinod Kumar v. State of Kerala, Supreme Court of India (2014) https://indiankanoon.org/doc/188149660/

Vishakha v. State of Rajasthan, Supreme Court of India (1997) https://indiankanoon.org/doc/1031794/

Chapter 13
The Continuous Struggle for the Existence of Females in the Construction Industry in the 21st Century

Gaganpreet Kaur
Amity University, India

Nandita Mishra
Linkoping University, Sweden

Puja Singhal
https://orcid.org/0000-0003-1927-5517
National Centre for School Leadership-NIEPA, India

ABSTRACT

The construction industry in India holds second place in the development of the country after the agriculture industry. The construction industry consists of the employment of the most diverse culture of people employed, and the issue of gender inequality is one of the main problems associated with this industry. This chapter focuses on the various issues related to the diversity of the people employed and the gender inequality prevailing among them. A questionnaire was designed which was to be filled by the workers, and a total of 220 respondents were interviewed from different sites of Delhi and NCR. Various questions related to the issues such as gender inequality and other problems faced by the female employees apart from the troubles of the routine problems were asked. The application of various tests applied on the data collected helped to study the issues in detail. Based on the field study, various suggestions and recommendations are provided.

DOI: 10.4018/978-1-7998-8594-8.ch013

INTRODUCTION

In the development of any country construction industry plays a very important role. This industry not only helps build the economy of the country but also makes it structurally beautiful. And the benefits of this industry are not limited to the above mentioned factors but along with this it generates employment also (Tripathi & Jha, 2018). In India, construction industry holds the second most critical part in the development of the nation's economy after agriculture. This industry employs around 33 million people who are engaged in the construction of road, power projects, buildings, factories, highways, metro projects, airports and many more. Apart from this industry employing a huge number of people yet there are maximum number of accidents (Patel, Moitra, Momin, & Kantharia, 2012)occur and the number of the occurrence of death during work is highest than any other industry (Zikriyoev & Crane, 2019). The sort of work involved is highly perilous and high level of safety is recommended, but the reality is far from the word satisfactory. The reason behind this could be many but discussing few of them are the uneducated, poor workers, time, cost associated with projects, lack of proper implementation of the rules laid by the Government allied with safety and health precaution to be taken (Tiwary & Gangopadhyay, A review on the occupational health and social security of unorganized workers in the construction industry, 2011). Insecurity of wages, dangerous working conditions and lack of access to any kind of health care are the few descriptions of the construction workers. The workers associated with the construction industry are essentially poor and most of them are migrants (Thenguzhali & Veerachamy, 2009). Accidents are the outcomes of the unsafe acts and unsafe working conditions (Shirur & Torgal, 2014). Majority of the accidents occur due to the lack of induction training (Pheng & Hou, 2019)which is to be provided at the time of recruitment of new worker and also regular training which is to be provided on regular basis to reduce the happening of accidents (Shamsuddin, Ani, Ismail, & Ibrahim, 2015). But the problem of this industry is not restricted to the lack of safety measures only there are many other factors adding and making the situation worst (Srivastava R., 2014). There are many health issues and the troubles associated with it (Saha, 2014). Construction workers are the one who work in the most torturing working conditions, working directly under the sun with the temperature sometimes rising to 50 degree Celsius (Sparks, Faragher, & Cooper, 2001). There was a need to regulate the safety, health, and welfare measures for the betterment of the construction workers, (Selvam A, Krithika Priyadarshini) by some regulatory authority. An act was passed by the Government named as Building and Other Construction Workers (Regulation of Employment and Conditions of Service) Act was passed in the year 1996. Under this various rules and regulations are laid so as to safeguard the safety, health and welfare conditions of the workers (Saha, 2014).

REVIEW OF LITERATURE

There are number of safety as well as health risks associated with construction industry and they are now being recognized by the name of occupational safety and health issues now. Many studies have been done on the occupational safety and health measures and the root cause of accidents, (Sageer, Rafat, & Agarwal, Identification of variables affecting employee satisfaction and their impact on the organnization, 2012). Lack of occupational safety as well as lack of the knowledge to use the safety equipment, (S.Chockalingam and T.Sornakumar, 2011) lack of induction as well as regular training provided to the workers, and this situation is even worst when the workers are not provided any safety equipment (S.Kanchana, P.sivaprakash and Sebastian Joseph, 2015). A survey conducted by International Labour organization stated that, "165 out of every 1000 workers are injured during work".

In India there are 3226 construction companies which are presently developing the country's infrastructure. Out the above total mentioned the private sector holds the majority in this sector with 3189 companies, whereas public companies holds only 28 companies and government holds a minimal number which is just 9 companies. The major issues with the safety and health issues in the construction industry is that apart from the rules and regulations being laid down by the Government the implementation of these are not even close to satisfactory. Construction work has been regarded by the International Labour Organization (ILO) as the most dangerous, the most accident prone job than any other. This sector is also considered as stated by ILO due to the nature of the work associated with it such as working on extreme heights, working with dangerous equipments such as cutters, drilling machines, welding, vibrators, cranes etc (Ofori, 2000). Work being done in the construction industry is way far from the extreme limits (Nyambura & Simon, 2018)which are recommended by the occupation safety and health standards (Mann J. S., 2007) either it is for men or even for women (Sang & Powell, 2012). The condition of women is even more worst as it has been the most female unfriendly industry than any other (Tiwary G., et al., 2012). "The types of the hazards that workmen are exposed to in the workplace are frequently classified as: physical (e.g. noise, thermal stress, ergonomic, stressors, ionizing and non-ionizing radiations), chemical (e.g. solvents, heavy metals, pesticides, and pharmaceuticals), biological (e.g. human immunodeficiency virus (HIV), hepatitis B and C) and psychological (stress and violence)" Occupational health Hazards- Analysis of the present Legal Framework, (Singh K., 2014). Some of the health risk associated with this industry is:

- Ø Musculoskeletal disorder: injuries related to muscle, joint or back
- Ø Hand-arm vibration syndrome: use of vibrating tools causing numbness and pain in the hands and in the fingers.

Ø Dermatitis: hazardous substances such as cements and other solvents causing redness and inflammation in the skin being exposed to.
Ø Hearing loss: high level of noise pollution caused from various machines used causing deafness and even sounds of ringing in the ears.
Ø Asbestos: Irritation caused by the fibers causing difficulty in breathing

Many substances used are harmful and there effects are even harsher on health if used with bare hands. Direct contact to them causes allergy, mild redness to the skin, in severe cases it also causes oil acne caused by the bitumen based products, skin ulcers from corrosive substances, dermatitis.

Lack of Facilities for Women Workers

One of the most important factors responsible for propelling of any sector is the satisfaction of its employees (Singh R. S., 2014). Absenteeism is one of the outcomes which are influenced directly or indirectly by the working conditions, industrial relations, environmental hazards, poor occupational health services. Absenteeism and labour turnover is the biggest obstacle on the path of success, efficiency and experience.

The unbelievable fact which is true is that according to the social justice bench of the Supreme Court of India consisting of the Justices Madan B Lokur and U.U Lalit an amount of Rs.1796.63 crores has been collected till 30 June 2016 by the Government of Delhi as levy for the labour welfare from the construction companies but the Government has spent just Rs.39 crores for the betterment of the Delhi workers. Despite of the Supreme Court orders at least an amount of Rs27000 crores which was meant for the welfare of the casual workers in the construction sector remained unutilized. Because of the fact that some states had misused the fund collected in the form of 1% cess on the construction companies, it has directed the Delhi government to return an amount of Rs.2.7 crores which being utilized for the purpose of publicity over the years.

RESEARCH METHODOLOGY

Ø With the changes that have taken place in the working of the construction industries a questionnaire was designed and survey was conducted in the construction sites in Delhi and NCR region. Targeting those companies and construction sites that employ more than 250 workers so as to check the rules and regulations which they have to follow under the BOCW Act (Building and Other workers Act, 1996). Various questions relating to the health and safety of the workers

Table 1. Reliability Statistics

Cronbach's Alpha	N of Items
.931	15

were asked and the labours were made to fill them. The 8 pages questionnaire addresses the many safety issues and health related questions were also. The total of 220 respondents were questioned out them 135 were male and 85 were female labours.

DATA INTERPRETATION

The data interpretation considers the various gender related issues prevailing in the construction companies and the problems being faced by the women employed there in. particularly this study interest on the following aspect of the issues:

Ø Equality in providing the safety measures
- Are men and women provided with equal safety measures?
- What are the conditions of these equipments?

Ø Health measure being provided.
- What health measures are taken into concern by the companies?
- Are the companies concered about the health of the labour?

Ø Welfare issues given to the women labour
- Are female workers treated equally?
- Are they provided with basic facilities?

Various test depending upon the data collected were applied and based on the outcomes the interpretations have been given. Below are the various test performed in order to fulfil the above mentioned objectives of the study.

Table1 shows the Cronbach's Alpha when applied came out to be 0.931 which indicates that the alpha coefficient for the 15 items have relatively high internal consistency. This further explains that the value of cronbach's alpha will increase when the inter correlation among the test items increases.

Table-2 shows the item's total score table, in this table the last column shows the Cronbach's alpha value if the item is deleted. As the Alpha value as shown in the 1st table came out to be .931 all the values in the last column are less than this value except the last which gives us the value of 0.939. In other words it says that

Table 2. Item-Total Statistics

	Scale Mean if Item Deleted	Scale Variance if Item Deleted	Corrected Item-Total Correlation	Cronbach's Alpha if Item Deleted
TOILETS	55.55	125.148	.723	.924
LABELLING	54.91	130.098	.649	.927
TOILETCLEANLINESS	55.27	124.879	.791	.923
TOILETVENTILATION	55.21	126.907	.757	.924
ACCESSIBILITY	55.00	129.463	.629	.927
TOILETLIGHTING	55.18	130.425	.619	.927
WATERINTOILETS	55.15	127.312	.613	.927
PRIVACY	55.20	121.363	.720	.924
HYGIENE	55.24	124.927	.675	.926
SANITATIONINLABOURCOLONIES	55.75	125.391	.720	.924
SEPARATEWASHROOMS	55.10	124.146	.623	.928
VENTILATIONOFWASHROOMS	55.42	125.245	.771	.923
OVERALLFACILITIES	55.46	125.222	.780	.923
DRAINAGEINLABOURCOLONIES	55.45	124.918	.754	.923
RATESAFETYEQUIPMENTS	54.98	132.334	.312	.939

if this item is deleted then the value of the Cronbach's alpha will increase rest in other cases the value decreases from the present value. Hence deleting any other item will decrease in the alpha value.

1. TESTING THE SAFETY EQUIPMENTS PROVIDED TO THE WORKERS USING T-TEST:

T-test was used to compare the means of the two groups (Ruxton, 2006) of gender that is male and female to know if there was any significance difference in them.

1. Gender
2. Safety equipments provided

SETTING THE HYPOTHESIS

H0=(NULL HYPOTHESIS) There is no significance difference between the mean of gender of workers in context to the safety equipments provided to them.

H1=(ALTERNATIVE HYPOTHESIS) There is a significance difference between the mean of the gender of workers in context to the safety equipments provided to them.

Table 3. Group Statistics

	GENDER	N	Mean	Std. Deviation	Std. Error Mean
RATESAFETYEQUIPMENTS	MALE	135	3.81	1.598	.138
	FEMALE	85	4.86	.726	.079

Table-3 shows that there are total of 220 workers out which 135 are male and 85 are female workers. The mean of which comes as 3.81 and 4.86 respectively.

Table-4 the Levene's test for equality variance shows that the significance value comes out to be .000 which further states that it is less than the value of 0.005 hence guiding us further to follow the lower values stated under Equal variances not assumed. Further on checking the significance value under 2-tailed test is again less than the value of 0.05 which states that we reject the null hypothesis stating and concluding that there is a significance difference between the gender and the safety equipments provided to them. Checking the result at 95% confidence interval level. This further states the safety equipments given to the male and female are not same in spite of the factor that they are working in same industry.

Table 4. Independent Samples Test

		Levene's Test for Equality of Variances		t-test for Equality of Means						
		F	Sig.	t	df	Sig. (2-tailed)	Mean Difference	Std. Error Difference	95% Confidence Interval of the Difference	
									Lower	Upper
RATESAFETYEQUIPMENTS	Equal variances assumed	130.626	.000	-5.661	218	.000	-1.044	.184	-1.407	-.681
	Equal variances not assumed			-6.586	201.688	.000	-1.044	.159	-1.357	-.731

Table 5. Model Summary

Model	R	R Square	Adjusted R Square	Std. Error of the Estimate
1	.728[a]	.530	.525	.740
a. Predictors: (Constant), TOILETS, HYGIENE				

2. TESTING THE CONCERN OF THE COMPANIES FOR HEALTH AND WELFARE OF WORKERS USING VARIABLES LIKE HYGIENE AND ADEQUATE NUMBER OF TOILETS USING REGRESSION

The regression analysis is used to check the relationship between the dependent variable and the independent variable. Here this test was used to check the relationship between the concerns of the companies for the health of the workers with regards to their health. For this

Ø Dependent variable taken is concern for the workers
Ø And independent variables taken are toilets and hygiene.

Below are the results of the regression analysis.

Table-5 shows the value of .530 as the R Square which when explains means that 53% of the variability in the dependent variables which is concern for the workers is explained by the independent variables that is toilets and hygiene in this model. There is not big discrepancy between the value of R square and Adjusted R square which further explains that the independent variables used in this model are not redundant.

DEFAULT HYPOTHESIS FOR THE BELOW TABLE IS

H0= The Model has the Explanatory Power

The significance value in table-10 come out to be .000 which is less than the .05 which further helps us to conclude that the model has no explanatory power or the model is useless. Hence we reject the null hypothesis.

Ø The default hypothesis for the below table is that
Ø HO=The independent variable does not help us to predict the dependent variable

Table 6. ANOVA

Model		Sum of Squares	Df	Mean Square	F	Sig.
1	Regression	133.730	2	66.865	122.232	.000[a]
	Residual	118.706	217	.547		
	Total	252.436	219			
a. Predictors: (Constant), TOILETS, HYGIENE						
b. Dependent Variable: CONCERNFORWORKERS						

Ø The model predicts that one unit increase in the hygiene variable will increase the dependent variable that is the concern for workers by 0.548 units being the other independent variables, toilets fixed and vice versa.

Ø The model predicts that one unit increase in toilets will increase the concern for the health of the workers by 0.219 units and vice versa being the other independent variable hygiene fixed.

Ø In table-7 the significance value comes less than .05 which means that we reject the null hypothesis and state that the independent variable do help us to predict the dependent variable. More over these coefficients have the positive correlation among them which means that the more concern for the workers will increase with the increase in the hygiene factor and the number of the toilets and vice versa.

2. (G) (3) To Test Whether Safety Induction Training are Given to Male and Female Workers Equally.

HO16= (NULL HYPOTHESIS) there is no significance difference between the safety induction training given to male and female workers

To test the above hypothesis Chi-Square test was applied on the two variables:

Table 7. Coefficients

Model		Unstandardized Coefficients		Standardized Coefficients	t	Sig.
		B	Std. Error	Beta		
1	(Constant)	.699	.205		3.413	.001
	HYGIENE	.548	.045	.613	12.288	.000
	TOILETS	.219	.048	.229	4.600	.000
a. Dependent Variable: CONCERNFORWORKERS						

*Table 8. Gender * Do you get any safety induction training at the time of employment? Crosstabulation*

Count				
		Do you get any safety induction training at the time of employment?		Total
		NO	YES	
Gender	MALE	261	54	315
	FEMALE	129	6	135
Total		390	60	450

1. Gender
2. Safety induction training

From the above test researcher wanted to know whether there was any difference in providing the training to male and the female workers. For studying this, above mentioned variables were taken under study.

From the above table result came out to be that there are 261 male and 129 female workers who did not receive any safety induction training before starting the construction work. There were 54 male and only 6 female workers who had received the safety induction training and the safety knowledge for performing the construction work safely.

Table 9. Chi-Square Tests

	Value	df	Asymp. Sig. (2-sided)	Exact Sig. (2-sided)	Exact Sig. (1-sided)
Pearson Chi-Square	13.187[a]	1	.000		
Continuity Correction[b]	12.111	1	.001		
Likelihood Ratio	15.685	1	.000		
Fisher's Exact Test				.000	.000
N of Valid Cases[b]	450				
a. 0 cells (.0%) have expected count less than 5. The minimum expected count is 18.00.					
b. Computed only for a 2x2 table					

In the above table the significant value is 0.000 which is less than 0.005.

P (0.000) <0.05

Table 10. Symmetric Measures

		Value	Approx. Sig.
Nominal by Nominal	Phi	-.171	.000
	Cramer's V	.171	.000
N of Valid Cases		450	

The result of the Chi-Square rejected the null hypothesis which meant that there was significant difference in giving the safety induction training to male and female workers. There was more emphasis laid on providing the safety training to the male workers than to the female workers. The reason behind this was that there were only 6 female workers out of the total 135 who responded positive of having the training, whereas there were 54 male workers out of total of 315 who had safety training at work.

From table:10 it comes out that there is a negative and low relation among the variables. Due to the reason that the number of female workers who were having the safety induction training were less moreover if their number increases in the population then this outcome will tend to decrease due to the fact that female workers are not given the safety induction training but as these two variables further share low relation as well the downfall in the outcomes will come with slow pace.

FINDINGS AND SUGGESTIONS

After undergoing the study of the various gender issues prevailing in the construction companies of Delhi NCR it came out that the issues faced by women in the construction industry is same irrespective of area. This industry majorly being a male dominating has either no women employee or if in case they have, then their numbers are kept just to qualify the minimum requirement. They are employed as unskilled workers and are always made to do the same (Saari & Judge, 2004).

Women workers majorly being uneducated are made to accept the gender discrimination as the ultimate truth. Thus eradicating any rebellious behaviour of being underpaid in advance from women. The main issue lies when women are not considered equally capable of performing construction work. They are not provided with equal training as of male. Safety equipment, safety trainings are given considering more about the male safety, whereas women are treated as their helpers.

Many tests have been conducted to show the real picture statistically. There is a huge difference between the working conditions for male and female (S.Singh, 21 October 2014). Most of the sites have not provided with the basic safety equipment

(Priya, Kothai, & Kohilambal, 2016) to the workers and in case where they have been provided it has only been given to male workers due to the fact that they are engaged in performing difficult task unlike female workers (Pries & Janszen, 1995). There is almost negligible health care facility available on sites. As this industry involves the most dangerous tasks but the facilities available for its health, safety measures do not match. There are no rest rooms provided to the female workers, (Prasad, Rao, & Nagesha, 2011) as a result they are left with no other option but to feed their little ones openly, which have resulted in many case of harassment. Lack of proper sanitation facilities at site and even at labour colonies have forced them to go for sanitation in open (Ringen & Seegal, 1995). No separate washrooms and the conditions of the partitions are worst (Hindu, 2013). The companies have found perfect loopholes of not providing the basic facilities to the female by employing less than 50 female workers. But the working conditions of the construction companies need serious attention because the situation in which they are working is worth discussing (Hinze, 2013). There is a need to educate the women about their rights (Fielden, Davidson, Gale, & Davey, 2000). Carrying their young ones at site is highly dangerous situation and there is a need to provide proper crèches for them irrespective of the count of female workers. Male and female must be given equality in case of pay and safety equipments, (Dester & Blockley, 1995) as the work is dangerous for both the genders equally. While talking about "SWACHH BHARAT ABHIYAN" how can we deploy them from the basic sanitation facilities?

WOMEN AND DIGITALISATION

It has been observed that educated women are a boom for the society (Mahalakshmi, 2015). Educating women will also help in minimising the accident rates (Kanshana, Sivaprakash, & Joseph, 2015). Providing equal training and safety equipment to women (Dalmia, 2012) will not only minimise the accident rates but will also boost their morale to bring healthy competition to other gender (Landford, Rowlinson, & Sawacha, 2000).

REFERENCES

Ahmed, S., Islam, H., Hoque, I., & Hossain, M. (2018). Reality check against skilled worker parameters and parameters failure effect on the construction industry for Bangladesh. *International Journal of Construction Management*, 1-10.

Arndt, V., Rothenbacher, D., Brenner, H., Fraisse, E., Zschenderlein, B., Daniel, U., & ... . (2015, March 14). Older workers in the construction industry: Results of a routine health examination and a five year follow up. *Occupational and Environmental Medicine*, 686–691.

Bala, S. (2016). *Gender Dimensions at Work and Employment: A Case of Sexual Harassment.* Noida: V.V.Giri National Labour Institute.

Bhattacharjee, S. (2015). An overview of labour welfare measures in India in response to globalization. *Journal of Developing Societies, 30*(1), 66–76.

Bishnu, I. (2004). Accidents in and out of the course of employment and the theory of national extension. *Labour law Journal.*

Boateng, E. B., Davis, P., & Pillay, M. (2019). Role of human safety intervention on the impact of safety climate on workers safety behaviours in construction projects: A conceptual model. *International conference on applied human fcators and ergonomics* (pp. 190-200). Springer.

Bust, P. D., Gibb, A. G., & Pink, S. (2008). Managing construction health and safety: Migrant workers and communicating safety messages. *Safety Science, 46*(4), 585–602.

Chawada, B., Gharat, V., Bansal, R., & Kantharia, S. (2012). Plight of female construction workers of surat city. *Indian Journal of Community Health*, 19–22.

Chockalingam & Sornakumar. (2011). An effective Total Construction Safety Management in India. *Scientific Information Database*, 405-416.

Choudhary, R. M., & Fang, D. (2008, April). Why operatives engage in unsafe work behaviour: Investigating factors on construction sites. *Safety Science, 46*(4), 566–584.

Dalmia, A. J. (2012, June). Strong women, weak bodies, muted voices. *Women construction workers in Delhi, 47*(26), 249-255.

Danna, K., & Griffin, R. W. (1999). Health and well-being in the workplace: A review and synthesis of the literature. *Journal of Management, 25*(3), 357–384.

Danso, H. (2012). Construction workers' satisfaction with work provision requirement dimensions in Ghana's construction industry. *IACSIT International Journal of Engineering and Technology*, 1613–1619.

Dester, W. S., & Blockley, D. I. (1995). Safety-beahviour and culture in construction. *Engineering, Construction, and Architectural Management, 2*(1), 17–26.

Devi & Kiran. (2013). Status of Female workers in Construction Industry in India: A Review. *IORS Journal of Humanities and Social Science.*

Devi & Kiran. (2013). Status of Female Workers in Constructtion Industry In India: A Review. *IOSR Journal of Humanities and Social Science* .

Everett, J. G., & Frank, P. B. Jr. (1996). Costs of accidents and Injuries to the construction Industry. *Journal of Construction Engineering and Management*, 158–164.

Field, A. (2009). *Discovering statistics using SPSS.* Sage Publication.

Fielden, S. L., Davidson, M. J., Gale, A. W., & Davey, C. L. (2000). Women in construction: The untapped resource. *Construction Management and Economics*, *18*(1), 113–121.

Gaganpreet Kaur, D. M. (2017). *Undulating struggle of women in changing scenario.* New Delhi: Bloomsbury.

Ganesan, S. (2018). *Employment, technology and construction development.* Taylor and Francis Group.

Henson, R. K., & Roberts, J. K. (2006). Use of Explorartory Factor Analysis in Published Research. *Educational and Psychological Measurement*, *66*(3), 393–416.

Hindu, T. (2013, December). *Protecting Women at workplaces.* Academic Press.

Hinze, J. (2013). *Improving safety performance on large construction.* CIB Working Commission W.

Jayakrishnan, T., Thomas, B., Rao, B., & George, B. (2013). Occupational health problems of construction workers in India. *International Journal of Medicine and Public Health*, 225–229.

Kanchana, Sivaprakash, & Joseph. (2015). Studies on Labour safety in Construction Sites. *TheScientificWorldJournal*, 6.

Kanshana, S., Sivaprakash, P., & Joseph, S. (2015). Studies on labour safety in construction sites. *TheScientificWorldJournal.*

Kulkarni, G. (2007). Construction industry: More needs to be done. *Indian Journal of Occupational and Environmental Medicine*, *11*(1).

Kumar, A. P., & Vishnuvarthan, C. K. (2014). A study on construction jobsite safety management. *International Journal of Innovative Research in Science, Engineering and Technology, 3*(1), 44-52.

Kumar, B. (2013). Gender discrimination among construction workers with reference to Vijaywada. *Journal of Sociology and Social Work, 1*(1), 42-53.

Kumar, M. D. (2013). Inimitable Issues of Construction Workers: Case Study. *British Journal of Economics, Finamnce and Management Sciences*, 42-53.

Kumar, R. (2019). *Research Methodology A step by step guide for beginners.* Sage Publication.

Kumar, S., & Bansal, V. K. (2013). Construction safety knowledge for practitioners in the construction industry. *Journal of Frontier in Construction Engineering*, *2*(2), 34–42.

Landford, D., Rowlinson, S., & Sawacha, E. (2000). Safety behaviour and safety management: Its influence on the attitudes of workers in the UK construction industry. *Engineering, Construction, and Architectural Management*, *7*(2), 133–140.

Laskar, A., & Murty, C. R. (2004). *Challenges before construction industry in India*. Academic Press.

Lee, J. C. (1951). Coefficient alpha and the internal structure of tests. *Psychometrika*.

Lette, A., Ambelu, A., Getahun, T., & Mekonen, S. (2018). A survey of work- related injuries among building construction workers in southwestern Ethiopia. *International Journal of Industrial Ergonomics*, *68*, 57–64.

M, D. D. (April 2013). Inimitable Issues of Construction Workers: Case Study. *British Journal of Economics, Finamnce and Management Sciences*, 42-53.

Mahalakshmi, J. (2015). Protection to women in India: A judicial Perspective. *Labour Law Journal*, 29-33.

Majumdar, R. (2016, May 12). *Migrant labourers: Stuck in a web of contractors, builders, lack of unions, welfare schemes*. Retrieved Dec 25, 2016, from Thozhilalar Koodam: https://tnlabour.in/migrant-workers/3680

Malhotra, V., Papola, T., Yugandhar, B., Sengupta, A. K., Kannan, K. P., & Srivastava, R. S. (2000). *Social security for Unorganised Workers: Report.* New Delhi: National Commission for Enterprises in the Unorganised Sector.

Mann, J. S. (2007). Welfare and protection measures pertaining to the construction worker in India. *Labour Law Journal*, 36-41.

McHugh, M. (2013). *The Chi-square test of independence*. Lessons in Biostatistics.

Moavenzadeh, F. (1978). Construction industry in developing countries. *World Development*, *6*(1), 97–116.

Mohamed, S. (2002). Safety climate in construction site environment. *Journal of Construction Engineering and Management*, *128*(5), 375–384.

Mouleeswaran, K. (2014). Evaluation of safety performance level of construction firms in and around erode zone. *International Journal of Innovative Research in Science, Engineering and Technology*, *3*(1), 1586–1594.

Moyce, S. C., & Schenker, M. (2018). Migrant workers and their occupational health and safety. *Annual Review of Public Health*, *39*, 351–365.

Nagaseshamma, S. (2014). Upliftment of construction Labour through social security laws. *Labour Law Journal*, 27-34.

Nyambura, M. M., & Simon, K. (2018). Employee performance in power transmission companies in Kenya. *International Journal of Business Management and Finance*.

Ofori, G. (2000). Globalization and construction industry development: Research opportunities. *Construction Management and Economics*, *18*(3), 257–262.

Osborne, J., & Waters, E. (2002). Four assumptions of multiple regression that researchers shouls always test. *Practical Assessment, Research & Evaluation*.

Patel, H. C., Moitra, M., Momin, M. H., & Kantharia, S. L. (2012). Working conditions of male construction worker and its impact on their life: A cross sectioanl study in Surat city. *National Journal of Community Medicine*, *3*(4), 652–656.

Pheng, L. S., & Hou, L. S. (2019). *Construction Quality and the Economy*. Springer.

Prasad, N., Rao, V. K., & Nagesha, H. N. (2011). Study on building and other construction workers welfare schemes/ amenities in Karnataka. *SAS Tech Journal*, *10*, 59–66.

Pries, F., & Janszen, F. (1995). Innovation in the construction industry: The dominant role of the environment. *Construction Management and Economics*, 43–51.

Priya, M., Kothai, P., & Kohilambal, E. (2016). Study on safety practices and their performance in the construction industry. *International Journal of Modern Trends in Engineering and Research*, 284-293.

Rajanna. (2015). Nature of Work, Working Conditions and Problems of Women Construction Workers: A Case Study. *International Journal of Business Quantitative Economics and Applied Managment Research*.

Ramesh, A. (n.d.). Safety Control in the Construction Industry in India. Academic Press.

Ringen, K., & Seegal, J. (1995). Safety and health in the construction industry. *Annual Review of Public Health, 16*(1), 165–188.

Ruxton, G. (2006). The unequal variance t-test is an underused alternative to Student's t-test and Mann- Whitney U test. *Behavioural Ecology*, 688–690.

Saari, L. M., & Judge, T. A. (2004). Employee attitudes and job satisfaction. *Human Resource Management, 43*(4), 395–407.

Sageer, A., Rafat, S., & Agarwal, P. (2012). Identification of variables affecting employee satisfaction and their impact on the organnization. *Journal of Business and Management*, 32–39.

Saha, A. (2014, February). Unsafe conditions and deaths in construction sites and governement inaction. *Thozhilalar Koodam*.

Sang, K., & Powell, A. (2012). Gender inequality in the construction industry: Lessons from Pierre Bourdieu. In *Proceedings of the 28th Annual ARCOM Conference* (pp. 237-247). Edinburgh, UK: Association of Researchers in Construction Management.

Satish Kumar, V. (2013). Construction safety Knowledge for Practitioners in the Construction Industry. *Journal of Frontiers in Construction Engineering*, 34-42.

Selvam & Priyadarshini. (n.d.). Safety management and Hazards Control measures in Construction. *IOSR Journal of Mechanical and Civil Engineering*, 97-101.

Shamsuddin, K., Ani, M., Ismail, A., & Ibrahim, M. (2015). Investigation the safety, health and environment (SHE) protection in construction area. *International Research Journal of Engineering and Technology*, 624-635.

Shirur, S., & Torgal, S. (2014, April). Enhancing safety and health management techniques in Indian construction industry. *International Journal of Engineering and Technical Research, 2*(4), 52-56.

Singh, R. (2014). *India: Overview of the Sexual Harassment of women at workplace.* Indian Corporate Counsel Association.

Singh, K. (2014). Safety in Indian Construction. *International Journal of Engineering Research & Technology (Ahmedabad).*

Singh, R. S. (2014, October 21). *India: Overview of the Sexual Harassment of women T Workplace*. Academic Press.

Sparks, K., Faragher, B., & Cooper, C. (2001). Well-being and occupational health in the 21st centuryworkplace. *Journal of Occupational and Organizational Psychology*, 489–509.

Srivastava, R. (2014). *Documenting the lack of labour rights in India's construction sector*. Centre for Development Policy and Research.

Thenguzhali, T., & Veerachamy, P. (2009). Occupational health hazards of women construction workers: A critical survey of the literature. *Indian Journal of Dermatology, 15*(8).

Tiwary, G., & Gangopadhyay, P. (2011). A review on the occupational health and social security of unorganized workers in the construction industry. *Indian Journal of Occupational and Environmental Medicine*.

Tiwary, G., Gangopadhyay, P. K., Biswas, S., Nayak, K., Chatterjee, M. K., & Chakroborty, D. (2012). Social-economic status of women of building construction industry. *Indian Journal of Occupational and Environmental Medicine*, 66–71.

Tiwary & Gangopadhay. (2011). A Review on the Occupational Health and Social security of Unorganized workers in the Construction Industry. *Indian Journal of Occupational & Environmental Medicine*, 18-24.

Tripathi, K., & Jha, K. (2018). An empirical study on factor leading to the success of construction organizations in India. *International Journal of Construction Management*.

Veerachamy. (2009). Occupational health hazards of women construction workers: A critical survey of the literature. *Indian Journal Dermatol.*

Zikriyoev, A. S., & Crane, R. A. (2019). Prevention of social cost in occupational health and safety is sustainable development for the construction industry. *International Scientific Journal Theoretical & Applied Science, 74*(6).

Chapter 14
Boosting Financial Literacy in the 4th IR Amongst Working and Non-Working Women in India

Shruti Bhuttani
Jagannath International Management School, Vasant Kunj, India

Suchitra Srivastava
Jagannath International Management School, Vasant Kunj, India

Vipul Singh
Jagannath International Management School, Vasant Kunj, India

ABSTRACT

The concept of financial literacy is of vital importance both for the individual and the economy as a whole. The chapter analyses the different components of financial literacy from the Indian perspective. It is an attempt to throw light and carry out a comparative analysis between the financial acumen of working and non-working Indian women. The results of the study may serve as important inputs to the policy makers to develop strategies to enhance financial literacy among Indian women in particular and thereby help in nation building.

INTRODUCTION

"Teach your daughter economic independence so, in the future, she can have a partner, not a master. Teach: your son to do housework so, in the future, he can

DOI: 10.4018/978-1-7998-8594-8.ch014

have a partner, not a servant."

The concept of financial literacy has evolved in recent times whereby the market is volatile and there is no job security. Most of the individuals are employed in the Private sector where the future is not secured as an employer is not responsible for providing pension to employees. Since 2005 government of India has also discontinued the practice of paying retirement pensions to its employees. The government is moving down the path of encouraging their citizen to undertake the responsibility for their retirement incomes and to focus on sound financial planning and not be dependent on the pension provided by the government. As a result, financial literacy has become essential for working individuals to be able to survive in modern society and to take prudent financial decisions for their future as there is a challenge to understand the complex financial products and services offered by various companies. In today's time's people need to be more knowledgeable about superannuation funds and how they operate and evaluate the returns that they promise.

The financial market is much more complex compared to the earlier times. The option of financial investments and credit facilities has increased manifolds since yesteryears. In such a complicated market knowing financial instruments and markets has become imperative. From the very early stage, a youth needs to understand the importance of planning for long-term investment and short-term saving to meet the need of funds for vacation, down payment for a house, a loan for education, a car loan, children education, secured retirement, etc. Researchers all over the world have reported inadequate financial literacy among the youth. Most developed countries such as the USA, UK, Canada, Australia, and several countries of Europe have reported financial literacy rates between 55 -75% (Figure 1).

India has a long way to go to achieve comparable financial literacy rates as the developed countries. Among the several challenges posed to our country in achieving the status of developed nations, perhaps the biggest in women's empowerment. This is achievable only when the women of the country will be educated, financially literate. and independent. Financial Literacy implies the capability to make effective decisions regarding the use of monetary resources. In the words of Noctor et al. (1992), a financially literate individual was capable of making intellectual judgments and adopting effective choices regarding the usage and management of money. In our country, women are at par with men in almost all fields but when it comes to financial decision-making, they are still dependent on the male members of their families. Our country is burdened with numerous challenges. The major ones are burgeoning population, unemployment, illiteracy, skewed distribution of wealth, poor health infrastructure, etc. Considering the distribution of wealth, illiteracy, and poor health indices, it becomes essential to educate the women and make them financially literate women to shoulder the responsibilities equally with men and fuel the engine of growth, thus contributing to the economic growth of the nation.

Instances of extreme poverty have been reported by women post the death of the earning member of the family. Such instances of dire poverty and financial misery could have been avoided with future financial planning, contingency savings, and emergency funds. At times, women are aware of such products but are reluctant to take the initiative to go for such options due to poor and incomplete information or lack of confidence. Comparing the women of developed countries with the women of developing countries it is found that women of developed countries are better financial planners, they are to manage money in a much better way, and the reason for this probably is that the women of developed countries score high on financial literacy. Financial Literacy not only involves knowing the systems and methods of financial prudence, but it also implies practical implementation of the concepts and theories of financial literacy. Bridging the gap between theory and practice is a challenge and the real test of a financially prudent person is that he or she can apply it today to day operations.

If we study the financial planning trend of Indian women, it is found that there is a tremendous scope of improvement in the area of money management (budgeting), investments, debt management, asset management, risk cover, etc. According to an annual Mastercard index prepared for measuring financial literacy (2013), "India is at the bottom among 16 countries in Asia-pacific region in terms of overall financial literacy." With 59 points. In our study, we undertake to assess the financial literacy level amongst working women in the state of Rajasthan. Most individuals in the United States and other countries cannot perform simple calculations and do not understand basic financial concepts such as interest compounding, the difference between nominal and real values, and risk diversification. Knowledge of more complex concepts, such as the difference between bonds and stocks, the workings of mutual funds, and basic asset pricing, are even scarcer. Financial illiteracy is widespread among the general population and particularly acute among specific demographic groups, such as women, the young and the old, and those with low educational attainment. I conclude with a brief discussion of the importance of incorporating financial literacy into school curricula as well as directions for future work.

Meaning of Financial Literacy

Financial literacy has been defined widely. Some researchers perceive it as a required talent, defined as the ability to obtain and interpret financial information, which may be measured through comprehension of financial principles as well as financial performance. Financial Literacy has been defined by the National Foundation for Education Research of UK as "the ability to make informed judgments and to take an effective decision regarding the use of management of money". The ANZ Bank's research on adult financial literacy in Australia described the concepts of financial literacy in the following way: "Financial literacy is about enabling people to make informed and confident decisions regarding all aspects of their budgeting, spending and saving and their use of financial products and services, from everyday banking through to borrowing, investing and planning for the future" (RMR,2003,p.1; CAN,2005,p.6). Atkinson and Messy (2012) have defined financial literacy as "a combination of awareness, knowledge, skill, attitude, and behavior necessary to make sound financial decisions and ultimately achieve individual financial wellbeing". Organization for Economic Co-operation and Development (2005) defines financial literacy as "A combination of awareness, knowledge, skill, attitude, and behavior necessary to make sound financial decisions and ultimately achieve individual financial wellbeing". According to Lusardi, and Mitchell (2014), Financial Literacy is interchangeably used with financial capability and economic literacy. Financial literacy is the ability to understand and apply various financial skills, including financial planning, wealth management, budgeting, and investing. Financial knowledge, behavior, and perception are directly or indirectly dependent on financial literacy.

NEED FOR FINANCIAL LITERACY

Financial literacy is important from the point of view of all stakeholders. The three important stakeholders such as Government, society, and economy are interdependent on one another. The Government wants the people of the county to be financially literate so they can take care of their financial needs. This will reduce the burden on the government. Having a good level of Financial knowledge will persuade the people of the society to invest confidently in the financial instruments. This will boost the circulation of money and bring prosperity to all the stakeholders. Financial security will also guarantee the happiness of society.

Government Perspective

The Government of India has a very clear agenda for increasing financial literacy in the country in collaboration with the four financial sector regulators namely, RBI, SEBI, IRDAI, and PFRDA. Financial literacy leads to better informed financial decisions. And this also supports the government's vision of financial inclusion. The government implemented the first National Strategy for Financial Education(NSFE,2013-18) and monitored the progress in these five years and it was found to be satisfactory and now the government has prepared the revised

NSFE,2020-25 after the successful review. The Government realizes very well the need for financial education and inclusion and therefore, Pradhan Mantri Jan Dhan Yojana was initiated by the government in the year 2014. Prioritizing the Need, the Government has set up the National Centre for Financial Education in the year 2013 to boost financial literacy by developing appropriate content and ensuring its spread across various sections of the society.

NCFE has adopted the '5 C' approach of strategy which includes emphasis on the development of relevant content in the curriculum in schools, colleges, and training establishments, developing Capacity among intermediaries involved in providing financial services, leveraging the positive effect of Community-led model for financial literacy through appropriate Communication strategy, and, enhancing Collaboration among various stakeholders. The three pillars of a growing economy are financial literacy, financial stability, and financial inclusion, and as there is a lack of financial education amongst the people and therefore it becomes an immense matter of concern in an economy. Hogarth (2002) found that "financial literacy is important because well-informed, well-educated consumers should make better decisions for their families; increase their economic security and well-being; contribute to vital, thriving communities; and foster community economic development". Standard & Poor's Financial Services LLC (S&P) global survey (2017) reported that less than 25% of adults are financially literate in South Asian countries. Financial literacy is yet to become a priority for an average Indian. The study also shows that nearly 76% of its adult population does not understand even the basic financial concepts. Hence, there is a need to put conscious efforts to provide financial literacy/education and in improving the financial knowledge of all sections of the society jointly by the financial institutions, banks, government bodies, and insurance companies.

Beal and Delpachitra (2003) stated that "the need for financial literacy has grown rapidly over the last decade because financial markets have been deregulated and credit has become easier to obtain, as financial institutions compete strongly with each other for market share". The priority is to reach the economically backward, poor, and uneducated who have limited access to financial services and provide them financial education about basic financial concepts free of cost. Also, there is a need to target schools, colleges, the working middle class, the educated, and even the rich and famous to provide knowledge about various investment opportunities and wealth maximization for their personal development and the development of the society as a whole. Health and Retirement Study conducted in 2004 on financial literacy by gender highlighted the sharp sex differences in financial literacy. It displayed a very low level of financial knowledge among women than men. It indicated that in comparison to man-woman possess less knowledge in understanding the concepts of compound interest, inflation, rise in the price of a stock, and risk diversification. (Figure 1). Lusardi and Mitchell (2008) examine this issue in more detail and warn about the difficulties women may face in making financial decisions, particularly after the death of a spouse. Lusardi and Mitchell (2011c) show that these gender differences hold across countries as well.

IR 4.0 AND IMPLICATION FOR FL

Schwab (2016), coined the phrase "The Fourth Industrial Revolution" in 2016. According to him, "like the revolutions that preceded it, the Fourth Industrial Revolution has the potential to raise global income levels and improve the quality of life for populations around the world." He cautioned that "The changes are so profound that, from the perspective of human history, there has never been a time of greater promise or potential peril."

The Fourth Industrial Revolution, popularly also referred to as 4IR or Industry 4.0 may be described as the "blurring of boundaries between the physical, digital, and biological worlds." These distinct boundaries and scopes have now been reduced with the fusion of concepts such as artificial intelligence (AI), robotics, the Internet of Things (IoT), 3D printing, genetic engineering, quantum computing, and other technologies. It is an amalgamation of these technologies that have shaped the production and consumption patterns and are fast becoming indispensable to modern life. It has been radically affecting our lifestyles and holds the potential to disrupt our day-to-day activities in major ways. Industry 4.0 conceptualizes the new practices in the manner goods are produced and delivered. It deals with the advancement towards industrial automation and the concept of the flexible factory. The aim is to remain competitive and the method is by leveraging the industrial internet of things (IIoT) and digitalization. These concepts would make both the factories and the warehouses much more agile, efficient and responsive to customer requirements.

With industries going in for the automation of many processes, secure wireless connectivity is a boon that facilitates industrial automation on a much larger scale. Industrial automation holds the promise of increased productivity and performance many folds. Huge gains also await industries that go wireless. In manufacturing, wireless cellular connectivity enables flexible production by allowing smart factories to rapidly changeover production lines and to shorten lead times. Hence, we may summarize that Industry 4.0 would make smart machines smarter, factories more efficient in producing products strictly as per specifications less wasteful processes, flexible production lines, and higher productivity. As rightly pointed out by experts, there were four main effects that the Fourth Industrial Revolution had on business. These may be enumerated as the impact on customer expectations, product enhancement, collaborative innovation, and organizational reforms.

Customer expectations were bound to increase given the access to information from myriad sources. Products of enhanced quality in terms of functionality and reliability are manufactured through improved processes. Innovations that were facilitated with the advancements in designing and testing with teams collaborating across the globe. Organizational reforms and restructuring to harness creativity and promote collaboration. The Fourth Industrial Revolution heralds the complete restructuring of workplaces. Ebony Frelix, Executive Vice President and Chief Philanthropy Officer at Salesforce.org, believes that businesses and governments need to share responsibility for upskilling workers and may do so by adopting nontraditional skill-building measures. According to Zvika Krieger, co-leader of the World Economic Forum's Center for the Fourth Industrial Revolution, "Companies need to be thinking about enabling their employees to code in new languages, but also to change their mix of soft skills." He added, "as AI begins to impact the workforce and automation replaces some existing skills, we're seeing an increased need for emotional intelligence, creativity, and critical thinking". With the rapid advancements in the production and delivery of goods, it becomes relevant to make advancements at the consumption front. Making the best use of the financial resources available, consumers may benefit from the fruits of IR 4.0. In this regard, the concept of financial literacy is of paramount importance. Only a financially literate person will be able to judiciously invest, save and improve his/her quality of life.

IMPORTANCE OF FINANCIAL LITERACY

Being financially literate is strongly and positively related to planning (Lusardi and Mitchel, 2008). It enables one to carry out judicious planning of one's day-to-day and future planning. The same researchers have put forth that there is a positive relationship between personal wealth and financial literacy. (Lusardi and Mitchel, 2011). Hence we may summarize that the benefits of financial literacy as follows:

1. **Creating a Budget:** making a budget is an essential tool for maintaining one's finances. A budget is a statement of Income and expenditure of an individual, household, or organization/Economy. It is imperative to maintain to have prudent fiscal management so that the expenses can be managed within the income.
2. **Understanding Interest Rates**: Knowing the concepts like simple and compound interest will facilitate the understanding of financial literacy. . The mathematical computation of these interests can facilitate an understanding of the returns on different investments for different periods. This also helps one to

invest in different schemes offered by the government and private institutions by assessing one's requirement of finances in the future.

3. **Prioritizing Savings:** saving are an important aspect of maintaining a healthy financial situation. A habit of saving goes a long way in inculcating financial prudence by eliminating unnecessary expenditure. It helps in the systematic planning of one's purchasing decisions. It also helps in harnessing a habit of restraint.
4. **A research report by YouGov**, a marketing research organization, revealed that saving or increasing savings was the main financial goal of more than a third of urban Indians in 2020. The findings state that 37% of urban Indians considered saving their main financial goal in 2019 relative to 32% in 2019 (BFSI,2020).
5. **Credit-Debt Cycle Traps Meaning**: Credit, if managed correctly can be a very useful tool. It is also critical to gather information regarding debt. An understanding of both can help avoid rash decision-making and thereby avoid the credit–debt cycle trap. The idea is to develop an understanding of the tools and concepts which are applied in the credit practices as early as possible. As far as the credit is concerned it is very easy to lose credibility as compared to gaining it is concerned and it requires planning to be done.
6. **Assets and liabilities:** It helps in understanding the difference between assets and liabilities.
7. **Financial stability and freedom:** It helps to achieve financial stability and financial freedom.
8. **Retirement Planning**: adequate knowledge about retirement schemes can help one plan for an independent and stress-free retired life. This would also assure one of a peaceful life at the present without worrying much about the future.

BENEFITS OF BEING FINANCIALLY LITERATE

Some researches (Hilgert et al., 2002; Perry and Morris, 2005) showed a positive association between financial literacy rates and the levels of education and income. A higher financial literacy rate is recommended as per the guidelines as it leads to optimal decision making by the consumers and it can be termed as positive financial behavior which is exhibited by the consumers leading to better financial wellbeing. (Hilgert, et al., 2003; Lusardi and Mitchell, 2007). Furthermore, Beverly and Burkhalter (2005) and Martin and Oliva (2001) argued that the development of financial knowledge and skills acquired by young people is important to create a foundation for prudent financial behavior in the future and financial wellbeing.

Figure 1. Global Variation in Financial Literacy

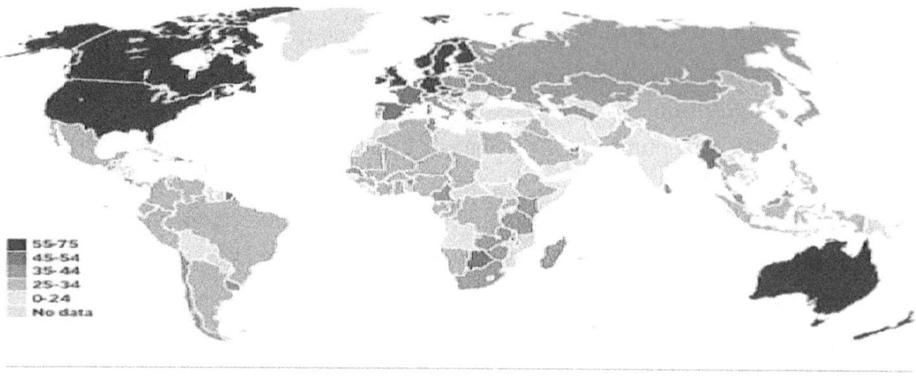

Financial skills should be acquired early in life. Casardi & Mitchell (2011) have stated that there is a positive association between personal wealth and financial literacy. Rosacker et al (2009) stated that obtaining sufficient education and understanding of basic financial knowledge and skills would enable them(University students) to be more productive and successful members of society. Sound financial behavior and wellbeing would be ensured by measurement of financial literacy of young people [Brenly & Burkhalter(2008) and Martin & Olivia (2001)]

FINANCIAL LITERACY IN THE WORLD

S&P Global conducted the FinLit Survey in 2014 on literacy which included the measurement of four fundamental concepts of financial decision making like risk diversification, inflation, numeracy, and interest compounding.

The results shown in figure 1 of the survey indicated that countries with the highest financial literacy rates were the Netherlands, Germany, Israel, Australia, Denmark, the United Kingdom, Canada, Norway, Finland, and Sweden, with about 65 percent or more of adults being financially literate. Looking at the other perspective, some economies of South Asia reported the lowest financial literacy scores, with about a quarter or lower number of adults being financially literate. In major advanced countries like Germany, the United States, Canada, Japan, Italy, France, and the United Kingdom the financial literacy in adults was found to be about 55 percent on an average. While, In the BRICS countries (Brazil, the Russian Federation, India, China, and South Africa)—on average, around 28 percent of adults are found to be financially literate. Studying the case of India and South Africa major disparity was found among them India at 24% and South Africa at 42%.

Figure 2. Position of Women compared to Men in Financial Literacy
(Source: Leora Klapper,Annamaria Lusardi,Peter van Oudheusden, 2011)

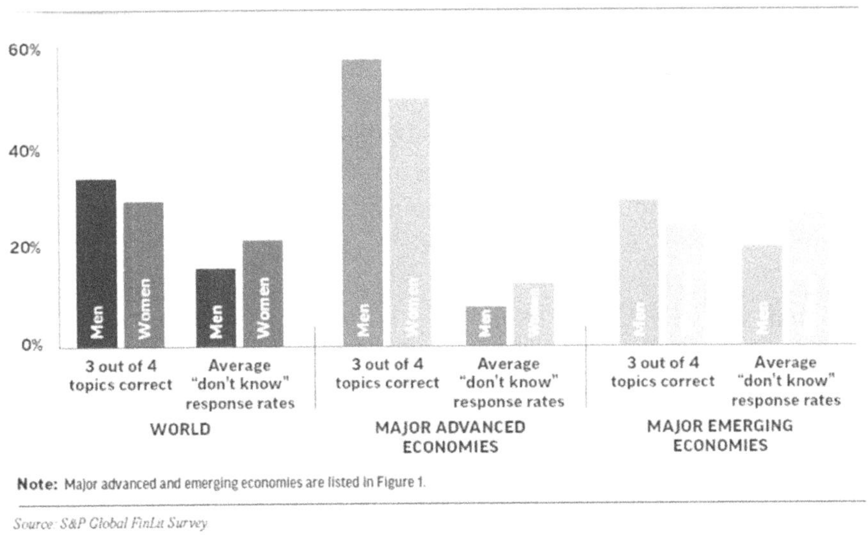

FINANCIAL LITERACY AMONG WOMEN AND THE POOR AROUND THE WORLD

According to the report by S & P, financial literacy rates were computed based on the characteristics such as age, education level, gender, income. The Worldwide statistics are as follows, 30% of women and 35% of men are financially literate. While women are less likely to provide correct answers to the financial literacy questions, they are also more likely to indicate that they "don't know" the answer, a finding consistently observed in other studies as well (Lusardi and Mitchell, 2014).

This gender gap was found in both advanced economies and emerging economies. The survey concluded that women had weaker financial skills compared to men even considering variations such as age, country, education, and income. The average gender gap in financial literacy was 5 percentage points in the developing economies which were not different from the worldwide gap. The gap was absent in China and South Africa (where financial literacy was equally low for both women and men). There is also a gap in financial literacy when looking at relative income in the BRICS economies. Thirty-one percent of the rich in these economies are financially literate, compared to only 23 percent of the poor.

The Organization for Economic Co-operation and Development (OECD) is an intergovernmental economic organization with 36 member countries, founded in 1961 to stimulate economic progress and world trade. It recognized that financial literacy is a key prerequisite for financial development and inclusion. With this objective, it invited countries to participate in an international data collection exercise for measuring financial literacy and financial inclusion. It provides the opportunity for countries developing or implementing national strategies for financial education to collect reliable baseline data and benchmark their progress against other countries in similar circumstances. Additionally, it provides an important signal that the participating countries are following international good practices and actively participating in the international financial literacy agenda.

FINANCIAL LITERACY IN INDIA

Reserve Bank of India (RBI) has been conducting Financial Literacy Week (FLW) every year since 2016 to propagate financial education messages on a particular theme across the country. During February 10-15, 2020, the theme of the Financial Literacy Week was 'MSME'. It helped create awareness about the different aspects relating to formalization, collateral-free loans, discounting of receivables, rehabilitation of stressed units, and timely repayments. According to a report by CNBC (2018), a literacy rate of 74 percent in India and not every adult individual having even a savings account, indicated a poor state of financial literacy in India. Despite the impetus received through the Pradhan Mantri Jan Dhan Yojna, a lot remained to be done to achieve a financially inclusive society where the citizens understood the importance of savings and had access to credit. The same agency quoted the results of a survey conducted by Standard & Poor's Financial Services, which stated that less than 25 percent of South Asian countries' adult population was financially literate. They also added that no data was available on financial literacy in India.

In India, virtually women are the main spender of the family whereas men are the principal earner of the family. Women are good at budgeting and managing household expenses but many women find themselves not competent to take high-value financial decisions and they generally trust their spouses, fathers, brothers, etc to be good at making the bigger financial decisions, as they feel that these men are having better knowledge about managing investment and analyzing risk and return. A minimum basic level of financial literacy is very essential for every woman so that they can live their life according to their own choices hence contributing to the healthy and prosperous life of their family as a whole.

Research Methodology

The attempt has been made to assess the financial literacy level among the working and non-working women in Delhi and NCR region. The study also aims to compare the financial literacy among working and non-working women. This is a Descriptive study based on Probability Sampling. The study was conducted on a sample of 200 out of which 100 were working women and 100 non working women. An equal number of working and non-working women was also considered while selecting the sample. A self-structured questionnaire was formed using the scales OECD for data collection. The financial literacy of women was assessed taking into account three parameters such as financial knowledge, behavior, and attitude of the respondents. The basic financial knowledge of the repondents is assessed utilizing a performance test in areas such as division, interest rate, compounding, inflation effects, time value of money, risk diversification, etc. The financial behavior of the people is assessed on the affordability of goods, behavior related to making timely payment of their bills, planning, and monitoring of the household budget, active saving habits, and borrowing requirements. The financial attitude of the people is assessed on the extent of belief in planning, tendency to save, and propensity to consume. The socio-demographic information from women was also taken such as domicile, age, marital status, level of education, educational background, household income, and housing living condition. It was been done with the purpose to show the association between the level of financial literacy and demographic variables of the survey respondents. The discussion on this is presented in tabular form in a subsequent section.

OBJECTIVE

The study was conducted under the following objective:

To assess the level of financial literacy of working and non-working women on three parameters such as financial knowledge, behavior, and attitude of the respondents.

RESULTS AND DISCUSSION

Table 1 presents details concerning domicile, age, marital status, level of education, educational background, household income, household debts, housing living conditions.

Concerning the occupation status of women, the sample contained 100 working women and 100 non-working women. This is the equal share of the sample that had been taken for both the working and non-Working Women. Regarding the residential location,66(33%) belonged to the rural area while 134 (67%)belonged to the urban area. Concerning the age of the respondents, it has been found that 53 (26%) respondents belonged to the age group of 18-30, 76(38%) belonged to 31-45,

Table 1. Demographic Data: Based on the responses of Working and Non-Working Women

S.NO	Item	SubItems	Working (100)	Non-Working (100)	Total(200)
1.	Domicile	Rural	30	36	66 (33%)
		Urban	70	64	134 (67%)
2.	Age (Years)	18-30	29	24	53 (26%)
		31-45	41	35	76 (38%)
		46-60	21	28	49 (25%)
		61 and above	9	13	22 (11%)
3	Marital Status	Married	63	57	120 (60%)
		Single	30	32	62 (31%)
		Separated/ Widower	7	11	18 (9%)
4.	Level of Education	Below Grade 10th	9	14	23(12%)
		Grade 10th	10	11	21(11%)
		Grade 12th or Metric	11	9	20 (10%)
		Graduation or Diploma	24	31	55 (27%)
		Post-Graduation (PG)	33	29	62 (31%)
		Doctorate or any qualification above PG	13	6	19 (9%)
5.	Education Background	Finance *	41	46	87(44%)
		Non –Finance	59	54	113 (56%)
6.	Household Income Group (Monthly)	Below 10,000	11	14	25 (13%)
		10000- 50000	23	19	42 (21%)
		50000-1,00,000	34	45	79(40%)
		Above 1, 00,000	32	22	54(27%)
7.	Housing Living Condition	Own parental house	42	48	90(45%)
		Rented House	39	46	85 (43%)
		Own House (With Regular EMI**)	19	6	25(13%)

- ** Graduation in Commerce-related subject is considered as Finance Background.*
- ***Equated Monthly Installment*

49 (25%) were from the age group 46-60, 22 (11%)respondents belong to the age group of 61 and above. It can be observed here that, majority of the respondents belong to the age group of 31-45 years.

On interpreting the marital status, it was seen that 120 (60%) respondents were married, 62 (31%) were single and 18 (9 percent) were separated or widowed. The share of married respondents is more among both the working and non-working as compared to the share of a woman in single and separated or widowed respondents. While considering the educational qualification of the respondents, about 19 (9%) respondents were highly educated (Ph.D. or Doctorate).62 (31%) respondents were Post Graduates, 55 (27%) of them were only graduates, 20 (10%) were educated up to 12th standard (HSC), 21 (11%) were educated only up to 10th standard and the remaining 23 (12%) had only high school or primary level Education. The share of respondents above Post Graduation and Post-Graduation were more among working women as compared to non-working women. While the share of women who haven't competed in 10th Grade also is seen more in the non-working women as compared to working women. With regards to the educational background of women is concerned, it has been found that 87 (44%) completed their education in finance or finance-related subjects while the remaining 113 (56%) haven't studied finance or finance-related subjects in graduation or post-graduation. In the case of the monthly income of respondents, 25 (13%) respondents had a monthly income of below Rs.10000. 42 (21%) of them had a monthly income between Rs. 10000-50000, 79 (40%) of the respondents had a monthly income between 50001 -1,00,000 and the rest 54 (27%) respondent's monthly income was above Rs1,00,000.

Regarding the housing living condition, 90 (45%) of women were living in their own parental owned house, 85(43%) living in a rental house while the remaining 25 (13%) were living in houses owed as there is a regular monthly EMI's becomes due on those so-called owned houses.

Assessment of Financial Knowledge

The financial knowledge of the respondents was assessed in areas such as division, interest rate, compounding, inflation effects, time value of money, risk diversification, etc. A performance-based test having eight questions was administered. The respondents were categorized as sound, fair and poor based on their financial knowledge. The results are depicted in Table 2

The key highlights of table 2 analysis were that 21% of the working women and 48% of the non-working women were having poor financial knowledge. The other findings were also consistent with the expectations of having a greater financial knowledge with age, marital status, and level of education.

Table 2. Assessment of Financial Knowledge and Demographic Variables

S.NO	Item	SubItems	Financial Knowledge			
			Sound	**Fair**	**Poor**	**Total**
1.	**Occupation Status**	**Working**	33	46	21	100
		Non-Working	20	32	48	100
2.	**Domicile**	**Rural**	6	34	20	66
		Urban	17	58	64	134
3.	**Age**	**18-30**	15	15	23	53
		31-45	32	39	5	76
		46-60	25	20	4	49
		61 and above	14	15	3	22
4.	**Marital Status**	**Married**	46	48	26	120
		Single	12	20	30	62
		Separated/ Widower	9	5	4	18
5.	**Level of Education**	**Below Grade 10th**	0	4	19	23
		Grade 10th	2	5	14	21
		Grade 12th or Metric	5	7	8	20
		Graduation or Diploma	26	15	14	55
		Post-Graduation (PG)	31	20	11	62
		Doctorate or any qualification above PG	11	5	3	19
6.	**Education Background**	**Finance**	21	38	28	87
		Non -Finance	13	38	62	113
7.	**Household Income Group (Monthly)**	**Below 10,000**	1	9	15	25
		10001- 50000	8	6	28	42
		50001-1,00,000	18	31	30	79
		Above 1, 00,000	12	22	20	54
8.	**Housing Living Condition**	**Own parental house**	12	36	42	90
		Rented House	19	29	48	85
		Own House (With Regular EMI)	6	11	8	25

Assessment of Financial Behaviour:

The study also attempts to analyze the financial behavior of women in the way they look after their finance. To understand how women behaved while handling money in their daily lives, the respondents were asked to respond to eight statements of the OECD Survey. The Likert scale of 1 to 5 is used where the respondents were supposed to respond from completely agree to disagree.

The statements(S) used are as follows:

S 1: Affordability: Before I buy something I carefully consider whether I can afford it.
S 2: Future Planning: I tend to live for today and let tomorrow take care of itself.
S 3: Saving Habits: I find it more satisfying to spend money than to save it for the long term
S 4: Timely Payment of Bills: I pay my bills on time.
S 5: Risk Taking Ability: I am prepared to risk some of my own money when saving or making an investment.
S 6: Monitoring of Household Budget: I keep a close personal watch on my financial affairs
S 7: Planning of Household Budget: I set long-term financial goals and strive to achieve them.
S8: Future Security: Money is there to be spent.

To confirm the responses, certain questions were also asked regarding the above statements. A score of 1 was allotted to each correct response. The respondents scoring 6 or above were considered as having positive behavior toward handling finances for daily needs. The respondents with 3-5 were considered neutral and below 3 were categorized under negative financial behavior.

The key highlights of table 3 were that 63% of the working women and 37% of the non-working women displayed positive financial behavior. About 47% and 37% of the married possessed sound and neutral financial behavior.

Assessment of Financial Attitude

The study has also attempted to understand the financial attitude of women towards financial planning and decision-making. The Survey questions of OECD were used to assess the financial attitude of women which sought responses towards:

The extent of belief in planning
Tendency to save, and
Propensity to consume.

Table 3. Assessment of Financial Behaviour and Demographic Variables

S.NO	Item	SubItems	Financial Behavior			
			Positive	**Neutral**	**Negative**	**Total**
1.	***Occupation Status***	***Working***	63	27	10	100
		Non-Working	37	48	15	100
2.	***Domicile***	***Rural***	27	20	19	66
		Urban	63	39	32	134
3.	***Age***	***18-30***	11	17	25	53
		31-45	37	20	19	76
		46-60	20	23	6	49
		61 and above	10	8	4	22
4.	***Marital Status***	***Married***	56	44	20	120
		Single	22	27	13	62
		Separated/ Widower	10	4	4	18
5.	***Level of Education***	***Below Grade 10th***	2	8	13	23
		Grade 10th	3	6	12	21
		Grade 12th or Metric	5	7	8	20
		Graduation or Diploma	15	12	28	55
		Post-Graduation (PG)	34	15	13	62
		Doctorate or any qualification above PG	10	5	4	19
6.	***Education Background***	***Finance***	42	28	17	87
		Non -Finance	33	33	47	113
7.	***Household Income Group (Monthly)***	***Below 10,000***	12	7	6	25
		10001- 50000	22	16	4	42
		50001-1,00,000	28	37	14	79
		Above 1, 00,000	29	15	10	54
9.	***Housing Living Condition***	***Own parental house***	28	42	20	90
		Rented House	39	29	17	85 (43%)
		Own House (With Regular EMI)	15	6	4	25(13%)

The responses are scored based on desirability and the maximum score for each item is 4 while the minimum score for each item is 0. The scores across the three items were then averaged. An average score of 3 or above was considered a positive attitude while a score of 2 was considered neutral and less than 2 was classified as a negative financial attitude. The scoring has been done following Agarwla et al., (2013).

From Table 4, it was evident that 50% of working and 43% of non-working women demonstrated a positive attitude regarding the three parameters of planning, saving, and propensity to consume. Comparing the place of residence, the urban women who constituted about 52% displayed a positive attitude in comparison to their rural counterparts. Among the unmarried women, about 48% displayed a neutral financial attitude. The impact of the level of education and age was consistent with the expectation of an increased positive attitude.

Financial Literacy

To analyze data, various response categories for financial literacy statements were assigned scores. The scoring pattern for the current study was adopted from Agarwala et. al. (2013).

The scoring pattern was as follows:

Correct answer:3, Do not know:2 and Wrong answer: 1

It is to be noted that, "Do not know" answers were given higher scores because admitting "don't know" is something less dangerous than not knowing something and claiming the opposite. With this scoring scheme, individuals could score a maximum of 30 (all correct answers) and a minimum of 10 (all wrong answers). Respondents who scored 25 and above (approximately 83% and above) were considered to have sound financial literacy. Those with scores ranging from 20 to 24 (approx. 67% to 83%) were considered to have fair financial literacy. Those with a score below 20 (below 67%) are considered as having poor financial literacy.

CONCLUSION

In the present study, instead of arriving at the Financial Literacy scores, on the whole, an attempt was made to analyze its constituent elements and their relationship with the socio-economic data of the working and non-working women. In this regard, the conceptual model proposed and validated by Potrich et al., (2016) was used. The adapted version of the model is given below.

Potrich et al. (2016) carried out a study on financial literacy among Brazilian students. Some of the students had opted for courses related to finance while others

Table 4. Assessment of Financial Attitude and Demographic Variables:

S.NO	Item	SubItems	Financial Attitude			
			Positive	Neutral	Negative	Total
1.	Occupation Status	Working	50	35	15	100
		Non-Working	43	37	20	100
2.	Domicile	Rural	25	25	16	66
		Urban	70	30	34	134
3.	Age	18-30	10	27	16	53
		31-45	40	20	16	76
		46-60	25	20	4	49
		61 and above	6	7	9	22
4.	Marital Status	Married	66	30	24	120
		Single	20	30	12	62
		Separated/ Widower	12	6	2	18
5.	Level of Education	Below Grade 10th	5	8	10	23
		Grade 10th	5	10	6	21
		Grade 12th or Metric	8	5	7	20
		Graduation or Diploma	22	20	13	55
		Post-Graduation (PG)	30	25	7	62
		Doctorate or any qualification above PG	11	3	5	19
6.	Education Background	Finance	40	35	12	87
		Non -Finance	45	50	18	113
7.	Household Income Group (Monthly)	Below 10,000	10	9	6	25
		10001- 50000	23	15	4	42
		50001-1,00,000	38	23	18	79
		Above 1, 00,000	39	10	5	54
9.	Housing Living Condition	Own parental house	20	46	24	90
		Rented House	45	25	15	85 (43%)
		Own House (With Regular EMI)	18	4	3	25(13%)

Figure 3. Conceptual Model
Source: Adapted from Potrich et al.(2016)

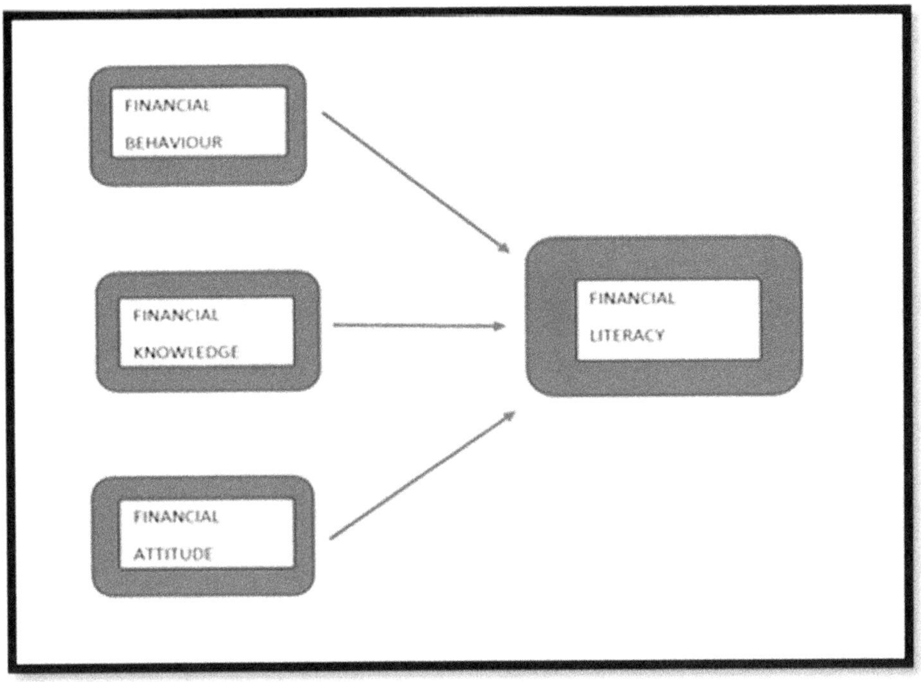

had not. Hence, there are two commonalities with the present study. Firstly, both the populations belong to developing country i.e India and Brazil. Secondly, in both the population there were people from finance and non-finance background. Hence, we have adopted the same model for our study assuming it to hold for the Indian population. Such a model was conceptualized to gain an understanding of the factors influencing financial literacy at the micro-level. This would facilitate the design and implementation of programs and initiatives that would enhance the financial knowledge of both working and non-working women. Further studies may be carried out to find out whether courses have to be designed keeping in mind the level of education and exposure of the recipients. Once the knowledge is enhanced, the attitude and behavior are bound to improve. This would ultimately lead to improved levels of financial literacy.

REFERENCES

Abreu, M., & Mendes, V. (2010). Financial Literacy and Portfolio Diversification. *Quantitative Finance*, *10*(5), 515–528. doi:10.1080/14697680902878105

Behrman, J. R., Mitchell, O. S., Soo, C. K., & Bravo, D. (2012). The Effects of Financial Education and Financial Literacy: How Financial Literacy Affects Household Wealth Accumulation. *The American Economic Review*, *102*(3), 300–304. doi:10.1257/aer.102.3.300 PMID:23355747

Beverly, S. G., & Burkhalter, E. K. (2005). Improving financial literacy and practices of youths. *Children & Schools*, *27*(2), 121–124. doi:10.1093/cs/27.2.121

BFSI. (2020). *'Saving' is the main financial goal for Indians in 2020: YouGov*. Retrieved from https://bfsi.economictimes.indiatimes.com/news/financial-services/saving-is-the-main-financial-goal-for-indians-in-2020-yougov/73185770

CNBC. (2018). *How financially literate is India? The answers will surprise you.* Retrieved from https://www.cnbctv18.com/personal-finance/how-financially-literate-is-india-the-answers-will-surprise-you-975361.htm

Dayal, Y. (2020). *Financial Literacy Week 2020*. Retrieved from https://www.rbi.org.in/Scripts/BS_PressReleaseDisplay.aspx?prid=49349

Hilgert, M. A., Hogarth, J. M., & Beverly, S. G. (2003). Household financial management: The connection between knowledge and behavior. *Federal Reserve Bulletin*, *89*, 309–322.

Jariwala, H. V., & Sharma, M. S. (2016). Assessment of Behavioural Outcomes of Financial Education Workshops on Financial Behaviour of the Participants: An Experimental Study. In T. Harrison (Ed.), *Financial Literacy and the Limits of Financial Decision-Making*. Palgrave Macmillan. doi:10.1007/978-3-319-30886-9_15

Klapper, L., Lusardi, A., & van Oudheusden, P. (2011). Financial literacy around the world: An overview. *Journal of Pension Economics and Finance*, *10*(4), 497–508. doi:10.1017/S1474747211000448 PMID:28553190

Lusardi & Tufano, (2015). Debt Literacy, Financial Experiences, and Over Indebtedness. *Journal of Pension Economics and Finance, 14*(4), 332-328.

Lusardi, A., & Carlo de Bassa, S. (2013). *Financial Literacy and High-Cost Borrowing in the United States*. NBER Working Paper 18969.

Lusardi, A., & Mitchell, O. (2007). Financial literacy and retirement preparedness: Evidence and implications for financial education. *Business Economics (Cleveland, Ohio)*, *42*(1), 35–44. doi:10.2145/20070104

Lusardi, A., & Mitchell, O. S. (2011). *Financial Literacy and Planning: Implications for Retirement Wellbeing*. Oxford University Press.

Lusardi, A., & Mitchell, O. S. (2014). The Economic Importance of Financial Literacy: Theory and Evidence. *Journal of Economic Literature*, *52*(1), 5–44. PMID:28579637

Martin, A., & Oliva, J. (2001). Teaching Children About Money: Applications of Social Learning and Cognitive Learning Developmental Theories. *Journal of Family and Consumer Sciences: From Research to Practice, 93*.

Organization for Economic Co-operation and Development (OECD). (2005). *Improving financial literacy: Analysis of issues and policies*. OECD.

Perry, V., & Morris, M. D. (2005). Who Is in Control? The Role of Self-Perception, Knowledge, and Income in Explaining Consumer Financial Behavior. *The Journal of Consumer Affairs*, *39*(2), 299–313. doi:10.1111/j.1745-6606.2005.00016.x

Potrich, A. C. G., Vieira, K. M., & Mendes-Da-Silva, W. (2016). Development of a financial literacy model for university students. *Management Research Review*, *39*(3), 356–376. doi:10.1108/MRR-06-2014-0143

Standard and Poor. (2015). *Financial Literacy Around the World: Insights From The Standard & Poor's Ratings Services Global Financial Literacy Survey*. Retrieved from https://gflec.org/initiatives/sp-global-finlit-survey/

Stango, V., & Zinman, J. (2009). Exponential Growth Bias and Household Finance. *The Journal of Finance*, *64*(6), 2807–2849. doi:10.1111/j.1540-6261.2009.01518.x

Compilation of References

Abreu, M., & Mendes, V. (2010). Financial Literacy and Portfolio Diversification. *Quantitative Finance*, *10*(5), 515–528. doi:10.1080/14697680902878105

Accenture. (2016). *Getting to equal: How digital is helping close the gender gap at work*. https://instituteforpr.org/wp-content/uploads/Accenture-IWD-2016-Research-Getting-To-Equal.pdf

Acker, J. (1989). *Doing Comparable Worth*. Temple University Press.

Acker, J. (1992). The Future of Women and Work: Ending the Twentieth Century. *Sociological Perspectives*, *35*(1), 53–68. doi:10.2307/1389368

Adams, R. B., & Ferreira, D. (2009). Women in the Boardroom and their Impact on Governance and Performance. *Journal of Financial Economics*, *94*(2), 291–309. doi:10.1016/j.jfineco.2008.10.007

Agarwal, B. (1985). Women and Technological Change in Agriculture: The Asian and African Experience. *Technology and Rural Women*, 67-114.

Agénor, P., & Agénor, M. (2014). Infrastructure, women's time allocation, and economic development. *Journal of Economics*, *113*(1), 1–30. doi:10.100700712-013-0358-0

Aggarwal, P. (2021). Impact of mandatory corporate social responsibility on corporate financial performance: The Indian experience. *Social Responsibility Journal*. Advance online publication. doi:10.1108/SRJ-09-2020-0394

Ahmed, I. (1985). *Technology and rural women*. Academic Press.

Ahmed, S., Islam, H., Hoque, I., & Hossain, M. (2018). Reality check against skilled worker parameters and parameters failure effect on the construction industry for Bangladesh. *International Journal of Construction Management*, 1-10.

AISHE. (2019). *All India Survey on Higher Education, 2018-19*. Department of Higher Education, Ministry of Education, Government of India.

AISHE. (2020). *All India Survey on Higher Education, 2019-20*. Department of Higher Education, Ministry of Education, Government of India.

Akter, S., Krupnik, T., Rossi, F., & Khanam, F. (2016). The Influence of Gender and Product Design on Farmers' Preferences for Weather-Indexed Crop Insurance. *Global Environmental Change*, *38*, 217–229. doi:10.1016/j.gloenvcha.2016.03.010 PMID:27212804

Albadr, B. (2003). E-commerce. *Science and Technology*, *65*, 14–19.

Alliance for Financial Inclusion. (2016). Policy Frameworks to Support Women's Financial Inclusion. Kuala Lumpur: Alliance for Financial Inclusion.

Anderson, E. (2020). *3 Challenges of Industry 4.0 and how to address them*. https://www.forescout.com/blog/3-challenges-of-industry-4-0-and-how-to-address-them/

Anonymous. (2017). *How will the fourth industrial revolution impact the future of work?* Change. https://www.changerecruitmentgroup.com/knowledge-centre/how-will-the-fourth-industrial-revolution-impact-the-future-of-work

Anonymous. (2020). *Industry 4.0 and sustainable manufacturing*. Future Bridge. https://www.futurebridge.com/industry/perspectives-mobility/industry-4-0-and-sustainable-manufacturing

Antonio & Tuffley. (2014). *Future Internet, The Gender Digital Divide in Developing Countries*. www.mdpi.com/journal/futureinternet

Aparna Bhat v. State of Madhya Pradesh, Supreme Court of India (2021) https://www.livelaw.in/pdf_upload/aparna-bhat-v-state-of-mp-168-390769.pdf

Apple. (2018). *Employer Information Report EEO-1*. Apple.

Argentina, W. (2018). *Digital inclusion communique*. Retrieved from w20argentina.com/wp-content/uploads/2018/07/comm_digital_inclusion_2.pdf

Arndt, V., Rothenbacher, D., Brenner, H., Fraisse, E., Zschenderlein, B., Daniel, U., & .... (2015, March 14). Older workers in the construction industry: Results of a routine health examination and a five year follow up. *Occupational and Environmental Medicine*, 686–691.

Arun, T., & Kamath, R. (2015). Financial inclusion: Policies and practices. *IIMB Management Review*, *27*(4), 267–287. doi:10.1016/j.iimb.2015.09.004

Asian Development Bank. (2011). Women and labor markets in Asia: Rebalancing towards gender equality in labor markets in Asia. ILO Regional Office for Asia and the Pacific. Bangkok: ILO.

Azman, H., & Mustapha, M. (2018). Benefits and challenges of corporate social responsibility implementations: Evidence from manufacturing sector in Malaysia. *International Journal of Engineering & Technology, 7*, 215-218.

Badagliacco, J. M. (1990). Gender and Race Differences in Computing Attitudes and Experience. *Social Science Computer Review*, *8*(1), 42–63. doi:10.1177/089443939000800105

Bae, K. B., & Skaggs, S. (2019). The impact of gender diversity on performance: The moderating role of industry, alliance network, and family-friendly policies – Evidence from Korea. *Journal of Management & Organization*, *25*(6), 896–913. doi:10.1017/jmo.2017.45

Bajpai, G. (2018). Gender of justice. *The Indian Express*. Retrieved 19 July 2021, from https://indianexpress.com/article/opinion/columns/gender-of-justice-appointment-of-female-judges-5452591/

Bala, S. (2016). *Gender Dimensions at Work and Employment: A Case of Sexual Harassment.* Noida: V.V.Giri National Labour Institute.

Baliki, G., Bruck, T., Ferguson, N. T. N., & Stojetz, W. (2019). *Rural youth in the context offragility and conflict.* 2019 Rural Development Report. International Fund for Agricultural Development (IFAD). https://www.ifad.org/documents/38714170/41187395/14_Baliki+et+al._2019+RDR+BCKGROUND+PAPER.pdf/a0003ba0-3e4f-3fbd-8d2b-654bf75176e8

Banerjee, M. (2019). Gender equality and labour force participation: Mind the Gap. *Indian Journal of Women and Social Change*, *4*(1), 113–123. doi:10.1177/2455632719831827

Baral, R. (2016). Women Managers & Professionals: Work-Family Conflict & Job Satisfaction. *Indian Journal of Industrial Relations*, *51*(3), 432–446.

Basistha, S., & Pathak, D. M. (2020). Participation of Women in the Emerging Trade Union Activities in the Tea-Gardens of Assam. *International Journal of Research and Innovation in Social Science*, *4*(3), 321–324.

Baughman, R., DiNardi, D., & Holtz-Eakin, D. (2003). Productivity and Wage Effects of family-Friendly' Fringe Benefits. *International Journal of Manpower*, *24*(3), 247–259. doi:10.1108/01437720310479723

BBC News. (2018, February). *Bangladesh country profile*. https://www.bbc.com/news/world-south-asia-12650940

Behrman, J. R., Mitchell, O. S., Soo, C. K., & Bravo, D. (2012). The Effects of Financial Education and Financial Literacy: How Financial Literacy Affects Household Wealth Accumulation. *The American Economic Review*, *102*(3), 300–304. doi:10.1257/aer.102.3.300 PMID:23355747

Beji, R., Yousfi, O., Loukil, N., & Omri, A. (2020). Board diversity and corporate social responsibility: Empirical evidence from France. *Journal of Business Ethics*. Advance online publication. doi:10.100710551-020-04522-4

Beneria, L., &Sen, G. (1981). *Accumulation, Reproduction and Women's Role in Economic Development: Boserup Revisited in Signs*. Academic Press.

Benkraiem, R., Hamrouni, A., Lakhal, F., & Toumi, N. (2017). Board independence, gender diversity, and CEO compensation. Corporate Governance: The International. *Journal of Business and Society*, *17*(5), 845–860.

Bertoni, S. (n.d.). *How do we win the mobile wallet war? be like Starbucks*. Retrieved July 28, 2017, from https://www.forbes.com/sites/stevenbertoni/2014/02/21/how-do-you-win-the-mobile-wallet-warbe-like-starbucks/

Beverly, S. G., & Burkhalter, E. K. (2005). Improving financial literacy and practices of youths. *Children & Schools*, *27*(2), 121–124. doi:10.1093/cs/27.2.121

BFSI. (2020). *'Saving' is the main financial goal for Indians in 2020: YouGov*. Retrieved from https://bfsi.economictimes.indiatimes.com/news/financial-services/saving-is-the-main-financial-goal-for-indians-in-2020-yougov/73185770

Bhadra, B. (2001). Janani O Prayukti: Lingakaran O Kshamatayaner Sahabastan (Bengali ed.) Yojana.

Bhattacharjee, S. (2015). An overview of labour welfare measures in India in response to globalization. *Journal of Developing Societies*, *30*(1), 66–76.

Bhatti, A., & Ali, R. (2021). Women constructing leadership identities in academia: Intersection of gender and culture. *Issues in Educational Research*, *31*(1), 1–18.

Bilton, N. (2014). Facebook tries, tries again on a smartphone. *The New York Times*.

Bimber, B. (2000). Measuring the gender gap on the internet. *Social Science Quarterly*, *81*(3), 868–876.

Bishnu, I. (2004). Accidents in and out of the course of employment and the theory of national extension. *Labour law Journal*.

Boateng, E. B., Davis, P., & Pillay, M. (2019). Role of human safety intervention on the impact of safety climate on workers safety behaviours in construction projects: A conceptual model. *International conference on applied human fcators and ergonomics* (pp. 190-200). Springer.

Boden, C. K., & Sorgner, A. (2018). Labor market opportunities for women in the digital age. *Economics: The Open-Access, Open-Assessment E-Journal, 12*, 1–8. doi:10.5018/economics-ejournal.ja.2018-28

Bøhren, Ø., & Staubo, S. (2014). Does mandatory gender balance work? Changing organizational form to avoid board upheaval. *Journal of Corporate Finance*, *28*, 152–168. doi:10.1016/j.jcorpfin.2013.12.005

Bora, S. U., & Sinha, D. (2011). Are India Women Scientists victims of the glass ceiling? *Current Science*, *100*(4), 837–840.

Borgonovi, F., Centurelli, R., Dernis, H., Grundke, R., Horvát, P., Jamet, S., Keese, M., Liebender, A. S., Marcolin, L., Rosenfeld, D., & Squicciarini, M. (2018). *Bridging the Digital Gender Divide: Include, Upskill, Innovate*. OECD.

Boston, F. R. (2012). *Mobile Phone Technology: smarter than we thought*. Retrieved 2019, from https://www.bostonfed.org/bankinfo/payment-strategies/publications/2012/mobile-phone-technology.htm

Boston, F. R. (2017). *Mobile phone technology: smarter than we thought.* Retrieved from https://www.bostonfed.org/bankinfo/payment-strategies/publications/2012/mobile-phone-technology.htm

Bourque & Warren. (1987). Technology, Gender, and Development. *Daedalus, 116*(4). https://www.jstor.org/stable/20025130

Bourque, S. C., & Warren, R E. (1987). Technology, Gender, and Development. *Learning about Women: Gender, Politics, and Power,* 173-197. https://www.jstor.org/stable/20025130

Bridging The Digital Gender Divide Include. (2018). *Upskill, Innovate*. OECD.

Briscoe, A., & Pfafflin, S. (1979). *Expanding the Role of Women in the Sciences. Expanding the Role of Women in the Sciences*. New York Academy of Sciences, Association for Women in Science.

Bullough, A., De Luque, M., Abdelzaher, D., & Heim, W. (2015). Developing Women Leaders through Entrepreneurship Education and Training. *The Academy of Management Perspectives, 29*(2), 250–270. doi:10.5465/amp.2012.0169

Bureau of Labor Statistics. (2016). *Labor force participation: What has happened since the peak?* https://www.bls.gov/opub/mlr/2016/article/labor-force-participation-

Busch, T. (1995). Gender differences in self-efficacy and attitudes toward computers. *Journal of Educational Computing Research, 12*(2), 147–158. doi:10.2190/H7E1-XMM7-GU9B-3HWR

Bust, P. D., Gibb, A. G., & Pink, S. (2008). Managing construction health and safety: Migrant workers and communicating safety messages. *Safety Science*, *46*(4), 585–602.

Caputo, D., Paiano, A., & Foltynowicz, Z. (2019). Corporate social responsibility for industry 4.0. the case study of the Italian company operating in Poland. *Proceedings from the Basiq International Conference "New Trends in Sustainable Business and Consumption."*

Carr, M. (2008). *Mobile payment systems and services: an introduction*. Retrieved from http://venturewoods.org/wp-content/uploads/2008/06/mobile-payment-systems-and-services.pdf

Carrington, D. (2018). *Merchants will decide the fate of Apple's mobile wallet.* Retrieved from http://blogs.forrester.com/denee_carrington/14-09-04-merchants_will_decide_the_fate_of_apples_mobile_wallet

Carr, M. (1984). *Technologies Appropriate for Women.* Intermediate Technology Publications.

Castaño, C. (2008). *La segunda brecha digital.* Ediciones Cátedra.

CATALYST. (2017). *Women On Corporate Boards Globally*. Author.

Central Intelligence Agency. (2021). *South Asia, Bangladesh.* https://www.cia.gov/library/publications/the-world-factbook/geos/bg.html

Centre for Information Technology. (2015). *Unlocking markets for women to trade.* Retrieved from https://www.intracen.org/uploadedFiles/intracenorg/Content/Publications/women_in_trade_web.pdf

Chakravarty, S., Das, S., & Vaillant, J. (2017). *Gender and youth employment in Sub-Saharan Africa: A review of constraints and effective interventions.* Policy Research Working Paper No. 8245. World Bank. https://openknowledge.worldbank.org/handle/10986/28905

Chandra, A. (2019). Gender Gap in skill development: An analytical review. In S. Bala & P. Singhal (Eds.), *Gender issues in technical and vocational education programs* (pp. 158–182). IGI Publishers. doi:10.4018/978-1-5225-8443-8.ch008

Chappelow, C. T. (2004). 360-degree feedback. In C.D. McCauley & E.Van Velsor (Eds.), The Centre for Creative Leadership handbook of leadership development (2nd ed., pp.58-84). Jossey-Bass.

Chastain, E., Thickett, B., Unnikrishnan, S., & Woods, W. (2014). *Bridging the entrepreneurship Gender Gap: The power of networks.* Boston Consulting Group.

Chaudhary, M., Sodani, P. R., & Das, S. (2020). Effect of COVID-19 on the economy in India: Some reflections for policy and programme. *Journal of Health Management, 22*(2), 169–180. doi:10.1177/0972063420935541

Chawada, B., Gharat, V., Bansal, R., & Kantharia, S. (2012). Plight of female construction workers of surat city. *Indian Journal of Community Health*, 19–22.

Cho, S. Y., Kang, P. K., Lee, C., & Park, C. K. (2020). Financial reporting conservatism and voluntary CSR disclosure. SSRN *Electronic Journal.* doi:10.2139/ssrn.3556255

Chockalingam & Sornakumar. (2011). An effective Total Construction Safety Management in India. *Scientific Information Database*, 405-416.

Chote, R., Nickell, S., & Parker, G. (2015). *Welfare trends report responsibility.* Office of Budget Responsibility. London: HMSO. https://obr.uk/wtr/welfaretrends-report-june-2015

Choudhary, R. M., & Fang, D. (2008, April). Why operatives engage in unsafe work behaviour: Investigating factors on construction sites. *Safety Science, 46*(4), 566–584.

CNBC. (2018). *How financially literate is India? The answers will surprise you.* Retrieved from https://www.cnbctv18.com/personal-finance/how-financially-literate-is-india-the-answers-will-surprise-you-975361.htm

Cohen, P. N., & Huffman, M. L. (2007). Working for the Woman? Female Managers and the Gender Wage Gap.'. *American Sociological Review, 72*(5), 681–687. doi:10.1177/000312240707200502

Colum, A. (2020). *COVID-19 and what digital divide means for people's livelihoods in Kenya.* https://www.heart-resources.org/blog/covid-19-and-what-the-digital-divide-means-for-peoples-livelihoods-in-kenya/

Companies Act 2013. (n.d.). http://ebook.mca.gov.in/Actpagedisplay.aspx?PAGENAME=17923

Constant, L., Edochie, I., Glick, P., Martini, J., & Garber, C. (2020). *Barriers to employment that women face in Egypt: Policy challenges and considerations*. https://www.rand.org/pubs/research_reports/RR2868.html

Cooper, J. (2006). The digital divide: The special case of gender. *Journal of Computer Assisted Learning*, *22*(5), 320–334. doi:10.1111/j.1365-2729.2006.00185.x

Cooper, J., & Weaver, K. D. (2003). *Gender and Computers: Understanding the Digital Divide*. Lawrence Erlbaum Associates, Inc. doi:10.4324/9781410608932

Cruz-Jesus, F., Oliveira, T., & Bacao, F. (2012). Digital divide across the European Union. *Information & Management*, *49*(6), 278–291.

Cullian, R. (2018). In Collaborative Work Cultures, Women Carry More of the Weight. *Harvard Business Review*. https://hbr.org/2018/07/in-collaborative-work-cultures-women-carry-more-of-the-weight

Daley, S. (2021). *Women in tech statistics show the industry has a long way to go*. https://builtin.com/women-tech/women-in-tech-workplace-statistics

Dalmia, A. J. (2012, June). Strong women, weak bodies, muted voices. *Women construction workers in Delhi*, *47*(26), 249-255.

Danna, K., & Griffin, R. W. (1999). Health and well-being in the workplace: A review and synthesis of the literature. *Journal of Management*, *25*(3), 357–384.

Danso, H. (2012). Construction workers' satisfaction with work provision requirement dimensions in Ghana's construction industry. *IACSIT International Journal of Engineering and Technology*, 1613–1619.

Das, S., & Kotikula, A. (2019). *Gender-based employment segregation: Understanding causes and policy interventions*. Jobs (Working Paper No. 26). https://documents.worldbank.org/curated/en/483621554129720460/Gender-Based-Employment-Segregation-Understanding-Causes-and-Policy-Interventions

Dastin, J. (2018). *Amazon scraps secret AL recruiting tool that showed bias against women*. Thomson Reuters. https://www.reuters.com/article/us-amazon-com-jobs-automation-insight/amazon-scraps-secret-ai-recruiting-tool-that-showed-bias-against-women-idUSKCN1MK08G?feedType=RSS&feedName=topNews&utm_source=twitter&utm_medium=Social

Davis, A. E., & Kalleberg, A. L. (2006). Family-Friendly Organizations? Work and Family Programs in the 1990s. *Work and Occupations*, *33*(2), 191–22. doi:10.1177/0730888405280446

Dayal, Y. (2020). *Financial Literacy Week 2020*. Retrieved from https://www.rbi.org.in/Scripts/BS_PressReleaseDisplay.aspx?prid=49349

de la Rey, C. (2005). Gender, Women, and Leadership. Agenda. *Empowering Women for Gender Equity*, (65), 4–11.

Deanne, K., Hilfinger, M., Im, E., Page, A., Regev, H., Spiers, J., Yoder, L., & Meleis, A. (1997). Defining and Redefining Work: Implications for Women's Health. Gender and Society, 11(3), 296-323.

Deborah, F. (2005). *How Women and Men Use the Internet*. Pew Internet & American Life Project.

Deepti, K.C. (n.d.). *Financial Inclusion: Government Promoted Initiatives*. IFMR CMF, Thematic Fact Sheet 8.

Deloitte. (2018). *Preparing tomorrow's Workforce for the Fourth Industrial Revolution*. Deloitte Touche Tohmatsu Limited. https://www2.deloitte.com/content/dam/Deloitte/global/Documents/About-Deloitte/gx-preparing-tomorrow-workforce-for-4IR.pdf

Deloitte. (2019). *Opportunity or Challenge? Empowering women and girls in India for the Fourth Industrial Revolution*. Deloitte Touche Tohmatsu Limited. https://www2.deloitte.com/content/dam/Deloitte/in/Documents/about-deloitte/UNGCNI_black_final%20v6%20web%20high%20res.pdf

Demirguc-Kunt, A., Klapper, L., Singer, D., & Van Oudheusden, P. (2015). *The Global Findex Database 2014 - Measuring Financial Inclusion Around the World.* World Bank Policy Research Working Paper No 7255.

Demirguc-Kunt, A., Klapper, L., Singer, D., Ansar, S., & Hess, J. R. (2018). *The Global Findex Database 2017: Measuring Financial Inclusion and the Fintech Revolution*. World Bank Group. doi:10.1596/978-1-4648-1259-0

Dester, W. S., & Blockley, D. I. (1995). Safety-beahviour and culture in construction. *Engineering, Construction, and Architectural Management*, *2*(1), 17–26.

Devereux, S., & Wheeler, S. R. (2004). *Transformative social protection*. Working Paper No. 232. Brighton, UK: Institute of Development Studies.

Devi & Kiran. (2013). Status of Female workers in Construction Industry in India: A Review. *IORS Journal of Humanities and Social Science*.

Devi & Kiran. (2013). Status of Female Workers in Constructtion Industry In India: A Review. *IOSR Journal of Humanities and Social Science* .

Dholakia, R. R., Dholakia, N., & Pedersen, B. (1994). Putting a byte in the gender gap. *American Demographics*, *16*(12), 20.

Digital Economy and Society Index — DESI. (2019). Retrieved from: https://ec.europa.eu/digital-single-market/en/desi

Digital Evolution Index – DEI. (n.d.). Retrieved from https://newsroom.mastercard.com/eu/files/2014/09/Digital-Evolution-Index_MC-Key-Findings-FINAL.pdf

Dr. Punita K. Sodhi v. Union Of India, Delhi High Court (2010) https://indiankanoon.org/doc/87321004/

DST. (2010). *Evaluating and enhancing women's participation in scientific and technological research: Indian initiatives. Report of National Task Force for Women in Science*. Ministry of Science and Technology, Department of Science and Technology, Government of India.

Dubochet. (2014). Why India Needs the Women's, Reservation Bill (No10).

Dugdale, A. (2013). *One fifth of women in the developing world think Internet use is inappropriate for them.* Available online: http://www.fastcompany.com/3004797/one-fifth-women-developingworld-countries-think-internet-use-inappropriate-them

Duppati, G., Rao, N. V., Matlani, N., Scrimgeour, F., & Patnaik, D. (2020). Gender diversity and firm performance: Evidence from India and Singapore. *Applied Economics*, *52*(14), 1553–1565. doi:10.1080/00036846.2019.1676872

Economic Commission for Latin America and the Caribbean (ECLAC). (2013b). Economía digital para el cambio estructural y la igualdad (LC/L.3602). Author.

Economic Times. (2019). *Fintech startups paving way for a financially smart India with global recognition.* Retrieved from economictimes.indiatimes.com/articleshow/68610868.cms?utm_source=contentofinterest&utm_medium=text&utm_campaign=cppst

Ehrbeck, T. (2014, July 23). Can India Achieve Financial Inclusion within the Next Few Years? *The Huffington Post.*

EIGE (European Institute for Gender Equality). (2017). *Cyber violence against women and girls.* http://eige.europa.eu/rdc/eige-publications/cyber-violence-against-women-and-girls

Encyclopedia of Corporate Social Responsibility. (2013). *Definition of CSR reporting*. Retrieved from https://linkF.springer.com/referenceworkentry/10.1007%2F978-3-642-28036-8_145

E-Participation Index — EPART. (n.d.). Retrieved from: https://publicadministration.un.org/publications/content/PDFs/E-Library%20Archives/UN%20E-Government%20Survey%20series/UN%20E-Government%20Survey%202014_Russian.pdf

Erasmus, B. (1997). Women Power: Aspects of Work-Life. *Agenda: Empowering Women for Gender Equity*, *13*(35), 35–44. doi:10.2307/4066087

Everett, J. G., & Frank, P. B. Jr. (1996). Costs of accidents and Injuries to the construction Industry. *Journal of Construction Engineering and Management*, 158–164.

Facebook. (2019). *Diversity Report 2019: Advancing diversity and inclusion*. Facebook. https://about.fb.com/news/2019/07/2019-diversity-report/

Field, A. (2009). *Discovering statistics using SPSS.* Sage Publication.

Fielden, S. L., Davidson, M. J., Gale, A. W., & Davey, C. L. (2000). Women in construction: The untapped resource. *Construction Management and Economics*, *18*(1), 113–121.

Filmer, D., & Fox, L. (2014). *Youth employment in Sub-Saharan Africa. Africa Development Forum.* Washington, DC: World Bank and Agence Française de Développement. https://openknowledge.worldbank.org/handle/10986/16608

Folke, O., Rickne, J., Tanaka, S., & Tateishi, Y. (2020). Sexual Harassment of Women Leaders. *Daedalus, 149*(1), 180–197. doi:10.1162/daed_a_01781

Food and Agriculture Organization of the United Nations. (2011). *The state of food and agriculture: Women in agriculture, closing the gender gap in development.* https://www.fao.org/3/i2050e/i2050e.pdf

Fry, R., & Stepler, R. (2017). *Women may never make up half of the U.S. workforce.* https://www.pewresearch.org/fact-tank/2017/01/31/women-may-never-make-up-half-of-the-u-s-w0orkforce/

Fundinger, D. (2015). *What is a mobile wallet and how does it work?* Retrieved from http://asmarterplanet.com/mobile-enterprise/blog/2015/01/what-is-a-mobilewallet.html

Fundinger, D. (2019). *What is a Mobile Wallet and How does it work?* Retrieved from http://asmarterplanet.com/mobile-enterprise/blog/2015/01/what-is-a-mobilewallet.html

Future Bridge. (n.d.). *Industry 4.0 and Sustainable Manufacturing.* Future Bridge. Retrieved from https://www.futurebridge.com/industry/perspectives-mobility/industry-4-0-and-sustainable-manufacturing/

Gaganpreet Kaur, D. M. (2017). *Undulating struggle of women in changing scenario.* New Delhi: Bloomsbury.

Gallego-Álvarez, I., García-Sánchez, I. M., & Rodríguez-Dominguez, L. (2010). The influence of gender diversity on corporate performance. *Revista de Contabilidad, 13*(1), 53–88. doi:10.1016/S1138-4891(10)70012-1

Gallén, M. L., & Peraita, C. (2017). The relationship between femininity and sustainability reporting: Femininity and sustainability reporting. *Corporate Social Responsibility and Environmental Management, 24*(6), 496–508. doi:10.1002/csr.1423

Gallup; International Labor Office (ILO). (2017). *Towards a better future for women and work: Voices of women and men.* ILO.

Gandhi, M., & Sen, K. (2021). Missing women in Indian university leadership: Barriers and facilitators. *Educational Management Administration & Leadership, 49*(2), 352–369. doi:10.1177/1741143219896048

Ganesan, S. (2018). *Employment, technology and construction development.* Taylor and Francis Group.

Garg, P. (2016). CSR and corporate performance: Evidence from India. *Decision (Washington, D.C.), 43*(4), 333–349.

Gauging the disruptive potential of digital wallets. (2019). Retrieved from www.mckinsey.com

Gay, G. (2019). Best Practices in Diversity: Companies Keeping Advancement of Women a Priority. *Women of Color Magazine*, *19*(1), 32–36.

Gay, G. (2020). Supporting Women in the Workplace: A Priority For Companies Large And Small. *Women of Color Magazine*, *20*(1), 28–31.

Gefen, D., & Straub, D. (1997). Gender differences in perception and adoption of e-mail: An extension to the technology acceptance model. *Management Information Systems Quarterly*, *21*(4), 389–400. doi:10.2307/249720

Gender and law synergies between SDG 5 and 16. (n.d.). https://www.idlo.int/fr/news/highlights/gender-and-rule-law-synergies-between-sdg-5-and-16

Gender Diversity Survey – 2020 Proxy Season Results. (n.d.). *Fenwick & West LLP*. https://www.fenwick.com/insights/publications/gender-diversity-survey-2020-proxy-season-results

Gender equality in decision-making positions. (2017). https://www.intereconomics.eu/contents/year/2017/number/1/article/gender-equality-in-decision-making-positions-the-efficiency-gains.html

Gender equality in decision-making positions. (n.d.). https://www.intereconomics.eu/contents/year/2017/number/1/article/gender-equality-in-decision-making-positions-the-efficiency-gains.html

Gender gap and sensitization in judiciary. (n.d.). https://www.drishtiias.com/daily-updates/daily-news-analysis/gender-gap-and-sensitisation-in-judiciary

GEO. (2018). *Reducing the gender pay gap and improving gender equality in organisations: Evidence-based actions for employers*. London: HMSO. gender-pay-gap.service.gov.uk

Gilliard, J., & Iweala, O. N. (2021). *Women and Leadership: Real Lives, Real Lessons*. The MIT Press.

Glass, J., & Estes, S. B. (2007). Do Flexible Work Practices Influence Time Spent in Domestic Labor? *Journal of Family Issues*, *28*, 263–288. doi:10.1177/0192513X06292703

Glass, J., & Fujimoto, T. (1995). Employer Characteristics and the Provision of Family Responsive Policies. *Work and Occupations*, *22*, 380–384.

Glass, J., & Riley, L. (1998). Family Responsive Policies and Employee Retention Following Childbirth. *Social Forces*, *76*, 1401–1435. doi:10.2307/3005840

Glauber, R. (2011). Limited access: Gender, Occupational Composition, and Flexible Work Scheduling. *The Sociological Quarterly*, *52*(3), 472–494. doi:10.1111/j.1533-8525.2011.01215.x PMID:22081800

Global Banking Alliance for Women. (2018). *The mobile wallet version 1-0*. GSM Association.

Global Connectivity Index – GCI. (n.d.). *Huawei*. Retrieved from: https://www.huawei.com/minisite/russia/gci2018rus/materials/gci2018.pdf

Global FinTech Adoption Index. (2019). Retrieved from https://www.ey.com/en_gl/ey-global-fintech-adoption-index

Godbole Rohini, M., & Ramakrishna, R. (2013). *Women scientists in India*. The Association of Academies and Societies of Sciences in Asia (AASSA). Annexure 3.

Goodstein, J. D. (1994). Institutional Pressures and Strategic Responsiveness: Employer Involvement in Work-Family Issues. *Academy of Management Journal*, *37*(2), 350–382.

Google. (2018). *Google Diversity Annual Report 2018*. Google.

Google. (2018). *Internet Saathi: Bridging the online gender divide in rural India*. https://www.google.com/about/values-in-action/internet-saathi/

Goos, M., & Manning, A. (2007). Lousy and lovely jobs: The rising polarization of work in Britain. *The Review of Economics and Statistics*, *89*(1), 118–133.

Grönlund, A., & Magnusson, C. (2016). Family-friendly policies and women's wages - is there a trade-off? Skill investments, occupational segregation and the gender pay gap in Germany, Sweden and the UK. *European Societies*, *18*(1), 91–113. doi:10.1080/14616696.2015.1124904

GSMA & ATKearny. (2015). *Accelerating the Digital Economy: Gender Diversity in the Telecommunications Sector*. https://www.atkearney.com/documents/10192/5580445/Connected+Women+2015- WDReport.pdf/d3c08b0a-fab6-431c-80c0-0d332b9e882d

GSMA. (2015). *Accelerating digital literacy: empowering women to use the mobile Internet*. GSMA.

GSMA. (2015a). *Connected Women 2015: Bridging the Gender Gap: Mobile Access and Usage in Low- and Middle-income Countries*. www.gsma.com/mobilefordevelopment/wp-content/uploads/2016/02/ConnectedWomen-Gender-Gap.pdf

Gulati, S., Nadeau, M.-C. N., & Rajgopal, K. (2015). *Gauging the disruptive potential of digital wallets*. McKinsey.

Hacker, A. (1986). Women and Work. *The New York Review of Books*, 26–32.

Hafkin, N. (2007). Women and gender in ICT statistics and indicators for development. *Information Technologies and International Development*, *4*, 25–41.

Hafkin, N., & Taggart, N. (2001). *Gender, IT and Developing Countries: An Analytic Study*. Center for Education Innovations.

Hargittai, E., & Shafer, S. (2006). Differences in Actual and Perceived Online Skills: The Role of Gender. *Social Science Quarterly*, *87*(2), 432–448. doi:10.1111/j.1540-6237.2006.00389.x

Harjoto, M. A., & Rossi, F. (2019). Religiosity, female directors, and corporate social responsibility for Italian listed companies. *Journal of Business Research*, *95*, 338–346. doi:10.1016/j.jbusres.2018.08.013

Harris, B. (2017). *What is gender gap and why it is getting wider?* World Economic Forum. https://www.weforum.org/agenda/2017/11/the-gender-gap-actually-got-worse-in-2017/

Haw, M. (1982). Women, Work, and Stress: A Review and Agenda for the Future. *Journal of Health and Social Behavior, 23*(2), 132–144. doi:10.2307/2136510 PMID:7108179

Heavey, S. (2013). *Women in India, Other Developing Countries Lag in Internet Use.* Available online: http://in.reuters.com/article/2013/01/10/internet-access-women-india-developingidINDEE90902820130110

Henson, R. K., & Roberts, J. K. (2006). Use of Explorartory Factor Analysis in Published Research. *Educational and Psychological Measurement, 66*(3), 393–416.

Her Lordship. (2021). *The Indian Express.* Retrieved 28 July 2021, from https://indianexpress.com/article/opinion/editorials/her-lordship-indian-judiciary-supreme-court-women-lawyers-association-7276985/

Heruti-Sover, T. (2019). *Study: Women run only 12% of top Israeli companies.* https://www.haaretz.com/israel-news/business/study-women-run-only-12-of-top-israeli-companies-1.6999800

Hilbert, M. (2011). Digital gender divide or technologically empowered women in developing countries? A typical case of lies, damned lies, and statistics. *Women's Studies International Forum, 34*(6), 479-489. doi:10.1016/j.wsif.2011.07.00

Hilbert, M. (2011). Digital gender divide or technologically empowered women in developing countries? A typical case of lies, damned lies and statistics. *Women's Studies International Forum, 34*, 479–489.

Hilgert, M. A., Hogarth, J. M., & Beverly, S. G. (2003). Household financial management: The connection between knowledge and behavior. *Federal Reserve Bulletin, 89*, 309–322.

Hindu, T. (2013, December). *Protecting Women at workplaces.* Academic Press.

Hinze, J. (2013). *Improving safety performance on large construction.* CIB Working Commission W.

Hoang, T. C., Abeysekera, I., & Ma, S. (2018). Board diversity and corporate social disclosure: Evidence from Vietnam. *Journal of Business Ethics, 151*(3), 833–852. doi:10.100710551-016-3260-1

Holloway, K., Rouse, R., & Niazi, Z. (2017). *Women's Economic Empowerment Through Financial Inclusion.* Innovations for Poverty Action.

How many women judges in supreme court and high court. (n.d.). https://www.thequint.com/voices/women/how-many-women-judges-in-supreme-court-and-high-court

Howcroft, D., & Rubery, J. (2018). Gender equality prospects and the fourth industrial revolution. In M. Neufeind, J. O'Reilly, & F. Ranft (Eds.), *Work in the Digital Age: Challenges of the fourth industrial revolution.* Rowman & Littlefield.

Hua, D., Mahmood, N., Zakaria, W., Lin, L., & Yang, X. (2018). The relationship between work-life balance and women leadership performance: The mediation effect of organizational culture. *IACSIT International Journal of Engineering and Technology*, *7*(4.9), 8–13. doi:10.14419/ijet.v7i4.9.20608

Huawei. (2019). *2018 Sustainability Report: Bring digital to every person, home and organization for a fully connected, intelligent world*. Huawei Investment & Holding Co, Ltd.

Hultin, M., & Szulkin, R. (2003). Mechanisms of Inequality: Unequal Access to Organizational Power and the Gender Wage Gap. *European Sociological Review*.

Hunter, R. (2015). *More than Just a Different Face? Judicial Diversity and Decision-making*. Academic Press.

Hwang, Y. (2010). The moderating effects of gender on e-commerce systems adoption factors: An empirical investigation. *Computers in Human Behavior*, *26*(6), 1753–1760. doi:10.1016/j.chb.2010.07.002

IBM. (2019). *Toward a mobile digital wallet*. Retrieved from https://domino.watson.ibm.com/library/CyberDig.nsf/1e4115aea78b6e7c85256b30066f0

IDI 2017 Rank. (2017). Retrieved from https://www.itu.int/net4/ITU-D/idi/2017/index.html

ILO. (2016a). Global Wage Report 2016/17. ILO.

ILO. (2016b). Women at Work: Trends 2016. ILO.

ILO. (2017a). World Employment and Social Outlook: Trends for women 2017. ILO.

ILO. (2017b). *World Social Protection Report 2017–19: Universal social protection to achieve the Sustainable Development Goals*. ILO.

ILO. (2018). *Trade Unions Need To Strategize To Reach Youth and Vulnerable Workers*. https://www.ilo.org/newdelhi/info/public/fs/WCMS_649893/lang--en/index.htm

ILO. (2018a). World Employment and Social Outlook: Trends 2018. ILO.

ILO. (2018b). *Women and men in the informal economy: A statistical picture* (3rd ed.). ILO.

ILO. (2019). *Work for a brighter future – Global Commission on the future of work*. International Labor Organization.

IMD World Digital Competitiveness Index — WDCI. (2018). IMD World Competitiveness Center.

IMF. (2018). *India Country Report, No 18/4*. https://www.imf.org/~/media/Files/Publications/CR/2018/cr1804.ashx

India Brand Equity Foundation. (2021). *Services Sector in India*. Retrieved on 8 July 2021 from https://www.ibef.org/industry/services.aspx

India Budget. (2021). *Expenditure profile 2021-22*. India Budget, 2020-21, Ministry of Finance, Government of India. https://www.indiabudget.gov.in/doc/eb/stat13.pdf

Indian Young Lawyers Association v. State of Kerala, Supreme Court of India (2018) https://indiankanoon.org/doc/163639357/

Infoplease. (n.d.a). *Bangladesh*. https://www.infoplease.com/world/countries/bangladesh

Infoplease. (n.d.b) *Israel map*. https://www.infoplease.com/atlas/middle-east/israel-map

Infoplease. (n.d.c). *Kenya map*. https://www.infoplease.com/atlas/africa/kenya-map

Infoplease. (n.d.d). *Map of the United States*. https://www.infoplease.com/atlas/north-america/united-states

INSA. (2004), Science career for Indian women: an examination of Indian women's access to and retention in scientific careers. The report, Indian National Science Academy (INSA).

Intel & Dalberg. (2012). *Women and the Web. Bridging the Internet and Creating New Global Opportunities in Low and Middle Income Countries*. Intel Corporation and Dalberg Global Development Advisors. https://www.intel.com/content/dam/www/public/us/en/documents/pdf/women-and-theweb.pdf

International Labor Office (ILO). (2015). Women in business and management: Gaining momentum. Global report. ILO.

International Labour Organization. (2009). *Final report: Survey and assessment of formal and informal apprenticeships in Bangladesh*. http://www.ilo.org/ wcmsp5/groups/public/@asia/@ro-bangkok/@ilodhaka/documents/publication/wcms_ 106575.pdf

International Labour Organization. (2012). *Bangladesh Skills Vision - 2016*. http://www.ilo.org/wcmsp5/groups/public/@asia/@ro-bangkok/@ilo-dhaka/documents/publication/wcms_176772.pdf

International Labour Organization. (2018). *The Gender Gap in employment: What's holding Women back?* https://www.ilo.org/infostories/en-GB/Stories/Employment/barriers-women#intro

International Labour Organization. (2020). *Empowering Women at Work- Trade Union Policies and Practices for Gender Equality*. ILO.

International Labour Organization. (2021). *COVID-19 and the world of work*. https://www.ilo.org/global/topics/coronavirus/lang--en/index.htm

International Trade Administration. (2021). *Kenya-Country Commercial guide: Information, Communications and Technology (ICT)*. https://www.trade.gov/knowledge-product/kenya-information-communications-and-technology-ict

I-SCOOP. (2017). *Industry 4.0: The fourth industrial revolution–guide to Industrie 4.0*. https://www.i-scoop.eu/industry-4-0/

Issa, A., Hanaysha, J., Elfeky, M., & Ullah, I. (2019). The Impact of Board Gender Diversity on Firm Value: Evidence from Kuwait. *International Journal of Applied Science and Research*, *2*(1), 1–21.

Issue of gender gap in judiciary explained pointwise. (n.d.). https://blog.forumias.com/issue-of-gender-gap-in-judiciary-explained-pointwise/

Jackson, E. (2015). Global Information Technology Strategy. *Jackson Journal of Information Technology*, *1*(2), 6–9.

Jackson, E. (2015). Global Information Technology Strategy. *Journal of Information Technology*, *1*(2), 6–9.

Jadhav, V. V., Mahadeokar, R., & Bhoite, S. D. (2019). *The Fourth Industrial Revolution (I4.0) in India: Challenges & Opportunities. International Journal of Trend in Scientific Research and Development.* https://www.ijtsrd.com/papers/ijtsrd23076.pdf

Jahan, R., & Mumtaz, S. (1996). The Elusive Agenda: Mainstreaming Women in Development. *Pakistan Development Review*, *35*(4), 825–834. doi:10.30541/v35i4IIpp.825-834 PMID:12294613

Jaisingh, I. (2019). An Open Letter From Indira Jaising to the Chief Justice of India on Women's Day. *The Wire.* Retrieved 10 July 2021, from https://thewire.in/law/open-letter-indira-jaising-to-cji-womens-day

Jaquette, J., & Staudt, K. (1985). *Women 'At Risk' Reproducers: Biology, Science, and Population in U.S. Foreign Policy. In Women, Biology and Public Policy*. Sage Publication.

Jariwala, H. V., & Sharma, M. S. (2016). Assessment of Behavioural Outcomes of Financial Education Workshops on Financial Behaviour of the Participants: An Experimental Study. In T. Harrison (Ed.), *Financial Literacy and the Limits of Financial Decision-Making*. Palgrave Macmillan. doi:10.1007/978-3-319-30886-9_15

Jayakrishnan, T., Thomas, B., Rao, B., & George, B. (2013). Occupational health problems of construction workers in India. *International Journal of Medicine and Public Health*, 225–229.

Jivani, A. (2020). Gender Lens to the Future of Work. *Daedalus*, *149*(1), 134–143. doi:10.1162/daed_a_01778

Joiner, R., Messer, D., Littleton, K., & Light, P. (1996). Gender, computer experience and computer-based problem solving. *Computers & Education*, *26*(1-3), 179–187. doi:10.1016/0360-1315(96)00008-5

Jones, F., Burke, R. J., & Westman, M. (2013). *Work-life balance: A psychological perspective.* Psychology Press.

Josefsson, E. (2019). *Industry 4.0 can be game changer for climate action.* https://www.ericsson.com/en/blog/2019/9/industry-4.0-can-be-a-game-changer-for-climate-action

Judicial appointments should reflect social diversity: CJI. (2021). *The Hindu*. Retrieved 4 July 2021, from https://www.thehindu.com/news/national/judicial-appointments-should-reflect-social-diversity-cji/article34730621.ece

Judith, M., Mayne, G., Aneja, U., & Sorgner, A. (2018). *Gender Economic Equity Bridging the Gender Digital Gap, Kiel Institute for the World Economy & John Cabot University, T-20*. Argentina.

Kanchana, Sivaprakash, & Joseph. (2015). Studies on Labour safety in Construction Sites. *TheScientificWorldJournal*, 6.

Kanshana, S., Sivaprakash, P., & Joseph, S. (2015). Studies on labour safety in construction sites. *TheScientificWorldJournal*.

Kapur, M. A. (2020). Union Budget 2020–21: A Critical Analysis from the Gender Perspective. *Economic and Political Weekly*, *55*(16).

Karamahmutoğlu, M. L., & Kuzey, C. (2016). The effect of board gender diversity on firm performance: Evidence from Turkey. *Gender in Management*, *31*(7), 434–455. doi:10.1108/GM-10-2015-0088

Karlan, D., & Kendall, J. (2016). *Research and impacts of digital financial services*. National Bureau of Economic Research. (Original work published 2016) doi:10.3386/w22633

Keeping the gender diversity conversation going – Women. (n.d.). https://www.hotelierindia.com/business/13878-keeping-the-gender-diversity-conversation-going

Kelan, E., & Stars, R. (2012). Developing Millennial Women as Leaders. Palgrave Macmillan.

Keohane, N. (2020). Women, Power & Leadership. *Daedalus*, *149*(1), 236–250. doi:10.1162/daed_a_01785

Khan, A., & Turowski, K. (2016a). *A Perspective on Industry 4.0: From Challenges to Opportunities in Production Systems*. University of Magdeburg. https://www.scitepress.org/Papers/2016/59297/59297.pdf

Khan, A., & Turowski, K. (2016b). A *Perspective on Industry 4.0: From Challenges to Opportunities in Production Systems*. University of Magdeburg. https://www.scitepress.org/Papers/2016/59297/59297.pdf

Khan, I., Khan, I., & Asim Afridi, M. (2021). Does board diversity matter for the quality of CSR disclosure? Evidence from the financial sector of Pakistan. *Review of Business Management*, 104–126.

Khan, I., Khan, I., & Şentürk, I. (2019). Board diversity and quality of CSR disclosure: evidence from Pakistan. In *Corporate Governance*. Emerald Publishing Limited.

Klapper, L., Lusardi, A., & van Oudheusden, P. (2011). Financial literacy around the world: An overview. *Journal of Pension Economics and Finance*, *10*(4), 497–508. doi:10.1017/S1474747211000448 PMID:28553190

KPMG & AIMA. (2018). *Industry 4.0 India INC Gearing up for change*. All India Management Association (AIMA) and KPMG. https://resources.aima.in/presentations/AIMA-KPMG-industry-4-0-report.pdf

KPMG. (2020). *Towards gender-balanced boards*. Retrieved from http://www.kpmg.com/IN

Kuhn, S., & Bluestone, B. (1987). Economic Restructuring and the Female Labor Market: The Impact of Industrial Change on Women. In L. Beneria & C. R. Stimpson (Eds.), *Women, Households, and the Economy* (pp. 3–32). Rutgers University Press.

Kularski, C., & Moller, S. (2012). The digital divide as a continuation of traditional systems of inequality. *Sociology*, *5151*, 1–23.

Kulkarni, G. (2007). Construction industry: More needs to be done. *Indian Journal of Occupational and Environmental Medicine*, *11*(1).

Kumar, A. P., & Vishnuvarthan, C. K. (2014). A study on construction jobsite safety management. *International Journal of Innovative Research in Science, Engineering and Technology*, *3*(1), 44-52.

Kumar, B. (2013). Gender discrimination among construction workers with reference to Vijaywada. *Journal of Sociology and Social Work*, *1*(1), 42-53.

Kumar, M. D. (2013). Inimitable Issues of Construction Workers: Case Study. *British Journal of Economics, Finamnce and Management Sciences*, 42-53.

Kumar, R. (2019). *Research Methodology A step by step guide for beginners*. Sage Publication.

Kumar, S., & Bansal, V. K. (2013). Construction safety knowledge for practitioners in the construction industry. *Journal of Frontier in Construction Engineering*, *2*(2), 34–42.

Lagarde, C., & Ostry, J. D. (2018). *Economic gains from gender inclusion: Even greater than You thought*. https://blogs.imf.org/2018/11/28/economic-gains-from-gender-inclusion-even-greater-than-you-thought/

Landford, D., Rowlinson, S., & Sawacha, E. (2000). Safety behaviour and safety management: Its influence on the attitudes of workers in the UK construction industry. *Engineering, Construction, and Architectural Management*, *7*(2), 133–140.

Larsson, A & Viitaoja, Y. (2020). *Identifying the digital gender divide: How digitalization may affect the future working conditions for women*. doi:10.4324/9780429317866-142018a

Laskar, A., & Murty, C. R. (2004). *Challenges before construction industry in India*. Academic Press.

Laudon, K., & Traver, C. (2007). *E-commerce: business, technology, society*. Pearson Prentice Hall.

Lawal, E., May, G., & Stahl, B. (2017). The significance of corporate social disclosure for high-tech manufacturing companies: Focus on employee and community aspects of sustainable development: Significance of corporate social disclosure for high-tech companies. *Corporate Social Responsibility and Environmental Management*, *24*(4), 295–311. doi:10.1002/csr.1397

Lee, J. C. (1951). Coefficient alpha and the internal structure of tests. *Psychometrika.*

Lette, A., Ambelu, A., Getahun, T., & Mekonen, S. (2018). A survey of work- related injuries among building construction workers in southwestern Ethiopia. *International Journal of Industrial Ergonomics*, *68*, 57–64.

Lohr, S. (2020, July 13). The Pandemic Has Accelerated Demands for a More Skilled Work Force. *The New York Times.*

Loretto, W., & Vickerstaff, S. (2015). Gender, age, and flexible working in later life. *Work, Employment and Society*, *29*(2), 233–249. doi:10.1177/0950017014545267

Lowen, A., & Sicilian, P. (2009). Family-Friendly Fringe Benefits and the Gender Wage Gap. *Journal of Labor Research*, *30*(2), 10. doi:10.100712122-008-9046-1

Lusardi & Tufano, (2015). Debt Literacy, Financial Experiences, and Over Indebtedness. *Journal of Pension Economics and Finance, 14*(4), 332-328.

Lusardi, A., & Carlo de Bassa, S. (2013). *Financial Literacy and High-Cost Borrowing in the United States.* NBER Working Paper 18969.

Lusardi, A., & Mitchell, O. (2007). Financial literacy and retirement preparedness: Evidence and implications for financial education. *Business Economics (Cleveland, Ohio)*, *42*(1), 35–44. doi:10.2145/20070104

Lusardi, A., & Mitchell, O. S. (2011). *Financial Literacy and Planning: Implications for Retirement Wellbeing.* Oxford University Press.

Lusardi, A., & Mitchell, O. S. (2014). The Economic Importance of Financial Literacy: Theory and Evidence. *Journal of Economic Literature*, *52*(1), 5–44. PMID:28579637

M, D. D. (April 2013). Inimitable Issues of Construction Workers: Case Study. *British Journal of Economics, Finamnce and Management Sciences*, 42-53.

Madanda, A., Kabonesa, C., & Bantebya-Kyomuhendo, G. (2007). Challenges to Women's Empowerment through ICTs: The Case of Makerere University. Agenda. *Empowering Women for Gender Equity*, (71), 81–88.

Mahalakshmi, J. (2015). Protection to women in India: A judicial Perspective. *Labour Law Journal*, 29-33.

Majmudar, U., Rana, N., & Sanan, N. (2015). *India's Top Companies for CSR & Sustainability.* Indian Institute of Management, Udaipur. Retrieved from https://www.iimu.ac.in/upload_data/main_containts/about/SocialResponsibility/IIMU_CSR_REPORT.pdf

Majumdar, R. (2016, May 12). *Migrant labourers: Stuck in a web of contractors, builders, lack of unions, welfare schemes*. Retrieved Dec 25, 2016, from Thozhilalar Koodam: https://tnlabour.in/migrant-workers/3680

Malhotra, V., Papola, T., Yugandhar, B., Sengupta, A. K., Kannan, K. P., & Srivastava, R. S. (2000). *Social security for Unorganised Workers: Report.* New Delhi: National Commission for Enterprises in the Unorganised Sector.

Mallawaarachchi, C. (2019). Significant Influences of digital literacy to promote gender equity and equality in education: Digital Literacy perspective. In Gender Issues in Technical and Vocational Education Programs. Academic Press.

Mallawaarachchi, C. (2014). Significant of Information Rich Contents in Technology-based marketing communication channels to reach knowledge savvy customers. *International Journal of Scientific and Research Publications*, *4*(10), 1–5.

Mallawaarachchi, C. (2015). Impacts of media literacy to enhance right to know and access to information: Democracy perspective. *International Journal of Scientific and Research Publications*, *5*(11), 257–261.

Mallawaarachchi, C. (2016). Universal responsibilities and challenges towards changing the landscape of knowledge access in higher education. *International Journal of Scientific and Research Publications*, *6*(10), 343–350.

Mallawaarachchi, C. (2019). The Application of artificial intelligence and interactive voice recognition in the banking industry in Sri Lanka. *Journal of Modern Accounting and Auditing*, *15*(8), 315–321. doi:10.17265/1548-6583/2019.06.004

Mandal, C. K. (2013). Concept and Types of Women Empowerment. *International Forum of Teaching and Studies, 9*(2).

Mann, J. S. (2007). Welfare and protection measures pertaining to the construction worker in India. *Labour Law Journal*, 36-41.

Marinova, J., Plantenga, J., & Remery, C. (2016). Gender diversity and firm performance: Evidence from Dutch and Danish boardrooms. *International Journal of Human Resource Management*, *27*(15), 1777–1790. doi:10.1080/09585192.2015.1079229

Mariscal, J., Mayne, G., Aneja, U., & Sorgner, A. (2019). Bridging the Gender Digital Gap. *Economics*, *13*(1), 1–12. doi:10.5018/economics-ejournal.ja.2019-9

Markel, K. (2016). Options and opportunities for women's workplace engagement. *Work, Employment and Society*, *30*(1), 192–197. doi:10.1177/0950017015590342

Marquis, C., & Lee, M. (2013). Who is governing whom? Executives, governance, and the structure of generosity in large US firms. *Strategic Management Journal*, *34*(4), 483–497. doi:10.1002mj.2028

Martin, A., & Oliva, J. (2001). Teaching Children About Money: Applications of Social Learning and Cognitive Learning Developmental Theories. *Journal of Family and Consumer Sciences: From Research to Practice, 93*.

Masum, A., Abdul Aziz, H. H. H. A., & Ahmad, M. H. (2020). Corporate Social Responsibility and its Effect on Community Development: An Overview. *IOSR Journal of Business and Management, 22*(1).

McHugh, M. (2013). *The Chi-square test of independence*. Lessons in Biostatistics.

McKinsey. (2019). *Digital India: Technology to transform connected nation*. McKinsey Global Institute. https://www.mckinsey.com/~/media/mckinsey/business%20functions/mckinsey%20digital/our%20insights/digital%20india%20technology%20to%20transform%20a%20connected%20nation/digital-india-technology-to-transform-a-connected-nation-full-report.ashx

McKinsey. (2021). *Women in the Workplace, 2021*. https://www.mckinsey.com/featured-insights/diversity-and-inclusion/women-in-the-workplace

Medha Kotwal Lele v. Union of India, Supreme Court of India (2012) https://indiankanoon.org/doc/48293767/

Mell, P., & Grance, T. (2011). The NIST definition of Cloud Computing. *Computers & Security*, 2.

Microsoft. (2019). *Corporate Social Responsibility Report 2018*. Microsoft.

Mishra, S., & Saur, D. (2010). Does Corporate Social Responsibility Influence Firm Performance of Indian Companies? *Journal of Business Ethics, 95*(4), 571–601. doi:10.100710551-010-0441-1

Mitrevska, T. C. (2017, March). *Land and gender: Macedonian experience*. Paper presented at the 2017 World Bank Conference on Land and Poverty, Washington, DC.

Moavenzadeh, F. (1978). Construction industry in developing countries. *World Development, 6*(1), 97–116.

Mohamed, M. (2018). Challenges and Benefits of Industry 4.0: An overview. *International Journal of Supply and Operations Management, 5*(3), 256–265.

Mohamed, S. (2002). Safety climate in construction site environment. *Journal of Construction Engineering and Management, 128*(5), 375–384.

Moolman, J., Primo, N., & Shackleton, S. (2007). Taking a byte of technology: Women and ICTs. *Empower. Women Gend. Equity, 21*, 4–14.

Moore, R., Vitale, D., & Stawinoga, N. (2018). *The Digital Divide and educational equity: A look at students with very limited access to electronic devices at home*. https://files.eric.ed.gov/fulltext/ED593163.pdf

More women judges need in judiciary. (n.d.). https://www.hindustantimes.com/cities/chandigarh-news/more-women-judges-needed-in-judiciary-101623059014130.html

Mouleeswaran, K. (2014). Evaluation of safety performance level of construction firms in and around erode zone. *International Journal of Innovative Research in Science, Engineering and Technology*, *3*(1), 1586–1594.

Moyce, S. C., & Schenker, M. (2018). Migrant workers and their occupational health and safety. *Annual Review of Public Health*, *39*, 351–365.

Mukesh v. State For Nct Of Delhi, Supreme Court of India (2017) https://indiankanoon.org/doc/68696327/

Muttakin, M. B., Khan, A., & Subramaniam, N. (2015). Firm characteristics, board diversity and corporate social responsibility: Evidence from Bangladesh. *Pacific Accounting Review*, *27*(3), 353–372. doi:10.1108/PAR-01-2013-0007

Nagaseshamma, S. (2014). Upliftment of construction Labour through social security laws. *Labour Law Journal*, 27-34.

Namrata, G. (2014). Uneven playing field: Women scientists in research laboratories. *Current Science*, *106*(11).

NASI. (2016). A road map for women in Science & Technology-A vision document, Inter-Academy Panel on "Women in Science" in India. The National Academy of Sciences in India (NASI).

NationalC. S. R. Portal. (n.d.). https://csr.gov.in/index20.php

NEP. (2020). National *Educational Policy 2020*. Ministry of human Resource Development, Government of India.

Networked Readiness Index — NRI. (n.d.). Retrieved from: https://www3.weforum.org/docs/GITR2016/WEF_GITR_Chapter1.1_2016.pdf

NFHS, (2019-21). *National Family Health Survey (NFHS-5), India Fact Sheet, Compendium of factsheets, India & 14 States/UTs (Phase II)*. International Institute for Population Sciences (IIPS).

Nicholson, G., & Newton, C. (2010). The role of the board of directors: Perceptions of managerial elites. *Journal of Management & Organization*, *16*(2), 204–218. doi:10.5172/jmo.16.2.204

Nilashi, M., Ibrahim, O., Mirabi, V. R., Ebrahimi, L., & Zare, M. (2015). The role of security, design, and content factors on customer trust in Mobile commerce. *Journal of Retailing and Consumer Services*, *26*, 57–68. doi:10.1016/j.jretconser.2015.05.002

Norwood, J. (1992). Working Women: Where Have We Been? Where Are We Going? *Population and Environment*, *14*(1), 95–103. doi:10.1007/BF01254609

NTIA (National Telecommunications and Information Administration). (1995). *Falling through the Net: A Survey of the "Have Nots" in Rural and Urban America*. Retrieved August 2, 2009, from https://www.ntia.doc.gov/ntiahome/fallingthru.html

NTIA (National Telecommunications and Information Administration). (1999). *Falling through the Net: Defining the Digital Divide. A Report on the Telecommunications and Information Technology Gap in America. Revised.* U.S. Government Printing Office, Superintendent of Documents. https://www.ntia.doc.gov/ntiahome/fttn99/contents.html

Nyambura, M. M., & Simon, K. (2018). Employee performance in power transmission companies in Kenya. *International Journal of Business Management and Finance.*

OECD. (2001). Understanding the Digital Divide. Paris, France: OECD (Organization for Economic Co-operation and Development).

OECD. (2013). *Women and Financial Education: Evidence, Policy Responses, and Guidance, OECD Publishing.* Organization for Economic Co-operation and Development.

OECD. (2015a). *The ABC of Gender Equality in Education: Aptitude, Behaviour, Confidence.* OECD Publishing. http://dx.doi.org/10.1787/9789264229945-en

OECD. (2017). Going Digital: The future of work for women. The pursuit gender equality: an uphill battle. Paris: OECD Publishing.

Official Statistics of Republic of Belarus. (n.d.). Retrieved from www.belstat.gov.by/en/ofitsialnaya-statistika/

Ofori, G. (2000). Globalization and construction industry development: Research opportunities. *Construction Management and Economics, 18*(3), 257–262.

Organisation for Economic Cooperation and Development. (2001). *Understanding the Digital Divide.* https://www.oecd.org/sti/ieconomy/1888451.pdf

Organisation for Economic Cooperation and Development. (2016). *Closing gender gaps in the labour markets of emerging economies: The unfinished job.* https://www.oecd.org/employment/oecd-employment-outlook-19991266.htm

Organisation for Economic Cooperation and Development. (2018). *Bridging the Digital Gender Divide: Include, upskill, innovate.* https://www.oecd.org/digital/bridging-the-digital-gender-divide.pdf

Organization for Economic Co-operation and Development (OECD). (2005). *Improving financial literacy: Analysis of issues and policies.* OECD.

Osariemen, A., Edosa, J. A., Uwuigbe, U., & Uwuigbe, O. R. (2018). Audit committee attributes and audit quality: A benchmark analysis. *Business: Theory and Practice, 19*(0), 37–48. doi:10.3846/btp.2018.05

Osborne, J., & Waters, E. (2002). Four assumptions of multiple regression that researchers shouls always test. *Practical Assessment, Research & Evaluation.*

Osterman, P. (1995). Work-Family Programs and the Employment Relationship. *Administrative Science Quarterly, 40*(4), 681–687. doi:10.2307/2393758

Pande, R. (2008). Digital Divide, gender, and the Indian experience in IT. In E. Trauth (Ed.), *Encyclopaedia of Gender and Information Technology* (pp. 191–199). IGI Global Publishers. doi:10.4018/978-1-59904-939-7.ch105

Patel, H. C., Moitra, M., Momin, M. H., & Kantharia, S. L. (2012). Working conditions of male construction worker and its impact on their life: A cross sectioanl study in Surat city. *National Journal of Community Medicine*, *3*(4), 652–656.

PCMag. (2014). *Definition of Direct Carrier Billing*. Retrieved from www.pcmag.com: http://www.pcmag.com/encyclopedia/term/63496/direct-carrier-billing

Perry, V., & Morris, M. D. (2005). Who Is in Control? The Role of Self-Perception, Knowledge, and Income in Explaining Consumer Financial Behavior. *The Journal of Consumer Affairs*, *39*(2), 299–313. doi:10.1111/j.1745-6606.2005.00016.x

Petrides, K. V., & Furnham, A. (2000). Gender Differences in Measured and Self-Estimated Trait Emotional Intelligence. *Sex Roles*, *42*(5/6), 449–461. doi:10.1023/A:1007006523133

Pew Research Center. (2014). *Online Harassment*. http://assets.pewresearch.org/wpcontent/uploads/sites/14/2014/10/PI_OnlineHarassment_72815.pdf

Pheng, L. S., & Hou, L. S. (2019). *Construction Quality and the Economy*. Springer.

Pitroda, S., & Desai, M. (2010). The march of mobile money: the future of lifestyle management. *The Mobile Wallet*, 127-155.

PLFS Annual Report 2019-20. (n.d.). National Statistical Office, Ministry of Statistics and Program Implementation (MOSPI), Government of India.

PMJDY. (2018). *Pradhan Mantri Jan-Dhan Yojana*. https://www.pmjdy.gov.in/scheme

Pohl, R. F., Bender, M., & Lachmann, G. (2005). Autobiographical Memory and Social Skills of Men and Women. *Applied Cognitive Psychology*, *19*(6), 745–759. doi:10.1002/acp.1104

Pollitzer, E. (2017). *Will the '4th Industrial Revolution' be gender-blind?* Elsevier. Retrieved on July 7, 2020, from https://www.elsevier.com/connect/will-the-4th-industrial-revolution-be-gender-blind

Potrich, A. C. G., Vieira, K. M., & Mendes-Da-Silva, W. (2016). Development of a financial literacy model for university students. *Management Research Review*, *39*(3), 356–376. doi:10.1108/MRR-06-2014-0143

Pradhan Mantri Jan-Dhan Yojana. (n.d.). http://www.pmjdy.gov.in/schemedetail.aspx

Prasad, N., Rao, V. K., & Nagesha, H. N. (2011). Study on building and other construction workers welfare schemes/ amenities in Karnataka. *SAS Tech Journal*, *10*, 59–66.

Premuzic, T., & Gallop, C. (2020). 7 Leadership Lessons Men Can Learn From Women. *Harvard Business Review*. https://hbr.org/2020/04/7-leadership-lessons-men-can-learn-from-women

Prevention of Sexual Harassment at the Workplace (POSH). (2020). Retrieved from https://www.nishithdesai.com/fileadmin/user_upload/pdfs/Research%20Papers/Prevention_of_Sexual_Harassment_at_Workplace.pdf

Pries, F., & Janszen, F. (1995). Innovation in the construction industry: The dominant role of the environment. *Construction Management and Economics*, 43–51.

Priya, M., Kothai, P., & Kohilambal, E. (2016). Study on safety practices and their performance in the construction industry. *International Journal of Modern Trends in Engineering and Research*, 284-293.

Provasi, R., & Harasheh, M. (2021). Gender diversity and corporate performance: Emphasis on sustainability performance. *Corporate Social Responsibility and Environmental Management*, *28*(1), 127–137. doi:10.1002/csr.2037

Pucheta-Martínez, M. C., Bel-Oms, I., & Olcina-Sempere, G. (2018). The association between board gender diversity and financial reporting quality, corporate performance and corporate social responsibility disclosure: A literature review. *Academia (Caracas)*, *31*(1), 177–194. doi:10.1108/ARLA-04-2017-0110

Qin, Z., Chang, Y., Li, S., & Li, F. (2014). *E-commerce strategy*. Springer Berlin. doi:10.1007/978-3-642-39414-0

Queisser, M., Adema, W. & Clarke, C. (2020). *COVID-19, employment and women in OECD countries*. London: VoxEU.

Rafaeli, S., Leck, E., Albo, Y., Oppenheim, Y., & Getz, D. (2018). *An innovative approach for measuring the Digital Divide in Israel: Digital trace data as means for formulating policy guidelines*. https://www.neaman.org.il/Files/Measuring_the_Digital_Divide_%20in_Israel_Final_July_29.pdf

Rafique, Q., Al-Mamun, A., & Ahmed, I. (2017). Corporate Social Responsibility and Gender Diversity: Insights from the Asia Pacific: Gender Diversity, Corporate Social Responsibility. *Corporate Social Responsibility and Environmental Management*, *24*(3), 210–221. Advance online publication. doi:10.1002/csr.1400

Ragnedda, M., & Muschert, G. W. (2013). Introduction. In M. Ragnedda & G. W. Muschert (Eds.), *The Digital Divide: The Internet and Social Inequality in International Perspective* (pp. 1–14). Routledge.

Rahman, D., & Singh, R. (2019). An overview of CSR taken by TATA Group. *International Journal of Developmental Research*, *9*(1).

Raja v. State of Karnataka, Supreme Court of India (2016) https://indiankanoon.org/doc/134419727/

Rajanna. (2015). Nature of Work, Working Conditions and Problems of Women Construction Workers: A Case Study. *International Journal of Business Quantitative Economics and Applied Managment Research*.

Rajgopal, K. (2012). *McKinsey on payments: Payment wave, commerce ocean.* Academic Press.

Raj, S. (2015). Financial Inclusiveness: The role of mobile money and digital financial services. *Socrates, 3*(1), 95–112.

Ramesh, A. (n.d.). Safety Control in the Construction Industry in India. Academic Press.

Rao, K., & Tilt, C. (2016). Board diversity and CSR reporting: An Australian study. *Meditari Accountancy Research, 24*(2), 182–210. doi:10.1108/MEDAR-08-2015-0052

Rashid, L. (2017). *Enhancing decent employment opportunities for women and marginalized groups in growth sectors.* https://www.un.org/development/desa/dspd/wp-content/uploads/sites/22/2017/04/BRAC-Skills-present

Redefining Women's Work. (2000). *Economic and Political Weekly, 35*(52/53), 4591–4592.

Reiko, K., Lopez, M., Sasaki, J., & Settecase, M. (2019). *W-20, Policy Brief.* The Digital Gender Gap.

Ringen, K., & Seegal, J. (1995). Safety and health in the construction industry. *Annual Review of Public Health, 16*(1), 165–188.

Roese, J. (2021). *COVID-19 exposed the Digital Divide. Here's how we can close it.* https://www.delltechnologies.com/en-us/perspectives/covid-19-exposed-the-digital-divide-here-s-how-we-can-close-it/?gacd=9643275-1040-5761040-266682520-0&dgc=st&gclid=CjwKCAjwoZWHBhBgEiwAiMN66eQ0xNIcBEqodudgWf8aH6NjUq4v1RyZQmnUKrLN0K1Q_PEj0rfuRoC7YQQAvD_BwE&gclsrc=aw.ds&nclid=vmlAo9V_McM-fNsg2vhYo6-FXU6B5npe066lyRCEAhTzIrCssL85yE2ty_gM9xjL

Rogers, E. M. (2001). The digital divide. *Convergence, 7*(4), 96–111. doi:10.1177/135485650100700406

Ruehl, M., & Kynge, J. (2019, Dec. 12). Fintech: the rise of the Asian 'super app'. *Financial Times.*

Rupley, K. H., Brown, D., & Marshall, R. S. (2012a). Governance, media, and the quality of environmental disclosure. *Journal of Accounting and Public Policy, 31*(6), 610–640. doi:10.1016/j.jaccpubpol.2012.09.002

Ruxton, G. (2006). The unequal variance t-test is an underused alternative to Student's t-test and Mann- Whitney U test. *Behavioural Ecology*, 688–690.

Sa'nchez-Franco, M., Villarejo, A., & Martı'n, F. (2009). The moderating effect of gender on relationship quality and loyalty toward internet service providers. *Information & Management, 46*(3), 196–202. doi:10.1016/j.im.2009.02.001

Saari, L. M., & Judge, T. A. (2004). Employee attitudes and job satisfaction. *Human Resource Management, 43*(4), 395–407.

Sageer, A., Rafat, S., & Agarwal, P. (2012). Identification of variables affecting employee satisfaction and their impact on the organnization. *Journal of Business and Management*, 32–39.

Saha, A. (2014, February). Unsafe conditions and deaths in construction sites and governement inaction. *Thozhilalar Koodam.*

Sahay, S. (1998). *Women and Empowerment: Approaches and Strategies.* Discovery Publishing House.

Salgaonkar, S., & Salgaonkar, P. (2009). Panchayats and Women Self Help Groups: Understanding the Symbiosis. *Indian Journal of Poultry Science, 70*(2), 481–494.

Samsung Electronics. (2019). *A Fifty Year journey towards a sustainable future. Sustainability Report 2019.* Samsung Electronics. https://images.samsung.com/is/content/samsung/assets/ve/our-values/resource/SustainabilityReport2019v2-en.pdf

Sang, K., & Powell, A. (2012). Gender inequality in the construction industry: Lessons from Pierre Bourdieu. In *Proceedings of the 28th Annual ARCOM Conference* (pp. 237-247). Edinburgh, UK: Association of Researchers in Construction Management.

Satish Kumar, V. (2013). Construction safety Knowledge for Practitioners in the Construction Industry. *Journal of Frontiers in Construction Engineering*, 34-42.

Satria, Y., Mahadwartha, P. A., & Ernawati, E. (2020). The effect of gender diversity on company financial performance. In *Proceedings of the 17 Th International Symposium on Management (INSYMA 2020).* Paris, France: Atlantis Press. 10.2991/aebmr.k.200127.094

Scandura, T., & Lankau, M. (1997). Relationships of Gender, Family Responsibility and Flexible Work Hours to Organizational Commitment and Job Satisfaction. *Journal of Organizational Behavior, 18*(4), 377–391. doi:10.1002/(SICI)1099-1379(199707)18:4<377::AID-JOB807>3.0.CO;2-1

Scherer, J. L. (2020). *The Digital Transformation People:- Renault-an Industry 4.0 case study.* https://www.thedigitaltransformationpeople.com/channels/the-case-for-digital-transformation/renault-an-industry-4-0-case-study/

Schneider, G. (2014). *Electronic Commerce.* Cengage Learning.

Schomer, I., & Hammond, A. (2020). Stepping up women's STEM careers in infrastructure: An overview of promising approaches. ESMAP Paper. Washington, DC: World Bank.

Schueller-Weidekamm, C., & Kautzky-Willer, A. (2012). Challenges of work–life balance for women physicians/mothers working in leadership positions. *Gender Medicine, 9*(4), 244–250.

SED's Report on Status of Women Scientists in Delhi. (2011). *Status of women scientists in S&T/R&D institutions in Delhi.* Academic Press.

Selvam & Priyadarshini. (n.d.). Safety management and Hazards Control measures in Construction. *IOSR Journal of Mechanical and Civil Engineering*, 97-101.

Selwyn, N. (2004). Reconsidering political and popular understandings of the digital divide. *New Media & Society, 6*(3), 341–362. doi:10.1177/1461444804042519

Sen A. (1985-86). *Women, Technology and Sexual Divisions*. Trade and Development, United Nations.

Setthasakko, W. (2009, July 24). Barriers to implementing corporate environmental responsibility in Thailand. *The International Journal of Organizational Analysis*, *17*(3), 69–83. doi:10.1108/19348830910974905

Shamsuddin, K., Ani, M., Ismail, A., & Ibrahim, M. (2015). Investigation the safety, health and environment (SHE) protection in construction area. *International Research Journal of Engineering and Technology*, 624-635.

Shankar, U., & Chowdhury, S. (2019). Representative judiciary in India: An argument for gender diversity in the appointment of judges in the supreme court. *ILI Law Review*. Retrieved from https://www.ili.ac.in/pdf/uss.pdf

Shashaani, L. (1994). Gender-differences in computer experience and its influence on computer attitudes. *Journal of Educational Computing Research*, *11*(4), 347–367. doi:10.2190/64MD-HTKW-PDXV-RD62

Shekhara, R., & Raza, R. (2020). *The Value of Dissent in Supreme Court Judgments*. Retrieved 17 July 2021, from https://www.theleaflet.in/dissent-judgments-supreme-court/

Shira, D. (2021). *Corporate Social Responsibility in India*. Retrieved on 7 July 2021 from https://www.india-briefing.com/news/corporate-social-responsibility-india-5511.html/

Shirur, S., & Torgal, S. (2014, April). Enhancing safety and health management techniques in Indian construction industry. *International Journal of Engineering and Technical Research*, *2*(4), 52-56.

Shruti, J. (2020). STEM and the digital economy for women. *India Matters*. https://www.orfonline.org/expert-speak/stem-and-the-digital-economy-for-women/

Silver, H., & Goldscheider, F. (1994). Flexible Work and Housework: Work and Family Constraints on Women's Domestic Labor. *Social Forces*, *72*(4), 1103–1119. doi:10.2307/2580294

Sinclair, A. (2014). A feminist case for leadership. In J. Damousi, K. Rubenstein, & M. Tomsic (Eds.), *Diversity in Leadership: Australian women, past and present* (pp. 17–36). ANU Press. doi:10.22459/DL.11.2014.01

Singh, R. (2014). *India: Overview of the Sexual Harassment of women at workplace*. Indian Corporate Counsel Association.

Singh, R. S. (2014, October 21). *India: Overview of the Sexual Harassment of women T Workplace*. Academic Press.

Singh, K. (2014). Safety in Indian Construction. *International Journal of Engineering Research & Technology (Ahmedabad)*.

Singh, M. B., & Chandra, A. I. (2019). Industry 4.0 and Future of Work in India. *FIB Business Review*, *8*(1), 9–16.

Skewed justice. (2020). *The Indian Express*. Retrieved 30 July 2021, from https://indianexpress.com/article/opinion/editorials/supreme-court-women-judges-kk-venugopal-7088348/

Slyke, V., Comunale, C., & Belangr, F. (2002). Gender differences in perceptions of web-based shopping. *Communications of the ACM*, *45*(7), 82–86. doi:10.1145/545151.545155

Smartphone users worldwide will total 1.75 billion in 2014. (2014). Retrieved from http://www.emarketer.com: http://www.emarketer.com/Article/Smartphone-Users-Worldwide-Will-Total-175-Billion-2014/1010536#sthash.UnbdaSGM.dpuf

Smith, A. (2015). On The Edge of a Glass Cliff: Women in Leadership in Public Organizations. *Public Administration Quarterly*, *39*(3), 484–517.

Smith, N., Smith, V., & Verner, M. (2006). Do Women in Top Management Affect Firm Performance? A Panel Study of 2,500 Danish Firms. *International Journal of Productivity and Performance Management*, *55*(5), 569–593. doi:10.1108/17410400610702160

Smithson, J., Lewis, S., Cooper, C., & Dyer, J. (2004). Flexible working and the gender pay gap in the accountancy profession. *Work, Employment and Society*, *18*(1), 115–135. doi:10.1177/0950017004040765

Soares, S. E., & Sidun, N. M. (2021). Women leaders during a global crisis: Challenges, characteristics, and strengths. *International Perspectives in Psychology: Research, Practice, Consultation*, *10*(3), 130–137. doi:10.1027/2157-3891/a000020

Sorgner, A., Bode, E., & Krieger-Boden, C. (2017). *The Effects of Digitalization for Gender Equality in the G20 Economies, Women 20 study*. https://www.ifw-kiel.de/pub/e-books/digital_women-final_report.pdf

Souchet, S. (2021a). *Industry 4.0 case study: - Lamborghini shifts gears into smart manufacturing's fast lane*. KPMG. https://home.kpmg/xx/en/home/insights/2018/11/industry-4-0-case-studies.html

Souchet, S. (2021b). *Industry 4.0 case study: Transforming a pharmaceutical giant*. KPMG. https://home.kpmg/xx/en/home/insights/2018/11/industry-4-0-case-studies.html

Souchet, S. (2021c). *Industry 4.0 case study: Smart farming blooms in South Korea*. KPMG. https://home.kpmg/xx/en/home/insights/2018/11/industry-4-0-case-studies.html

Sparks, K., Faragher, B., & Cooper, C. (2001). Well-being and occupational health in the 21st centuryworkplace. *Journal of Occupational and Organizational Psychology*, 489–509.

Srivastava, R. (2014). *Documenting the lack of labour rights in India's construction sector*. Centre for Development Policy and Research.

SSESS. (2017). *Final Report – Status of women in science among select institutions in India: policy implications*. Society for Socio-Economic Studies and Services (SSESS).

Standard and Poor. (2015). *Financial Literacy Around the World: Insights From The Standard & Poor's Ratings Services Global Financial Literacy Survey*. Retrieved from https://gflec.org/initiatives/sp-global-finlit-survey/

Stango, V., & Zinman, J. (2009). Exponential Growth Bias and Household Finance. *The Journal of Finance*, *64*(6), 2807–2849. doi:10.1111/j.1540-6261.2009.01518.x

Statistical Yearbook. (2019). The National Statistic Committee of the Republic of Belarus.

STIP. (2013). *Science, Technology, and Innovation policy, 2013*. Government of India, Ministry of Science & Technology. https://dst.gov.in/sites/default/files/STI%20Policy%202013-English.pdf

Sudhansu Sekhar Sahoo v. State Of Orissa, Supreme Court of India (2002) https://indiankanoon.org/doc/76278/

Suen, S. (2013). *The education of women as a tool in development: Challenging the African maxim*. http://journals.ed.ac.uk/hydra/article/view/720

Sujatha, R. (2017). Gender, and Science, A Case for Inclusion and Diversity. *Economic and Political Weekly*, *52*(17).

Sundström, A., Hyder, A. S., & Chowdhury, E. H. (2020). Market-oriented CSR implementation in SMEs with sustainable innovations: An action research approach. *Baltic Journal of Management*, *15*(5), 775–795. doi:10.1108/BJM-03-2020-0091

Sweeney, J. J., & Nussbaum, K. (1989). *Solutions for the New Work Force*. Seven Locks Press.

Sweet, J. (2016). *Access to digital technology accelerates global gender equality*. https://hbr.org/2016/05/access-to-digital-technology-accelerates-global-gender-equality

Swift v. Castle, 23 Ill. 209, Illinois Supreme Court (1859) https://cite.case.law/ill/23/209/

Tandon, J., & Gupta, H. (2019). *A study of Corporate Social Responsibility (CSR) practices in select Indian companies with special reference to environmental aspects*. Paper presented at the National Conference on "Achieving excellence through sustainability and innovation" organized by Delhi Institute of Advanced Studies.

Tapver, T., Laidroo, L., & Gurvitš-Suits, N. A. (2020). Banks' CSR reporting – Do women have a say? *Corporate Governance*, *20*(4), 639–651. doi:10.1108/CG-11-2019-0338

Target judicial patriarchy, not the judge. (2021). *The Hindu*. Retrieved 18 July 2021, from https://www.thehindu.com/opinion/lead/target-judicial-patriarchy-not-the-judge/article34030694.ece

Tata Trusts. (2020). *India Justice Report 2020*. Retrieved from https://www.tatatrusts.org/Upload/pdf/ijr-2020-overall-report-january-26.pdf

The Global Economy.com. (2021). *Israel: Labor force: Percent female*. https://www.theglobaleconomy.com/Israel/Labor_force_percent_female/

The Global Innovation Index – GII. (n.d.). Retrieved from https://www.wipo.int/edocs/pubdocs/en/wipo_pub_gii_2018.pdf

The UN Global E-Government Development Index – EGDI. (n.d.). Retrieved from https://publicadministration.un.org/publications/content/PDFs/UN%20E-Government%20Survey%202018%20Russian.pdf

Thenguzhali, T., & Veerachamy, P. (2009). Occupational health hazards of women construction workers: A critical survey of the literature. *Indian Journal of Dermatology*, *15*(8).

Thorton, G. (2017). *India's readiness for Industry 4.0- A focus on Automotive sector*. Grant Thorton India. https://www.grantthornton.in/globalassets/1.-member-firms/india/assets/pdfs/indias_readiness_for_industry_4_a_focus_on_automotive_sector.pdf

Tilting the Scale: Gender Imbalance in the Lower Judiciary. (2018). *Vidhi Centre for Legal Policy*. Retrieved 20 July 2021, from https://vidhilegalpolicy.in/research/report-on-gender-imbalance-in-the-lower-judiciary/

Tinker, I. (1981). New Technologies for Food-Related Activities. Academic Press.

Tiwary & Gangopadhay. (2011). A Review on the Occupational Health and Social security of Unorganized workers in the Construction Industry. *Indian Journal of Occupational & Environmental Medicine*, 18-24.

Tiwary, G., & Gangopadhyay, P. (2011). A review on the occupational health and social security of unorganized workers in the construction industry. *Indian Journal of Occupational and Environmental Medicine*.

Tiwary, G., Gangopadhyay, P. K., Biswas, S., Nayak, K., Chatterjee, M. K., & Chakroborty, D. (2012). Social-economic status of women of building construction industry. *Indian Journal of Occupational and Environmental Medicine*, 66–71.

Top 100 stocks by Market Capitalization: BSE Listed stocks Market Capitalization. (n.d.). https://www.bseindia.com/markets/equity/eqreports/topmarketcapitalization.aspx.com/markets/equity/eqreports/topmarketcapitalization.aspx

Toronto Centre. (2018). *Advancing Women's Digital Financial Inclusion.*

Tripathi, K., & Jha, K. (2018). An empirical study on factor leading to the success of construction organizations in India. *International Journal of Construction Management.*

Trivelli, C., & De Los, R. (2014). *Creating Financial Assets: the case for Saving Accounts as means for Economic Independence and Empowerment for Women*. Proyecto.

Tshoaedi, M. (2012). Women in the Forefront of Workplace Struggles in South Africa: From Invisibility to Mobilization. Labour, Capital and Society / Travail. *Capital EtSociété*, *45*(2), 58–83.

Tuokuu, F. X. D., & Dartey-Baah, A. (2016). Corporate social responsibility: Is it an alternative to the government? *Journal of Global Responsibility*, *7*(1), 26–38. doi:10.1108/JGR-05-2015-0007

U.S. Bureau of Labor Statistics. (2013). *Women in the labor force: A Databook.* https://www.bls.gov/cps/wlf-databook-2012.pdf

U.S. Bureau of Labor Statistics. (2014). *Women in the Labor force: A Databook.* https://www.bls.gov/cps/wlf-databook-2013.pdf

U.S. Bureau of Labor Statistics. (2021). *Labor force statistics from the current population survey.* https://www.bls.gov/cps/cpsaat03.htm

UGC. (2012). *Annual Report, 2011-12.* University Grants Commission (UGC).

UN Statistics. (2016). Table 7: Population by age, sex and urban/rural residence: latest available year, 2007- 2016. In *Demographic Yearbook – 2016* [database]. United Nations Statistics Division. https://unstats.un.org/unsd/demographic-social/products/dyb/index.cshtml

UN Women Watch. (2018). *Facts & figures: Rural women and the millennium development goals.* www.un.org/womenwatch/feature/ruralwomen/facts-figures.html

UN Women. (2005). *Gender Equality and Empowerment of Women through ICT.* UN Division for the Advancement of Women, Department of Economic and Social Affairs of the United Nations Secretariat. www.un.org/womenwatch/daw/public/w2000-09.05-ict-e.pdf

UN Women. (2018a). *Turning promises into action: Gender equality in the 2030 Agenda for sustainable development.* www.unwomen.org/en/digital-library/publications/2018/2/gender-equality-in-the2030-agenda-for-sustainable-development-2018#view

UNESCO and Equal Skills Coalition. (2019). *I'd blush if I could: Closing gender divides in digital skills through education.* Policy paper. UNESCO. https://en.unesco.org/Id-blush-if-I-could

UNESCO EQUALS Skills Coalition. (2019). *I'd blush if I could: closing gender divides in digital skills through education.* Author.

UNESCO. (2003). *Towards a more equitable information society: How and why of gender mainstreaming.* http://portal.unesco. Org/ci/en/file_ download. Php/ 250561f24133814c18284feedc30bb5egender_issues. Pdf

UNESCO. (2007). Science, Technology and Gender: An International Report. UNESCO.

UNESCO. (2015). *UNESCO Science Report –Towards 2030, India.* United Nationals Educational Scientific &Cultural Organization.

UNESCO. (2017). *Literacy rates continue to rise from one generation to the next.* Fact Sheet No. 45, September, FS/2017/LIT/45. http://uis.unesco.org/sites/default/files/documents/fs45-literacy-rates-continuerise-generation-to-next-en-2017.pdf

UNESCO. (2019). *Women in science, Fact Sheet No. 55 June 2019 FS/2019/SCI/55.* UNESCO Institute for Statistics.

UNESCO. (2021). *Women a minority in Industry 4.0 fields.* https://en.unesco.org/news/women-minority-industry-40-fields

UNICEF. (2020). *Towards an equal future: Reimagining girls' education through STEM*. https://www.unicef.org/media/84046/file/Reimagining-girls-education-through-stem-2020.pdf

UNIDO. (2019). *UNIDO addresses the need for enhanced women's inclusion in Industry 4.0*. https://www.unido.org/news/unido-addresses-need-enhanced-womens-inclusion-industry-40

United Nations. (2015). *The World's Women 2015: Trends and statistics*. https://unstats.un.org/unsd/gender/downloads/worldswomen2015_report.pdf

Van Marrewijk, M. (2003). Concepts and definitions of CSR and corporate sustainability: Between agency and communion. *Journal of Business Ethics*, *44*(2), 95–105. doi:10.1023/A:1023331212247

VanderBrug, J. (2013). *The Global Rise of Female Entrepreneurs*. Harvard Business School.

Veerachamy. (2009). Occupational health hazards of women construction workers: A critical survey of the literature. *Indian Journal Dermatol*.

Vehovar, V., Sicherl, P., Hüsing, T., & Dolnicar, V. (2006). Methodological challenges of digital divide measurements. *The Information Society*, *22*(5), 279–290.

Venkatesh, D. (2020). *India Manufacturing Seeing Innovations*. ARC Advisory Group. https://www.arcweb.com/industry-best-practices/india-manufacturing-seeing-innovations

Venkatesh, V., & Morris, M. (2000). Why Don't Men Ever Stop to Ask for Directions? Gender, Social Influence, and Their Role in Technology Acceptance and Usage Behavior. *Management Information Systems Quarterly*, *24*(1), 115–139. doi:10.2307/3250981

Verdin, R., & Jacqueline O.R. (2021). *A gender agenda for the future of work in a digital age of pandemics: Jobs, skills and contracts*. WSI Study, No. 24. HansBöckler-Stiftung, Wirtschafts- und Sozialwissenschaftliches Institut (WSI).

Vinnicombe, S., Singh V., Burke, R.J., Bilimonia, D., & Huse, M. (2008). Women on Corporate Board of Directors. In *International Research and Practice*. Edward Elgar Publishing Ltd UK.

Vinod Kumar v. State of Kerala, Supreme Court of India (2014) https://indiankanoon.org/doc/188149660/

Vishakha v. State of Rajasthan, Supreme Court of India (1997) https://indiankanoon.org/doc/1031794/

Watzlawek, L. M. (2018). *Implementation of Industrie 4.0 in Purchasing: A Case Study*. University of Twente, The Faculty of Behavioural, Management and Social Sciences. https://essay.utwente.nl/75246/6/watzlawek_BA_BMS.pdf

Webster, K. (2018). *How to make it in mobile commerce*. Retrieved from www.humnwallet.com/article/-the-evolution-of-the-wallet-ancient-to-modern-times

WEF. (2016). *The Future of Jobs: Employment, Skills and Workforce Strategy for the Fourth Industrial Revolution*. Global Challenges Insight Report. Geneva: World Economic Forum.

WEF. (2018). *The Global Gender Gap Report 2018.* World Economic Forum. https://www.weforum.org/reports/the-global-gender-gap-report-2018

WEF. (2018a). *The fourth industrial revolution can smash gender equality-or deepen it.* https://www.weforum.org/agenda/2018/03/the-fourthindustrial-revolution-could-smash-gender-inequality-or-reinforce-it/

WEF. (2018b). *Future of Jobs.* https://www.weforum.org/reports/the-future-of-jobs-report-2018

WEF. (2018c). *Will the fourth industrial revolution be a revolution for Women?* https://www.weforum.org/agenda/2018/01/gender-inequalityand-the-fourth-industrial-revolution/

WEF. (2019). *Global Gender Gap Report 2020.* Insight Report. Geneva: World Economic Forum. Available at: https://www3.weforum.org/docs/WEF_GGGR_2020.pdf

WEF. (2021). *Global Gender Gap Report 2021.* WEF.

Weingarten, E. (2013). *The Developing World Needs More Female Internet Users.* Available online: http://www.slate.com/articles/technology/technology/2013/01/a_new_report_on_female_internet_ users_from_the_developing_world.html

Widyasari, P. A., & Ayunda, N. F. (2020). CSR Reporting: Perspective of Female Audit Committee Having Financial Expertise. In *Proceedings of the 17th International Symposium on Management (INSYMA 2020).* Atlantis Press.

Women and the Web. (2013). Available online: http://www.intel.com/content/www/us/en/technology-in-education/women-in-the-web.html

Women's World Banking. (2016). Women's Financial Inclusion: A Driver for Global Growth. New York: Women's World Banking.

World Bank Group. (2018). *The Global Findex Database.* Author.

World Bank. (2015, May). *Bangladesh's ICT industry: A boon for Women's employment.* https://www.worldbank.org/en/news/feature/2015/05/08/bangladeshs-ict-industry-a-boon-for-womens-employment

World Bank. (2017). *Breaking the glass ceiling challenges to female participation in technical diploma education in Bangladesh.* South Asia Region, Education Global Practice Report. http://documents.worldbank.org/curated/en/ 717771486560820977/

World Bank. (2017). *The Global Findex Database.* Retrieved from worldbank.org/curated/en/332881525873182837/The-Global-FindexDatabase-2017-Measuring-Financial-Inclusion-and-the-Fintech-Revolution

World Bank. (2018). *Labour Force Participation Rate.* https://data.worldbank.org/indicator/SL.TLF.CACT.ZS

World Economic Forum. (2016). *The Industry Gender Gap Women and Work in the Fourth Industrial Revolution.* Retrieved from https://www3.weforum.org/docs/WEF_FOJ_Executive_Summary_GenderGap.pdf

World Economic Forum. (2016). *Women and Work in the Fourth Industrial Revolution.* https://reports.weforum.org/future-of-jobs-2016/women-and-work-in-the-fourth-industrial-revolution/

World Economic Forum. (2017). *The Global Gender Gap Report.* https://www3.weforum.org/docs/WEF_GGGR_2017.pdf

World Economic Forum. (2017, July). *Accelerating Workforce Reskilling for the Fourth Industrial Revolution.* Author.

World Economic Forum. (2018). *Our Shared Digital Future: Building an Inclusive Trustworthy and Sustainable Digital Society.* Author.

World Economic Forum. (2019). *Global Gender Gap Report 2020.* https://www3.weforum.org/docs/WEF_GGGR_2020.pdf

World Employment and Social Outlook. (2018). *Trends for Women Global snapshot.* International Labor Office.

Worldometer. (2021a). *Bangladesh population (Live).* https://www.worldometers.info/world-population/bangladesh-population/#:~:text=Bangladesh%202020%20population%20is%20estimated,(and%20dependencies)%20by%20population

Worldometer. (2021b). *Israel population (Live).* https://www.worldometers.info/world-population/israel-population/

Worldometer. (2021c). *Kenya population (Live).* https://www.worldometers.info/demographics/kenya-demographics/

Worldometer. (2021d). *United States population (Live).* https://www.worldometers.info/world-population/us-population/

Wright, P. (2011). Women and Leadership Style. *Group, 35*(3), 247–253.

Wynn, A. (2009). *An investigation of the contributions of gender, shopping orientation, online experience and website's interactive features to consumers' intentions to engage in apparel e-commerce shopping.* Nova South-Eastern University.

Yarram, S. R., & Adapa, S. (2021). Board gender diversity and corporate social responsibility: Is there a case for critical mass? *Journal of Cleaner Production, 278*, 123319. doi:10.1016/j.jclepro.2020.123319

Zikriyoev, A. S., & Crane, R. A. (2019). Prevention of social cost in occupational health and safety is sustainable development for the construction industry. *International Scientific Journal Theoretical & Applied Science, 74*(6).

About the Contributors

Shashi Bala, an economist is Fellow at V.V. Giri National Labour Institute, NOIDA (An Autonomous Body of Ministry of labour & Employment, Government of India). She was awarded PhD from the Centre of Study for Diplomacy, International Law and Economics, School of International Studies, Jawaharlal Nehru University, New Delhi. She was the Visiting Researcher in 2008 at the Korean Labour Institute, Seoul, South Korea. Presently, she is coordinating the activities of the Centre for Gender & Labour Studies and Centre for Agrarian Relations, Rural Labour and Behaviour Studies at the Institute. She organizes training programmes and conducts research on various dimensions pertaining to Labour economics & development policies; Skill development; Social security; Gender budgeting; Behavior skill management, etc., with the central focus on gender and related issues. She has been a member of the Task Force on Gender Equality in the World of Work, Ministry of Labour & Employment, Government of India, INDIA.

Puja Singhal is Assistant Professor at **National Centre for School Leadership (NCSL)**, NIEPA, **New Delhi**. She is a gold medalist in Economics and has a Doctorate from the Jai Narain Vyas University, Jodhpur (Rajasthan). She has also worked with V.V.Giri National Labor Institute (Ministry of Labor and Employment) and was involved in policy-oriented projects. Now she organizes workshops, training programs on gender and leadership at NCSL and works as a National Co-ordinator of five states of India. In 2015, she presented her paper at 4th **European and International** Conference for Learning Innovations and Quality (LINQ), at **Brussels (Belgium).** She has published extensively in the form of books, research papers, and articles in peer-reviewed and reputed academic journals, like Emerald, IGI Global, Inderscience, etc., and also received the best paper award twice. Her areas of special interest are Vocational Education, Gender issues, E-Learning and Innovation in education, Skill Development, School Leadership. She can be accessed at pujasinghal@niepa.ac.in.

* * *

Salwa Alinat-Abed earned a Ph.D. degree in Islamic and Middle Eastern studies from the Ben-Gurion University of the Negev in Israel. She serves as post-doctorate with the European Scientific Institute (ESI), the Dan David Institute at the Tel-Aviv University and Truman Institute for Peace at Hebrew University of Jerusalem. Alinat-Abed's primary research focuses on the experiences of women in the Islamic Movement in Israel in specific and Political Islam in the Middle East in general.

Bhoomika Batra is a doctorate in the Department of Accounting and Taxation from IIS deemed to be University, Jaipur, India. Her research interests are Corporate Governance, Accounting, Social Welfare, Digitalization, and Corporate Finance. She is a Founder of an online research academy EdBhoomi: Ground for Education with two years of experience in data analysis. ORCHID ID: 0000-0003-3747-9812.

Anjuli Chandra is an M.Sc., Ph. D. in Anthropology from University of Allahabad, Central University, Uttar Pradesh, India. Social Anthropology, Environmental Anthropology, Tribal Studies and Social Exclusion are her areas of specialization. Completed 04 minor and one major research project on Health Exclusion of Arunthatiyars in Tamil Nadu, sponsored by UGC, New Delhi. Last eleven years she is working as Assistant Professor cum Assistant Director, in the Centre for Study of Social Exclusion and Inclusive Policy (CSSEIP), Gandhigram Rural Institute (Deemed to be University), Gandhigram, Dindigul, Tamil Nadu.

Robert Cobb, Jr. is an Associate Professor responsible for the development and evaluation of skills, knowledge, and dispositions pertinent to the manipulation of engineering design graphics technologies used to generate two- and three-dimensional visual artifacts of parts, products and built environments. His outreach initiatives intend to motivate and prepare secondary students to pursue and persist toward life-long learning and career aspirations in disciplines where persons from disinvested communities are marginalized and underrepresented by harnessing the autonomy in distance learning technologies providing them access to educational opportunities, experiences, resources, and environments. His research agenda involves inquiries concerning the integration of self-regulated learning strategy instruction to develop and deploy learning and motivational strategies creating inclusive online learning environments and experiences and eradicating the symbolic violence caused by environments facilitated by computer and information technologies.

Paula E. Faulkner joined North Carolina Agricultural and Technical State University in 2007. She is as a Professor in the Department of Agribusiness, Applied Economics and Agriscience Education. She instructs and advises undergraduate and graduate students in agricultural education. Her research addresses the needs of underrepresented populations in agriculture including limited resource and minority farmers, women farmers in less developed countries as well as identifying strategies for increasing the number of minority students in the food, agriculture, natural resources and human (FANH) sciences. She serves as a board member for the North Carolina Fulbright Alumni Association and on the editorial board for the European Scientific Journal (ESJ). For her research efforts, Faulkner was selected as the University's Outstanding Young Investigator of the Year (2013-2014) and as her College's Senior Researcher of the Year (2016-2017).

Gaganpreet Kaur is an Assistant Professor (visiting faculty) in Amity University Uttar Pradesh. She has an academic experience and expertise of teaching human resource and company law. She has also worked in S.D.College and led many group training sessions. She also possess research experience and have many research papers published in National and International Journals like serial publications, transstellar publication, bloomsberry and has also received the best paper award. She has attended and presented many research papers in conferences and completed her Ph.D in labour laws.

Nimra Khan is working as an Academic Associate at the department of Human Resource Management at the Indian Institute of Management, Amritsar, India. Prior to that she was working as Research Associate at V.V Giri National Labour Institute, Noida, India on various research projects pertaining to Agrarian relations, rural camps and behavioral studies with specific focus on Gender .She is post Graduate in Commerce with specialization in Business Management from Jamia Millia Islamia, New Delhi, India.

Thomas Kipkurgat is the Managing Director of Rivatex East Africa Limited, a leading integrated textile company in Kenya. He holds a Ph.D., in Agricultural Economics and Management from Texas Tech University and extensive expertise in economics and marketing management. He is a columnist on topical agricultural economics in national media. He has authored published his research in several publications. Kipkurgat has been lecturing and supervising both Master's and PhD students at Moi University and Donghua University in China. He has also attended and presented in numerous seminars, conferences and workshops internationally.

C. A. Kamakshi Mehta is an Assistant Professor at Amity University, Haryana, India, with experience of 23 years. She has completed her CA from ICAI in 1998 and her Master's degree in commerce from Mahatma Gandhi University, Meghalaya. At present she is pursuing her doctorate from JNU, Rajasthan. She has also qualified for her NET in Commerce in the year 2019. She has secured 8th Rank in BCom (Hons) from Guwahati university 1994 .She has presented papers at various international and national conferences and published research papers in the journals of repute. Her research interests include Forensic Audit , Frauds, NPA, Banks, Sustainability. Orcid ID: 0000-0002-3709-2338.

Nandita Mishra is a Professor in Accounting and Taxation with a demonstrated history of working in the higher education industry for nearly two decades. Ambassador to International Integrated Reporting Council (IIRC) London and Country Director- India -HETL (Higher education teaching and learning). A researcher and academician in the fields of finance & accounting, corporate governance, sustainability, and integrated reporting. A Cost and Management Accountant by profession with a doctorate in corporate governance.

Rajesh Sannegadu is a full academic at the University of Mauritius and a holder of a PhD in Business Management from the North West University, South Africa. He has been lecturing International Business, entrepreneurship and SMEs management since the last ten 10 years. Prior to joining academia, he worked in the public service and the private sector (construction industry and the banking sector). During his employment as a Business Analyst in one of the leading banks in Mauritius, he was responsible to assess Business Plans from corporate clients seeking financial assistance. He also participated in different workshops to contribute to the development of the National Export Strategy for Mauritius. As principal investigator, he has also completed several projects funded by the Mauritius Research Council. ORCHID ID: 0000-0001-7789-0599.

Vaishali Trivedi is an Associate Professor at St Kabir Institute of Professional Studies, Ahmedabad. She holds a PhD in HR, Master's of Business Administration with dual specialization in HR and Marketing. She possess 8 years of experience in academics wherein she is actively engaged in disseminating knowledge about various HR and Marketing subjects. Her academic areas of interest are Talent Management, Diversity and Inclusion, Performance Management , Brand Management. She has published papers in many national and international journals.

Vikas Trivedi is an Assistant Professor at Institute of Law, Nirma University. He holds a master's degree in Management and Law and a PhD from MLS University. He has also qualified National Eligibility Test in Management and Law conducted by University Grants Commission. He possess a teaching experience of more than 12 years. His areas of interest include Consumer Law, Contract Law and Human Resource Management. Before joining academia, he worked with organizations like- Indiabulls Securities, ICICI Bank and HDFC Bank.

Index

www.ingramcontent.com/pod-product-compliance
Lightning Source LLC
LaVergne TN
LVHW081343300926
849161LV00008B/2048